Revitalizing the Northeast

Revitalizing the Northeast

Prelude to an agenda

Edited by George Sternlieb and James W. Hughes

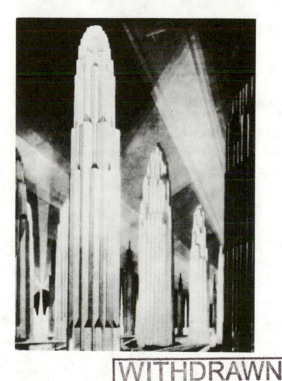

CENTER FOR URBAN POLICY RESEARCH

THE CENTER FOR URBAN POLICY RESEARCH
RUTGERS UNIVERSITY
BUILDING 4051 / KILMER CAMPUS
NEW BRUNSWICK, NEW JERSEY 08903

Cover design by Francis G. Mullen.

Copyright, 1978, Rutgers—The State University of New Jersey.

All rights reserved. Published in the United States by the Center for Urban Policy Research, New Brunswick, New Jersey 08903.

ISBN: 0-88285-047-4

Library of Congress Cataloging in Publication Data

Main entry under title:

Revitalizing the Northeast.

  Bibliography: p.

  1. Northeastern States—Economic conditions— Addresses, essays, lectures.

  2. Northeastern States—Economic policy—Addresses, essays, lectures.

  I. Sternlieb, George.

  II. Hughes, James W.

HC107.A115R48   309.1'74'04   78-669
ISBN 0-88285-047-4

Contents

Acknowledgments

Acknowledgments are the most pleasant of duties particularly when they are addressed to a group whose services and insights were as fruitful as those secured by the editors in the course of this study. First and foremost we owe a great deal of gratitude to all of the participants. Despite what must have seemed to some of them as interminable requests and editorial juggling they preserved their equanimity in a most heartwarming fashion. Over and above the direct conference participants, we were indeed fortunate to secure—either directly or indirectly—additional contributions and commentary from John E. Smith of the Energy Office of New York State; Eric Markell, New York State Energy Research and Development Authority; and Walt Rostow of the University of Texas. In addition Timothy B. Clark, editor and publisher of the *Empire State Report,* and the Temporary Commission on New York City Finances graciously permitted us to reproduce material that had been developed under their aegis.

Our associates at the Center for Urban Policy Research have provided always a constant stream of insight and inspiration. We would like to single out in this context Robert Burchell, Kristina Ford, Robert Lake, David Listokin and Connie O. Michaelson. Mrs. Mary Picarella and Jill Millerand supervised the complicated details of conference management and correspondence. We would particularly like to extend our gratitude for the typing efforts of Joan Frantz, Lydia Lombardi and Anne Hummel as well as the editorial inputs of Dan Sohmer and Barry Jones. The flaws that remains are the editors'.

About The Contributors

Gurney Breckenfeld is a member of the Board of Editors, Fortune Magazine.

Thomas A. Clark is Assistant Professor of Urban and Regional Planning at Rutgers University.

Janice Cogger is a City Planner of the Cleveland City Planning Commission.

Norman I. Fainstein is Associate Professor in the Department of Urban Affairs and Policy Analysis of the New School for Social Research.

Susan S. Fainstein is Professor of Urban Planning and Policy Development at Rutgers University.

William C. Fruend is Vice President and Chief Economist of the New York Stock Exchange.

Bennett Harrison is Associate Professor of Economics and Urban Studies at the Massachusetts Institute of Technology.

John G. Heiman is the former Commissioner of the New York State Division of Housing and Community Renewal. He is presently Comptroller of the Currency.

James W. Hughes is Research Associate at the Center for Urban Policy Research and a Professor of Urban and Regional Planning at Rutgers University.

Sandra Kanter is Assistant Professor of the College of Public and Community Services at the University of Massachusetts-Boston.

Norman Krumholz is presently Director, Department of Community Development, City of Cleveland, Ohio.

Sar A. Levitan is Director of the Center for Social Policy Studies at George Washington University.

Paul A. London is Director of the New England Economic Research Office.

D. Quinn Mills is Professor of Business Administration and Labor Relations at Harvard Business School.

W. W. Rostow is Professor of Economics and History at the University of Texas at Austin.

Roger Starr is Henry Luce Professor of Urban Values at New York University.

George Sternlieb is Director of the Center for Urban Policy Research and Professor of Urban and Regional Planning at Rutgers University.

Wilbur R. Thompson is Professor of Economics at Wayne State University.

Martin Tolchin is Congressional Correspondent of the *New York Times*.

Prologue: Prelude to an Agenda

Introduction

THE CYCLES OF ECONOMIC HISTORY have long been the subject of intensive study. For example, the dissection of the intimacies of the business cycle, of the traumas associated with the phenomena of economic boom leading to bust, of food production advancing beyond demand and then alternately succumbing to the latter, have traditionally served as a mainstay of economic analysis and investigation. Consequently, it should be of little surprise that the long-term swings in relative economic fortune have been newly rediscovered as the nation's aging industrial regions increasingly appear to be entering the negative phase of such cycles. While these models of cause and effect provide useful typological devices, simplifying and ordering day-to-day occurrences into understandable patterns, they pose an ever-present danger. The transition from recognizing the logical sequencing of events to establishing their causality—i.e., event B not only follows event A, but is the inevitable result of it—is hazardous, particularly as we turn to the intersection of politics and economic development.

Despite the risk of invoking the perspective, it is perhaps useful to place the North-South regional growth issue of the United States in a longer term framework. This approach is particularly seductive as we

1

preside over an apt bridge point in American history. At this writing the Bicentennial is barely a year in the past. The first half of the era was one in which the North flourished increasingly as an industrial locus, supported in very large part by what were then referred to as federally financed "internal improvements." Indeed in the first century of our existence—up until 1876—the northern share of such efforts was ten times that of the South; the state of New York by itself secured more than the total South.

The year 1876 has particular significance in this context. As a result of the agreement which permitted Rutherford Hayes to assume the presidency in a disputed election, the last troops of occupation were withdrawn from the South, and significant concessions involving federal expenditures in the area were made—not least of them a new major transcontinental railroad which was planned to sweep through the region. It was at that moment of time that southern political leadership broadly and explicitly opted for economic development and industrialization. But the foundation for industrial urbanization had already been set in the North, upon which the era of city building reached full crescendo, and with it, economic dominance for the next half century.

Meanwhile, beset by the problems of race and poverty, initial progress in the South was relatively slow. Indeed much of it was hindered by a variety of business practices on the national level which reflected the political power of entrenched northern interests. Characteristic of these elements was the so-called basing point system, which set freight charges on iron and steel products, regardless of their origin, as if they were shipped from Pittsburgh. Thus a steel plant at Birmingham would have no freight advantage in selling to a user in Mobile as against the equivalent facility located in Pittsburgh or Cleveland. The cheap labor available in the South faced the internal problem of racial discrimination and the external problem of competition with the tide of foreign immigrants flooding the urban areas of the North. The latter could and did compete successfully with the agrarian displacees of the South.

So little progress had been made in revitalizing the South as a region that it became the primary target of popular literature as a symbol of backwardness. As we view the South in terms of the flourishing Sunbelt, a region of rising income and, increasingly, of racial equity, the era reflected by *Tobacco Road* and the early novels of Faulkner fade into history. All too frequently, however, they mirrored a sad reality—if only a portion of it. One of the primary targets, therefore, of early New Deal legislation was an effort to bring new vigor to the region and its people. The conjunction of the enormous level of capital investment and federal spending of World War II provided the crucial launching platform. This was aided and abetted by a pattern of population redistribution as the northern industrial centers, hungry for labor, absorbed in ever increasing numbers black agrarian displacees. The path of this latter process had been initially defined in World War I. The change in immigration laws in the early 1920s reduced the customary European source of inexpensive labor for the North to a mere trickle. While the rate of South to North migration was slowed by the Depression, the revitalization of the economy during World War II served as an enormous aid in the South's unloading of redundant population.

In retrospect the broad sweep of events which made the South's takeoff possible becomes more evident:

1. The first wave of black migration from the South to the North was induced by the industrial labor demands of the North during World War I.
2. The virtual cessation of European immigration, based on the new immigration laws of the early 1920s, provided an additional and continuing rationale for the utilization of black labor in the North.
3. The New Deal programs targeted extensive aid to the South, beginning the modernization of its infrastructure, agricultural and natural resources bases.
4. The increasing mechanization of southern agriculture during the Depression forced more and more people, both black and white, from the land.
5. Subsequently, there was the selective absorption of this heretofore redundant labor force in the era of World War II, with many of the blacks—given the better opportunities that existed for them there—seeking northern defense related employment, while their white equivalents were anchored into the newly burgeoning native industry in the South.

But the long-term results of the New Deal exceeded that of southern economic development. It provided the legal base for a broad sweep of unionization. The process, however, was most effective in the North while largely bypassing the South. This in turn implied not merely substantial variations in regional wage levels but also in work practices. One of the editors of this volume had occasion to study the relocation of a major textile producer from New England to Georgia. The number of looms per worker accepted in the latter site was half again as high as that accepted as a maximum in the older location. In many cases it was a simple matter of an aged, somewhat hostile labor force in the North versus a newly hired, anxious-to-please and young labor pool waiting in the South. In the North there was a multigenerational labor force heritage all too well aware of the tenuous nature of its position—and thus open for unionization. In the South by contrast there were first generational agricultural displacees carrying with them the tradition of "every person for himself."

But the South still labored under the difficulties of race, of an image of backwardness, and of limited public infrastructure—particularly in higher education—which limited its capacity to attract high technology enterprise. These difficulties were slowly but inexorably mitigated by the dominance of southern congressmen, based on the seniority system, in the crucial investment oriented sectors of the federal government. The armed services—long a stronghold of southern tradition, perhaps by default of equivalent business opportunity—developed an officers corps largely staffed by southerners. Of parallel significance was the role played by southern representatives and senators on the equivalent armed services committees both in the House and Senate, leading to significant investment both in military installations and high technology defense contracts. What evolved was a crucial bridge facilitating the upgrading of southern economic enterprise from a raw material and cheap labor orientation—the classic roles of semicolonial areas—to one increasingly of high technology manufacture. In conjunction with other federal investments in southern infrastructure—the interstate highway system, canal and river improvements, and port development—as well as the evolution of other development facilitators—such as air conditioning which mitigated climatic differentials—the South gained full citizenship in the nation's broader economic system.

This was a process that was generally viewed favorably by most Americans. The South had moved from the most backward area of the nation to one of increasing modernity, with the rewards amicably shared regionally—particularly as improvement was secured not merely for whites but for blacks as well. The exact point at which southern achievement suddenly became viewed as a threat to the North is obscure. While complaints of the export of southern human problems to northern cities had long been raised as well as their impact in specific industries, it was not until the early 1970s—when recession buffeted the aging industrial regions of the country; when the energy and natural resources crises bestowed increased advantage to exporting territories; and when foreign industrial competition challenged American economic hegemony —that doubts of the future, and with them general fear of southern competition, arose in the North. The lingering effects of these shifts —which are increasingly recognized as chronic, long-term phenomena—

have triggered a response, which is manifested by the growth of regional pressure groups within Congress.

The alliance between northern congressmen and those of the older sectors of the Midwest, who seemingly represent areas suffering from the same malaise, is showing increasing vigor at analyzing pork barrel legislation and broader measures in terms of their very specific impacts upon the regions that they represent.

But is redress for the northern decline, or for that matter southern growth, properly to be found in Washington? This point will be raised in several of the essays of this volume. It is the editors' opinion, however, that if the new awareness should lead only to regional rivalry, it will be self destructive. Have we progressed so little as to require a reinvention of the Civil War? Must we view the problem of regional growth as a zero sum game in which the winnings of one sector must be at the cost of the other? Is there a possibility, rather than setting in motion a series of raids and counter-raids on the national fisc, to view the end of the era described here as the opportunity for a new rapprochement and the beginnings of a true national growth endeavor?

Americans have been long on de facto economic growth stimuli and regional incentives and very short on their de jure growth equivalent. There has never been a formally acknowledged or avowed national growth policy. Congress has mandated a major White House report on national growth objectives which is currently scheduled for the end of 1977. Can it provide a baseline not for North versus South, or West versus East, but rather for a national coalition for advancement? What are the elements that must go into such policies? What present inequities are there in resource allocation which must be cured so as to provide this base? It is our hope that this volume may provide an insight into the process.

THE RECENT CONTEXT

The popular media's probing of the plight of the Northeast and its complement, the burgeoning fortunes of the Sunbelt, has rapidly gained parity with the attention lavished upon the urban maladies and the suburban frontiers of the 1960s. Suddenly, the invocation of the regional dimension for evaluating a host of concerns is now commonplace. Unfamiliar phrases have quickly become not only standard articles of media discourse, but also staples of political rhetoric. The images they invoke and concepts they represent have become embedded so firmly that it is difficult to recall a time without them. The conventional wisdom of the previous decade has become obsolete in a remarkably brief span of time.

While this new reference framework has suddenly "rejuvenated" the efforts of those whose task it is to focus on the continuing, but shopworn, litany of the nation's pockets of decline, the public and private leadership of the Northeast is confronted with a seemingly remorseless sequence of urban evolution on an unprecedented scale. Past realities and instrumentalities appear inadequate to meet an emerging set of priorities.

The awakening to this evolving state of affairs began with tentative interpretations of ambiguous information. As the post-1970 data tabulations slowly interfaced to reveal apparently new patterns of metropolitan and regional change, only limited reservations about the continuities of past assumptions initially surfaced. However, when fragmentary accounts pyramided into uncontestable evidence, a new reality gradually came into focus. Obscured by the convention of a decennial census system, as well as the booming national economy in the late 1960s, was the belated recognition of a long-term transformation in the nation's social and economic parameters. The aging industrial heartland of America—stretching from New England to the upper Midwest—began to experience unique residual strains emanating from persistent industrial relocation and population migration to the southern rimlands on a national scale. The problems encapsulated by the older central cities of the Northeast and North Central states—the historical loci of the nation's manufacturing activity—were compounded by the gathering momentum of regional shifts, and began to diffuse and spread across entire metropolitan and subregional areas. The traditional bases of industrial America have become prisoners of their earlier history and are experiencing the dislocations caused by accelerating technological change, a maturing economy, and an increasingly mobile and footloose population.

It is clear that long-term structural readjustments are going to dominate the patterns of social and economic life, particularly in the Northeast, as we proceed into the final quarter of twentieth century. No facet of the political and planning environment can escape the daily repercussions of the phenomenon. It is not surprising, therefore, that the region's political agenda is and will increasingly be dominated by confrontations with the processes and consequences of the forces in motion.

THE OBJECTIVE

The task of this volume can be described best as a prelude to an operational policy agenda. It is our premise that there are scant prospects for immediate deflections of powerful trendlines and long-term swings in relative fortune; it would be positively misleading to endorse simple, painless mechanisms of change promising immediate results. Indeed, hastily formulated interventions influencing the lives of the region's citizenry may well have unanticipated consequences working against their long-term interests, as well as those of the region. Given the momentum of the basic transition, the policy response must correspondingly be long-term in nature, scope, and application. Hence, it is essential to focus on the basic guidelines that should shape the policies devised in the years to come. Where it is in our capacity, specific interventionary procedures will be evaluated, particularly those which have been casually promulgated without adequate forethought. But the major concern will be with the main principles, critical elements, and basic constraints which should constitute the boundaries and guidelines of a policy response agenda.

The first task attendant to this objective is an examination of facts and realities of regional change, and an analysis of the underlying logic of the web of causal forces and processes.

The Dynamic Trendlines

Three broad, major phenomena have coalesced into a dynamic shaking the very foundations of the older industrial heartland of America:

1. The accelerating regional shift
2. Metropolitan-nonmetropolitan tensions
3. Expanding intrametropolitan differentials

The problems facing the Northeast and adjacent industrial states are the product of these forces converging, interfacing, and reinforcing one another within the same time frame and geographic loci. While they are thoroughly intertwined, their isolation is useful for analytical purposes so as to gain a starting point for policy evaluations.

THE ACCELERATING REGIONAL SHIFT

A very powerful momentum has built up over the past fifteen years, sweeping employment and population growth away from the older metropolitan centers of the Northeast and North Central states to the newer growth poles of the South and West. The "rise of the sunbelt" and the "decline of the Northeast" are not inventions of the popular media, but are ominous long-term realities.

As evidence stand the overall performances of the national and regional economies of the past fifteen years. Total employment change from 1960 to 1975 (the long-term trend) has markedly favored the South and West, with the Northeast in general, and the Middle Atlantic Division (a subset of the Northeast comprising New York, New Jersey and Pennsylvania) in particular, lagging significantly.

1960-1975 TOTAL EMPLOYMENT CHANGE

	Number	Percent
U.S. Total	23,879.2	46.6
Northeast Region	3,305.9	21.7
Middle Atlantic Division	2,118.7	18.7
North Central Region	5,534.9	36.2
South Region	9,662.3	69.9
West Region	5,376.1	69.5

NOTE: Numbers in thousands.

More importantly, in the 1970 to 1975 period (the short-term trend), when the nation's total employment increased by six million jobs, the Northeast lost almost 36,000. (Indeed, the South secured 55.8 percent of the national increase.) However, within the Northeast, the Middle Atlantic Division lost approximately 224,000 jobs, 1.6 percent of its 1970 total. Both New York City and Philadelphia contributed heavily to this decline, each losing approximately 11.5 percent of its 1970 employment total.

1970-1975 TOTAL EMPLOYMENT CHANGE

	Number	Percent
U.S. Total	5,925.9	8.5
Northeast Region	−35.7	−0.2
Middle Atlantic Division	−223.5	−1.6
Philadelphia City	−108.8	−11.8
New York City	−438.5	−11.5
North Central Region	872.1	4.4
South Region	3,305.1	16.4
West Region	1,784.1	15.8

NOTE: Numbers in thousands.

The economies of the Northeast and North Central regions have historically been predicated on manufacturing. Ominously, the long-term swings of this employment sector underpin the total employment trendlines. From 1960 to 1975, the United States added nearly 1.5 million manufacturing jobs, as did the South. In contrast, the Northeast Region lost 781,000 manufacturing jobs, 627,000 of which were in the Middle Atlantic Division. In percentage terms, the Northeast lost 13.9 percent of its manufacturing jobs, while the Middle Atlantic Division lost 15.0 percent.

1960-1975 Manufacturing Employment Change

	Number	Percent
U.S. Total	1,469.3	8.8
Northeast Region	−781.4	−13.9
Middle Atlantic Division	−625.7	−15.0
North Central Region	234.4	4.2
South Region	1,469.0	41.0
West Region	520.3	27.8

NOTE: Numbers in thousands.

The bulk of these losses accrued in the 1970 to 1975 period, with the Northeast experiencing a decline of some 936,000 manufacturing jobs, 724,000 of which were lost in the Middle Atlantic Division. Again, New York City and Philadelphia contributed significantly to this decline, both losing approximately 30 percent of their 1970 manufacturing employment totals. Concurrently, the South has evolved into the dominant manufacturing locus of the nation.

1970-1975 Manufacturing Employment Change

	Number	Percent
U.S. Total	−1,467.0	−7.4
Northeast Region	−936.2	−16.2
Middle Atlantic Division	−724.1	−17.0
Philadelphia City	−72.3	−30.4
New York City	−244.3	−29.9
North Central Region	−579.8	−9.1
South Region	23.9	0.5
West Region	25.1	1.1

NOTE: Numbers in thousands.

The question raised by these trendlines concerns the degree to which the overall divisional and regional experience is a function of the "writing off" of obsolete industrial infrastructures from the inventory of operational and competitive means of production.

In this regard, an important guide to the future is the replenishment of the capital plant of the Northeast. The region's share of the nation's total authorized private nonresidential construction dropped from 21.7 percent in the 1967 to 1969 period to 11.4 percent in 1976. In contrast, the South's increased from 29.1 percent to 35.8 percent for the same benchmark periods. The Northeast, therefore, is not securing a commensurate share of investment in new capital plant and infrastructure.

1967-1976 Percentage Share of the Valuation of Total Private Nonresidential Construction Authorized

Period	U.S. Total	North-east Region	North Central Region	South Region	West Region
1967-1969	100.0%	21.7%	26.7%	29.1%	22.5%
1970-1972	100.0	18.5	23.9	33.2	24.5
1973-1975	100.0	15.9	24.7	34.3	25.1
1976 [1]	100.0	11.4	24.9	35.8	28.0

NOTE: 1. First seven months, preliminary.

A basic foundation of urban economic modeling and analysis is that people tend to follow jobs; population movements mirror the pattern of basic industry shifts. From 1960 to 1975, when the total United States population increased by 18.8 percent, the Northeast's expanded

1960-1975 Percentage Population Change

	1960-1975	1960-1975	1970-1975
U. S. Total	18.8%	13.4%	4.8%
Northeast Region	10.7	9.8	0.8
Middle Atlantic Division	9.0	8.9	0.1
North Central Region	11.7	9.6	1.9
South Region	23.9	14.3	8.4
West Region	35.0	24.2	8.7

by only 10.7 percent. In the 1970 to 1975 period, the Northeast's growth rate declined to the 0.8 percent level, compared to the nation's 4.8 percent and the South's 8.4 percent levels.

Again it is the Middle Atlantic Division which has lagged even the broader northeastern performance, particularly in the 1970 to 1975 period (0.1 percent versus 0.8 percent).

Moreover, the significance of absolute population change is underscored by migrational data. Migration is a telling criterion of location shift by choice, of people seeking out "better" places to live. Whether because of climate, jobs, sheer restlessness, or whatever—migration data tend to gauge the locational preferences of Americans. And in this context, the Northeast Region demonstrates extremely unfavorable patterns. During the latest time period (1970 to 1975) the Middle Atlantic Division alone had a net out-migration of 758,000 people, while the South had a net in-migration of 2,624,000 people.

1960-1975 NET MIGRATION

	1960-1975	1970-1975
Northeast Region	375	−686
Middle Atlantic Division	59	−758
North Central Region	−752	−878
South Region	592	2,624
West Region	2,854	1,467

NOTE: Numbers in thousands.

Correlating with these tendencies are the per capita personal income changes which occurred from 1960 to 1975. While the national increase stood at 162.6 percent, the Northeast lagged at 147.6 percent; in contrast, the South surged forward with a 192.5 percent gain in per capita personal income.

1960-1975 PERCENTAGE PER CAPITA INCOME CHANGE

U.S. Total	162.6%
Northeast Region	147.6
Middle Atlantic Division	147.0
North Central Region	162.1
South Region	192.5
West Region	152.4

The patterns of residential dwelling unit starts also parallel the population movements. In the 1964 to 1966 period, the Northeast secured 17.8 percent of the total national residential starts. By 1976, the region's share declined to the 10.4 percent mark.

1964-1976 PERCENTAGE SHARE OF RESIDENTIAL
DWELLING UNIT STARTS

Period	U.S. Total	North-east Region	North Central Region	South Region	West Region
1964-1966	100.0%	17.8%	23.7%	38.9%	19.5%
1967-1969	100.0	15.4	24.7	40.5	19.4
1970-1972	100.0	14.0	20.0	43.5	22.5
1973-1975	100.0	13.4	23.1	41.8	21.8
1976 [1]	100.0	10.4	25.3	38.4	25.9

NOTE: 1. First seven months, preliminary.

Both private nonmanufacturing and government employment are generally construed as population-serving activities, dependent on population growth. From 1960 to 1975, private nonmanufacturing employment in the Northeast increased by 36.5 percent, while the South had a 77.8 percent growth. The Middle Atlantic Division's 30.2 percent increase was the slowest in the nation.

1960-1975 PRIVATE NONMANUFACTURING EMPLOYMENT CHANGE

	Number	Percent
U.S. Total	15,932.0	58.9
Northeast Region	2,798.1	36.5
Middle Atlantic Division	1,821.8	30.2
North Central Region	3,799.1	50.6
South Region	5,868.3	77.8
West Region	3,466.5	80.1

NOTE: Numbers in thousands.

From 1970 to 1975, while the Northeast's private nonmanufacturing growth rate was only 5.1 percent, the Middle Atlantic Division lagged at the 3.0 percent level. Both Philadelphia and New York City experienced declines in the vicinity of 7 percent. In contrast, the South's growth rate was more than four times that of the Northeast—22.2 percent.

1970-1975 PRIVATE NONMANUFACTURING EMPLOYMENT CHANGE

	Number	Percent
U.S. TOTAL	5,386.5	14.3
Northeast Region	506.3	5.1
Middle Atlantic Division	226.9	3.0
Philadelphia City	−36.4	−6.9
New York City	−211.9	−8.7
North Central Region	1,131.8	11.1
South Region	2,434.0	22.2
West Region	1,314.1	20.3

NOTE: Numbers in thousands.

Total government employment change shows narrower inter-regional differentials. From 1960 to 1975, the Northeast's growth rate (66.6 percent) was closely competitive with the South's 87.7 percent. However, the latter's more vigorous expansion in the private sectors is perhaps indicative of a stronger fiscal support basis for its governmental activities.

1960-1975 TOTAL GOVERNMENT EMPLOYMENT CHANGE

	Number	Percent
U.S. TOTAL	6,477.9	78.1
Northeast Region	1,289.2	66.6
Middle Atlantic Division	992.4	67.1
North Central Region	1,501.4	68.3
South Region	2,298.0	87.7
West Region	1,389.3	90.6

NOTE: Numbers in thousands.

The short-term time period (1970 to 1975) shows growing gaps analogous to the other employment sectors.

1970-1975 TOTAL GOVERNMENT EMPLOYMENT CHANGE

	Number	Percent
U.S. TOTAL	2,006.7	13.6
Northeast Region	394.2	13.9
Middle Atlantic Division	273.3	12.4
Philadelphia City	–0.1	–0.1
New York City	17.7	3.1
North Central Region	320.1	9.5
South Region	847.2	20.8
West Region	445.2	18.0

NOTE: Numbers in thousands.

Included within total government employment change is the federal civilian subsector, whose economic impact may approximate that of a basic industry. Over the fifteen-year time span (1960 to 1975), the rate of growth occurring in the South (31.9 percent) was virtually ten times greater than that taking place in the Northeast (3.3 percent).

1960-1975 FEDERAL CIVILIAN EMPLOYMENT CHANGE

	Number	Percent
U.S. TOTAL	488.6	22.4
Northeast Region	15.9	3.3
Middle Atlantic Division	12.9	3.6
North Central Region	73.4	17.3
South Region	269.7	31.9
West Region	129.6	29.9

From 1970 to 1975, the Northeast actually lost 12,400 federal civilian jobs, aggravating the problems engendered by private employment contractions. The South and West regions, in contrast, show continued expansion of federal employment.

NOTE: Numbers in thousands.

1970-1975 FEDERAL CIVILIAN EMPLOYMENT CHANGE

	Number	Percent
U.S. TOTAL	42.9	1.6
Northeast Region	−12.4	−2.5
Middle Atlantic Division	−5.8	−1.5
North Central Region	−0.8	−0.2
South Region	38.4	3.6
West Region	17.7	3.2

NOTE: Numbers in thousands.

In summary, the long-term trends (1960-1975) show a marked depletion of the Northeast Region's economic vitality compared to the southern and western parts of the nation. Over the past five years (1970 to 1975), a rapid acceleration of these trendlines is evident, documenting the sagging fortunes of the region, and raising important questions as to the recovery capacity of the region's economy.

METROPOLITAN-NONMETROPOLITAN TENSIONS

The Northeast not only is the victim of regional dynamics, but also is affected by metropolitan-nonmetropolitan development trends. A marked shift in historical metropolitan growth patterns took place in the post-1970 period.

For the past several decades, metropolitan areas were the dominant growth poles of the nation. This is no longer the case. In the 1970 to 1974 period, the growth rate of nonmetropolitan areas exceeded that of metropolitan areas in total.

The twenty largest metropolitan areas of the United States experienced a net out-migration of 1.2 million people while nonmetropolitan areas had a net in-migration of 1.5 million people (1970-1974). And it was the major metropolitan centers of the Northeast and North Central regions which led this transformation.

The out-migration from the northeastern metropolises actually comprises two separate phenomena. The first is primarily an exurban flow to areas adjacent, but external, to formally defined SMSAs; this is the extension of the classic exposition of metropolitan growth outward from the urban core, and may simply be the result of lagging definition.

But the major movements are regional, contributing to the flows of population and jobs out of the Northeast to the southern rimlands on a national scale.

This nonmetropolitan resurgence may mark the endpoint of the historic industrial metropolis. A new "post-suburban" metropolitan format may be emerging from origins as diverse as the aging industrial concentrations in the North to the rural growth poles in the South. The new arrangement appears to be predicated on geographically dispersed clusters of service functions and decentralized bands of economic activity.

EXPANDING INTRA-METROPOLITAN DIFFERENTIALS

The regional dimension is also the product of expanding intrametropolitan differentials. The older central cities of America—the centerpieces of industrial urbanization—have been buffetted by severe stresses the last several decades. These massed population concentrations, the basis for the Northeast's historical economic supremacy, are on the verge of even more marked deterioration.

For the first time (1970 to 1974), the nation's 243 central cities, in total, lost population, and did so quite markedly. From 1970 to 1974, their losses totaled 1.2 million people, or 1.9 percent of their 1970 base. In contrast, their suburban rings expanded by 6.2 million people (8.4 percent).

These declines were principally registered by the central cities of the nation's largest metropolitan areas (those with more than one million people). These cities have lost 3.8 percent of their population from 1970 to 1974 (1.3 million people).

Racial shifts have also accelerated, with America's central cities being vacated by whites at increasingly alarming rates. With the momentum of black suburbanization, partial vacuums are opening up in older cities, evidenced by fractured landscapes of abandoned housing and empty commercial and industrial shells.

In the 1970 to 1974 period, as a function of selective in-and out-migration (coupled with the net decline in population), the purchasing power of central city residents declined by $29.6 billion. This implies a loss of support capacity, for example, of $37 billion in residential realty (1.5 million housing units), and 23 million square feet of supermarket space.

This evidence of contraction is intimately tied to the inter-regional shifts of manufacturing activity, as well as to the passing of the age of manufacturing in the United States. The bonds between urban centers and manufacturing activity have been weakened, as have the linkages between extant central city economic activity and urban residential populations.

The Underlying Processes

The many contours of the nation's social and economic life, then, have gradually altered their course to the detriment of the aging northeastern landscape. The logic of this transformation is complex and the leverage points to ease the transition are vague. How, then, do we begin to move from the descriptive realm to the prescriptive—the molding of policy parameters?

Obviously, it would be desirable to place the subsequent analysis of interventionary strategies within a formal evaluative framework defined by the underlying forces and their web of interrelationships. However, their integration into logical connective chains severely taxes present theoretical capacities as well as empirical resources. Indeed, the converse phenomenon—industrialization and urbanization—has been a part of America for over a century. Yet analysts of this growth analog have yet to fabricate any simple direct lineage among its determinants. As Maury Klein and Harvey A. Kantor observe:

> The modern industrial city is the product of several forces and factors coming together at a certain time in a unique way . . . . There is no single "cause" or set of "causes" . . . [It] was the product of all these factors interacting with and reinforcing each other. The crucial point is not the individual factors but the nexus of relationships among them. They are so thoroughly intertwined that it is difficult even to discuss them in isolation.[1]

Analogously, while we do consider a myriad of underlying processes, the reality of circular interrelationships has to be recognized; to adopt the logic of Klein and Kantor, it is probable that the connective chain is not so much circular as it is a spiral in which the driving forces reinforce one another and gain momentum as they move through time.[2] Similarly, while the construction of the aggregative decline scenario proves elusive—except in broader conceptual terms—there is little we can do but be cognizant of this limitation and make it explicit.

At this time we must be content, for the most part, to consider the overall dynamic as sets of discrete factors, partitioned into two broad groupings—the economic (and political) process, and residential choices and growth resynthesis—and employ them as a preliminary baseline for policy evaluation.

THE ECONOMIC PROCESS

Arching over the set of specific factors of change are the broader historical parameters of economic growth. As W. W. Rostow notes, there is a distinct tendency of latecomers to modern economic growth to catch up to those who began earlier. In the early stages of a nation's development, regional growth differentials increase as modern industrial technologies are absorbed by regions and areas endowed either with appropriate resources, or location, or with particularly creative entrepreneurs. As an economy matures, a process of regional convergence commences for two reasons. First, the latecomers to industrialization have a large backlog of modern technologies to absorb; the more mature regions must depend on the flow of new technologies while carrying a heavier weight of old or obsolescent industrial plant. Second, as regions (the early leaders) become more affluent, more resources are allocated to lower productivity services, dampening the potential for continued high rates of growth. Thus Rostow sees the relative rise of the Sunbelt as a consequence of natural regional evolution—as Veblen would have put it—the advantage of being last.

Within this broad sweep of regional economic evolution, however, the following particulars are of direct relevance.

Aging Capital Plants. The industrial infrastructure of our older regions and cities relate to production methods and approaches which are no longer competitive. The shifts of jobs and the declining shares of capital investment within these regions indicate that obsolescence is not being countered effectively.

Rationalization of Labor Intensive Industries. A virtual revolution has occurred in the technologies of goods production, information processing, and communications. While automation and technological change may possibly produce new jobs equivalent in number to those replaced, it is clear that their geographic loci do not necessarily coincide, nor do the skills and work patterns of the individuals concerned.

Declining Urban Linkages. The historic linkage between manufacturing activity and urban location has been terminated as a result of the rationalization of labor intensive industries. America's older cities were predicated on manufacturing industries. The passing of the golden age of manufacturing—the great industrial transformation —has left us with a number of overgrown "factory towns."

Absorption and Locational Decisionmaking. Older linkages have also been weakened with the emergence of conglomerates and multnational corporations absorbing what were previously locally owned firms, perhaps insulating locational decisionmaking from such subjective factors as historical ties, *i.e.,* family-owned businesses may be loath to stray too far from their traditional setting. While arguments could be made to the contrary, larger scale organization may imply the increasing economic rationality of locational decisions, with industries becoming increasingly "footloose."

The Dissolution of the Industrial Metropolis. The transition into the post-industrial era lends question not only to the rationale of the manufacturing city, but also to the historic industrial metropolis encompassing it. New spatial formats of industrial activity are synthesizing, rendering older configurations obsolete.

Accelerating Industrial Evolution. It is apparent that the growth in service and white-collar functions has not been able to compensate for urban manufacturing losses. The latter have occurred just as the rationalization and automation of paper and information handling has finally come to fruition, limiting effective increases in labor force commensurate with increased levels of activity.

Hardening of the Arteries. Aging regions develop a variety of conflicting property interests in the broader sense of the term, creating inhibitors that limit their ability to adapt to new industrial realities, thereby reducing their desirability for new entrants.

Hostile Business Environment. As a consequence, the costs of conducting economic activity in the Northeast have reached ominous levels in comparison to the new growth areas. Taxation, unionization, and a long developing anti-business milieu all impinge upon the locational decisionmaking process.

Spatial Homogenization. Broader technological changes—such as the interstate highway system domestically and dry bulk cargo shipping internationally—undermine the locational advantage once inherent in the Northeast. Similarly, alternative developments—such as the communications revolution—have made heretofore bypassed areas now directly competitive.

Receptivity to Growth. Locational decisionmakers are subject not only to basic economic constraints, but also to subtle, yet vital, interactions with local political structures. And in the growth areas outlined above, receptivity to potential new industrial relocatees is high, in contrast to older settings. The lower-business-cost package in the South in particular is a specific manifestation of its receptivity to economy activity.

The Enclaves of Private Enterprise. The business community in the broadest of senses may perceive the basic tenets of capitalism under increasing attack from all quarters. According to this thesis, the regional flows of economic activity may be interpreted as strategic withdrawals to enclaves characterized by political ideologies congruent to private enterprise. Capitalism making its last stand in Texas is a frequently voiced notion.

The Federal Expenditure Matrix. The dynamics of federal spending have tended to replicate the pattern of private economic activity flows. Whether they have been channeled in this fashion because of market realities (*i.e.*, federal grants may tend to follow people and jobs) or, conversely, have actually served to structure market forces, is as yet unclear. Whatever the case, they assuredly have aggravated the economic posture of the Northeast.

The Washington-New York City Transformation. The growing regulatory power of the national government has come to dominate many dimensions of American society. The gravitation of the nation's major public and private decisionmaking apparatus to the Washington locus implies the demise of New York City as the capital and headquarters of private enterprise, and contributes significantly to the Northeast's diminished economic stature.

The Fifth Kondratieff Cycle. W. W. Rostow suggests that capitalist economies are subject to long cycles, four or five decades in length, initiated by upward shifts in the prices of food, energy, and raw materials relative to the prices of manufactures. The post-1970 period is the fifth time in the past two hundred years a rise in the relative prices of basic commodities has occured. This helped convert a relatively benign pattern of regional shift into much more substantial flows. Development in the Sunbelt was accelerated, since it exported energy and agricultural resources to the balance of the nation; the relative price shift decelerated the already slower rate of expansion in the Northeast and North Central regions.

Energy Importation. More specifically, the Northeast region depends more heavily on petroleum for residential and industrial uses compared to the Sunbelt, which utilizes far less expensive natural gas for the bulk of its energy needs. The Northeast has few indigenous energy resources and is a major importer. In 1972, $7 billion was spent by its member states on fuel importation; this total ballooned to $20.7 billion by 1975.[3] With the growth leaders of the 1970's being the energy producing states, it is clear that the changing energy matrix has contributed significantly to the Northeast's diminished economic posture.

RESIDENTIAL CHOICES AND GROWTH RESYNTHESIS

The emerging concentrations of economic activity cannot be asymmetric to the complementary patterns of population settlement. Encouraging similar transitions are the major premises affecting the residential location decisions of individual households.

Facilitating Mechanisms. Earlier in this century, the impetus toward population decentralization—suburbanization—was underlaid by two factors. The first centered about facilitating mechanisms. The pyramiding of successive technological innovations made feasible the habitation of territories beyond formal city boundaries. To cite but one example, the widespread use of air conditioning has permitted the larger-scale equivalent of suburbanization to occur by equalizing regional climates.

Social and Cultural Predispositions. A second factor, basic social desires, must act in conjunction with the first to produce large-scale migrations. The vacation of settings thought of as undesirable socially or environmentally for more pristine and/or amenity-rich alternatives has now been permitted to work itself out over the entire geography of the nation. Suburban flight has given way to regional shift.

Complexity vs. Autonomy. The complex infrastructure inherent in the aging industrial metropolises of the "snowbelt" has become one of their principal liabilities. As discipline wanes, this high state of interdependence places individuals in fragile environments susceptible to external events. Autonomy becomes desirable and is sought in the less complex, more primitive habitats in the sunbelt.

The Decline of Agricultural Migration. The past fifteen years appear to mark the terminal shift of population as a function of the agricultural revolution. The dissolution of labor intensive farming has run its course. The northern metropolises have been relieved of a significant source of population replenishment.

The Expanding Retirement Vehicle. The elderly and retired have become a major force in American society. Their segregation into specialized residential subcommunities throughout the Sunbelt has an economic impact approximating that of a basic (exporting) industry, in that they generate an income flow (pensions and social security) from territories external to their new refuges. Moreover, the transfer of their fixed asset positions represents a net increment in wealth for the growth regions.

The Critical Mass Phenomenon. As the growing concentrations of people and jobs form the support threshold for the development of "urban' amenities and functions, the infrastructures of older areas become redundant. The translation of income flows to new areas fosters the rapid replication of older facilities, undermining the economic rationale of the passed-over resources.

Shifting Market Loci. The sustained higher growth rates in the southern and western regions of the country over the last several decades, as well as the emergence of the preceding two phenomena, make the Northeast increasingly distant from the growing markets of America. It is to these markets that population-serving economic activities are linked, and whose development reinforces the momentum of the overall trendline.

Declining Export Functions. The latter factor also translates into declining export functions for the Northeast economy, while the South concurrently undergoes "import substitution." The locational calculus that dictated the historic concentrations of wealth and economic activity in the Northeast has been visibly altered; the region may well be overdeveloped relative to its waning export role in the future. Self-sufficiency in the South implies contraction in the Northeast.

Shifting Criteria of Locational Decisionmaking. Gaining increased significance for locational decisionmaking are the basc residential preferences of the more important employee subgroups. Select industries have become "footloose" with the homogenization of the economic attributes of "place," and follow their key personnel. Hence residential desires, as depicted above, become a force in themselves for the locational settings of economic activity.

The amorphous web of contributory forces underscores the complexity of the dynamic that has been set in motion. Its gathering momentum is a result, as Wilbur Thompson suggests, of a process that is disequilibrating, cumulatively expansionary in the Sunbelt and cumulatively contractionary in the Northeast. Indeed, each individual impetus tends to reinforce the other, amplifying the magnitude and severity of the total process.

This lends question to any attempt at devising an itinerary of singular policy responses confronting point by point a package of simplified causal premises. It would be unwise to voice a set of easy prescriptions —institutional and legislative changes and actions—promising immediate and effective results. The reality is one of very difficult readjustments—social, political, and economic—and equally complex policy responses, formulated and modified over a very long time frame.

A BIOMODAL PHENOMENON?

Moreover, the participants in the policy dialogue must be cognizant of two distinct attributes bisecting the overall problem. The first concerns the fundamental maturation of the American economy, as well as the life style preferences of its citizenry. The process of regional equalization is the product of these phenomena and is facilitated by deep-seated forces virtually immune to substantial deflection. Like the central city of yore, the Northeast is enveloped in a process serving to reduce its historic functional role. While there is little chance of its being reversed, fundamental adjustments are possible to mitigate its consequences.

But there is also a puzzling dimension to the overall pattern of decline which appears to exceed benign evolution. Whether this is a result of self-imposed regional deficiencies and counterproductive policies— such as the pervasiveness of income redistribution at subregional scales —or of inadvertent (or covert) patterns of federal spending and investment, is as yet unclear. But it is a virtual certainty that the malaise is far deeper than that implied by regional equalization and raises the question of the *will*, as well as the political capacity, of the Northeast to recapture lost momentum. Both of these concerns deserve priority on any agenda, and must be seriously addressed.

A CAVEAT

The later dimension also invokes the requirement to raise two distinct caveats before directing attention to the organization for response. For the most part, the analyses that follow are contained within an intra-national perspective. It is entirely plausible that the phenomena under discussion are manifestations of broader shifts in the international arena—the barely perceptible residuals of an evolving worldwide inter-dependence and the inroads of challenges to American economic supremacy. If there is validity to this concept, then the overall national framework may have to assume new dimensions, superseding the very conceptual focus which immediately follows, and adding further complexity to the question of where the national interest lies. The tentative stirrings of concern on this matter will be more fully elaborated in the latter stages of this prologue.

Second, the problem of an uncompromising, aggressive regionalism, while most severe within the latter framework, may in any case pre-cipitate severe national divisions. Assertiveness in many instances is both warranted and vital in the protracted competition for select federal resources. Yet it should not be so inflexible as to diminish the nation's fundamental capacity for concerted national response.

The Organization for Response

Assuming the validity of these trendlines and causal processes, and accepting the premise that the resultant dislocations represent the very harsh future facing our older regions, how do we begin to establish the baselines for public policy and interventionary strategies? As an appro-priate starting point, it is essential to step back and review what we perceive to be the conceptual policy alternatives presently facing the Northeast Region. While the typology does not cover all possible options, it is probably inclusive of the major stances and postures for responding, either implicitly or explicitly, to the task at hand.

THE POLICY FRAMEWORK

The first alternative would be extreme on any continuum—*noninter-vention*. The philosophy inherent in this position is that the market works efficiently, has structured, rather than *been* structured by, federal spending in recent years (i.e., the same forces directing the flows of private economic activity have governed the public sector) and should be left to run its course. According to this thesis, any intervention will serve to lessen overall national efficiency and productivity by perpetuating older obsolete formats of industrial activity, either functionally or geographically. Moreover, if the episode of central city decline is a prologue to regional destiny, such intervention is envisioned as futile in the long run, wasteful of resources, and entails significant opportunity costs. Other elaborations of this philosophy are certainly possible, but most policymakers would probably reject this alternative with due consideration of its consequences. As W. W. Rostow points out, "economic decline is not a graceful process. It is painful, socially contentious, and potentially quite ugly in the political moods and problems it generates . . . regions which choose to go down in the style to which they have become accustomed find it a difficult or even tragic path to follow."

A second policy approach would seek solely the *modification of the parameters of federal expenditures and investments* while letting market forces work themselves out as they may. Underlying this position is the belief that government activities are of varying import in structuring the market, such as the provision of large-scale infrastructures (freeway networks, canal systems, and the like) to which private economic activities respond.

William C. Fruend, an advocate of this position, suggests that:

> In addition to natural economic forces, there have been important policies, man-made in Washington, which have aggravated the northern loss of population, jobs, and incomes . . . . If we discover, as we probably will, that natural economic forces have played a dominant role in producing the economic decline of the Northeast, then policies designed to counter or reverse these trends will not only be futile but inconsistent with national objectives of economic growth and productivity . . . . To the extent that the decline has been due to deep-seated basic longer-run economic forces, there should be no intervention in the form of artificial restraints or incentives . . . . To the extent that the decline of the Northeast has been due to federal

programs such as defense, transit, and welfare expenditures, these programs need to be carefully reexamined.

While Fruend's posture bespeaks a grudging recognition of the federal role—although clearly subservient to "natural" economic forces—an alternative philosophy can derive the same conclusion. Actions of the federal government—discriminatory patterns of federal expenditures and other deliberate policies—are perceived as channeling people and resources away from the Northeast. Market forces are considered subsidiary to and dependent on the role of government in influencing all facets of American life. Hence modifications to the allocation matrix of federal resources are viewed as the only serious response vehicle.

However, the logic of these positions may not be complete. Acceptance of a federal causal role implies that actions and policies of states and municipalities may also shape market forces, and refine the impacts of federal policies. Indeed, any federal response could well be muted by counterproductive behavior by lower-level governments, as well as existing institutional and public strictures. Additionally, the singular focus on the federal domain reduces the effective policy strategy to a "shopping list" of changes demanded of Washington. Nothing difficult is asked of the region itself; no harsh preliminaries to change are necessary. Unfortunately, such "easy" prescriptions often have the tendency to deliver very few substantive results. For example, one of the major issues of federal government support for New York City bonds was the fear that if it were too readily available it would inhibit necessary— if painful—reforms.

Moreover, to passively regard the movements of private economic activity while attempting to redefine the regional parameters of federal outlays may produce the consequence that will be elaborated subsequently: the contours of change may become etched so deeply that even with ultimate federal restructuring, the Northeast may become so depleted that its revitalization capacity wanes. When the critical mass of population, buying power, and economic activity become firmly wedded to new geographic loci, it is difficult to turn back the clock of history and reverse the currents of change, no matter what level of regional parity finally comes to fruition.

This leads to the final end of our abbreviated policy spectrum—*maximum feasible reshaping of government at all levels*—which recognizes that the nation has evolved via close interdependencies between all its public and private sectors. Every level of public governance, as well as the actions of its citizenry, not only defines the broader policy settings of private enterprise, but also provides the infrastructures on which it is vitally dependent.   Hence the role of both the federal and nonfederal public sectors in channeling private market forces is clearly recognized by this perspective, and is encompassed by the overall response strategy.

This set of policies, then, would seek to intervene in the process of federal resource allocation while concurrently attempting to modify state and local environments, and infrastructures, tailoring them to future economic requirements.   It is upon the consideration of this strategy, obviously, that this set of proceedings is premised.

This position, however, is not an easy one to assume, since many recommendations may tend to be unpalatable to the region's political system.   Demanding more federal resources is inherently painless and politically attractive; but the attempt to specify the effective actions the region itself can undertake will undoubtedly require the imposition of costs on its citizenry and political institutions.   As W. W. Rostow notes:

> The problems of the North will not be resolved, then, by incantation or by somewhat enlarged flows of federal funds. . . . Structural trans-formations are clearly possible if there is a common will to accom-plish them, a sense of direction, and a general environment of rapid economic growth. . . .   Part of that process will prove to be the re-gathering of momentum in the North.

Hence within this policy stance it is necessary to examine the political realities of the Northeast—recognizing the hazardous nature of attempt-ing to generalize in this area—for no matter how effective any set of responses could be, their utility is minimal without some measure of basic political feasibility.

The Political Realm

It is via this perspective that the political ambience of the Northeast —the forum and arena of public policy deliberation in the broadest of senses—must be approached.   What are the realities of this environment as it interacts with the residuals of decline and recommendations for intervention?   Before we attempt this elaboration, it is perhaps useful to briefly review the inherent conflict between politics and planning, since this general dilemma will permeate any attempt to forge long-range policies encompassing the entire region.

THE DILEMMA OF POLITICS AND PLANNING

Democracies do well at war, but long-range planning and policy-making have always been troublesome for them.   The political feasibility of the latter is dependent upon consensus, upon the recognition of definable common purposes, and upon a collective perception by major societal groups of a long-term overriding "public interest." These political prerequisites rarely synthesize except in times of threatening crises because they require short-range self-interest and advantage to be submerged. The imposition of immediate costs—burdens not borne equally by political subgroups—is concomitant to efforts designed to achieve future objectives and benefits, whose full range of potential impacts is uncertain and can never be precisely assured. This constraint has a tendency to be overlooked, since "planning" is often promulgated as a means of efficiency, a promise to uncover painless optimum solutions. But long-range decisionmaking often requires the absorption of unavoidable front-end costs—social, political, and economic—which political actors are loath to accept. Political horizons are manifestly short-run; unrelenting pressures for reelection dictate actions predicated on immediate attractiveness, whatever the long-term consequences.

In jurisdictions afflicted by decline, the prerequisites necessary to entertain long-range solutions appear even more difficult to achieve, despite an impending crisis ambience. The affected parties find it difficult to accept short-range burdens when they stand as unique to a limited area rather than general. If alternative habitats are unaffected and insulated, providing a potential refuge for both businesses and individuals, their visibility renders sacrifice even more unpalatable.

Moreover, major reforms also entail rearrangements of existing patterns of accommodation which are in delicate balance due to resource scarcity. For vested interests, the latter condition implies limited options for adapting to circumstances involving reallocation; hence the existence of intensely held beliefs that major policy shifts will only make things worse, since the status quo represents an optimum position for many key parties. Consequently, environments of limited or shrinking resources may be characterized by a plethora of hostilities to long-range strategies if they conflict (which is a virtual certainty) with the positions and immediate needs of select subgroups. The dilemma is that acceding to the demands of the latter tends to preclude the former.

Certainly, we do not want to give the impression of naïvely decrying political realities and constraints. We are well aware and appreciative of the responsibilities of political leaders to their constituencies. Yet we would be remiss not to suggest, as Paul McCracken stresses, that those in political life also have responsibility for the larger- and longer-run good.[4] Nonetheless, one must not lose sight of the reality of the very significant tensions between day-to-day strictures and long-range considerations, particularly when resources are limited. Consequently, it is useful to examine the salient characteristics of the political environment of decline, for they impinge upon every remaining policy variable considered in this discussion.

THE POLITICAL ENVIRONMENT OF DECLINE

The political behavior within decline settings must be seen as evolving from the very process of decline, as well as contributing to and reinforcing its operative parameters. Similarly, at this stage of regional evolution, political constraints may represent an obstacle to the deflection and alteration of the extant trendlines. What we now are able to discern on the regional scale may have been presaged by the urban political scene in the last decade. Its accretion may be considered a logical complement to the spread of urban socioeconomic transformations to metropolitan and regional scales.

At the risk of both oversimplification and overgeneralization, it is now apparent that the nation's declining cities never really had the political capacity to face the fact of economic disinvestment. As Norton Long has observed, the basic reality that the total costs of doing business in cities far exceeded the same cost package prevailing elsewhere—even if recognized—was submerged by a philosophy of income redistribution and maintenance in order to sustain a standard of public and private consumption.[5] The end result of a shrinking economic base—burgeoning social and economic needs of large affected subgroups—created significant demands on a limited urban fisc. Any focus on long-range threshold changes to restore economic vitality—the alteration of the cost structures of conducting economic activity or the contraction of the public sector's functions commensurate with levels of private activity support—was precluded by more immediate pressures on political leadership. Moreover, policy adjustments centering on reductions cause displacements in living patterns and have an inherent tendency to undermine public support. To ignore these pressures was and is political suicide in the absence of a potent constituency supportive of long-range readjustments.

In hindsight it is not difficult to discern that such political behavior often acted as a positive feedback mechanism. Actions plausibly intended to mitigate the residuals of decline—at best outgrowths of real compassion; at worst, self-serving attempts to draw political advantage —served in the long run to accelerate the very dynamics of decline. Was such a political milieu also characteristic of the broader region?

MEDIA EVENTS AND DISSIPATION OF POLITICAL CAPITAL

The New York City congressional delegation, diagnosed by Martin Tolchin, appears to be prototypical of the genre.

> It's a media oriented delegation . . . lacking any clout . . . without a single chairman. The reason . . . was because New York politicians never regarded Congress as an important place. They regarded it as a stepping stone for mayor, or governor, or senator . . . they also happen to be the champions of unpopular causes, champions of Vietnam, the poor, the blacks, etc.

Briefly, the tendency to subvert the long-term substantive interests of the region for short-term popular issues and symbolic actions so often surfacing in "media events"—issues staged on the basis of their theatrical and dramatic potential so as to achieve maximum publicity—have in the past paralleled their urban counterparts.

Paul London expresses similar sentiments in reference to the recent fuel shortages this past winter (1976-1977). The political focus on short-term consumer advocacy may represent the *dissipation of political capital* that is desperately needed to forge a long-term energy resolution truly meaningful to the region's future. Similarly, the seeming compulsion to waste political capital and the region's money on dying neighborhoods and obsolete moribund industry—symbolic gestures so attractive to the media but insignificant in terms of long-term positive accomplishments—tends to submerge the advocates of very rational, but very difficult, policies which at least have the potential to redirect the future.

Moreover, there appears to be a symbiotic linkage between the intellectual climate of the region and such political attitudes. As London suggests, politicians in general always face dilemmas and conflicts in making choices between what is politically appealing and what is economically useful in the long term. Rarely do the two coincide. Unfortunately, as London observes, the intellectual community may also have become infected by the same championing of popular causes —the politically attractive issues—thereby making it easier for politicians to do what they do best anyway—choose the short-term popular political expedient.

THE BROADER INTELLECTUAL AMBIENCE

The environment for "doing business" and for political decision making is not always subject to rigorous quantification; one dimension of a complex ambience is the end product of the behavioral attitudes of a subarea's elite.   Roger Starr differentiates the characteristic differences of the elite as they vary by the growth and decline (shrinkage) phases of urban and/or regional evolution.   Such attitudinal profiles may provide a qualitative index of the range of politically feasible options in areas where the shrinkage phase becomes dominant.

1. In the growth phase, the elite are environmentally indifferent. In the decline state, they are oversensitive. The environmental reception accorded the steamboat in New York in the nineteenth century (favorable) was a marked departure from that granted the Concorde (SST) presently (hostile), although the former represented a more fundamental quantum change in technology and environmental impact.

2. In the growth phase, the elite are marginally compassionate; they are sensitive only to hardship they cannot escape observing. In the decline phase, the elite are guilt-ridden, their compassion has a wider scope—the cities' poor in their entirety.

3. In the expansion phase, the elite are tolerant of and even tend to celebrate growth inequality among individuals. Respect and adulation is granted to business leaders and the major "winners." In the shrinkage context, egalitarianism and outrage against growth inequality among persons is manifest.

4. In the period of growth, the elite are prepared to assess individual responsibility and to assert it against those who break what they regard as a necessary code of society. In the shrinkage phase, a great reluctance to impose individual responsibility is exhibited, even in the case of criminal acts.

5. In the growth phase, the elite are culturally aggressive; in the decline phase, they are culturally defensive, e.g., the opposition to the expansion of the Metropolitan Museum in Central Park.

6. In the growth period, the elite are politically asleep; politics are simple with people inert to them. In the shrinkage stage, they are politically insomniac. There is no subject too small, no matter nor decision too tiny to escape political interest.

It is this set of attitudes, suggests Starr, that has limited what political jurisdictions can do when they start on a downward path, a path that stimulates acceleration. When the elite reinforce inherent political tendencies, the potential for initiation of long-range policy-making and the imposition of threshold changes becomes questionable.

A BASIC PREREQUISITE

Within this attitudinal maze—the intellectual climate and the basic pressures impinging upon political decisionmaking—Paul London isolates a necessary prerequisite for broad meaningful regional responses: we (planners and appointed officials) have an obligation to recognize the kind of issues and dilemmas that politicians face, and to make it easier for politicians to chose the long-term over the short-term. We have a responsibility to reorient the intellectual climate so that politicians can make the tough votes. A support structure must be formed to bolster the feasibility of meaningful policy choices that engender immediate inconveniences. *There are no simple, painless mechanisms of change; if the region is to alter its downward path, the decisionmaking climate must be supportive of the politically difficult choices.*

What London is actually advocating, in reference to the planning profession, is a redirection of recent conventions. Planning's intellectual heritage, predicated on the notions of "public interest" and "general welfare," was subjected to close scrutiny the past decade, and thoroughly rejected in some quarters. Lisa Peattie reflects the sentiments of the latter:

> We believed, and still do, that the concept of a "general welfare" as a guide to policy was a mirage, that societies and cities included in fact a number of particular interests, and that (planning) was actually a political instrument which represented some particular segment of these possible interests, and determined who got what, where, and how . . . the planning process favored the more wealthy and the more powerful. . . .[6]

The response, obviously, was advocacy planning, which attempted to politicize planning and decisionmaking. While not disputing the validity of these sentiments, the extremes of this position have the potential, at best, to thwart many regional initiatives. The revisionist position suggested by London calls for a reaffirmation of a climate that gives weight to select overriding concerns which transcend endless rounds of competitive infighting.

THE CONSENSUS DILEMMA

A potential retardant to the preceding recommendation arises from the extreme breadth of interests encompassed by the Northeast Region and similarly afflicted North Central states. The difficulty of fusing a consensus in such an extended sphere is understandable. Accommodation and any measure of unanimity were rarely achieved in singular political jurisdictions encompassing the "urban crisis." Their attainment within a broad multistate region, whose heterogeneity and multiplicity of interests represent a quantum leap over the urban analog, will be that much more difficult.

This reality has been obscured, however, by the tendency to speak of the Northeast as if it were homogeneous, and its problems as characteristic of the whole rather than of selective subareas and unique interest groups. Regarding simply the larger political parameters of the region, D. Quinn Mills suggests:

> It is extremely difficult to generalize about the Northeast. New York is quite different from New Jersey; Pennsylvania is special in many ways; Massachusetts could not be more different from New Hampshire and, in fact, each state exists in the form that it does because they are adjacent to each other and to a substantial degree they are a reaction to each other.

Hence, fragmentation will be an ever-present threat to any regional initiative, whether the focus is on the federal expenditure maze or on self-generated internal responses. To weave consensus from a seemingly incoherent web of political threads will be a difficult undertaking. But, the hallmark of any effective and meticulous planning accomplished within the region will be the ability to understand, and function within, this constraining political milieu.

The Policy Framework: The Federal Domain

While the implications of the preceding discussion exert their maximum presence on attempts at intra-regional restructuring, they also bear considerable weight on the process of marshaling the region's political clout in forays against the federal treasury. Before entertaining the most prominent targets of such actions, it is useful to explore the foundation which must be firmly embedded to ensure sustained, long-term efforts.

ESTABLISHING REGIONAL CONSCIOUSNESS

Pursuant to preparing initiatives designed to enlist the federal arsenal in attacking the Northeast's economic woes is the process of constructing a *regional perspective*—a regional consciousness. The broader public must comprehend the significance of the regional dimension as it affects their lives and institutions, and modify their beliefs and attitudes accordingly. A process of constituency building has to commence, generating a climate for regional interests. An informed citizenry and organized support base may enable public pressure to impress itself upon the region's political representatives in Washington, providing a stimulus to recalcitrant leadership elements.

Integral to this process—and a necessary preliminary to the forging of consensus—is the task of convincing the relevant parties that the region's current difficulties are not temporary phenomena, but represent the cutting edge of the future. Indeed, Wilbur Thompson suggests that:

> One of the very first steps to be taken in formulating a strong program of economic redevelopment for the Northeast is for its populace to face up to the basic and persisting nature of industrial relocation and population migration . . . . The challenge . . . is to convince the many parties at interest throughout the region that the events of the past half-dozen years are not a transitory aberration but are rather a very deep and persisting trend—or, better, a long swing in relative fortunes. It will be very difficult to formulate good public policy if the Northeast thinks in terms of months or years instead of decades.

Presently, however, with attention focusing heavily on the region's plight, political leadership may not require impetus from the electorate. It may now be *au courant* for the region's federal lawmakers to board the regional bandwagon, since substantial political capital may be gleaned by railing against inequitable federal policies. Few negatives can be associated with attempts to gain greater shares of federal largess; moreover, a convenient scapegoat stands available to mask other real shortcomings and deficiencies.

But while issues and concerns leap into prominence and achieve center stage, they ultimately fade from public consciousness. Thus, an "issue-attention cycle"—heightened public interest followed by boredom and eventual stasis, whatever resolution ensues—must ultimately be confronted. When maximum political advantage has been squeezed from the regional issue, and when public concern dims via oversaturation, will present efforts wane? It is possible, and even probable, that after a frantic series of funding formula adjustments and legislative changes are pursued, a new concern may well rise to the fore.

A LONG-TERM CONSTITUENCY

Yet the region's difficulties are not going to correspondingly wither and fade away. They are the consequence not of transient but of chronic conditions, and are typical of what the future holds unless very long-term programs of regional initiative are seriously, and continuously, entertained. Hence, it is necessary to build a continuing regional constituency—an institutionalized advocacy for regional concerns over time—which strives to maintain the gathering momentum. Perhaps the beginnings of such a constituency have formed as a by-product of the transition from problem recognition to response operationalization—the setting of a regional agenda.

A REGIONAL AGENDA

As Paul London emphasizes, "consciousness-raising on the Northeast-Sunbelt issue is dangerous unless you know what you want to do after you have raised consciousness." The evolution from vague intention to substantial achievement is a difficult one. The task of identifying concrete action foci had been initiated earlier (1972) when New England congressmen and a regional business group pooled resources to create the New England Congressional Caucus and Research Office. The subsequent formation in 1976 of the Coalition of Northeast Governors (CONEG) and the House of Representatives' Northeast-Midwest Economic Advancement Coalition, as well as their respective research groups—the Policy Research Center, Inc., and the Northeast-Midwest Research Institute—has provided the initial toeholds for forging an agenda and represents the embrionic foundation for long-term constituency building.[7]

Yet abstract consensus arising from general problem awareness often has a tendency to dissipate when concrete issues are confronted. Even when targeted at the federal expenditure matrix, Paul London warns:

> I'm not sure that the wider groupings are going to focus on the regional dimensions of the issues. They may get into formulas on which I believe they will find everybody voting their district and not the region.

Despite these forebodings—some of which have already been experienced—Martin Tolchin is nonetheless optimistic about the tightening of the political bonds within the region.

> The Northeast-Midwest Coalition does put the spotlight on 208 members of the House of Representatives. It also, incidentally, provides a data base for them. It makes them much more effective, much more knowledgeable on the implications of all legislation . . . not only on their own districts, but on the region as a whole. . . . The groundwork has been laid, and when new aid formulas and legislation come up, we are going to see the vast majority of these people will be voting together . . . the rest are going to have to explain to their constituents why they are departing from the coalition.

Elaborating further, Tolchin emphasizes that the same media orientation which has produced problems in the past is working to focus public attention on regional congressional delegations. The public is evidencing an awareness of the traditional self-serving behavior and will begin to exert pressure on members situated in the Northeast-Midwest corridor to unite:

> There is going to be definite political pressure on them that just may overwhelm their personal needs and personal political ambitions. The same will probably hold true for the relationship between congressmen and governors. . . . With the public spotlight focused on them, it could be very politically disadvantageous for them not to unite.

The Guidelines. One of the major foci of these groups has been to seek redress on inequitable federal expenditure allocations on a regional base. To varying degrees, all federal expenditures influence regional growth. These implications demand quantification, evaluation, and explication. *The question must be asked whether the national interest requires regional imbalance.*

As Martin Tolchin observes, technology has really meant a new day for congressional formulas. With the use of the computer, print-outs are available literally within hours after the development of any distributional formula. Hence the analytical means exist for examining the regional implications of any proposed legislation or allocation scheme. *At the forefront of any agenda, then, stands the requirement for the constant monitoring of each and every legislative package, ascertaining and disseminating its effect on the regional flow of expenditure dollars.*

Indeed, in the current session of Congress (1977), nine grant-in-aid programs will be considered for extension, all of which redistribute national income via distributional criteria.[8] As this legislation proceeds, it is apparent that regional efforts have already secured increased allotments for the northeastern states, with the coverage by the popular media evidencing keen awareness of the regional allocation debate. For example, countercyclical revenue sharing, a special aid program to areas of high unemployment, provides funds to hard-pressed state and local governments. Its objective is to maintain the recipient jurisdictions' regular levels of employment while avoiding tax increases which could negate the stimulative effect of other federal antirecession policy. The enlargement and extension of the program provides increased resources to states and municipalities of highest unemployment. Despite the efforts of Sunbelt and Midwest legislators to gain greater coverage—ensuring a little bit for everybody—the reworked distribution formula concentrates greater shares of aid to the most severely impacted jurisdictions, i.e., the Northeast. But with the legislation providing for a reexamination of the allocation mechanism after a year's period, it is clear that such efforts may well have to be institutionalized on a day-to-day basis. Nonetheless, the recent experience appears to gauge the emergency of a new northeastern consciousness, as well as the potential effectiveness of the embrionic coalitions.

But whatever immediacies press forth, a period of detached and vigorous study must simultaneously commence. Many relevant issues and legislation will have long periods of gestation. Welfare, for example, stands prototypical. As analysts have noted, "the politics of welfare revisions are among the most complicated ever to swirl around a domestic issue . . . welfare reform could take many years to obtain and that in many respects reform could hurt, rather than help . . . (regional) financial plights." [9] With high benefit levels in the northeastern states representing onerous fiscal burdens—with all the repercussions of the costs of conducting economic activity—early reform proposals emanating from the region called for complete federal financing of the entire system (whose costs it now shares with states and localities in widely varying proportions) and minimum national payment levels. These revisions, as first assumed, would diminish the fiscal stress throughout the Northeast by transferring the bulk of the system's costs to the federal government, while lessening the drawing power of the Northeast for welfare clientele.

Closer examination, however, challenged the virtues of this prescription. If the revenue source for the expanded scope of the program comprised general federal taxes, the Northeast could well experience a net loss, given the region's disproportionate share of federal tax burdens. The reform proposal's substitution of federal for local resources would not compensate the region's contribution to the federal treasury.[10]

Consequently, the redressing of inequitable federal spending patterns is a dual natured task, with both short- and long-term dimensions. The region must continually confront legislative immediacies as they arise, while simultaneously preparing well-researched initiatives regarding major longer-range programatic issues, both in the context of proposed national reforms of fundamental governmental responsibilities— such as welfare—and in the questioning of long-standing predilections —for example, is it in the national interest to deplete the Northeast's inventory of military facilities? For the latter issues, a barrage of hastily initiated actions will not suffice in the long run.

But gaining parity with regard to the balance of general federal tax and expenditure flows is not sufficient by itself to attack the deeper structural problems of the region, nor to recapture lost economic momentum. Affirmative investment policies are required which address the long-term economic potential of the region. Paul London suggests the task should center about the creation of a twenty-first century infrastructure:

> What does a 21st century infrastructure for the Northeast look like? Our aim should be to get the federal government to buy us a 21st century infrastructure. . . . The Northeast should seek major investments in the energy area. Eight hundred billion dollars are going to be spent on energy investment in this country probably in the next ten or fifteen years. We should want a major share of this investment . . . . We will make jobs along the way building infrastructure as we will with energy investment. We should focus on tangible investments that lower the cost of doing business in the Northeast and not piddle our money out a dollar at a time through little programs that make people happy a day at a time.

Indeed, there appears to be an emerging recognition that the revitalization of the Northeast is a development task requiring investment outlays as distinguished from transfer payments.

The operative mechanisms for such policies appear to be rooted in the alphabet-laden institutions of the New Deal era—the TVA, NRA, RFC, and CCC—which helped modernize the South during the Great Depression. As Paul London remarks:

> I would look to the TVA and Bureau of Reclamation and Corps of Engineers and say we want the kinds of things they do. What does

a 21st century infrastructure look like and what does a 21st century Bureau of Reclamation look like. Let's have such agencies building infrastructure in the Northeast.

The same overall perspective is also expressed by W. W. Rostow:

It is likely that a national development bank will be required like the old Reconstruction Finance Corporation. Its authority should extend not only to the fields of energy and energy conservation, but also to the financing of water development, transport rehabilitation and other projects judged of high priority national interest. Wherever possible, such a bank should use its authority to guarantee or to marginally subsidize funds raised privately by state or local governments, rather than engage in full direct financing.

But interpentrating these themes—long-range investment and fundamental restructuring of the broader environment of conducting future economic activity—is the omnipresent pressure for immediate results. The latter represents a dangerous tendency to follow strategies rigidifying the region's structural deficiences. Efforts should not dissipate into programs supporting inefficient industries and subsidizing employment in marginal activities whose longevity is questionable. As William C. Fruend notes, shoring up the inefficient through artificial stimuli will reduce national productivity, and will only forestall the basic confrontation with the requirements to recapitalize the region's aging infrastructure.

If the political configurations within the Northeast can somehow abide by these guidelines, can they function successfully in the broader national political arena? A sense of fairness appears to have prevailed in the cited success in reformulating federal expenditure allocation procedures and distributional mechanisms. However, the same rationale may not suffice for initiating fundamentally new investment programs, which will face stern resistance from the political instrumentalities of the Sunbelt states.

Thus a critical parameter will be the ability of the Northeast to *interface successfully* with the nation's other regional clusters. The latter will increasingly face potential economic and social dislocations as the next decade proceeds—in the Southwest, for example, water will probably be the next great resource crisis, threatening a critical premise of its agricultural base, energy goals, production processes, and individual lifestyles. Whether such impending difficulties will be forced to serve as leverage for harsh inter-regional tradeoffs, or whether they will provide the means for more amiable constructive approaches toward grappling with the structural problems of the individual regions, is as yet uncertain. But as Rostow indicates, when the debate shifts from federal revenue allocation into these terms, an enlarged possibility exists for national policy development mitigating the tensions between regions.

Within this national framework, moreover, the Northeast will still have to make substantial concessions; among them may be *the acceptance of unpalatable and unattractive development*—noxious but necessary public facilities—inherent to infrastructure development. A regional energy policy, for example, may not be able to be predicated on the "raping" of other regions. Although a national phenomenon, there has been an extreme predilection in northeastern jurisdictions to disdain certain development formats. For example, thirteen out of fourteen oil refineries in New England in recent years have been successfully blocked by local opposition.[11] Plausible and understandable as such behavior may be, it stands as a threat to any regional agenda and has the potential to fracture inter-regional accommodations. Indeed, Rostow emphasizes that:

> With energy policy, we face the most potentially divisive issue in the nation. I cannot convey to you with sufficient force the depth of the feeling in the southern energy exporting states about some of the attitudes of the North. At one and the same time, the North appears to be demanding both low energy prices and refusing to develop its own energy resources on environmental grounds. This is seen in the South as a straightforward colonial policy of exploitation . . . it would not be difficult to split the nation, yielding an OPEC within it.

As should be apparent, then, the fundamental attribute of effective national action reduces the ability of the Northeast—in the broadest of senses—*to accommodate solutions within its own geographic sphere. The region must comprehend, address, and articulate what it is willing to do for itself—what risks and burdens its leadership and citizenry are willing to bear—before entering into serious national debate.* To engage in terminal consumerism—to refuse to intercede if it invokes the slightest personal inconvenience—no matter how noble the mantra, is a committment to stasis and decline.

The Internal Regional Response

The federal and regional partition is not a smooth one; the most significant federal actions may imply regional concessions. Moreover, perhaps the most critical juncture to be traversed concerns the natural and self-inflicted deficiences of the region and how they are approached. All of the requisite considerations discussed previously are magnified when the region itself attempts to restructure its basic environment. At the baseline levels—building regional consciousness, forging a constituency, and debating an agenda—a preliminary requirement is to dispel any comforting, but misleading, myths about self-corrective "equilibrating" forces dampening the powerful economic swings presently in effect. Such notions, which obviate facing up to hard and painful decisions, will be readily grasped unless countered effectively.

THE FALLACY OF REGIONAL EQUALIZATION

Perhaps as a subterfuge for confronting a very difficult and ominous reality, shelter has been sought in the notion that as the growth areas of the country mature, their advantageous business cost postures—land, labor, taxes, and so forth—will tend to diminish. Conversely, the parallel slackening of market pressures in the stagnant regions will foster downward adjustments in their cost structures. (Indeed, D. Quinn Mills provides some evidence that the latter may already be occurring.) The conclusion drawn is that, as the regional costs of doing business converge and approach parity, renewed developmental pressure will ensue with the Northeast becoming the focus of renewed industrial activity.

While such logic is, on the surface, plausible and comforting, it bears close similarity to the assumptions earlier invoked on the metropolitan scale, assumptions which never really came to fruition. As economic activity decentralized within metropolitan areas over the past two decades, the assertion was made that the suburban cost advantages were but temporary, due to fade with the passage of time. When the suburbs had to replicate urban services and amenities, when land prices soared, and when the all too familiar problems and externalities of urbanization surfaced, the competitive position of the cities would be restored. While the former have certainly been realized in the suburban arena, the repercussions that were to take place in the city never materialized. Many of the preconditions for the envisioned renaissance were evident, but the reversal of the evolutionary track simply did not occur.

Consequently, it may be hazardous to place faith in similar logics promulgated for eventual regional parity. The time frame necessary for regional equalization permits the flows of development to gain powerful momentum, establishing a critical mass of economic functions in growth areas, and correspondingly diluting the concentration of activity in older territories. Once the level of industrial concentration falls below a minimum threshold, competitive cost structures may not be sufficient by themselves to bolster diminished attractiveness.[12]

ADJACENT PRELIMINARIES

Other difficulties will abound as local political realities demand quick solutions, as well as avoidance of, what London terms, "the issues that require political guts." The desire for immediate results raises several concerns which penetrate the policymaking agenda. The first, expressed by D. Quinn Mills, revolves around the possibility of formulating strategies which would "rigidify the current situation and keep us in the business of supporting and maintaining inefficient industries." The end result would forestall coming to grips with the region"s basic problems, providing but a temporary respite from the fundamental transition. Instead, what needs to be done "is to identify what the future will look like, what the country wants it to look like, what industries will develop and grow, and what affirmative public policies will support and cushion the development."

A second concern, also raised by Mills, can be labeled the *negative feedback dilemma*. If it is possible to design policy initiatives which offer the promise of revitalizing the Northeast's economy, and if the economy is somehow stimulated, will it tend to be choked off by a resurgency of the same kinds of behavior that created the problem in the first place? Will the sacrifices made to restore economic vigor fall prey to renewed prosperity, returning the region to its present, inadequate competitive status? Such questions must be confronted throughout all stages of response consideration and design.

One final consideration is suggested by Wilbur Thompson. What may be a very basic necessity is the realization, perhaps grudgingly, that to be effective, response mechanisms may have to:

> work with, rather than oppose, current trends. Too often we try to turn completely around powerful market forces with relatively weak public policies when the best we could hope to do (within our political institutions) is to bend those trends a little and adjust more gracefully to their main thrust.

Heeding these preliminaries, how can the region's public sectors adjust to a process that has seemingly propelled its economic status into a plethora of negatives? Initial efforts, whose long-term impact is vague, have stressed the alteration of the broader environment for conducting economic activity—a concern inherent in several of the hypothesized factors of decline. Since subregional units of government directly influence sectors of the total business cost package, while standing helpless in regard to other causal processes, certain policies lend themselves to immediate consideration. The question is whether they can produce substantive results.

The Context. The broader settlement patterns of the Northeast—the chain of central cities forged in the industrial age—are of a complexity rarely paralled in the history of urbanization. Yet that same attribute—complexity—has become one of the principal liabilities of the region; as new technologies have evolved to prominence, the Northeast has remained a virtual hostage to the parameters of a distant past.

The historic industrial metropolis of the region was a unique conjunction in time and space, a special adaptation to mobility restrictions bounding the movements of individuals, goods, and services. Its form and structure permitted a set of interdependencies to be stretched beyond the confines of the former pedestrian city. Within its bounds flourished high levels of services and amenities which were just not feasible in more distant hinterlands. And the extent to which they could spread was defined by mature rail systems and early highway developments.

The evolution to suburbanization and subsequently to regional shift was the result of the increasing homogenization of mobility, which, in the context of other technological developments, loosened the strictures of spatial contiguity. While the Northeast in part adapted to these new parameters, with many of its lesser urban centers becoming voids in the regional land use pattern, a substantial legacy of the older order remains. This comprises not only an inefficient capital plant and the costs it imposes, but also a host of institutions whose longevity renders them virtually immune to alteration—relationships have become wedded to fixed patterns. As these concerns are translated into specifics—taxation, the labor force matrix, and infrastructure—factors are evident which plausibly define the economic competitiveness of the region. As such, they impact the cost of conducting economic activity and serve as preliminary policy focal points.

MODIFICATION OF THE BUSINESS COST PACKAGE

The traditional location decisionmaking calculus encompasses within its logic the minimization of the total costs of producing goods or services. While certain elements are inviolate to governmental strictures and policy stances, other components of the cost package are strictly defined by governmental parameters. Receiving foremost attention among the latter are state and local taxation and business disincentives. It is rare indeed when public utterances by private industry about locational choices do not invoke the spector of evacuating high tax jurisdictions for the virtues of low tax environments. And given the surface plausibility of these arguments, politicians have readily grasped at policies offering business tax relief.[13] What are the myths and realities of such contentions?

The Efficacy of Tax and Business Incentive Mechanisms. The effect of taxation on industrial location has been subject to sustained debate without clear resolution. This is not surprising, since it is virtually impossible to clarify its effects from that of a cluster of simultaneously interacting factors. But the latter are not subject to effective monitoring. In contrast, highly visible tax burdens—and their converse, business incentive mechanisms—have been ascribed importance since they are amenable to quantitative reduction and comparison.

While tax burdens have provided the publicly voiced justifications for vacating select geographies, Harrison contends, for the most part, that their contribution to the bottom line profitability of the firm may not be of the magnitude supposed.[14] Nonetheless, excessive taxation represents a cost that a firm does not have to bear willingly if more hospitable environs exist.

Whatever the ultimate economic significance of the taxation variable to the firm, its more subtle implications must be underscored. Recent studies of the Philadelphia economy—a prototype of the northeastern transformation—have stressed the importance of tax burdens as *signals*, both of a hostile business environment and as a prelude to further "exploitations" of private sector activities.[15] As these concerns filter into the locational decisionmaking process, it is apparent that their weight may be very significant indeed.

If we concede that high taxation can be a deterrent to economic viability, it is by no means established that the converse—reductions via tax incentive and subsidy mechanisms (such as tax abatements and low-cost loans)—assures the restoration of past virtues and competitive postures. Yet this assumption is very casually invoked. The wielding of locational incentives by the southern states has received ample publicity throughout the past several decades; their visibility and apparent success has led to their emulation by the older industrial states as their economies weakened. But again it is difficult to establish the significance of the impact of incentive strategies on the economic evolution of the

South.   Undoubtedly, however, their relevance is linked to the phenomenon of *obsolescence and threshold effects.*

Relocation decisionmaking is often bound to the economic reality of
threshold effects, i.e., unless broader cost "environments" are altered by
sufficient magnitudes over a specific period of time, the economic activities in question will probably ignore these alterations since the very
process of reacting to them may entail internal costs of similar magnitude.
Moreover, the returns to any attractive adaptation are always insecure.

For example, firms with relatively efficient facilities are not likely to
relocate solely on the basis of locational incentives, since the costs of
relocation may not be compensated by the anticipated savings.   Conversely, an enterprise with an obsolete physical plant, whose inefficiencies
may force a decision to move, i.e., it is at the threshold, may be more
likely influenced by differential tax provisions, but only within the context of the broader business cost package.

It is conceivable that the latter scenario encompasses some of the
events comprising the regional shifts of economic activity.   Although
definitive empirical evidence is lacking, we would suggest that portions
of the manufacturing losses of the Northeast represent the final stages
of obsolescence, both of very old facilities and production processes
as well as products superceded in the marketplace.   Major decisions of
relocation were faced since firms were at or near the threshold, and
marginal cost considerations—of which tax inducements were but one
—became important.   And as we have noted earlier, the broader business
environment—comprising the full complement of business costs and
benefits—are far superior in the southern growth sectors even in the
absence of tax subsidy provisions.

Situational Contexts: Differential Incentive Effects.   But what of the
converse—the institution by states in the Northeast of tax incentives to
maintain or stimulate employment?   This question cannot be approached
in general, but only in reference to the specifics of a range of unique
situations.   Locational decisionmaking varies industry to industry as well
as within each industry's or its component facilities' stage in life cycle;
the influence of incentives is certainly not constant over these possibilities.   Although the following contexts and conditions are not all inclusive,
they should assist in narrowing the policy perspective.

> *First,* activities which have relocated in the immediate past out of
> the region are, for the most part, no longer at a threshold position.
> Incentive mechanisms, at this point in their life cycle, probably would
> represent only a marginal alteration in their cost structures.   Con-

sequently, such firms are not likely to respond to any stimulus provided by vacated territories.[16]

Second, whatever the broader locational parameters, certain activities tend to settle near their markets. Given the increasing market strength of the Sunbelt, defined by rising personal income, firms predicated on the resulting demand may be spatially linked to it, rendering impotent any incentives provided by states geographically distant from the final market.[17]

Third, the Northeast and North Central states still represent strong markets in and of themselves, notwithstanding the growing affluence of the Sunbelt. Some minimum floor of manufacturing activity (as well as a much higher contingent of population serving activities) is intimately bound to the older regions by virtue of market considerations. In this context, subsidy mechanisms then produce what Harrison and Kanter term *incentive displacement*: since the recipients would have acted as they did in the absence of the subsidy—by employing their internal resources—the subsidy displaces, rather than complements, the effect of local investment resources.[18]

A *fourth* case or condition arises from *agglomeration economies,* which induce long-distance moves to be made in clusters, since certain industries are interdependent. If the primary moves, its dependents must likewise follow suit; conversely, the latter are place dependent (at least to some minimum distance) if the primary remains in place. Incentive provisions in this context would tend to induce either a displacement effect or be impotent.[19]

A *fifth* situation evolves from what Harrison and Kanter suggest is the *dual nature* of locational decisionmaking. Very different types of criteria bound decisions of interregional (long distance) and intraregional relocations. Regions are first chosen on the basis of broad qualitative considerations (the entire business environment/cost-benefit package). Once the region has been selected, then the choice of the particular state within that region may be predicated on the marginal costs of doing business. Business incentive mechanisms may be significant in this case; however, intraregional competition is precipitated, with states vying over limited economic activity. While this may be rational behavior at a statewide level, clearly the region—which in any case will capture the industry—as a whole may experience substantial opportunity costs.[20]

A *sixth* case may be construed as a subset of the fifth, arising from a process of *intraregional decentralization*. As the traditional industrial metropolis—which does not respect formal state boundaries—undergoes a spatial transformation into a "post-industrial" or "post-suburban" format, intraregional dispersion is fostered. The introduction of incentive provisions to activities enveloped within this matrix of change produces no new net increment of employment or investment in the broader region, and may only serve to reduce the region's tax income and increase its opportunity costs.[21]

Overriding this select range of situations is the relative significance of establishment relocation within the total process of employment growth and decline, as differentiated from expansion and contraction of establishments in place, and the formation of new and the demise of old establishments. Indeed one recent study of manufacturing employment change in New Jersey asserts that:

> The popular concern with relocation is misplaced. Establishment growth (in place) dominates the process of employment location change. Relocation is clearly *not* the most powerful process altering the distribution of employment.[22]

Hence the band of economic activities significantly affected by incentive availability may turn out to be quite narrow. If the subsidies then accrue mostly to firms for doing what they would have done anyway, then the costs of incentives may, as Harrison and Kanter suggest, outweigh the benefits received.

Policy Parameters. While they probably cannot promise or deliver immediate deflections of the trends in effect, tax incentive mechanisms may have to constitute a portion of a broader response package, if only to gain parity to the purported benefits offered by the Sunbelt states. Furthermore, *they may also be an essential signal of the region's willingness to respond to charges of unfavorable business postures. But it is essential that within the region there be coherence and equalization between each state's operative provisions.* If this is not the case, the region's overall response may dissipate into furious cutthroat interstate competition. Indeed, Norman Krumholz and Janice Cogger suggest that unrestrained "competition between states and amongst localities to attract new investment may result in something similar to a gasoline price war." Given this supposition, *this policy question may not be so much the employment of locational incentives—they are already a fact of life—but the standardization of provisions throughout the region in order to minimize the factional disputes between its member states.* The attempt to operationalize such a policy should constitute an effective test of the region's basic capacity for consensus.

Moreover, the probability that relocation may be substantially less important than the growth of establishments already in place lends credence to the observation of Krumholz and Cogger that the best approach to economic stabilization *"may not be to attract the new, but to hold on to what you have got."* Consequently, an appropriate role for incentive mechanisms may be the effectuation of this policy—the retention of economic activity already situated within the domain of the incentive granting institution. And in select jurisdictions, the fear that this represents an unwarranted subsidy in the face of overwhelming social needs is allayed by the fact that business tax burdens *are* onerous. In New York City, for example, differential assessment practices and rent control provisions may have effectively biased the distribution of taxation away from the residential sector. In such a context, the incentive mechanisms may in fact represent an equalization provision.

Moreover, the scope of the taxation variable cannot be confined to its impingement upon the corporate balance sheet; also of direct relevance is its impact on the economic postures of individual employees as reflected by personal tax levies and the cost of living matrix. While considerably less attention has been granted the personal counterpart to business tax burdens, its importance should not be underestimated. As we have suggested earlier, the basic residential and work environment preferences of the more important employee subgroups have secured increased consideration by the locational decisionmaking apparatus of footloose industries. If the personal tax burdens imposed by a jurisdiction tend to repel select employees, a deterrent to industrial stability and growth may result.

Indeed, as D. Quinn Mills points out, the combination of state and local taxes in New York state consume double the national percentage share of the income of high income families. It is not difficult to discern, then, the problem of establishments in New York City—where the burden is even higher—of attracting young management to this locale. Moreover, many corporate headquarters have also experienced difficulties in inducing their employees to accept transfers to New York City. Such experiences certainly bear more than limited scrutiny in assessing corporate relocation prospects. Economists in this age of "soft" locational decisionmaking have perhaps overstressed corporate profit motivation rather than the personal fisc of the decisionmaker.

It is puzzling, therefore, that New York City—while struggling to improve its business climate by redefining the business taxation package—is also considering increases in its commuter income tax levy, replacing one deterrent with another. What this scenario emphasizes is *the basic policy requirement of consistency with regard to the entire question of tax burdens and incentives. The simple respositioning of levies within the broader business environment is, to say the least, not conducive to long-term confidence in the economic viability of a particular regional setting, and negates other thrusts to foster a more affirmative climate for conducting business.*

The Labor Force Matrix. The preceding issue potentially represents a response tactic at its worst. A little tinkering with a mechanism susceptible to public intervention may spawn a political facade of vigorous counteraction, relieving the pressure for more fundamental intercessions. However, dilemmas arise in confronting adjacent concerns if they are substantively inviolate to the domain of the traditional governmental medium. To a degree, wage rates and productivity appear at first glance to be of this mold.

These factors have been stressed as leading attractions of the Sunbelt states. However, D. Quinn Mills, examining the extant wage rate statistics, finds it difficult

> to see the pressure of wage rates in general on the location of manufacturing industries or, for that matter, other kinds of industries, except to some degree in the New York City area. Now that is not to say that in certain industries that pressure does not exist. But across the broad range of manufacturing activities, the Northeast has been losing manufacturing jobs and relative positions substantially at a time when, with some few exceptions—New York City being the major one—its wage increases have not been above the national average.

Bernard L. Weinstein, comparing the business climates of New York and Texas, also suggests that lower labor costs in general cannot be pinpointed as a major factor attracting business investment to Texas.[23] Indeed, less tangible, ancillary factors—such as work attitudes—may impinge more heavily on the process of employment location, affecting productivity levels not adequately measured by the nation's basic economic accounts.

> The labor force in Texas seems to have more positive attitudes toward work than is the case in New York. Whether these attitudes stem from a strong fundamentalist tradition or the absence of viable alternatives to work—such as welfare or unemployment insurance— is unclear.[24]

If the latter is the case, Weinstein points to several public policy factors which help mold this attitudinal profile.

> Although Texas has large pools of both skilled and unskilled labor, only 13 percent of the workforce is unionized as compared to 38 percent in New York. Texas, like most other southern states, has a right-to-work law which prohibits union or agency shops. State labor laws also provide employers with extensive legal coverage for strikes, picketing, and boycotts. In addition, employer taxes for unemployment and workman's compensation are 70 percent below the national average.[25]

Hence unionism per se, as well as the public policies which enhance its institutionalization, is seen as a fundamental dimension of a negative business climate. As Mills points out:

> It happens—perhaps it shouldn't but it does—that there continues to be in our country a substantial element of business decisions about the location of plants and capital investment which involves the attempt to avoid unions.

If these views are correct, what are the policy guidelines for the region? Again the equalization argument stresses stamping the union label on the South's rapidly swelling and largely unorganized work force, fostering national parity of an essential element affecting economic activity location. Certainly, with national labor leaders observing once unionized jobs retreating to southern enclaves, a strong national campaign has been mobilized.[26] At the same time, however, fighting unions has become a major preoccupation of many corporate managements.[27] A conflict of major proportions is shaping up, but as Mills suggests, it can be assured that the unionization stance of the South is not going to change very fast.

With equalization but a tentative glimmer on a distant horizon, the Northeast must continue to look inward. As Harrison contends, the region would certainly not want to emulate the labor policies of a Taiwan or South Korea, favored bastions of labor intensive economic activities. *But the states of the Northeast must take an active role to facilitate ongoing cooperation between labor and management—and between the public and private sectors—molding an environment more conducive to economic viability.* The antibusiness posture, most perceptible in New York, must be countered.[28]

Certainly, the weight of the crisis dimension can enhance this possibility, by making such changes palatable through desperation. Yet two cited concerns still press forth. If action is only precipitated by the threshold level of "pain" induced by nonaction, substantial economic activity may be irretrievably lost. And if some immediate, but temporary, accommodations are reached, will they disintegrate upon the advent of any sustained economic vigor? Hence the policy requirement is for both immediate responses and permanent mechanisms and instrumentalities—the latter to enhance the long-term confidence of the private economic sector.

Energy and Infrastructure Rebuilding. The absence of indigenous and/or readily available energy resources has rendered the northeastern states dependent upon other regions of the nation and the balance of the world for their basic energy sustenance. Historically obscured by an environment of inexpensive abundance, the precarious status of importer (particularly of petroleum) has been rapidly thrust home by threshold changes in the world's energy order. Combined with the highest energy costs in the nation, the Northeast now experiences massive flows of capital out of the region, and with it, lost investment and industrial expansion potential. And as energy costs escalate, the states of the Northeast will experience a further diminishing of their business cost postures.

As the country begins the arduous task of forging a basic energy policy, it is incumbent that the region ensures its interests are properly advocated. What will probably emanate from the national debate are domestic energy resource projects—representing large federal investments—primarily situated in the western parts of the country. Invariably, such solutions will aggravate the Northeast's energy dependency problem—continued capital drains from the region—as well as stimulating private investment and employment in the energy–producing territories.

Unfortunately, the requirement to counter these tendencies, and to secure a share of such national investment, may not assure an effective response when the debate turns to particulars. The region's precarious position is not solely the consequence of natural resources endowment, or a lack thereof. As has been stressed previously, the intellectual and political milieu of the Northeast has been fine tuned to a state of consummate environmental awareness. Many self-help energy proposals have and will suffer the fate of politically repulsive issues. When seemingly innocuous and benign generalities as "shares of energy resource investment" and "infrastructure rebuilding and development" are transformed into operational specifics—coal burning and solid waste power plants, overhead electrical transmission lines, nuclear facilities, highway projects, and solid and liquid waste disposal facilities—manifest public resistance has the capacity to immediately induce political stasis. The transition of the region's economic assumptions— from abundant low–cost, but high pollution, energy to limited high-cost environmentally safeguarded energy—have produced a dilemma of rarely paralleled domestic complexity.

The exportation of environmental degradation cannot be achieved without the corollary flows of capital resources. It is a precarious regional bargaining position to demand cheap energy and benefits while insisting that other areas of the country shoulder the environmental costs. Public and political resistance to the siting of energy facilities raises the possibility of the Northeast mortgaging its future in order to avoid immediate burdens and unpleasantries. Continued reductions in relative and absolute economic stature will ultimately confront the region with all their harsh implications if the energy trendlines are not somehow arrested.

Nonetheless, one of the major proposals to facilitate this development centers on the creation of a regional energy development corporation, authorized with bonding power to raise and lend capital.[29] Its first priority would be to generate new energy systems and, secondarily, economic development. Initially to be created by interstate compact—in the mode of the Port Authority of New York and New Jersey—the entity has been recast into the format of a federally chartered regional corporation. The former had little chance of congressional approval if it did not first get the approval of the legislatures of the individual states; going to the states first presented the hazard of a single state's objecting to the proposal, thereby effectively scuttling it.[30] Since a federally chartered agency would not require approvals of state legislatures, such a directional tack probably serves as a barometer indicating the difficulty of the region's achieving some measure of internal consensus.

Although the functional activities of the corporation have not been fully clarified,[31] it is interesting to observe the rationale for its creation. Vigorously proposed by Felix Rohatyn—chairman of New York's Municipal Assistance Corporation (Big MAC) and a veteran of instituting politically infeasible measures—the following logic was suggested:

> With $15 billion in lending authority, Rohatyn said, the corporation could induce politicians "to do what they know they should do" but have not dared to do. "What you would have here," he said, "is an entity which could say to a governor, 'Look, here's a $2 billion investment. But before we can make it, we'll need the following changes in your tax structure. We'll need changes in union work rules. And so on.'"[32]

But to serve in this manner requires political autonomy, implying an inevitable tradeoff between efficiency and accountability—freedom to control. These are often conflicting phenomena; securing gains in one may yield a lessening of the other. The dangers inherent to such a vehicle—since it is predicated on an efficiency criterion—may generate resistance to the powers that can make it effective.

Indeed, the era of public authorities insulated from the electorate may be over. Even the independence of the once mighty Port Authority of

New York and New Jersey is questioned. *In our time reform must come from popular commitment.*

Policies for Transition: Reduction in Status. A visible dismantling of the industrial cities that emerged during the nineteenth century has been a corollary and contributing factor to the regional evolutionary process and the euphemistically labeled "maturation" of the northeastern economy. As these loci of decline expand concentrically, there is a concurrent regrouping of social and economic viabilities in postsuburban frameworks. Bands of affluence and centers of contraction represent the territorial expression of the region's fundamental transition.

Should the Northeast's new capital investment programs be used to enhance the development and strength of the exurban growth bands, where the attendant multiplier effects have a greater probability of being achieved, but at the cost of simultaneously hastening the demise of weaker, older centers? Or should they be targeted to the maintenance of some residuum of economic activity in areas undergoing sustained decline?

Again, these are considerations abundant with political hazard, since they may imply the virtual "writing off" of particular territories while simultaneously confronting the growth control dilemmas in the suburban and exurban arenas. But the marshaling of resources to expedite the development of the post-industrial metropolitan format—and to foster the powerful cumulative effects of new "urban" growth—may be a strategy necessary to meet the challenge of the emerging regional parameters of the next decade.

But what of the less fortunate jurisdictions? Is there a plausible strategy—as distinct from tenuous philosophic stances—for confronting ominous trendlines? For example, Newark's population in 1950 stood at 439,000. By 1975, it had declined to below 340,000 people, a loss of nearly a quarter of the base. In the 1970 to 1975 period alone, it registered a decline of 42,000 people. And this is not a unique phenomenon; contraction is a condition of marked proportions in our aging central cities. Images of an affluent and vigorous past cannot be resuscitated into expectations for the future. Can this basic reality be faced?

Planned Shrinkage. Although Roger Starr has the strong impression that his phrase "planned shrinkage" will run a poor second to "benign neglect" in the Unappreciated Phrases Derby, it remains that shrinkage or contraction is a fact of life for many jurisdictions in the Northeast.

To suggest any such strategy, however, has been to speak the unspeakable, generating negative emotional responses not ameliorated by reasoned qualification. Starr, for instance, has been accused of implicitly advocating racial genocide when his first utterances to this end were noted. Despite the hazards of pursuing the concept further, the rationale of a planned shrinkage strategy must be reviewed, if only because of the paucity of realistic alternative responses.

Given the dynamics sketched out earlier—including the notion that the Northeast is overdeveloped relative to its future economic role—it is apparent that more and more areas are not only characterized by declining populations and fiscal resources, but by redundant infrastructures. It is fiscal suicide to try to maintain a capital plant and service structure geared to a level of clientele associated with the distant past. Sooner or later, the reality has to be faced that an area cannot survive if the pattern of its costs remains the same for a smaller level of population and economic activity as it was for a larger. A planned shrinkage strategy, according to Starr, attempts to take notice of the fact of shrinkage and make some prudent efforts to outline a long-range set of municipal policies that accommodate to it. Since it is already happening, the transition may be eased by explicitly planning for it rather than refusing to recognize its existence.

Norman Krumholz presents several dimensions of a constructive shrinkage policy as they are currently being realized in the domain of Cleveland—divestiture of certain responsibilities while simultaneously accepting new ones. Standing as examples are the transfer of certain facilities and activities to other entities which can draw upon a broader base for their financial support, and moving into the land banking business. Krumholz has few illusions that there will be an immediate market for most of the land that the city will obtain through this process. But the assemblage of such parcels into large tracts—if not inefficiently disposed of due to immediate pressures—may present future opportunities to deal with the physical requirements of new economic and industry parameters, as well as the space to respond to a new or redefined infrastructure package.

But other elements of a shrinkage strategy may be less palatable, politically and socially. Select services reduction, rather than transfer, are painfully difficult. Indeed, Starr's concept of concentrating resources on select growth pockets within cities and withdrawing them from areas of incipient decline—albeit with affirmative policies to resettle and reconcentrate a shrinking population within the growth enclaves—has met fierce opposition. But ultimate restructuring can only be impeded by the region's municipalities saddling themselves with the maintenance and operation of what now appear to be redundant facilities, as well as inefficient service delivery to scantily inhabited neighborhoods. The fiscal burdens not only reduce the potential for expenditures having more productive impacts, but also act as accelerators to a continued path of economic contraction. Thus planned shrinkage, if it can rid itself of perverse connotations, implies facing up to, rather than postponing, the inevitable day of reckoning.

Clearly, the operational mechanisms of this strategy will have to be worked out over a considerable period of time. However, preliminary guidelines are offered by Krumholz and Cogger.

> *Imposition of Restraints*—the avoidance of committing resources to projects and programs offering few returns or public benefits, require high future operating costs, as well as proposals geared toward past realities. Efforts should stress holding on to existing assets rather than attempting to attract new ones, unless extraordinary circumstances so dictate.

> *Creative Investment Resources*—seeking opportunities to direct resources toward programs and projects which will result in long-term savings, make existing systems work more efficiently, or will channel private resources toward the fulfillment of public objectives.

> *Management Emphases*—the shifting of the traditional planning functions to the management of stasis and decline. The task is to provide a reasonable level of services, while fiscal resources and population levels decline, by working closely over long periods of time with operating departments.

> *Strengthening Community Organizations*—not traditional citizen participation but the alliance with neighborhoods already mobilized with active agendas. These would serve as the pivotal residential stabilization points in an overall shrinkage context.

Also stressed by Starr is the following guideline:

> *Internal Resettlement*—encouraging the natural flow out of areas that have lost general attraction, fostering concentration and social cohesion in territories that remain alive and making the provision of municipal services economical.

But a further extrapolation of the latter provision may be the logical complement to a planned shrinkage formula. If, as Wilbur Thompson has remarked previously, we find a way to admit, politically, that depopulation is not only a likely and logical consequence of the aging of urban capital, but is actually occurring and demands explicit policy, then what must concurrently be put to evaluation is the question of broader policies of *assisted out-migration*, as distinct from internal resettlement.[33]

Migrational Disincentives and Relocation Allowances. While the migration of America's citizenry to the Sunbelt may not exactly be of the floodtide that rhetoric so often imposed, it does signify a curious aspect of America's regional development policy—at least if one disdains assigning cynical motives to a past national administration. As D. Quinn Mills asserts, "historically we have a history of letting regional development go where it will." In somewhat analogous fashion, Starr observes that the national strategy of dealing with localized stasis or decline has simply been to open up frontiers and permit or encourage migration—with the western homesteading program standing as a case in point. The free flows to the southern rimlands reflect this history, except that an unanticipated impedence has made this migration a selective one. As Mills interprets:

> We have developed over the past thirty or forty years a whole series of social welfare programs—unemployment compensation, welfare, etc.—which regardless of how the financial burdens are distributed, find themselves acting to hold the population in areas where it now exists. So we have created for ourselves a society in which we have much more restraint on movement of population than we used to. To what degree are we prepared to adopt policies which have the function of smoothing these kinds of transitions in our economy?

Confronting the latter question head on, Wilbur Thompson suggests the need for public policies assisting out-migration, since "if depopulation will come sooner or later, a little contraction sooner that maintains productivity and income levels may eliminate the need for more contraction later."

> The strongest kind of case can be made for relocation allowances across much of the Northeast and Midwest, especially when they are contrasted with the prevailing inter-regional differentials in public assistance, unemployment compensation and other transfer payments. Various financial aids to migration could change the reward

structure to induce redundant labor to leave the Northeast while the present pattern of much higher transfer payments in this region acts as a strong incentive to stay on with the least excuse.

Certainly the increasing economic stature of the South and the West North Central states has in part been due to the "unloading" of redundant population as labor intensive agriculture declined. To suggest now that the Northeast likewise encourage a redundant—and perhaps overlapping, populace to move on sounds ominously like a policy to keep permanently transient a marginal subset of America's citizenry. But, as Thomas Clark points out, relocation allowances to stimulate out-migration have been a continuing center of attention as they have been implemented in the Appalachian region. And if the more mobile sectors of our society are freely pursuing the economic opportunity of the nation's growth zones, should not the less mobile be afforded a similar choice? As to its political feasibility, Thompson suggests:

> An urban area that does come to accept the probability that its local economy cannot support, for the foreseeable future, a population and labor force quite as large as the one it inherited from the past, may come to support relocation allowances and other aids to migration.

The entire issue, however, is much broader than merely providing incentives to exit. The territories to be ostensibly bestowed a population seeking full admittance to American society may not replicate the behavior that our urban centers have traditionally granted to new arrivals. As Peter A. Morrison has recently pointed out, the new potential destination areas, as well as the nation itself, may not explicitly address the questions Who gets to live where? and Who is to decide and by what criteria? But assuredly they may not avoid providing implicit answers, which in effect amount to rationing systems controlling local settlement patterns.[34] It is not inconceivable, then, to envision a habitually abject subcitizenry caught in an interminable migration cycle, permanently external to the nation's economic system.

The threatening cloud of this possibility forces a return to the opposite end of the political spectrum—not only the national will to confront this problem, but also its basic capacity in the face of compelling international economic challenge.

The Broader International Confrontation

Is the context of our current thinking too limited? Is the regional perspective merely a brief interlude on an evolutionary track leading to ever increasing scales of causal influence? Are we concentrating upon variations of regional growth rates at the very time when the nation should rather be focusing on the international equivalent? Is the true competition, which the lagging northern economies face, that of the South—or is it increasingly the aggressive and hard-hitting equivalent of a Japan or a Taiwan?

The history of efforts at revitalizing America's older industrial cities indicates that, regardless of the generosity or paucity of the tools that were brought to bear, their application was both too little and too late. The basic momentum of the shifts of high growth technology, of expanding industry, and of labor rationalization had already developed beyond either the capacity or will to cope with the shifts. Perceiving suburbia as a villain masked the very reality of economic evolution. Are we in danger of replicating the same phenomenon when we address northern decline as a product of southern growth?

It may be appropriate to suggest that any effort at regional redress which is not eventually placed within the international context may be doomed to failure, partaking of fighting this year's war with last year's weapons. Efforts to reinvigorate the North may have to be preceded by an agenda of the economic functions and objectives to be pursued competitively by the United States as a whole. Once these have been established, the regional requirements and their optimization can be considered. Failure to do the former, however, may make the latter process at best a transient, and a losing, exercise. But if steps are not taken promptly to revitalize the aging areas, the pattern of decline may be set. Today's inputs, or their lack, will determine the locational "rationality" of tomorrow's national planning.

WHERE IS THE NATIONAL INTEREST?

Much of the discussion summarized here reflects a basic premise of a zero sum game—one in which previous southern gains have been at the North's expense—with partisans of the latter area attempting to reverse the process. But neither the North or the South, nor the United States as a whole, functions or resides in a vacuum. Factored into the equation and its ultimate resolution must be the interests of the United States as an entity within an increasingly competitive world environment.

If we conceive of the United States as a single region, and extrapolate the developmental framework of W. W. Rostow, then we may perceive the balance of the world's regions catching up to the United States, whose economic position can only be maintained through continued infusions of advanced technology and increased productivity. Does the emergence of the Sunbelt signify an adaption to this emerging reality, with the North seemingly unable to restructure itself so as to restore its competitive position in the world arena?

The current national balance of payments deficit indicates the failure of our export industries and commodities to keep pace with the rising costs and quantities of both imported energy and other sustenance and consumption requirements. Indeed the relatively slow growth of United States economy—often excused by its absolute level—marks the clear danger of a declining worldwide competitive status. From the national viewpoint therefore, the primary issue may not be to redress the real or fancied imbalances between its internal regions, but rather to project national necessities and world realities and to utilize governmental policies so as to optimize those parameters. In this context, the rebuilding of the North at the expense of the South without attendant overall growth may be disastrous. It can lead to the deification of properly-past industrial endeavors and public spending patterns which cannot be maintained in the long run if they impede the vigor of national advancement.

The basic question, therefore, is whether the national interest is best served by policies optimizing present trends, i.e., following the current pattern of federal spending and development (which parallels and amplifies contemporary private shifts), rather than acting as a buffer against them. The analogy may be appropriate to public policy (both that which has been verbalized and that which has been implemented) toward central city revitalization. Despite much expostulation to the contrary, the realities of government policy have largely left behind the old infrastructure of industrial development in the central city.

The national highway program, for example, has been far more influential as a tool for generating vast shifts of employment opportunity than all of the expenditures on urban renewal. It should be noticed in this context that the latter in its entire history amounts to barely $10 billion—while the former may eventually reach ten times that. Tax policy has encouraged new development rather than the rehabilitation and revitalization of old, while government financing at all levels has substantially enhanced the capacity to develop the new outer ring infrastructure of housing, sewerage, waste treatment facilities, and the like in suburban and exurban areas. The vacuum of function and support in the central cities has been filled rather by essentially nongrowth economic inputs—of transfer payments for welfare and make-work tasks.

Without questioning the merits, or the lack thereof, of this de facto policy, we may well ask whether the same can be afforded for regions as a whole. Can we permit large stretches of the Northeast and Midwest to decline in economic function, in job base, and ultimately in population? Do we want to? Unfortunately there is little in the way of formal economic analysis or projective technique that has addressed the former area and little real consensus on the latter. However, "no policy" is clearly policy that has a high danger of leading to that result. The White House Conference on National Growth Objectives scheduled for mid-1978 may provide a formal baseline for a renewed public examination of the options. The performance, however, of prior goal-announced government planning efforts has been relatively poor in the past. For example, the congressionally mandated HUD *National Growth Reports* have been significant only in their insignificance.[35]

To repeat: there is a basic policy issue that cannot be avoided if significant federal intervention is undertaken. Should it take the shape of cutting back southern development funds or of increasing their northern equivalent? The quandary is that vigorous national growth may have to preface the latter, a requirement that may be dependent on our ability to flourish in an increasingly competitive world environment. Yet diverting resources from our own more competitive internal environs—the Sunbelt—may in turn diminish the posture of the United States, and its growth potential, within this broader arena. Do we risk slowing down the entire train, perhaps permanently, so the regional laggards can board, or do we by necessity attempt to stress its unity and optimize total speed and momentum? This is an essential question that must permeate the entire regional dialogue. Its resolution may place emphasis on the basic requirement for internal northern restructuring efforts, and the generation of the desire and will to recapture a lost dynamic. National commitment is essential but not sufficient—the base responsibility and required capacity lies within the region, its people and leaders.

NOTES

Quotes secured from the balance of the papers in this volume are not directly referenced to page numbers, nor are comments taken from the initial conference transcripts.

1. Maury Klein and Harvey A. Kanter, *Prisoners of Progress: American Industrial Cities, 1850-1920* (New York: Macmillan, 1976), p. 5.

2. *Ibid.*, p. 20.

3. Neal R. Pierce, "Northeast Governors Map Battle Plan for Fight over Federal Funds Row," *National Journal*, November 27, 1976, p. 1, 698.

4. Paul W. McCracken, "The Demagoguery of Energy," *The Wall Street Journal*, May 16, 1977, p. 18.

5. Norton E. Long, "A Marshall Plan for Cities," *The Public Interest* 46 (Winter 1977): 48-58.

6. Lisa Peattie, "Community Drama and Advocacy Planning," *Journal of the American Institute of Planners* 36, no. 6 (November 1970): 405.

7. Also of potential significance in this regard is the proposed mid-Atlantic regional commission—comprising New York, New Jersey, Pennsylvania, Delaware, and Maryland—that is seeking designation by the Department of Commerce as an economic development region. Approval would initially establish research and planning operations with the goal of ultimately capturing federal funds for specific economic development projects.

Previously funded in the latter stages of the Ford Administration was the Council for Northeast Economic Action that will eventually establish a permanent research institution to examine regional problems. However there are assertions that this group was formed to counter the Coalition of Northeast Governors. See: Timothy B. Clark, "The Frostbelt Fights for a New Future," *Empire State Report* 2, no. 9 (October-November 1976): 340.

8. Neal R. Pierce, "Northeast Governors Map Battle Plan for Fight over Federal Funds Row," *National Journal*, November 27, 1976, p. 1,703. At the present (June 1977), a greater sense of unity has been achieved in the Northeast and adjacent environs, and the success in the community development and countercyclical revenue sharing legislation marks this new, and apparently effective, consciousness. See: Edward C. Burks, "Northeast and Midwest Join in Congress in Bid for More Aid," *New York Times*, June 13, 1977, p. 32.

9. Steven R. Weisman, "Beame and Carey Advisors Find Welfare 'Reform' Less Attractive than U.S. Takeover," *New York Times*, May 24, 1977, p. 25.

10. For example, "the National Governor's Conference recently proposed a series of 'reforms' in the aid to dependent children category. Under the proposal, the federal government would raise its minimum share of such payments in every state to $2,400 annually. If states wanted to raise this level to $3,600, the federal government would pay 90 percent of this $1,200 increment. If a state wanted to raise the level another $1,200 to $4,800, the federal government would pay 50 percent of the extra amount. The affect of this proposal, according to one analysis, would be to pick up 50 percent of the $800 million cost that New York State and its localities pay for aid to dependent children ($400 million). However, the total cost of the program would be $10 billion, according to one calculation. New York State's share would be 13.3 percent—$1.3 billion—more than it is paying today for the same program." Ibid.

11. Alan L. Otten, "Not on My Block," *Wall Street Journal*, May 19, 1977, p. 22.

12. A recent *New York Times* analysis isolates the television industry as a case in point. New York and New Jersey, once national centers of such production, have experienced steep declines the past decade. Symbolic is General Electric's Electronics Park in Syracuse, where only 10 percent of the 12,000 member workforce existing in 1966 are left. To cope with the competitive pressure of imports, management shifted production south or overseas, responding to higher taxes, wages and unionization levels, and

aging plants. Still, of twenty-seven companies producing television sets in the United States in 1960, only twelve remain.

When the technological evolution to small transistor and color sets buffeted the black-and-white market, and when Japanese imports soared, the Northeast's production facilities—predicated on the big cabinet and black-and-white tube era—were undermined. As a belated response, trade negotiations have secured from Japan agreements to cut exports to the United States by 40 percent. But interviews with industry and union officials make dubious any assumption of this action's reviving employment in the Northeast—at best it might help maintain current depressed levels. It is too late to now shift production back from overseas (Ireland, Taiwan, Singapore, and Yugoslavia in the case of General Electric) or the South. Any increase in demand will be absorbed by the newer facilities in the South, which will assemble components predominantly fabricated overseas. The critical mass of up-to-date and competitive facilities is outside of the Northeast. The depletion of the latter has reached the point where it is virtually immune to the alteration of the broader parameters. See: Agis Salpukis, "GE's Plants a Symbol of TV Output Decline in Northeast," *New York Times*, May 28, 1977, p. 25.

13. This discussion is not limited only to tax incentives, but also includes the broader policy package—low interest loans, state guarantees of loans, etc.

14. For marginal firms, providing the least desirable jobs, taxes are a much more important element. However, larger, well endowed corporations, providing more substantive employment opportunities, are much less affected by the taxation variable.

15. See: George Sternlieb, Thomas Clark, and Kristina Ford, *Taxation and the Philadelphia Economy,* (New Brunswick, N.J.: Rutgers University, Center for Urban Policy Research, 1977).

16. For example, tax or financing incentives in New England, in all probability, stand little chance of attracting back the textile industries lost to the South decades earlier.

17. Large scale bakeries, for instance (as well as other select food processing activities), tied to growing southern markets, are virtually immune to northern incentive provisions.

18. Likewise, similar activities, as specified in note 13, may be relatively fixed, in a regional sense, by virtue of the markets they service.

19. Presently, many activities are spatially linked to the financial activities (stock markets and the like) in lower Manhattan. As long as the larger primaries remain in place, the subsidiary functions may be geographically immobile (at least on a regional basis). However, the latter may respond to incentives provided across the Hudson River in New Jersey.

20. For example, a regional brewery has migrated from New York City to suburban Allentown in Pennsylvania, where incentive mechanisms were extant. Apparently, the firm was at the threshold—its older facilities were probably inefficient across many dimensions—but it was tied to regional markets. The major decision, intra-regional site selection, may have hinged on marginal cost adjustments, with the resultant migration to Pennsylvania. From a regional perspective, the only likely change was in reference to foregone revenues.

21. The last example is also illustrative of this situation.

22. Franklin J. James, Jr., and James W. Hughes, "The Process of Employment Location Change: An Empirical Analysis," *Land Economics* 49, no. 4, (November 1973): p. 413.

23. Bernard L. Weinstein, "Why Texas Outdraws New York for Business," *The Empire State Report* 2, no. 9 (October-November 1976): 334.

24. Ibid.

25. Ibid.

26. Wayne King, "Labor Mounting Strong Campaign to Unionize South," *New York Times*, March 17, 1977, p. 1.

27. James C. Hyatt, "Firms Learn Art of Keeping Unions Out; Figures Indicate They're Passing Course," *Wall Street Journal*, April 19, 1977, p. 48.

28. New York, whose recent utterances raise homage to the need to foster a more hospitable business climate, is challenging a recent federal court decision invalidating a New York law providing unemployment payments to strikers beginning in the eighth week of a walkout. The decision said the law put the state on the side of strikes, encouraged long walkouts, and conflicted with federal laws. While an important victory for business and industry, the state's proposed challenge certainly lends question to the depth of its commitment to modifying its economic environment. See: Clyde Haberman and Milton Leebaw, "Jobless Benefits for Strikers are Invalidated," *New York Times*, May 29, 1977, p. 6.

29. See: Paul, Weiss, Rifkind, Wharton, and Garrison, "Northeast Energy and Economic Development Compact (Draft)," New York, April 19, 1977.

30. Agis Salpukis, "Northeast Will Tie Plan for Aid by U.S. to Energy Program," *New York Times*, May 5, 1977, p. 10.

31. Neal R. Pierce, "Northeast Governors Map Battle," p. 1,700. Under consideration are: "development of coal mines in Pennsylvania; improvements in rail service; building of industrial parks; assists in energy conservation; construction of transmission lines to bring relatively inexpensive Canadian power into the region; energy stockpiles to protect against the vagaries of OPEC pricing; and the development of offshore oil reserves." But final specifications will come forth as a national energy policy evolves to which the corporation wisely proposes to interface its undertakings.

32. Ibid.

33. Wilbur R. Thompson, "Economic Processes and Problems in Declining Metropolitan Areas," in George Sternlieb and James W. Hughes, eds., *Post Industrial America: Metropolitan Decline and Inter-Regional Job Shifts* (New Brunswick, N.J.: Rutgers University Center for Urban Policy Research, 1975), p. 192.

34. Peter A. Morrison, *Migration and Rights of Access: New Public Concerns of the 1970s*, P-5785, The Rand Paper Series (Santa Monica, Calif.: The Rand Corporation, 1977), p. 16.

35. See: Committee on Community Development, the Domestic Council, 1976 *Report on National Growth and Development: The Changing Issues for National Growth*, Third Biennial Report to the Congress, February 1976.

Section I

Regional Evolution and
The Policy Problem

Introduction

THREE DISCERNIBLE SPATIAL TRANSFORMATIONS—inter-regional, metropolitan-nonmetropolitan and intra-metropolitan—are recontouring the national landscape of every social and economic parameter in America. In
the aggregate, the new economic and social geography is the consequence
of the maturation of the nation's economy—a deep-seated evolution
toward regional equalization—and the extrapolation of both implicit and
manifest social and personal values. The result has been a virtual
repositioning of the status of the Northeast Region—if not quite atrophy,
at least visible reductions in its historic functional roles—and the ensuing
dislocations are seemingly immune from the conventional political wherewithal.

Several major developments over the past fifteen years—particularly
as they have accelerated in this decade—have altered the course of
American society, weakening the assumptions and conventions which
long channeled our thinking and expectations. While they arise from
different causes, their consequences are closely intertwined.

1. *Benign Evolution and Accelerated Dislocations.* The relatively
higher rates of growth in the lesser developed parts of the country have
always been the product of an evolving and maturing nation. But the
apparent threshold changes of the post-1970 period are partially a consequence of the explosion in energy costs. The cheap energy of the past

century fueled a production revolution that enriched the industrial Northeast Region. The passing of this era has shifted with a vengeance the balance toward the energy exporting regions.

2. *Political Thresholds.* While the national political scene has seen the critical mass of influence shift to the Sunbelt territories, after a generation of deliberate federal policy to stimulate their lagging economies, decisionmaking by popular acclaim has induced virtual political stasis in the Northeast. The latter is conceivably the product of nascent post-industrial values.

3. *Technological Dilemmas.* The technological revolution underpinning the changing fortunes of America's regions has yet to make its most significant impact. For example, information transfer by telecommunications will increasingly substitute for the physical movements of people and goods. While futurists' rhetoric has long encompassed the notion of highly sophisticated technologies superseding the very concept of spatial interdependency, this new reality is rapidly coming on line. The evolution of place-independent computer linkages has served to substantially homogenize space and time and radically alter patterns of connectivity. The older, centralized configurations of the Northeast have been undermined.

At one and the same time, the economic constraints of countertechnologies are being recognized as prohibitive. For example, the nation's transportation systems may be at the end of their evolutionary track. There is probably no fundamental economically feasible innovation—such as a sophisticated mass transit facility providing service equivalent to the automobile that can be retrofitted to older urban land use configurations—which will alter the transportation picture to any significant degree. Hence the Northeast stands not only as victim of the impacts of current technological change, but it is also victimized by the economic limits of technology, whereby developments having the potential to accentuate its positive attributes—such as in transportation and energy—are mired in an explosion of costs.

4. *Population Dynamics.* Gauged by declining birth rates and the increasing prevelance of divorce and shrinking household sizes, there is a fundamental alteration in the American family as well as individual life style preferences. As Wilbur Thompson suggests, the rapid rate of natural increase of the postwar period favored the existing distribution of the population; simple human inertia acted to confirm the vitality of established places and compensated for any out-migration. With lower rates of natural increase, migration has assumed greater significance. And with "life style" emerging to full prominence as fam-

ily mores change, positive decisions to migrate—for population to re-distribute itself elsewhere—abound to the detriment of the northeastern territories.

Certainly, a myriad of other causal influences have crosscut the entire Northeast trauma and are explicitly examined in the papers of this section. These developments are occasioning shifts on a very large scale, with the form and structure of new arrangements gradually coming into focus. Effective policy responses cannot be simple abstractions, but rather must be rooted in analyses of the critical phenomena as they have evolved over time. Integral to this task are empirical investigations undertaken with appropriate evaluative frameworks, challenging at every step the conventions and wisdom of the immediate past.

Perceptual Frameworks and Empirical Reality

The slowly moving tides, barely perceptible undercurrents, and rare but suddenly overwhelming tidal waves of change are subject to only limited quantification by the information accounts available to academician and practitioner alike. Compounding the difficulties of discerning these changes, even if imprinted on the ledgers of our data systems, is the predominance of older reference frameworks through which the information is filtered and interpreted. When the regional dynamics that are now beginning to dominate the national consciousness were synthesizing, our energies and attentions were narrowly restricted to the strains evolving from the urban-suburban transformation. Whatever limited lead time had been available to grasp the essence of an emerging reality was dissipated by our inability to supersede older conventions.

In hindsight, when economic and demographic statistics can be retro-fitted to a broadened evaluative framework, a remarkably clear picture emerges. In the first paper of this section, "The New Metropolitan and Regional Realities of America," the events of the past fifteen years are examined in three partitions—inter-regional, metropolitan-nonmetro-politan, and intra-metropolitan—with both long gathering and threshold changes isolated.

1. *From 1960 to 1965, a period of sluggish national growth, the South's overall economy significantly outperformed that of a moderately expanding Northeast Region. While this differential was reduced in the ensuing five-year period (1965 to 1970), under the auspices of a booming national economy, the South still held a commanding edge. However, the relatively rapid national expansion producing*

some growth in the Northeast obscured the sustained dynamic vigor of the South. As the performance of the national economy slackened in the post-1970 period, and the energy crisis ensued, the Northeast experienced a traumatic decline in its total employment, while the South gleaned over 50 percent of the nation's employment growth. Hence the 1970 to 1975 pattern was, in part, briefly prefaced by the events of ten years previous. The accelerated extrapolation was only temporarily interrupted by the boom years of the late 1960s.

2. *The component employment sectors provide a glimpse into the emerging process of northeastern decline. From 1960 to 1965, the Northeast actually registered declines in its manufacturing employment rolls, while the South captured almost three quarters of the national manufacturing growth. During this period, then, the Northeast's overall growth was sustained only by the rapid expansion of public and private service industries, that effectively concealed important underlying problems.*

3. *The rapid 1965 to 1970 national expansion revived the Northeast's manufacturing sector, providing perhaps the last full utilization of its obsolescent industrial plant. While the South still surged forward, the full import of the evolution was still obscured.*

4. *The 1970 to 1975 period brought home all of these latent and manifest tendencies. The Northeast experienced a devastating contraction of its manufacturing base. The expansion of retail trade, personal services, and the whole range of nonmanufacturing activities was no longer sufficient to cushion the impact of its declining export (manufacturing) sectors.*

5. *The South also saw a marked deceleration of its manufacturing growth rates during the post-1970 era. However, it had many unmet local trade and service needs arising from the previous rapid growth of its exporting sector. Hence private nonmanufacturing and government employment growth effectively compensated for its manufacturing slowdown. The Northeast's growth in these population dependent sectors had been used up the previous decade.*

6. *The Northeast's fiscal position weakened perceptively with these events, with New York City just the tip of a large urban iceberg. The large public service commitments of the previous decade— geared to the large black in-migration of the 1950s and 1960s— clashed head on with a diminished export base and declining population growth rates, i.e., a lagging fiscal support capacity.*

7. *From slow growth in the 1960s, the Northeast's population level remained virtually constant after 1970; net in-migration was trans- formed to net out-migration. In contrast, America's movers flocked to the South in increasing numbers drawn by economic opportunity and more subtle desires—e.g., life style and climate. It is this increasing population base—as well as the associated income shift —which has allowed the South's economy to flourish in spite of the national slowdown. Population serving activities are compen- sating for other lagging sectors.*

8. *The 1970 to 1975 period also saw the marked resurgence of non- metropolitan areas, and the corresponding slippage of the former metropolitan growth poles. This phenomenon represented a thresh- old change from all previous conventions, and was obscured by the limitations of a decennial census. The large metropolitan areas of the nation's manufacturing belt, centered on the historic industrial cities spawned in the nineteenth century, were the frontrunners in this transformation. Throughout the nation, a new spatial format of metropolitan functions was emerging, to the detriment of the Northeast's obsolescent configurations.*

9. *Within metropolitan areas in the past five years, the traumas of the central cities visibly deepened. Black suburbanization flows repli- cated the patterns of their white forebears, opening up partial vacuums in the once fabled loci of industrial urbanization.*

10. *The sheer measure of regional and metropolitan shifts clearly renders obsolete much of our political wisdom and folkway. It is evident that the older political instrumentalities—city, state, and subregional jurisdictions—simply do not have either the scale or the wherewithal which is required to grapple with these changes. The necessity for broader responses is present. The political will is as yet uncertain.*

The Longitudinal Perspective and Policy Parameters

Interpreting this chain of events, W. W. Rostow, with the perspective of an economic historian, provides the vital longitudinal framework, exploring their origins in the longer past.

1. *The present positions of the Northeast and the industrial Midwest result from deeply rooted structural elements which decree a greater relative load of obsolescent industries, a heritage of large past commitments to expensive social services, and a large concen-*

tration of poor in the central cities reflecting prior south-to-north population flows over a protracted period of time.

2. *These conditions stem from one of the best established but least well known characteristics of economic growth: the tendency of late comers to modern economic growth to catch up with those who began earlier. In the early stages of a nation's growth, regional disparities emerge. But with the passage of time and the availability of a diversified pool of unapplied technologies, the lagging regions begin to exploit their opportunities and catch up.*

3. *The Sunbelt's turning point toward convergence clearly came between 1930 and 1940, in the period of recovery from the Great Depression after 1929. Ensuing were four decades of sustained relative progress.*

4. *The rise of the Sunbelt, then, is a phenomenon some forty years old. It was accompanied by a large flow of black migrants to the North as a consequence of the modernization of agriculture. In the North, during the 1950s and 1960s, some trouble was experienced with the decline of the classic industries it had pioneered. But the high national growth rates of the 1960s and the rapid expansion of such service industries as education, health, and travel concealed these underlying potential problems.*

5. *In the post-1970 period, the relative rise in food and energy prices accelerated the development of a good many Sunbelt states that exported energy and agricultural resources to the rest of the country. Similarly, this shift in relative prices converted a slow-moving but endurable erosion of the relative position of the energy importing northern states into something of a crisis.*

6. *The Northeast also had committed itself to enlarged public and private services at a time when its manufacturing base, with high obsolescence in certain sectors, was decelerating or declining, its rate of population increase was slowing down, and an unfavorable shift in its terms of trade, as in Great Britain, occurred.*

Given this perspective, Rostow begins the task of outlining the parameters of policy toward regional change.

7. *Despite the region's seeking redress in terms of federal expenditure allocations, Rostow concludes that when the flow of federal grants is systematically correlated with various indicators of economic development in the states, no significant association emerges. Major*

regional changes in the country have been determined by deep and understandable historical forces. They have been only marginally shaped by the balance of federal tax and expenditure flows.

8. *The future of federal policy and outlays in the regions should be determined by the requirements of the several regions, viewed in terms of their structural problems and the larger interests of the nation as a whole. The major task of regional development is an investment one throughout all sectors of America.*

9. *The problem of the North is to regather momentum by bringing to bear its enormous potentials in technology, finance, and entre-preneurship; to exploit its energy resources in the new price environment; to rehabilitate its transport system in cost-effective ways; and to modernize the industrial sectors that hold the greatest promise for the future. This will require a new sense of regional purpose as well as intimate public-private collaboration.*

10. *The challenge to the Sunbelt is to complete its transition to industrial modernization; to develop its resources in energy and agriculture in both its own interest and that of the nation; to deal with its social problems under conditions of rapid population increase; and to do all these things while avoiding, to the degree possible, the environmental degradation that marked the urbanization of the North.*

11. *Once the debate shifts to these terms, the possibilities enlarge for national policies which would mitigate the tensions between regions. Within this framework, a number of prerequisites stand out:*

    a) A return to sustained full employment and high growth rates on a national basis would greatly ease the special problems of the Northeast by simultaneously reducing welfare requirements and expanding tax revenues. This should be achieved by expanded investment in energy and other resource development and conservation fields combined with outlays to reaccelerate the growth of productivity.

    b) These special investment areas can serve as leverage for serious and sustained efforts to bring into the working force people now caught up in marginal lives of poverty.

    c) A national energy policy is required to both enlarge our resources in all the regions and economize their use. The nation as a whole has to face up to the fact that energy is and will be expensive, that conservation and economy are required of us all, and that the energy potentials of the country as a whole—not merely the South and the West—must be promptly and fully exploited under environmental rules of the game that are firmly settled.

d) A basic requirement is a national welfare policy which would render more uniform the criteria for public assistance; the expense entailed implies that such a system will be viable and sustainable only in an environment of full employment and rapid growth.

e) Within the states and regions as well as at the national level, new forms of public-private collaboration will be necessary; we have to learn how to make the public and private sectors work together.

f) These problems cannot be dealt with if the states and regions look merely to Washington for salvation. The basic analyses, investment plans, and public-private consortia must be developed within the states and regions. The revitalization of the Northeast is a development task; and the firmest lesson of development economics is that it must be rooted in self-help, leaving to the federal government its proper share of effort.

g) There is a warning to be made about any proposal for an increased governmental role in the investment process: high standards of priority and productivity must be preserved. We cannot afford to compound existing tendencies toward declining rates of productivity increases by committing public funds to essentially wasteful enterprises.

The critical dimension permeating each of these concerns is, according to Rostow, the generation of a common will and sense of direction in the Northeast so that the regathering of momentum can commence.

Preliminary Policy Directions

Wilbur R. Thompson, a pioneer of urban economics, brings to bear his arsenal of knowledge to suggest initial policy directions as well as the pitfalls and false hopes to avoid. After adjusting the overall perspective to the disequilibrating and long-term nature of the regional swings, a number of important preliminary guidelines to the overall policy debate are put forth.

1. *What will prove eternally elusive in the quest to "solve" the economic downswing is a new industry about to enter its growth state, which demands high skills, and can afford the Northeast's high business cost structures—and even more ideally, has not come to anyone's attention and is patiently waiting for the Northeast to recognize and enhance its virtues. Nonetheless, the region should try to focus on new frontiers, since its competitive posture with respect to the old has dissipated markedly.*

2. *The Northeast's headstart in science and technology has rapidly succumbed to the process of regional convergence. While ideas are mobile and technological leads hard to maintain, the emphasis on science and technology is vital, since the manufacturing economies of the Northeast and Midwest—with their high cost structures—cannot hope to fall heir easily to firms leaving other areas. As Rostow also emphasizes, the South has and will continue to grow by acquiring larger shares of existing (older) industries. And when their growth begins to slow (in export industries), they can cushion the transition through "import substitution" growth, and by filling gaps in retail trade and services. The latter process has been completed in the Northeast.*

3. *The advantage the older, established industrial areas enjoy is strong state (Midwest) and private (Northeast) graduate schools which may serve—since they are difficult to replicate in the short term—as facilitators of the preceding strategy.*

4. *But a purely industrial approach may not be enough—more attention should be granted to occupational mixes to balance local labor markets. Focusing on industries with occupational structures amenable to highly educated women—manufacturing dependent economies have an acute shortage of such positions—may be essential to hold on to their highly educated male spouses.*

5. *The region could also follow a strategy of attracting and holding talented persons, who in the long run create new industries. To the extent that talented persons choose where they would like most to live and, directly and indirectly, force industries and businesses to come to them, the principal line of causation may run from the natural and man-made environment to the economic base of the community, rather than the reverse. Places that lack superior natural environments must then try harder to create superior man-made—physical and social—environments.*

6. *The Northeast's industrial cities—with their emerging historic districts—may yet have renewed potential for economic development if the preceding causal linkage proves true. Unique residential environments may leverage economic activity.*

7. *Yet a redundant labor force will remain a critical regional problem. Given the public policies that retard mobility, what may be necessary are relocation allowances that rearrange reward structures. Assisted out-migration and population contraction from a large population base is not likely to diminish appreciably the important gains that flowed from growth to that size.*

Perhaps the most significant factors facing the Northeast are the constraints limiting its options. As Thompson suggests, "if you accept the crisis theory of behavior, what you do have going for you in this time of hard choices is desperation . . . logical deduction and disciplined imagination is about all we have to go on. So hang in there, think big, and be patient."

The New Economic
Geography of America

GEORGE STERNLIEB
JAMES W. HUGHES

Introduction

THE FLYWHEEL OF HISTORY OFTEN SUSTAINS a vision of past realities long since overcome by time and change. For planners, and all who are concerned with public policy, obsolete reference frameworks are an ever-present peril. Models of reality are useful so long as they are predictive. When permitted to age without adjustment for new facts, they can be positively harmful.

Adding to this danger is the submergence of much planning and political activity within the immediacies of apparently localized problems. The ultimate effect is to obscure the broader picture of massive shifts taking place in the locus of economic and demographic development within the nation as a whole. Increasingly, however, the sum of particular incidents—of fiscal crisis in New York, of desperation municipal financing in Philadelphia, of federal housing subsidies ostensibly national in scope but regionally biased in practice, of widespread housing aban-

75

donment (regardless of the incidence of rent controls or of other specifics
to which it is attributed in individual communities), and of vast differences in local and regional unemployment rates (which ominously now
appear much more chronic than transient)—begins to evoke a requirement to define the basic factors that are at work.

The study that follows attempts to construct a data base pertinent to
three major phenomena which we believe will increasingly structure and
constrain the basic economic and political environment of planning for
the next decade. They have been nominally titled:

1. The Accelerating Regional Shift
2. The Emerging Metropolitan-Nonmetropolitan Dynamic
3. Expanding Intrametropolitan Differentials

We have attempted to overcome the lagging perception of these emerging forces by assembling extensive, and we believe compelling, sets of
data fully documenting their gathering momentum. Underlying causal
processes are suggested, but the principal concern for the moment is
with new realities. Regardless of their root foundation, the phenomena
are so monumental in their impact on local and national policy alike
as to require quantification. Local planners cannot act within the immediacies of their domains without taking cognizance of these realities.
The luxury of leaving them to the regional economist has ended.

The Accelerating Regional Shift

The "rise of the Sunbelt" and the "decline of the Northeast" are perceptions recently added to the lexicon of the popular media. Their
specifications and scale, however, have not been fully comprehended.
They encompass events which are not new but represent the accelerated
evolution of established trendlines. *A very powerful momentum has
built up over the past fifteen years, sweeping employment and population growth away from the older metropolitan centers of the Northeast
and North Central states to the newer growth poles of the South and
West.*

In the past decade, when this new dynamic was emerging, the major
political convulsions and confrontations centered on the internal shifts
taking place within metropolitan areas. Riveting our attentions and
energies were the tensions between the traumas of the central city and
the growth—and more recently the no-growth—aspirations of suburbia.
Unnoticed was the fact that the industrial belt from Boston to St. Louis,
which Wilbur Thompson calls the American Ruhr, was beginning a long-

Exhibit 1
Regions and Geographic Divisions of the United States

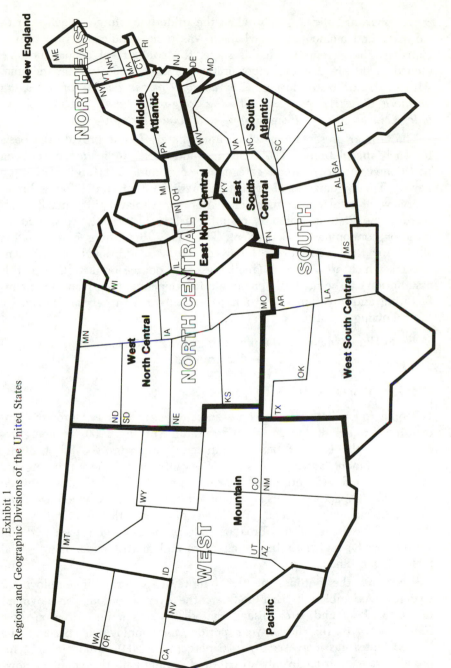

Source: U. S. Bureau of the Census, *Census of Housing: 1970,* General Housing Characteristics, Final Report HC(1)-A1 United States Summary.

term downward slide.[1] Only when the underlying forces reached critical mass, and momentum snowballed, was their significance fully appre-
ciated. When events reach this stage, the contours of change become
etched so deeply that the opportunities for their deflection are minimal
without drastic restructuring. *The analogy of the decline of the aging
northern industrial crescent with the long-term transformation of our
older central cities is increasingly—and uncomfortably—apt.*

The tabular presentations which immediately follow provide the basis
for such speculations. The economic and social indicators have been
partitioned into two broad categories, economic shifts and population
flows. The organizational format is predicated on providing a broad
overview of total employment change before isolating its specific subsectors, the first of which is manufacturing, historically construed as
basic or nonpopulation dependent. The many dimensions of population
shifts are then considered, followed by two additional employment
clusters which are assumed (realizing some degree of distortion in this
assumption) to be nonbasic or population dependent—private nonmanufacturing and government. Briefly, the analytical subsets are linked by
the following equation:

Total Employment = Manufacturing + Private Nonmanufacturing
+ Government.

EMPLOYMENT SHIFTS

People follow jobs—and people encourage employment growth. Increasingly much of the social programming of the 1960s is being re-
focused on the issue of basic employment opportunity. Job training,
skills enrichment, and all the other interventionary devices promulgated
over the past decade presumed that there were *structural gaps* between
the specific capacities of local inhabitants and the jobs which were assumed to be open to them. While in large part this is certainly still
the case, the issue of the broader pattern of general *job availability*
within specific regions is becoming more and more the dominant social
issue of our time.

What are the outlines of the long-term patterns of employment
change? Assembled in Exhibit 2 are the overall national employment
totals for 1960 and 1975 disaggregated by region and division (see
Exhibit 1). In this fifteen-year period, the employment base of the
United States has increased by 46.6 percent, or 23.9 million jobs. This
growth was far from evenly distributed throughout the country, however. While the Northeast secured only a 21.7 percent increase and

the North Central Region 36.2 percent, rates of growth far below the national average, employment in the South and West expanded by nearly 70 percent. Indeed, though the South's total employment in 1960, 13.8 million, was substantially below that of the Northeast's 15.2 million and the North Central Region's 15.3 million, by 1975 it evolved into the dominant employment locus of the country, encompassing 23.4 million jobs. Thus in fifteen years the South outdistanced both the Northeast and North Central regions, which hover slightly below and above the 20 million job mark, respectively.

EXHIBIT 2

TOTAL EMPLOYMENT CHANGE: 1960-1975[1]
BY REGION AND DIVISION
(Numbers in thousands)

Region and Division	1960	1975	Change 1960-1975 Number	Change 1960-1975 Percent
Northeast Region	15,229.5	18,535.4	3,305.9	21.7
Middle Atlantic Division	11,676.4	13,864.9	2,188.5	18.7
New England Division	3,553.1	4,670.5	1,117.4	31.4
North Central Region	15,291.8	20,826.7	5,534.9	36.2
East North Central Division	11,318.1	14,957.5	3,639.4	32.2
West North Central Division	3,973.7	5,869.2	1,895.5	47.7
South Region	13,818.0	23,480.3	9,662.3	69.9
South Atlantic Division	7,054.2	12,078.8	5,024.6	71.2
East South Central Division	2,606.0	4,353.0	1,747.0	67.0
West South Central Division	4,157.8	7,048.5	2,890.7	69.5
West Region	7,734.3	13,110.4	5,376.1	69.5
Mountain Division	1,765.9	3,353.9	1,588.0	89.9
Pacific Division	5,968.4	9,756.5	3,788.1	63.5
U. S. Total[2]	52,073.6	75,952.8	23,879.2	46.6

NOTES: 1. Employees on nonagriculture payrolls as of March of the respective years.
         2. Excludes Hawaii and Alaska.

SOURCE: U. S. Department of Labor, Bureau of Labor Statistics, *Employment and Earnings* (Washington, D.C.: U. S. Government Printing Office, Monthly).

When the focus is narrowed to the divisional partitions, the relative stagnation of the older industrial heartland is further highlighted. *The most laggard part of the United States is the Middle Atlantic Division, comprising New York, New Jersey, and Pennsylvania.* Here employment increased by less than two additional jobs for every ten existing in 1960. Even New England, whose long, historic decline in relative position has been oft observed, fared better, adding three jobs for every ten which existed in 1960. The East North Central Division's performance replicates that of New England, i.e., three additional jobs for every ten existing in 1960. The West North Central Division, on the other hand, added five jobs for every ten that preexisted. Even this last pattern stands in marked contrast to the divisional equivalents in the South and West, where even the weakest division shows growth on the order of seven additional jobs for every ten that existed in 1960.

Within this fifteen year span there are compelling patterns of variation, which speak to the near term future. Exhibit 3 details the regional shares of the nation's total growth for the three five-year periods between 1960 and 1975. The weakness of the Northeast and the growing strength of the South was clear from 1960 to 1965, a period of only modest national performance. The former accounted for only 14.5 percent of the United States employment gains, while the latter garnered 38.5 percent. The boom period of 1965 to 1970 obscured this differential, dampening the inter-regional spread. Yet, even under what now appears to have been an exceptional growth period in American history, the South encompassed 33.9 percent of the national expansion, and the Northeast only 20.7 percent.

The decline in the overall economy from 1970 to 1975 spawned a unique absolute job decline in the Northeast, with more than 35,000 jobs lost. The South, conversely, gained more than 3.3 million jobs, an addition which represents more than half of all the new economic growth in the United States from 1970 to 1975.

Within the Northeast, the variation between the Middle Atlantic and New England divisions is most striking. In the first ten years of the period, it is the former which maintained the Northeast's vitality, with shares of national growth double and triple that of New England. From 1970 to 1975, however, the situation changes quite markedly. While the Middle Atlantic states lost 224,000 jobs, New England concurrently gained 188,000. Clearly, New England may have been an early loser, but it is bottoming out and now appears to be stabilizing into a future of slow but steady growth. Nevertheless, it trails all the divisions save for the Middle Atlantic.

EXHIBIT 3

REGIONAL GROWTH SHARES OF TOTAL EMPLOYMENT CHANGE: 1960-1975[1]

(Numbers in thousands)

Region	Absolute Growth Increment			Percentage Share of National Growth		
	1960-1965	1965-1970	1970-1975	1960-1965	1965-1970	1970-1975
Northeast Region	875.7	2,465.9	−35.7	14.5	20.7	−0.6
Middle Atlantic Division	594.2	1,818.2	−223.9	9.8	15.3	−3.8
New England Division	281.5	647.7	188.2	4.7	5.4	3.2
North Central Region	1,422.2	3,240.6	872.1	23.6	27.2	14.7
East North Central Division	989.7	2,332.6	317.6	16.4	19.6	5.4
West North Central Division	432.5	908.5	554.5	7.2	7.6	9.4
South Region	2,323.6	4,033.6	3,305.1	38.5	33.9	55.8
South Atlantic Division	1,182.8	2,146.6	1,695.2	19.6	18.0	28.6
East South Central Division	509.4	668.5	569.1	8.4	5.6	9.6
West South Central Division	631.4	1,218.5	1,040.8	10.5	10.2	17.6
West Region	1,420.4	2,171.3	1,784.4	23.5	18.2	30.1
Mountain Division	322.8	493.7	771.5	5.3	4.1	13.0
Pacific Division	1,097.6	1,677.6	1,012.9	18.2	14.1	17.1
United States Total[2]	6,041.9[3]	11,911.4	5,925.9	100.0	100.0	100.0

NOTES: 1. Employees on nonagriculture payrolls as of March of the respective periods.
2. Excludes Hawaii and Alaska.
3. Numbers and percents may not add due to rounding.

SOURCE: U.S. Department of Labor, Bureau of Labor Statistics, *Employment and Earnings* (Washington, D.C.: U.S. Government Printing Office, Monthly)).

EXHIBIT 4

TOTAL EMPLOYMENT CHANGE, MIDDLE ATLANTIC DIVISION: 1960-1975[1]
(Numbers in thousands)

Division and State	1960	1965	Change 1960-1965		1970	Change 1965-1970		1975	Change 1970-1975	
			Number	Percent		Number	Percent		Number	Percent
Middle Atlantic Division ..	11,676.4	12,270.6	594.2	5.1	14,088.8	1,818.2	14.8	13,864.9	-223.9	-1.6
New York State	6,102.1	6,333.5	231.4	3.8	7,159.1	825.6	13.0	6,881.5	-277.6	-3.9
New York City	3,557.7	3,554.0	-3.7	-0.1	3,817.2	263.2	7.4	3,378.7	-438.5	-11.5
Balance of State	2,544.4	2,779.5	235.1	9.2	3,341.9	562.4	20.2	3,502.7	160.9	4.8
New Jersey State	1,943.0	2,163.0	220.0	11.3	2,580.6	417.6	16.0	2,637.6	57.0	2.2
Pennsylvania State	3,631.3	3,774.1	142.8	3.9	4,349.1	575.0	15.2	4,345.8	-3.3	-0.1
Philadelphia (City)[2] ..	N.A.	N.A.	N.A.	N.A.	919.4	N.A.	N.A.	810.6	-108.8	-11.8
Balance of State	N.A.	N.A.	N.A.	N.A.	3,429.7	N.A.	N.A.	3,535.2	105.5	3.1

NOTES: 1. Employees on nonagriculture payrolls as of March of the respective periods.
2. The data for Philadelphia city not available for 1960 and 1965. Additionally, the Philadelphia city totals are annual averages.

SOURCE: U.S. Department of Labor, Bureau of Labor Statistics, *Employment and Earnings* (Washington, D.C.: U.S. Government Printing Office, Monthly).

Is this a reflection of the Northeast's becoming the focus of marginal employment opportunities? Does it imply that this region requires very substantial national growth before its resources are brought into the main stream? And conversely, will it continue to lose out to more efficient and/or more desirable areas as soon as there is curtailment in the absolute levels of employment demand? In order to clarify these questions, further analysis of the underlying economic sectors is required. First, however, it may be useful to examine more closely the leading edge of decline in the Northeast—the Middle Atlantic Division.

The Middle Atlantic Division. In Exhibit 4 we have detailed the employment shifts for the states comprising this division (New York, New Jersey, and Pennsylvania), as well as for New York City, Philadelphia, and the balance of their respective states. The period 1960 to 1965 heralded the shifts which were to take place ten years later, with New York City losing jobs as the division in total added nearly 600,000 employees. If we consider New York State sans New York City, it fared almost as well as New Jersey. Bolstered by the suburbanization of New York City and Philadelphia deeper into its territories, New Jersey's 11.3 percent increase in employment dominated the positive side of the ledger.

The period from 1965 to 1970, one of enormous economic vigor for the country as a whole, raised the level of employment growth throughout the division, with the earlier intra-divisional balances being preserved. From 1970 to 1975, however, the situation changes very drastically—the division as a whole lost 224,000 jobs. However, it is extremely important to note that the decline of both New York City (439,000 jobs) and Philadelphia (109,000 jobs) completely obscures the positive growth of the balance of the division. Excluding these two decline sectors, the Middle Atlantic states enjoyed an increase in employment of 324,000. This would appear to indicate, then, that areas of stability and vigor coexist in the presence of severe pockets of decline, even if the central cities of the older industrial metropolises of the Northeast are losing their economic rationales. The congruity of their plights is given emphasis by the virtual identity of New York City's and Philadelphia's rates of decline—11.5 and 11.8 percent, respectively.

The Role of Manufacturing. Viewing employment in the aggregate tends to obscure the varying performances of major industrial subsectors. In this context, it appears that a major swing element has been the change in manufacturing employment.

Manufacturing employment in the United States, as shown in Exhibit 5, has experienced minimal growth in the fifteen years between 1960 to 1975—increasing by less than 1.5 million jobs or 8.8 percent. This pattern may not be unique to the United States, but rather is representative of the evolution that takes place within an advanced technological society. The linkage of productivity increases (generated by new approaches to job rationalization and increased capital investment) with the export of labor intensive manufacturing activity to lower cost, foreign areas, imposes effective limits on employment growth. But within this relatively static national picture, the shifts between regions have been monumental. *The Northeast has lost over 781,000 manufacturing jobs from 1960 to 1975, 13.9 percent of its 1960 total.* The North Central Region experienced only minimal change; but the South in-

EXHIBIT 5

MANUFACTURING EMPLOYMENT CHANGE: 1960-1975[1]
BY REGION AND DIVISION
(Numbers in thousands)

Region and Division	1960	1975	Change 1960-1975	
			Number	Percent
Northeast Region	5,620.6	4,839.2	−781.4	−13.9
Middle Atlantic Division	4,172.8	3,547.1	−625.7	−15.0
New England Division	1,447.8	1,292.1	−155.7	−10.8
North Central Region	5,579.9	5,814.3	234.4	4.2
East North Central Division	4,586.4	4,577.8	−8.6	−0.2
West North Central Division	993.5	1,236.5	243.0	24.5
South Region	3,650.5	5,146.5	1,496.0	41.0
South Atlantic Division	2,013.1	2,614.2	601.1	29.9
East South Central Division	823.2	1,245.0	421.8	51.2
West South Central Division	814.2	1,287.3	473.1	58.1
West Region	1,874.6	2,394.9	520.3	27.8
Mountain Division	248.9	411.2	162.3	65.2
Pacific Division	1,625.7	1.983.7	358.0	22.0
U.S. Total[2]	16,725.6	18,194.9	1,469.3	8.8

NOTES: 1. Employees on nonagriculture payrolls as of March of the respective years.
2. Excludes Hawaii and Alaska.

SOURCE: U. S. Department of Labor, Bureau of Labor Statistics, *Employment and Earnings* (Washington, D.C.: U. S. Government Printing Office, Monthly).

creased with enormous vigor, adding almost 1.5 million manufacturing jobs to its employment rolls. *Indeed the South, in and of itself, fully accounted for the total U. S. growth increment; the losses of the Northeast offset the relatively small growth totals of the North Central and West regions.*

In 1960 the Northeast was the dominant manufacturing center of the nation, as evidenced by its 5.6 million job total. The North Central Region was closely competitive, with employment at the 5.5 million level, while the South had only 3.6 million manufacturing jobs. By 1975, however, the South surpassed the Northeast and now challenges the stagnant North Central Region. The variation within the last region is particularly significant. The older East North Central industrial complex is substantially lagging the nation, showing an absolute loss in manufacturing employment over the fifteen-year time span. But it is the Middle Atlantic Division of the Northeast which leads this sad procession of manufacturing employment losers with a net decline of 625,000 jobs by 1975—fully 15 percent of its 1960 total.

Again, the long-term trends mask periodic variation of vital import in viewing the short-term future. The shifting patterns of growth are highlighted in Exhibit 6, which delineates the regional growth shares of manufacturing employment change by five-year intervals from 1960 through 1975. From 1960 to 1965, when the absolute growth in manufacturing employment nationally had slowed substantially, the Northeast lost 110,000 jobs. At the same time, the South secured the bulk—72 percent—of the national increase of 723,000 jobs. From 1965 to 1970, when the absolute national growth increment tripled, the Northeast benefitted substantially, securing more than 264,000 jobs. The South, however, was concurrently accumulating a greater and greater level of critical mass, with a net growth of 951,000 jobs.

The broader dynamics change quite drastically from 1970 to 1975 when the nation as a whole lost nearly 1.5 million manufacturing jobs. *Almost 64 percent, more than 936,000, were lost in the Northeast, a decline which represents the acceleration of the pattern established in the 1960 to 1965 period.* The North Central Region showed a major break in trend, losing more than 500,000 jobs. The South and the West, conversely, struggled through this period of national stress with small but significant gains.

The pattern that *The Regional Plan of New York and Its Environs* anticipated in the late 1920s for New York City (later confirmed in the late 1950s by Hoover and Vernon's key analysis for the New York Metropolitan Region Study)—that of a declining manufacturing base

EXHIBIT 6

Regional Growth Shares of Manufacturing Employment Change: 1960-1975[1]
(Numbers in thousands)

Region	Absolute Growth Increment			Percentage Share of National Growth		
	1960-1965	1965-1970	1970-1975	1960-1965	1965-1970	1970-1975
Northeast Region	-110.1	264.9	-936.2	-15.2	12.0	-63.8
Middle Atlantic Division	-89.4	187.8	-724.1	-12.4	8.5	-49.4
New England Division	-20.7	77.1	-212.1	-2.8	3.5	-14.4
North Central Region	189.7	624.5	-579.8	26.2	28.2	-39.5
East South Central Division	148.0	428.0	-585.4	20.5	19.3	-39.9
West North Central Division	41.7	195.7	5.6	5.8	8.8	0.4
South Region	520.6	951.6	23.9	72.0	43.0	1.6
South Atlantic Division	250.4	424.3	-73.6	34.6	19.2	-5.0
East South Central Division	157.1	233.3	31.4	21.7	10.5	2.1
West South Central Division	113.1	293.9	66.1	15.6	13.3	4.5
West Region	122.7	372.5	25.1	17.0	16.8	1.7
Mountain Division	25.4	82.9	54.0	3.5	3.7	3.7
Pacific Division	97.3	289.6	-28.9	13.5	13.1	-2.0
United States Total[2]	722.9[3]	2,213.4	-1,467.0	100.0	100.0	-100.0

NOTES: 1. Employees on nonagriculture payrolls as of March of the respective periods.
2. Excludes Hawaii and Alaska.
3. Numbers and percents may not add due to rounding.

SOURCE: U.S. Department of Labor, Bureau of Labor Statistics, *Employment and Earnings* (Washington, D.C.: U.S. Government Printing Office, Monthly).

within New York City—now seems to have spread to the entire region that dominates the older urban scene of America—the Northeast.[2] Increasingly enveloped within this transformation is the less senior, but still aging, industrial heartland of the United States, the North Central states. *Events once endemic to the metropolitan level—in particular, employment decentralization—appear to have been attenuated to new spatial scales and are now working themselves out over the entire geography of the country.*

But is this phenomenon solely the province of our older industrial heartland? Is the South Atlantic Division beginning to show equivalent signs of age? After securing 35.6 percent of total national manufacturing growth in the first five-year period, it accounted for only 19.2 percent from 1965 to 1970, and actually was the locus for 5 percent of the national *decline* in the last five-year period. And the West South Central Division appears to be replicating the earlier growth sequence over time, with even the East South Central states showing the beginning of lag. The pattern of high growth to slow, of stagnation to decline may not be unique to the Northeast (although these suggestions must be tempered in light of overall national growth swings). To the contrary, the data presented here indicate that it may be a remorseless sequence without fear of the Mason-Dixon line. Is there a pattern showing of growth leading to the inhibitors of growth and to the consequent shift to new areas? Certainly this is not a unique thesis. There is, however, evidence of a speeding up of this phenomenon that may leave the time cycle of the planner and policymaker behind.

And in this light, should or could these data have provided some anticipation of the demise of the real estate boom in several sectors of the South Atlantic Division? This question will be entertained in some detail after evaluating the internal dynamics of manufacturing employment change within the Middle Atlantic Division.

Exhibit 7 details, by five-year periods, the major subareas of the Middle Atlantic Division. It is strikingly evident that the decline in manufacturing employment during the first ten years of the period under consideration was solely the province of New York City. Presently (1970 to 1975) it is a dominant theme throughout all division subareas. Every state, including the balance of New York and Pennsylvania, i.e., excluding New York City and Philadelphia, respectively, shows an absolute decline in manufacturing employment. However, more than 316,000 of the net loss of 724,000 manufacturing jobs in the Middle Atlantic Division accrued to these two cities. Each, remarkably, lost approximately 30 percent of its manufacturing employment over

EXHIBIT 7

MANUFACTURING EMPLOYMENT CHANGE[1]
MIDDLE ATLANTIC DIVISION: 1960-1975
(Numbers in thousands)

Division and State	1960	1965	Change 1960-1965		1970	Change 1965-1970		1975	Change 1970-1975	
			Number	Percent		Number	Percent		Number	Percent
Middle Atlantic Division ..	4,172.8	4,083.4	−89.4	−2.1	4,271.2	187.8	4.6	3,547.1	−724.1	−17.0
New York State	1,927.9	1,810.0	−117.9	−6.1	1,838.5	28.5	1.6	1,462.4	−376.1	−20.5
New York City	988.7	866.2	−122.5	−12.4	816.9	−49.3	−5.7	572.6	−244.3	−29.9
Balance of State	939.2	943.8	4.6	0.5	1,021.6	77.8	8.2	889.8	−131.8	−12.9
New Jersey State	794.6	807.9	13.3	1.7	884.2	76.3	9.4	735.3	−148.9	−16.8
Pennsylvania State	1,450.3	1,465.5	15.2	1.0	1,548.5	83.0	5.7	1,349.4	−199.1	−12.9
Philadelphia (City)[2] ...	N.A.	N.A.	N.A.	N.A.	237.8	N.A.	N.A.	165.5	−72.3	−30.4
Balance of State	N.A.	N.A.	N.A.	N.A.	1,310.7	N.A.	N.A.	1,183.9	−126.8	−9.7

NOTES: 1. Employees on nonagriculture payrolls as of March of the respective periods.
2. The data for Philadelphia city not available for 1960 and 1965. Additionally, the Philadelphia city totals are annual averages.

SOURCE: U.S. Department of Labor, Bureau of Labor Statistics, *Employment and Earnings* (Washington, D.C.: U.S. Government Printing Office, Monthly).

the brief five-year span. The losses of the balance of the division hovered around the 10 percent level.

The question, therefore, to be raised concerns the degree to which the overall northeastern experience is a function of the "writing off" of obsolete industrial infrastructures from the inventory of operational, and competitive, means of production, analogous to the scrapping of New England's mills several generations past. Certainly, the landscapes of New York City and Philadelphia and the urban subcenters of their immediate hinterlands are dominated by aging multifloored industrial structures, tied into the nineteenth century rail network. Their scale of vacancies is increasingly ominous with local jurisdictions struggling frantically, but unsuccessfully, to uncover economically meaningful recycling formats.

Yet the balance of the division, which includes substantial pockets of similar structures, lost only 10 percent of its manufacturing employment, a rate of decline not inordinate in the light of the experience of the South Atlantic Division.

While absolute and proportionate shrinkage of manufacturing employment had been unique to the Northeast, in the 1970 to 1975 period the phenomenon as such was for the first time shared by the new classic growth area—the South Atlantic states. As shown in Exhibit 8, the South Atlantic Division as a whole lost 2.7 percent of its manufacturing jobs from 1970 to 1975. Indeed, only two states, North Carolina and Florida, had increases, showing gains of 2.3 and 5.2 percent, respectively. Moreover, if we exclude Washington, D.C., and Maryland, Georgia led this downturn with an 8.5 percent rate of decline, a performance perhaps more characteristic of the Middle Atlantic states.

It has become *au courant* in recent years to stress our societal transformation to a post-industrial format—one in which nonmanufacturing employment, rather than merely being a derivative of primary activity (manufacturing), manifests a life force of its own. While unquestionably there is much substance in such generalizations, the casual refutation of older reference frameworks may be dangerous. A significant linkage persists between manufacturing employment—and the wealth generated by it—and both producer- and consumer-oriented service industries, which in whole or part serve to absorb and multiply this largesse. The precise impact coefficient—the time lag between primary shrinkage and secondary effect—is yet obscure. It is further complicated by great shifts in transfer payments, as well as in absolute wealth, as the United States perhaps uniquely becomes the setting of vast migrations of the

EXHIBIT 8

MANUFACTURING EMPLOYMENT CHANGE [1]

SOUTH ATLANTIC DIVISION: 1960-1975

(Numbers in thousands)

Division and State	1960	1965	Change 1960-1965		1970	Change 1965-1970		1975	Change 1970-1975	
			Number	Percent		Number	Percent		Number	Percent
South Atlantic Division	2,013.1	2,263.5	250.4	12.4	2,687.8	424.3	18.7	2,614.2	-73.6	-2.7
Delaware	59.4	64.3	4.9	8.2	71.8	7.5	11.7	66.0	-5.8	-8.1
Washington, D.C.	19.8	20.3	0.5	2.5	20.0	-0.3	-1.5	16.3	-3.7	-18.5
Maryland	256.3	257.0	0.7	0.0	274.9	17.9	7.0	237.4	-37.5	-13.6
Virginia	271.5	310.0	38.5	14.2	363.1	53.1	17.1	357.8	-5.3	-1.5
West Virginia	128.6	125.4	-3.2	-2.5	127.7	2.3	1.8	123.2	-4.5	-3.5
North Carolina	493.5	564.5	71.0	14.4	698.6	134.1	23.8	714.5	15.9	2.3
South Carolina	238.5	286.1	47.6	20.0	334.5	48.4	16.9	324.0	-10.5	-3.1
Georgia	338.1	388.1	50.0	14.8	465.8	77.7	20.0	426.4	-39.4	-8.5
Florida	207.4	247.8	40.4	19.5	331.4	83.6	33.7	348.6	17.2	5.2

NOTE: 1. Employees on nonagriculture payrolls as of March of the respective years.

SOURCE: U.S. Department of Labor, Bureau of Labor Statistics, *Employment and Earnings* (Washington, D.C.: U.S. Government Printing Office, Monthly).

elderly, both from central cities and inhospitable climates, to the new retirement havens. Does such a phenomenon replicate the impact of exporting (manufacturing) industries: new regions of habitation accrue not only an income flow derived from external areas (pensions and Social Security payments), but also net increments in fixed wealth (the asset positions of the migrants)? These are vexing questions to which definitive answers have yet to be formulated. And in this light, the level of concern which must be invoked for the selected manufacturing declines in the South Atlantic states remains problematic. At the very least, however, caution may be warranted toward overexaggerations of widespread total affluence throughout the Sunbelt. Nevertheless it is difficult not to recognize the weight of current trendlines working strongly against the Northeast and North Central states and favorably toward the southern rimlands.

But are trends destiny? Certainly the answer to that question cannot simply be ascertained from the employment indicators presented so far. One critical input into any economic future is the level of investment in new capital plant and infrastructure, and its regional allocation. In general, new capital facilities are those which will ultimately be utilized in preference to the old. The vital question concerns where they are being put in place.

Nonresidential Construction. Exhibit 9 summarizes the valuation of total private, nonresidential construction authorized from 1967 through the first five months of 1976. Under this rubric are grouped all of the nation's activities in creating the physical places where economic activity is conducted. The pattern is an ominous one from the point of view of the older northern regions. The share of nonresidential investment developed in the Northeast shrank consistently through the period under consideration, from a 21.7 percent annual average from 1967 through 1969 to 15.9 percent for 1973 to 1975—and to a far from definitive but forebodingly low 11.4 percent in the first five months of 1976. The North Central Region, conversely, held relatively constant throughout these periods, generally capturing about 25 percent of the national investment. (The question of whether the entirety of the North Central Region is sharing in this consistent capital replenishment, or whether the deviation shown earlier between the East North Central and West North Central divisions is still operative still remains. Data are not available on a divisional basis.)

Once again it is the South and West which increasingly procure the bulk of new development, with the former enlarging its share from 29.1 percent to 35.8 percent from 1967 to 1976. The West's pattern of

EXHIBIT 9

VALUATION OF TOTAL PRIVATE,
NONRESIDENTIAL CONSTRUCTION AUTHORIZED
1967-1976

(Millions of dollars; numbers represent
annual averages for the periods indicated)

Period	U. S. Total	Annual Average Valuation			
		Northeast Region	North Central Region	South Region	West Region
1967-1969	11,683.3	2,504.7	3,119.8	3,395.8	2,627.0
1970-1972	14,277.5	2,641.1	3,409.5	4,734.4	3,492.5
1973-1975	17,932.1	2,848.4	4,431.2	6,157.5	4,495.0
1976 [1]	6,420.6	728.9	1,601.1	2,295.8	1,794.8
		Percent Distribution			
1967-1969	100.0	21.7	26.7	29.1	22.5
1970-1972	100.0	18.5	23.9	33.2	24.5
1973-1975	100.0	15.9	24.7	34.3	25.1
1976 [1]	100.0	11.4	24.9	35.8	28.0

NOTE: 1. First five months, preliminary.
SOURCE: U. S. Bureau of the Census, *Construction Reports*, Series C20 (Washington, D.C.: U. S. Government Printing Office, Monthly).

invigoration correlates significantly with that of the South; it is adding to and replenishing its nonresidential base accounting for 28.9 percent of current national totals, more than twice the magnitude of the Northeast. Significantly, the West was at parity with the latter area only eight years previous.

The Underlying Rationale. These trendlines emphasize what we believe to be the existence of a number of underlying processes that permeate many of the immediate concerns faced by planners in a variety of contexts. They also appear to represent key causal elements upon which broader public policy responses hinge.

    1. *Aging Capital Plants.* The industrial infrastructures of our older regions relate to production methods and approaches which are no longer competitive. The shifts of jobs and the declining shares of capital investment within these regions indicate that obsolescence is not being countered effectively.

2. *Rationalization of Labor Intensive Industries.* A virtual revolution has occurred in the technologies of goods production, information processing, and communications. While automation and technological change may possibly produce new jobs equivalent in number to those replaced, it is clear that their geographic loci do not coincide.

3. *Hardening of the Arteries.* Aging regions develop a variety of conflicting property interests in the broader sense of the term, creating inhibitors which limit their ability to adapt to new industrial demands, thereby reducing their desirability for new entrants.

4. *Spatial Homogenization.* Broader technological changes—such as the interstate highway system domestically and dry bulk cargo shipping internationally—undermine the locational advantages once inherent in older regions. Similarly, alternative developments—such as the communications revolution—have made heretofore bypassed areas now directly competitive.

5. *Receptivity to Growth.* Locational decisionmakers are subject not only to basic economic constraints, but also to subtle, yet vital, interactions with local political structures. And in the growth areas outlined above, receptivity to potential new industrial relocatees is high, in contrast to the older regions.

Certainly, other processes are of operational significance. Their existence will be suggested as the analogs of employment shifts—population flows—are examined in some detail.

POPULATION FLOWS

Within the continental United States, it is the shift of population which serves both as signal and as instigator of economic growth and decline. The new shopping center, in the absence of net new additional consumers to be serviced, can only flourish at the cost of the contraction of the old. The new field sales office, the growth of financial institutions, and the development of an interwoven set of service industries geared to local consumers are all directly linked to this key variable. (Indeed, in a following section, we demonstrate the negative impacts of population and income losses on the economic viability of local jurisdictions.)

The secular pattern of shift in the United States—as exemplified by westward movement—though perhaps as old as our history, has now been suddenly accentuated. Exhibit 10 tabulates the basic regional population changes which have occurred from 1960 to 1975. Of overriding consideration in viewing these regional performances is the *deceleration of national growth*—from 18.5 percent from 1950 to 1960, to 13.4 percent from 1960 to 1970, and to 4.8 percent (which translates to

EXHIBIT 10

Regional Population Change: 1960 to 1975

(Numbers in thousands)

Region	Population Totals			Numerical Change			Percentage Change		
	1960[1]	1970[2]	1975[3]	1960-1975	1960-1970	1970-1975	1960-1975	1960-1970	1970-1975
Northeast	44,678	49,061	49,461	4,783	4,383	400	10.7	9.8	0.8
North Central	51,619	56,593	57,669	6,050	4,974	1,076	11.7	9.6	1.9
South	54,973	62,812	68,112	13,140	7,839	5,300	23.9	14.3	8.4
West	28,053	34,838	37,878	9,825	6,785	3,040	35.0	24.2	8.7
U. S. Total	179,323	203,304	213,120	33,797[4]	23,981	9,816	18.8	13.4	4.8

NOTES: 1. April 1, 1960 census.
2. April 1, 1970 census as reported in source below.
3. July 1, 1975 provisional estimate.
4. Numbers may not add due to rounding.

SOURCE: U.S. Bureau of the Census, *Current Population Reports*, Series P-25, no. 640, "Estimates of the Population of States with Components of Change: 1970 to 1975" (Washington, D.C.: U.S. Government Printing Office, 1976).

an equivalent decade rate of 9.8 percent) from 1970 to 1975. For the entire 1960 to 1975 period, when the nation's population expanded by 18.8 percent, the Northeast and North Central states grew by only 10.7 and 11.7 percent, respectively. It was the South and West which by far gained the bulk of the population increases, as evidenced by growth rates of 23.9 and 35.0 percent, respectively. Indeed, in 1960 the West had only 60 percent of the population of the Northeast; by 1975, it broached the 75 percent mark. The South's 1960 population exceeded by ten million that of the Northeast; by 1975 this gap had nearly doubled.

Again the total shift masks intra-period patterns of differentiation. Slow growth in the Northeast and North Central states from 1960 to 1970 has been transformed into virtual stagnation in the post-1970 period. While even the West's growth has slowed somewhat, the South's has accelerated markedly, with a 1960 to 1970 decade growth rate of 14.3 percent followed by a 1970 to 1975 equivalent decade rate of 16.8 percent. *Briefly, both the South and the West are now growing at twice the national rate leaving the older northern sections of the country at best approaching a steady state condition.*

Total population change, moreover, is the product of both net natural increases (births minus deaths) and net migration. Given the overall decline in the nation's birth rate, the latter assumes increased significance. Migration is a telling criterion of location shift by choice, of people seeking out "better" places to live. Whether because of climate, jobs, sheer restlessness, or whatever—migration data tend to gauge the locational preferences of Americans. In Exhibit 11 these are clearly defined. *The period from 1960 to 1970 appears to mark the terminal shift of population as a function of the agricultural revolution.* The West North Central Division, the bread basket of America, lost nearly 600,000 people through net migration. Replicating this pattern was the East South Central Division; the dissolution of labor intensive farming resulted in a net out-migration of nearly 700,000 people.

Concurrently, the West Region was the destination of the bulk of the movers, with the Pacific Division alone gaining more than 2.5 million individuals. Its lure was paralleled by the South Atlantic Division, with the great boom of Florida the leading attraction; this total division gained more than 1.3 million individuals. The Northeast—in part because of overseas in-migration—enjoyed a net addition of 375,000 individuals, the bulk of them concentrated in the New England Division.

The dynamic changes which have occurred since 1970 are of enormous significance to the pressures on land use as they relate to the economic adjustments taking place in the nation. The aging industrial belt is

EXHIBIT 11

REGION AND DIVISION NET MIGRATION:
1960 TO 1970 AND 1970 TO 1975
(Numbers in thousands)

Region and Division	1960-1970	1970-1975
Northeast Region	375	−686 [1]
Middle Atlantic Division	59	−758
New England Division	316	71
North Central Region	−752	−878
East North Central Division	−153	−774
West North Central Division	−599	−103
South Region	592	2,624
South Atlantic Division	1,332	1,859
East South Central Division	−698	202
West South Central Division	−42	563
West Region	2,854	1,467
Mountain Division	307	832
Pacific Division	2,547	635

NOTE: 1. Numbers may not add due to rounding.
SOURCE: U. S. Bureau of the Census, *Current Population Reports,* Series P-25,
no. 640, "Estimates of the Population of States with Components
of Change: 1970 to 1975." (Washington, D.C.: U. S. Government
Printing Office, 1976).

increasingly being vacated as a matter of conscious choice. *The North Central Region's 1970 to 1975 net out-migration, for example, approached 900,000 persons—more than the loss experienced in the entire 1960 to 1970 decade.* Internally, moreover, the loss is shifting from the previous agricultural locus (the West North Central Division) to the industrial complexes of the East North Central Division. *The pattern in the Northeast is similar to the industrial Middle Atlantic Division buffeted by a net out-migration of over 750,000 people.*

The pattern of "winners" also changes markedly. From 1960 to 1970 the West had nearly five times as many in-migrants as the South. From 1970 to 1975, the South outdistanced the West by a factor approaching two. *Indeed, the entire South Region had a net in-migration of 2.6 million people—as much as the 1970 populations of Philadelphia (1.9 million) and Cleveland (751,000) combined.* Even the East South Central

Division, earlier the locus of major out-movement, has been a net gainer in the last five years, as has the booming, oil rich West South Central Division.

The pattern within the West also has shifted with the nation's former front runner, the Pacific Division, being outdistanced by the Mountain states. *To Horace Greely's earlier inspiration "Go west young man" must be added an admonition—selectively—and based on these data, an even more overriding injunction to consider the South.* For it is not only the realities of population concentration which are rapidly being altered —but also the income equivalent.

The Income Shift. As the popular media brim with accounts of northern cities and states desperately petitioning the federal government for economic aid, it is difficult to recall the conscious policy of the United States, since the early days of the New Deal, of focusing income growth in the South. The images of tobacco road, of the dust bowl, of the sharecropper and dirt-eating children have faded into the far reaches of our consciousness. It is perhaps far too easy to forget the triumph documented by the data shown in Exhibit 12: the revitalization of a region which was once America's shame.

EXHIBIT 12

PER CAPITA PERSONAL INCOME CHANGE:
1960 TO 1975
(Unadjusted dollars [1])

Region [2]	1960	1975	Change: 1960-1975	
			Number	Percent
Northeast	$2,546	$6,305	$3,759	147.6
North Central	2,293	6,011	3,718	162.1
South	1,760	5,148	3,388	192.5
West	2,484	6,269	3,785	152.4
U. S. Total	2,222	5,834	3,612	162.6

NOTES: 1.   Not in constant dollars.
2.   Regional incomes are population weighted means of divisional parameters.   Published data available only on a division basis.
SOURCE: U. S. Department of Commerce, Bureau of Economic Analysis, *Survey of Current Business* (Washington, D.C.: U. S. Government Printing Office, Monthly).

Even as late as 1960 per capita personal incomes in the South were only about two-thirds of their northeastern equivalent. But significant regional income homogenization has taken place the last fifteen years. While the Northeast on this basis remains the wealthiest part of the United States, and the South still the poorest (with the West and North Central divisions standing intermediate), the relative closing of the gap is most substantial. Moreover, differential interregional costs of living (not considered here) may serve to completely bridge the remaining spread. In the South, incomes have nearly tripled in the fifteen-year period under consideration, increasing 192.5 percent. (One should realize that this increment in southern income levels has occurred despite an enormous influx of retirees, many of whom have low incomes, but compensatingly strong asset positions.[3]) The Northeast had the slowest pattern of growth, recording an increase of 147.6 percent (see Exhibit 12).

When these data are viewed in the light of numerical changes in total population, the potency of increased southern buying power needs little amplification. For instance, total personal income in the South in 1975 stood at $350.7 billion, an increase of 261 percent over the 1960 total of $97.1 billion. In contrast, the Northeast fell sharply behind the South; its 1960 total personal income, $114.1 billion, increased by only 173 percent to the $311.8 billion level.[4] The Northeast's lagging pace correlates significantly with its corresponding performance in the economic and population sectors. And this pattern is reinforced by a key statistic related to population—new dwelling unit starts.

Residential Construction. Any study of housing vacancy rates would certainly mark the Northeast as a most marketable region for new housing starts. Its vacancy rates are substantially lower than those of the nation as a whole, and specifically in comparison to the high growth areas of the South and West. Yet it is the latter regions which have consistently attracted the bulk of the new dwelling unit starts in the country as a whole. Exhibit 13 presents the average annual housing starts for successive three-year increments from 1964 to 1975, with an addendum for the first seven months of 1976. While the absolute number of regional starts fluctuates in concert with the national pattern of activity, *the proportional share secured by the Northeast shows a long-term decline, from 17.8 percent in the 1964 to 1966 period to 10.4 percent for the first seven months of 1976.* In contrast, the South has consistently accounted for about 40 percent of the nation's starts, despite the enormous condominium glut in Florida the past several years. In

EXHIBIT 13

RESIDENTIAL DWELLING UNIT STARTS: 1964-1976
(Numbers in thousands; numbers represent annual
average starts for the periods indicated)

Period	U. S. Total	Housing Unit Starts Annual Average			
		Northeast Region	North Central Region	South Region	West Region
1964-1966	1,422.2	253.2	337.5	553.8	277.7
1967-1969	1,455.6	224.3	359.2	589.4	282.8
1970-1972	1,977.3	276.4	395.5	860.1	445.3
1973-1975	1,527.1	203.9	352.5	638.3	332.5
1976 [1]	863.5	90.2	218.3	331.0	223.5
		Percent Distribution			
1964-1966	100.0	17.8	23.7	38.9	19.5
1967-1969	100.0	15.4	24.7	40.5	19.4
1970-1972	100.0	14.0	20.0	43.5	22.5
1973-1975	100.0	13.4	23.1	41.8	21.8
1976 [1]	100.0	10.4	25.3	38.4	25.9

NOTE: 1. First seven months, preliminary.
SOURCE: U. S. Bureau of the Census, *Construction Reports,* Series C20
(Washington, D.C.: U. S. Government Printing Office, Monthly).

both cases, the pattern of building performance is congruent to the migration and population growth exhibited by these two regions.

The significance of housing starts has many facets. Not the least of them is its importance as a basic multiplier for the local economy, whether it is in providing jobs for construction workers, fabricators, architects, insurors, mortgage bankers, local furniture vendors, and all of those innumerable activities that cluster both directly and indirectly to housing. (Need we say planners!) Its importance, therefore, as a dynamic of local growth requires little amplification. As we suggested earlier, jobs may have attracted people, but subsequently people and their shelter demands add further impetus to economic viability. In addition, housing clearly augments a region's appeal to potential movers in a country which, with few exceptions, still thinks of *new* housing as *better*.

The Driving Forces. As in the case of economic activity shifts, the currents of regional population flows are shaped by a complex of forces affecting locational decisionmaking. In addition to the basic constraints of economic opportunity, we believe the following factors have direct relevance for both understanding and extrapolating recent events.

1. Earlier in this century, the impetus toward population decentralization —suburbanization—was underlaid by two factors. The first centered about *facilitating mechanisms*. The pyramiding of successive technological innovations made feasible the habitation of territories beyond formal city boundaries. To cite but one example, the widespread use of air conditioning has permitted the larger scale equivalent of suburbanization to occur by equalizing regional climates.

2. A second factor, social and cultural predispositions, must act in conjunction with the first to produce large-scale migrations.[5] The impetus to flee settings thought of as undesirable socially or environmentally for more pristine and/or amenity rich alternatives has now been permitted to work itself out over the entire geography of the nation. Suburban flight has given way to regional shift.

3. The complex infrastructure inherent in the aging industrial metropolises of the "snowbelt" has become one of their principal liabilities. As discipline wanes, this high state of interdependence places individuals in fragile environments susceptible to external events. Autonomy becomes desirable and is sought in the more primitive, less structure dependent habitats in the Sunbelt.

These factors certainly do not represent a definitive listing of the forces underpinning residential shifts. Additional concerns of significance will be put forth as they simultaneously affect metropolitan and nonmetropolitan population flows. However, one final task remains to complete the evaluation of regional growth cycles—population dependent employment—private nonmanufacturing and government job shifts.

PRIVATE NONMANUFACTURING EMPLOYMENT

Exhibit 14 details the long-term (1960 to 1975) changes in private nonmanufacturing employment (excluding government) on a regional and divisional basis. The South and West, as implied by their population growth totals, are the expansion leaders, evidencing growth rates of 77.8 and 80.1 percent, respectively, in total nonmanufacturing jobs (which are inclusive of the fire, insurance, and real estate; wholesale and retail trade; transportation and public utilities; service and miscellaneous;

contract construction; and mining employment subsectors). The Northeast (36.5 percent) and North Central (50.6 percent) regions again show significant lags in their growth rates.

EXHIBIT 14

PRIVATE NONMANUFACTURING EMPLOYMENT CHANGE:
1960 TO 1975 [1]
BY REGION AND DIVISION
(Numbers in thousands)

Region and Division	1960	1975	Change 1960-1975	
			Number	Percent
Northeast Region	7,672.4	10,470.5	2,798.1	36.5
Middle Atlantic Division	6,025.2	7,847.0	1,821.8	30.2
New England Division	1,647.2	2,623.5	976.3	59.3
North Central Region	7,512.5	11,311.6	3,799.1	50.6
East North Central Division	5,252.6	7,876.2	2,623.6	49.9
West North Central Division	2,259.9	3,435.4	1,175.5	52.0
South Region	7,547.4	13,415.7	5,868.3	77.8
South Atlantic Division	3,694.0	6,802.4	3,108.4	84.1
East South Central Division	1,285.5	2,243.4	957.9	74.5
West South Central Division	2,567.9	4,369.9	1,802.0	70.2
West Region	4,326.3	7,792.8	3,466.5	80.1
Mountain Division	1,113.9	2,136.5	1,022.6	91.8
Pacific Division	3,212.4	5,656.3	2,443.9	76.1
U. S. Total [2]	27,058.6	42,990.6	15,932.0	58.9

NOTES: 1. Employees on nonagriculture payrolls as of March of the respective years.
2. Excludes Hawaii and Alaska.

SOURCE: U. S Department of Labor, Bureau of Labor Statistics, *Employment and Earnings* (Washington, D.C.: U. S. Government Printing Office, Monthly).

On a divisional partition, the Middle Atlantic states are uniquely separable in terms of their low rate of expansion—30.2 percent. Significantly, the New England Division's performance (59.3 percent) does not evidence too severe a differential from the nation's faster growing divisions. At the leading edge of change are the Mountain states (with a 1960 to 1975 rate of increase of 91.8 percent) and the South Atlantic Division (84.1 percent). In the latter arena—which was shown to have experienced a somewhat troubled manufacturing sector in the post-1970 period—this growth apparently more than compensates for other lagging economic activities. As we suggested earlier, the growing retirement sector, and its external income flows, may replicate the support capacity of basic industries, acting as a spur to population serving activities.

The fifteen-year cycle, however, touching only two moments of time, conceals significant internal dynamics as shown in Exhibit 15. The interregional gaps—particularly the Northeast versus the South—evident during the 1960 to 1965 period, narrowed perceptibly during the years 1965 to 1970, a time when the national economy was operating at full force. *In the post-1970 period, the early 1960s gap is transformed into a virtual chasm, with the South's share of national growth (45.2 percent) almost five times greater than the Northeast's (9.4 percent).* Certainly, the loss of 247,300 private nonmanufacturing jobs in New York City and Philadelphia (not in exhibit) exaggerated the regional differentials; yet were we to compare the Northeast versus the South, excluding these two urban giants, we would find the gap not appreciably bridged.

GOVERNMENT EMPLOYMENT CHANGE

Completing the employment cycle is the governmental sector detailed in Exhibit 16, which provides total government employment change from 1960 to 1975. But these gross totals do not differentiate between federal employment and its state and local equivalents and, therefore, must be viewed with caution. The South's growth rate for the fifteen-year period (87.7 percent) surpasses that of both the Northeast (66.6 percent) and North Central states (68.3 percent), and is roughly comparable to the performance of the West Region (90.6 percent). The implications of these rate increments—which are considerably smaller compared to the other employment sectors—are troublesome. Do they represent onerous tax burdens on the older regions (the Northeast and North Central states) as they attempt to mitigate the losses, or slowed growth, of private economic activity? Or do they represent the belated provision of local public services to growth areas (the South and West), soon to be followed by increased local taxation and equivalent inhibitors to future growth? Or do the differentials constitute the selective place-

EXHIBIT 15

REGIONAL GROWTH SHARES OF PRIVATE NONMANUFACTURING EMPLOYMENT CHANGE: 1960 to 1975 [1]

(Numbers in thousands)

Region	Absolute Growth Increment			Percentage Share of National Growth		
	1960-1965	1965-1970	1970-1975	1960-1965	1965-1970	1970-1975
Northeast Region	660.9	1,630.9	506.3	17.8	23.9	9.4
North Central Region	848.3	1,819.0	1,131.8	22.8	26.6	21.0
South Region	1,284.5	2,149.8	2,434.0	34.6	31.5	45.2
West Region	919.9	1,232.5	1,314.1	24.8	18.0	24.4
U.S. Total [2]	3,713.6 [3]	6,832.2	5,386.2	100.0	100.0	100.0

NOTES: 1. Employees on nonagriculture payrolls as of March of the respective periods.
2. Excludes Hawaii and Alaska.
3. Numbers and percents may not add due to rounding.

SOURCE: U.S. Department of Labor, Bureau of Labor Statistics, *Employment and Earnings* (Washington, D.C.: U.S. Government Printing Office, Monthly).

ment of federal employment, whose impact may approximate that of a basic sector industry?

EXHIBIT 16

TOTAL GOVERNMENT EMPLOYMENT CHANGE:
1960 TO 1975 [1]
BY REGION AND DIVISION
(Numbers in thousands)

Region and Division	1960	1975	Change 1960-1975	
			Number	Percent
Northeast Region	1,936.5	3,225.7	1,289.2	66.6
Middle Atlantic Division	1,478.4	2,470.8	992.4	67.1
New England Division	458.1	754.9	296.8	64.8
North Central Region	2,199.4	3,700.8	1,501.4	68.3
East North Central Region	1,479.1	2,503.5	1,024.4	69.3
West North Central Division	720.3	1,197.3	477.0	66.2
South Region	2,620.1	4,918.1	2,298.0	87.7
South Atlantic Division	1,347.1	2,662.2	1,315.1	97.6
East South Central Division	497.3	864.6	367.3	73.9
West South Central Division	775.7	1,391.3	615.6	79.4
West Region	1,533.4	2,922.7	1,389.3	90.6
Mountain Division	403.1	806.2	403.1	100.0
Pacific Division	1,130.3	2,116.5	986.2	87.3
U. S. Total [2]	8,289.4	14,767.3	6,477.9	78.1

NOTES: 1.   Employees on nonagriculture payrolls as of March of the respective years.
        2.   Excludes Hawaii and Alaska.

SOURCE: U. S. Department of Labor, Bureau of Labor Statistics, *Employment and Earnings* (Washington, D.C.: U. S. Government Printing Office, Monthly).

Exhibit 17 provides some insight into these questions by isolating federal civilian employment for the same time period (1960 to 1975) and area partitions. The South and West clearly serve as the major focus of federal growth, reinforcing the private sector trendlines. Indeed, the South's 31.9 percent increase completely outpaces the North-east's 3.3 percent increase by a tenfold margin. If we deduct the South's 1960 to 1975 federal growth increment (269,700 jobs) from the total governmental increase of Exhibit 16 (2.3 million jobs), then the residual state and local growth (2.0 million jobs) represents an increase of 77 percent over the *total 1960* base. This is a rate much closer to the Northeast equivalent.

EXHIBIT 17

FEDERAL GOVERNMENT CIVILIAN EMPLOYMENT CHANGE
BY REGION AND DIVISION: 1960-1975 [1]
(Numbers in thousands)

Region and Division	1960	1975	Change 1960-1975	
			Number	Percent
Northeast Region	475.8	491.7	15.9	3.3
Middle Atlantic Division	362.7	375.6	12.9	3.6
New England Division	113.1	116.1	3.0	2.7
North Central Region	424.0	497.4	73.4	17.3
East North Central Division	282.2	322.3	40.1	14.2
West North Central Division	141.8	175.1	33.3	23.5
South Region	845.6	1,115.3	269.7	31.9
South Atlantic Division	516.6	723.9	207.3	40.1
East South Central Division	138.3	144.8	6.5	4.7
West South Central Division	190.7	246.6	55.9	29.3
West Region	433.1	562.7	129.6	29.9
Mountain Division	128.0	181.4	53.4	41.7
Pacific Division	305.1	381.3	76.2	25.0
U. S. Total [2]	2,178.5	2,667.1	488.6	22.4

NOTES: 1. As of December 31 of the respective years.
2. Excludes Hawaii and Alaska.

SOURCE: U. S. Civil Service Commission, *Monthly Review of Federal Civilian Manpower Statistics* (Washington, D.C.: U. S. Government Printing Office, Monthly).

Taking a Northeast versus the South perspective (assuming they correlate, respectively, to the North Central and West Regions) it is clear that the South is securing the bulk of federal civilian employment, paced by the South Atlantic Division, the locus of an extensive federal bureaucracy. But the growth rates of the nonfederal sector in the Northeast and South are not strikingly disparate. Thus the "softening" of the South's economic pulling power as a function of increased costs of business over time is *not* shown by this indicator. The scale of local public service employment must be commensurate with the fiscal support bases—of which the private employment sector (both manufacturing and nonmanufacturing) bulk significantly—if tax increases and the formation of similar inhibitors are to be avoided. Indeed, if we correlate then the governmental components (Exhibits 16 and 17) with their manufacturing (Exhibit 5) and nonmanufacturing (Exhibit 14) counterparts, the South's governmental employment growth appears to be much more congruent to the private sector expansion. In the Northeast, the exact opposite is true.

Intra-Period Variations. Exhibits 18 and 19 provide the intra-period (five-year) breakdowns for the four regions. The patterns of change of total government employment (Exhibit 18) correspond to both the long-term (fifteen-year) dynamic as well as to the intra-period variations demonstrated in the other employment categories, with but one exception. The Northeast, in the post-1970 period, did not manifest the service downturn that it experienced previously in the other economic sectors. Whether this represents cause or effect—i.e., whether the tax burdens associated with paying for government employment have acted as growth inhibitors, or whether the continued expansion is a necessary complement to a faltering private sector—remains a lingering, but significant, question.

In Exhibit 19, the federal sector is again isolated. On a regional basis, it is apparent that federal government contraction in the Northeast and North Central states from 1970 to 1975 must aggravate the readjustments fostered by their lagging private sectors. In contrast, the federal expansion in the South and West continually added to the overall matrix of growth. Moreover, in the South Atlantic Division as a whole (not in exhibit), the federal increment may have counterbalanced the shrinkage in manufacturing employment experienced in the 1970 to 1975 period. Indeed, it is again difficult not to recognize the baseline tendency, particularly the evidence of the post-1970 period, working strongly against the aging industrial sections of the nation.

EXHIBIT 18

REGIONAL GROWTH SHARES OF TOTAL GOVERNMENT EMPLOYMENT CHANGE: 1960 to 1975 [1]

(Numbers in thousands)

Region	Absolute Growth Increment			Percentage Share of National Growth		
	1960-1965	1965-1970	1970-1975	1960-1965	1965-1970	1970-1975
Northeast Region	324.9	570.1	394.2	20.2	19.9	19.6
North Central Region	384.2	797.1	320.1	23.9	27.8	16.0
South Region	518.5	932.3	847.2	32.3	32.5	42.2
West Region	377.8	566.3	445.2	23.5	19.8	22.2
U.S. Total [2]	1,605.4	2,865.8	2,006.7	100.0 [3]	100.0	100.0

NOTES: 1. Employees on nonagriculture payrolls as of March of the respective periods.
2. Excludes Hawaii and Alaska.
3. Numbers and percents may not add due to rounding.

SOURCE: U.S. Department of Labor, Bureau of Labor Statistics, *Employment and Earnings* (Washington, D.C.: U.S. Government Printing Office, Monthly).

EXHIBIT 19

REGIONAL GROWTH SHARES OF FEDERAL GOVERNMENT CIVILIAN EMPLOYMENT: 1960 to 1975 [1]

(Numbers in thousands)

Region	Absolute Growth Increment			Percentage Share of National Growth		
	1960-1965	1965-1970	1970-1975	1960-1965	1965-1970	1970-1975
Northeast Region	2.4	25.9	—12.4	1.3	10.0	—28.9
North Central Region	28.4	45.8	—0.8	15.2	17.7	—1.9
South Region	107.3	124.0	38.4	57.3	48.0	89.5
West Region	49.3	62.6	17.7	26.3	24.2	41.3
U. S. Total [2]	187.4	258.3	42.9	100.0 [3]	100.0	100.0

NOTES: 1. Employees on nonagriculture payrolls as of March of the respective periods.
2. Excludes Hawaii and Alaska.
3. Numbers and percents may not add due to rounding.

SOURCE: U.S. Department of Labor, Bureau of Labor Statistics, *Employment and Earnings* (Washington, D.C.: U.S. Government Printing Office, Monthly).

THE REGIONAL FUTURES

What will the future hold for America's regional jurisdictions? Clearly the state of the art forbids definitive answers; we would, however, like to speculate on several alternative possibilities, as well as to raise some questions of import.

1. It is difficult to refute the basic reality of the scale of economic prosperity tipping inordinately toward the South. As measured by long-term (fifteen-year) employment totals, the secular trendline appears very powerful, indeed. And in the short run (1970 to 1975), a marked acceleration of the regional disparities is apparent. Whether the recent avalanche-like events are temporary phenomena—consequences of a stagnant national economy and technological and energy cost readjustments—or rather a momentum having reached critical mass—whose deflectability becomes even more dubious—is a key question for the foreseeable future.

2. If the latter is the case, the analogy between the Northeast Region and the historical decline of the nation's central cities—and between the southern rimlands on a national scale and the traditional affluence of the nation's suburbs—is the appropriate, but distressing, future scenario. Differentials once evidenced by urban-suburban tensions will then be fully extended to much higher regional scales.

3. If the former encompasses the basic reality, then we will probably see a continuation of the long-term dynamic, one which does not preclude select areas of economic viability within the Northeast. However, urban decline, as indicated for New York City and Philadelphia, may not be curtailed. The repositioning of extant activity, and of new growth, will certainly be in a suburban/exurban format, with select spatial bands of activity predominating. Thus, while thriving accumulations of decentralized activity clusters may be the future scenario, increasingly painful readjustments—which we simply appear incapable of dealing with effectively—will concurrently confront older cities as their traditional roles continue to contract.

4. This possibility then raises the following questions and observations.

   a) Is the stabilization, or moderate revival, of New England, a harbinger of what may be anticipated in the Middle Atlantic Division given some lessening of seepage from its older cities?

   b) In this regard, do the demonstrated losses of manufacturing employment represent the final phasing out of the obsolete multi-floored urban industrial parcel, an industrial configuration related to a level of technology and rationalization which is no longer competitive? The degree to which New York City and Philadelphia dominate the losses may attest to this fact. Is the endpoint of this process in sight, with stability and moderate growth on the horizon, as hinted by the New England experience?

c) Are the older industrial states, whose aging central cities played the major historic role as job loci, capable of maintaining their employment base as the central cities in question shrink in employment?

d) In reference to the South Atlantic Division—into whose orbit an inordinate volume of development interest has swung—does the faltering of the manufacturing sector provide an advanced indicator of future general employment likelihoods? Is it possible that the manufacturing shifts signal for the South Atlantic states advanced signs of the earlier New England and present Middle Atlantic trauma? Or will the growth of their continuing dominance in governmental spending as well as the geographic shift of the affluent retirement sector provide more than compensatory sustaining elements?

4. The growth of federal employment in the South Atlantic Division is indicative of another phenomenon of national import—the Washington-New York City transformation. Historically, the establishment of the District of Columbia as the national capital, rather than New York, implied a basic separation of powers. Washington became the political capital, while New York and other cities became the capitals for virtually every other activity—economic, cultural, intellectual, and so forth. In contrast to many foreign nations, total power was never narrowly focused in one single city, e.g., a Paris or a London.

However, encompassed within the regional shifts may be the rise of an "imperial" Washington, correlating with the northeastern demise in general, and New York City specifically. The dynamic growth of the federal vehicle—with regulatory agencies influencing virtually every facet of our lives and industry—implies the gravitation to a single geographic focus of the nation's major public and private decisionmaking apparatus.

These are but some of the basic questions that will be facing planners and policymakers for the forseeable future. They are not solely a consequence of the regional dynamic, however. They are also interpenetrated by another major phenomenon—emerging metropolitan-nonmetropolitan growth tensions. It is to this matter we now turn.

The Emerging Metropolitan-Nonmetropolitan Dynamic

The decline of the central city and the resynthesis of many dimensions of American life in suburbia have been construed as the basic challenge of contemporary planning activity. The efforts put forth in ameliorating the intra-metropolitan problems of racial resegregation, of fiscal shortfall, and of infrastructure duplication have as yet not shown an appropriate awareness of a broader change of concommitant significance. *It is one in which the very role of the traditional industrial metropolis may soon be coming into question.*

The data in Exhibit 20 help define the basic transformations of the post-1970 era. From 1960 to 1970 the twenty largest metropolitan agglomerations of the United States experienced the final stages of their service as the nation's dominant growth poles—their average annual population increase (1.7 percent) exceeded that of lesser metropolitan places (1.5 percent), and far outdistanced nonmetropolitan territories (0.4 percent).[6] Significantly, in terms of net migration, the large metropolises secured 4.2 million newcomers, the remaining metropolitan settlements 2.2 million, while nonmetropolitan areas had a net migration loss of 3.2 million people.

The contrast with the most recent accounting period, 1970 to 1974 is jarring. *Large metropolitan areas have evolved into slow growth settings (an average annual population growth of 0.3 percent) as the smaller metropolitan areas have assumed the dominant focus of growth (1.5 percent). Yet the latter are being challenged by the marked resurgence of nonmetropolitan growth, where population increases averaged 1.3 percent annually.* In an equally telling transformation, the twenty largest metropolitan complexes experienced a net migration outflow of 1.2 million people, while nonmetropolitan territories had a net migration inflow of 1.5 million. Some of this shift undoubtedly signifies the drive toward exurbia, and can be attributed to the uncodified extension of the current nominal boundaries of metropolitan enclosure. However, the lagging pace of metropolitan delineation may only be a secondary explanation for the phenomenon.

REGIONAL CHANGE AND METROPOLITAN SHIFTS

The basic reality can only be ascertained in conjunction with the web of regional differentials highlighted in Exhibit 21, which partitions metropolitan and nonmetropolitan population growth patterns by regional location. It is the large metropolitan complexes of the Northeast which dominate the post 1970 experience of metropolitan decline, losing 0.3 percent of their population annually. Also exhibiting similar symptoms, although on a lesser plane, are their equivalents in the North Central states, which experienced annual population losses of 0.1 percent. In sharp contrast is the status of large metropolitan areas in the South and West, which demonstrated annual increases of 1.8 and 0.5 percent, respectively.

The major focal points of growth in the Northeast and North Central states are nonmetropolitan areas, which far exceeded even the positive

EXHIBIT 20

Metropolitan and Nonmetropolitan Population Change and Net Migration: 1960 to 1974
(Population numbers in thousands; migration in millions)

Metropolitan Status [1]	Population			Average Annual Percent Change		Net Migration	
	1960	1970	1974	1960-1970	1970-1974	1960-1970	1970-1974
Total Metropolitan	127,938	149,817	154,964	1.6	0.8	6.4	0.5
Large metropolitan [2]	69,262	81,471	82,548	1.7	0.3	4.2	−1.2
Other metropolitan	58,676	68,346	72,416	1.5	1.5	2.2	1.7
Nonmetropolitan	51,373	53,483	56,427	0.4	1.3	−3.2	1.5
U.S. Total	179,311	203,300	211,391	1.3	1.0	—	—

NOTES: 1. Current metropolitan area definition (1975).
2. Large metropolitan includes areas identified individually in Exhibit 22.

SOURCE: U. S. Bureau of the Census, *Current Population Reports*, Series P-25, no. 640, "Estimates of the Population of States with Components of Change: 1970 to 1975" (Washington, D.C.: U.S. Government Printing Office, 1976).

EXHIBIT 21

POPULATION AND AVERAGE ANNUAL PERCENT CHANGE
FOR REGIONS BY METROPOLITAN STATUS: 1960 to 1974
(Numbers in thousands)

Region	Population			Average Annual Percent Change	
	1960	1970	1974	1960-1970	1970-1974
Northeast					
Large Metropolitan	26,309	28,933	28,623	1.0	−0.3
Other Metropolitan	12,300	13,548	13,816	1.3	0.5
Nonmetropolitan	6,069	6,580	6,987	0.8	1.4
North Central					
Large Metropolitan	20,049	22,591	22,559	1.2	−0.1
Other Metropolitan	14,810	16,815	17,226	1.3	0.6
Nonmetropolitan	16,760	17,185	17,759	0.3	0.8
South					
Large Metropolitan	10,232	13,702	14,756	2.9	1.8
Other Metropolitan	22,347	26,112	28,122	1.6	1.7
Nonmetropolitan	22,382	22,998	24,299	0.3	1.3
West					
Large Metropolitan	12,672	16,245	16,610	2.5	0.5
Other Metropolitan	9,219	11,871	13,252	2.5	2.6
Nonmetropolitan	6,162	6,720	7,382	0.9	2.2

NOTE: 1. Large metropolitan includes areas identified individually in Exhibit 22. Metropolitan areas as defined in 1975.

SOURCE: U. S. Bureau of the Census, *Current Population Reports*, Series P-25, no. 640, "Estimates of the Population of States with Components of Change: 1970 to 1975" (Washington, D.C.: U. S. Government Printing Office, 1976).

growth performances of the smaller metropolitan areas. In the South and West, the bulk of the population growth on an absolute basis is taking place in smaller metropolitan settings. The linkage of regional and metropolitan growth patterns becomes apparent when it is realized

that the Northeast has nearly three-fifths of its total population concentrated in four large metropolitan areas.[7] Therefore, the virtual halt
in large metropolitan growth nationally has much greater effect in the
Northeast when compared to the South, where only one-fifth of the
population resides in large metropolitan settings. Similarly, the revitalization of the nonmetropolitan sector has negligible positive effects in
the Northeast, where only one-seventh of the population is nonmetropolitan; in contrast, the South, where one-third of the population so
resides, experiences much greater repercussions from nonmetropolitan
growth. Avoiding the question of which shift—regional or metropolitan
—is the primary causal factor, we can be certain that their interlinkage
is forging the critical dynamic for the immediate future.

When the data for the twenty largest metropolitan agglomerations
are further dissected, their losses appear more alarming. As shown in
Exhibit 22, *every one of the eleven major metropolises in the Northeast
and North Central regions experienced net out-migration from 1970 to
1974.* Yet in the South, only Washington, D.C. is similarly afflicted;
more than compensating for the latter's performance has been the phe-
nomenal growth of Houston, Miami, and Atlanta, clearly indexed by
very substantial numbers of in-migrants.

Surprisingly, the West exhibits a pattern similar to the older regions.
Los Angeles and Seattle, perhaps subject to the vagaries of the aircraft
industry, had negative migration balances while San Francisco's net
in-migration was far below its experience of the preceding decade.

And the magnitudes of the losses of the older regions' metropolises
are far from trivial. In New York, for example, the net out-migration
of 635,000 people represents 3.6 percent of its 1970 population, with
similar proportions (3.2 percent) moving from Chicago and Detroit.
The Cleveland and St. Louis agglomerations fared even worse, buffeted
by losses of 5.3 and 4.4 percent, respectively. Even the fastest growing
metropolitan areas of the Northeast and North Central states, in terms
of total population change from 1970 to 1974, are growing at a rate far
slower than all, but Seattle, of the southern and western metropolises.

In the past, the sheer growth in population, particularly through migration, generated much of the social and economic stress of the major,
older urban agglomerations. This pattern has now changed very markedly, providing both hope and new challenge to the social meliorist.
The problems of coping with increased housing demand, of overcrowded
schools and overstressed physical facilities may be somewhat alleviated
by the new conditions of population stability and decline; but in their
place is the question of the fiscal balance—of the economic wherewithal

within the older metropolitan settings with which to service the remaining population. These factors will be examined in more detail subsequently. Certainly, however, within the metropolitan arena are equally important and distressing patterns of change.

Before this task is entertained, however, it is appropriate at this juncture to speculate on several integral dimensions of the process generating the migration from metropolitan to nonmetropolitan places. As should be evident, they are closely intertwined within the web of regional forces suggested earlier.

1. The societal drives that gave impetus to the suburbanization wave of the last half century have grown to full national force. The urbanization of suburbia—and its concommitant externalities—has spawned successive population movements to adjacent nonmetropolitan territories, as well as to the amenity rich Sunbelt on a national scale.

2. The nonmetropolitan growth resurgence may mark the decline of the endpoint of industrial urbanization—the historic industrial metropolis.

3. We may not, however, be witnessing so much the vigor per se of Sunbelt nonmetropolitan areas—the surges of antiurbanism—but the resynthesis of new metropolitan areas as a result of the powerful cumulative effects of repositioned urban growth.[8] What may be emerging is the new post-industrial spatial adaptation of the social and economic functions once concentrated solely in the withering monuments to the industrial age.

4. Likewise, a new post-suburban format appears to be evolving out of the nation's older industrial metropolises—geographically dispersed clusters of service functions and decentralized bands of economic activity. It is entirely possible that the spatial patterns of American life are converging toward a common configuration, despite a wide spectrum of diverse origins.

5. As a result of this "critical mass phenomenon"—the growing concentrations of people and jobs forming the support threshold for the development of "urban" amenities and functions—the infrastructures of older areas become redundant. The empty shells which once housed these activities litter the fading cityscape. A virtual dismantling of the traditional urban complex may be starting to take place.

Expanding Intra-Metropolitan Differentials

The history of America's major cities is one of meeting—and surmounting—the problems of growth and change. *But for the first time, the nation's central cities in total are losing population, and doing so quite markedly.* From 1970 to 1974, their population losses totaled 1.2 million, or 1.9 percent (Exhibit 23), while the corresponding suburban

EXHIBIT 22

POPULATION AND NET MIGRATION FOR THE 20 LARGEST METROPOLITAN AGGLOMERATIONS: 1960 TO 1974[1]

(Numbers in thousands)

Region and Area	Population			Change 1960-1970		Change 1970-1974		Net Migration	
	1960	1970	1974	Number	Percent	Number	Percent	1960-1970	1970-1974
Northeast Region									
New York	15,779	17,494	17,181	1,715	10.9	-313	-1.8	301	-635
Philadelphia[2]	5,024	5,628	5,642	604	12.0	14	0.2	98	-105
Boston	3,457	3,849	3,918	392	11.3	69	1.8	61	-2
Pittsburgh	2,405	2,401	2,334	-4	-0.2	-67	-2.8	-166	-89
North Central Region									
Chicago	6,795	7,611	7,615	816	12.0	4	0.0	-6	-242
Detroit	4,122	4,669	4,684	547	13.3	15	0.3	15	-151
Cleveland	2,732	3,000	2,921	268	9.8	-19	-0.6	-36	-159
St. Louis	2,144	2,411	2,371	267	12.5	-40	-1.7	24	-105
Minneapolis-St. Paul	1,598	1,965	2,011	367	23.0	46	2.3	118	-26
Cincinnati[2]	1,468	1,611	1,618	143	9.7	7	0.4	-33	-43
Milwaukee	1,421	1,575	1,589	154	10.8	14	0.9	-29	-30

EXHIBIT 22 (continued)
POPULATION AND NET MIGRATION FOR THE 20 LARGEST METROPOLITAN AGGLOMERATIONS: 1960 TO 1974[1]
(Numbers in thousands)

Region and Area	Population			Change 1960-1970		Change 1970-1974		Net Migration	
	1960	1970	1974	Number	Percent	Number	Percent	1960-1970	1970-1974
South Region									
Washington, D.C.	2,097	2,909	3,015	812	38.7	106	3.6	429	-14
Dallas-Fort Worth	1,738	2,378	2,499	640	36.8	121	5.1	368	10
Houston	1,571	2,169	2,402	598	38.1	233	10.7	328	116
Miami	1,269	1,888	2,223	619	48.8	335	17.7	512	312
Baltimore	1,804	2,071	2,140	267	14.8	69	3.3	54	22
Atlanta	1,169	1,596	1,775	427	36.5	179	11.2	233	102
West Region									
Los Angeles	7,752	9,983	10,231	2,231	28.8	248	2.5	1,172	-84
San Francisco	3,492	4,424	4,585	932	26.7	161	3.6	489	45
Seattle	1,429	1,837	1,794	408	28.6	-43	-2.3	235	-91

NOTES: 1. Standard consolidated statistical areas and standard metropolitan statistical areas (SMSAs).
2. Small portions of Philadelphia and Cincinnati areas are in the South. Thus regional totals will differ slightly from those in Exhibit 21.

SOURCE: U.S. Bureau of the Census, *Current Population Reports*, Series P-25, no. 640, "Estimates of the Population of States with Components of Change: 1970 to 1975" (Washington, D.C.: U.S. Government Printing Office, 1976).

rings expanded by 6.2 million people or 8.4 percent. It is the largest
metropolitan areas, those with populations exceeding 1 million, which
account for all the decline. Their central cities have lost 3.8 percent
of their population in the four-year period under consideration (1.3
million people), while their suburban rings have gained 6.4 percent.
The central cities of the smaller metropolitan areas, those with populations of less than 1 million, have barely held their own. Their suburban rings, however, appear to be flourishing, showing a growth rate
(11.5 percent) far exceeding that of the nation as a whole (4.1 percent).
Again the broad data mask substantial internal variation in pattern.

EXHIBIT 23

POPULATION BY TYPE OF RESIDENCE, 1974 AND 1970
(1970 metropolitan area definition; numbers in thousands)

Type of Residence	1970	1974	Numerical Change 1970-1974	Percent Change 1970-1974
Metropolitan Areas, Total	142,043	137,058	4,985	3.6
Central Cities	61,650	62,876	−1,226	−1.9
Suburban Rings	80,394	74,182	6,212	8.4
Metropolitan Areas of 1 Million or More	81,059	79,489	1,570	2.0
Central Cities	33,012	34,322	−1,310	−3.8
Suburban Rings	48,047	45,166	2,881	6.4
Metropolitan Areas of Less Than 1 Million	60,985	57,570	3,415	5.9
Central Cities	28,638	28,554	84	0.3
Suburban Rings	32,347	29,016	3,331	11.5
U.S. Total	207,949	199,819	8,130	4.1

NOTE: Data exclude inmates of institutions and armed forces in barracks.
Therefore metropolitan totals may be inconsistent with those of
previous exhibits.

SOURCE: Vincent P. Barabba, "The National Setting," in George Sternlieb and
James W. Hughes, eds., *Post-Industrial America: Metropolitan De-
cline and Inter-Regional Job Shifts* (New Brunswick, N.J.: Rutgers
University, Center for Urban Policy Research, 1976).

RACIAL SHIFTS

America's central cities are being vacated by whites at an accelerating pace. Their departures represent a net loss of 5.1 percent from 1970 to 1974, almost 2.5 million people (Exhibit 24). Concurrently, the white population gains of the suburban rings were more than twice the central city loss (5.3 million). And despite the partitioning of metropolitan areas by size, their general pattern is pervasive.

In contrast stand the black population growth increments within central cities and suburban rings—their numbers increased 817,000 in the former and 554,000 in the latter. Hence, only one-third of the loss of whites within America's cities was offset by black increases. More-over, the pattern shown in Exhibit 24 documents the momentum of black suburbanization. While the absolute base is small, the 16.1 percentage change indicates the basic pattern of choice and preference. A partial vacuum is therefore opening up in central cities, given both the lagging pace of natural increase, and the pattern of net out-migration.

The implications of these data are manifold. *To cite but one example, the problem of the central city may no longer be the stimulation of additions to the housing stock, but rather the provision of take-out mechanisms for those units no longer required by a shrinking population.* While the issue may be offset temporarily by continued contraction in household size, to view such problems as residential abandonment in the abstract without studying the broader population shifts is to do them less than justice.

Within this perspective, Exhibit 25 summarizes the overall patterns of change by race and location of residence. The central cities' proportionate role of housing America's citizenry continues to wane; the suburban rings increasingly achieve critical mass. By 1974, the reversal of previous nonmetropolitan growth trends have pushed their proportional share of total population beyond that of the central city.

Significantly, on a percentage basis, it appears that the locational pattern of blacks is beginning to replicate the leading pattern of whites. From 1970 to 1974, the central cities' share declined (from 58.5 to 58.3 percent of the nation's total black population), counterbalanced by an increasing presence in the suburbs (15.6 to 16.9 percent). While in part this shift may represent the overflow of the central city into older adjoining suburbs, some of it unquestionably represents a much more radical, and welcome, diffusion.[9]

EXHIBIT 24

POPULATION BY RACE AND TYPE OF RESIDENCE,[1] 1974 AND 1970
(1970 metropolitan area definition; numbers in thousands)

Race and Type of Residence	1974	1970	Numerical Change 1970- 1974	Percent Change 1970- 1974
White				
U.S. Total	181,342	175,276	6,066	3.5
Metropolitan Areas, Total	121,739	118,938	2,801	2.4
Central Cities	46,427	48,909	−2,482	−5.1
Suburban Rings	75,313	70,029	5,284	7.5
Metropolitan Areas of 1 Million or More	68,336	67,721	615	0.9
Central Cities	23,215	25,007	−1,792	−7.2
Suburban Rings	45,120	42,714	2,406	5.6
Metropolitan Areas of Less Than 1 Million	53,404	51,217	2,187	4.3
Central Cities	23,211	23,903	−692	−2.9
Suburban Rings	30,192	27,315	2,877	10.5
Black				
U.S. Total	23,542	22,056	1,486	6.7
Metropolitan Areas, Total	17,713	16,342	1,371	8.4
Central Cities	13,726	12,909	817	6.3
Suburban Rings	3,987	3,433	554	16.1
Metropolitan Areas of 1 Million or More	11,243	10,715	528	4.9
Central Cities	8,897	8,664	233	2.7
Suburban Rings	2,346	2,051	295	14.4
Metropolitan Areas of Less than 1 Million	6,470	5,628	842	15.0
Central Cities	4,828	4,245	583	13.7
Suburban Rings	1,642	1,383	259	18.7

NOTE: 1. Data exclude inmates of institutions and armed forces in barracks. "Other" racial/ethnic groups excluded.

SOURCE: Vincent P. Barabba, "The National Setting," in George Sternlieb and James W. Hughes, eds., *Post Industrial America: Metropolitan Decline and Inter-Regional Job Shifts* (New Brunswick, N.J.: Rutgers University, Center for Urban Policy Research, 1976).

EXHIBIT 25

POPULATION BY RACE AND LOCATION OF RESIDENCE [1]
1950 TO 1974 [2]
(Percent distribution)

Race and Location of Residence	1950	1960	1970	1974
Total Population, U.S.	100.0	100.0	100.0	100.0
SMSA Total	62.5	66.7	68.6	68.3
Central Cities	35.5	33.4	31.5	29.6
Suburban Rings	27.0	33.3	37.1	38.7
Nonmetropolitan Areas	37.5	33.3	31.4	31.7
White Population, U.S.	100.0	100.0	100.0	100.0
SMSA Total	62.9	66.7	67.9	67.1
Central Cities	34.6	31.1	27.9	25.6
Suburban Rings	28.3	35.5	40.0	41.5
Nonmetropolitan Areas	37.1	33.4	32.1	32.9
Black Population, U.S.	100.0	100.0	100.0	100.0
SMSA Total	59.3	67.5	74.1	75.2
Central Cities	44.4	52.3	58.5	58.3
Suburban Rings	14.9	15.2	15.6	16.9
Nonmetropolitan Areas	40.7	32.5	25.9	24.8

NOTES: 1. 1970 metropolitan area definition.
2. 1950 and 1960 distributions based on total population; 1970 and 1974 distributions exclude inmates of institutions and armed forces in barracks.

SOURCES: U. S. Bureau of the Census, *U. S. Census of the Population; 1950 and 1960*, vol. 2.
Vincent P. Barabba, "The National Setting," in George Sternlieb and James W. Hughes, eds., *Post-Industrial America: Metropolitan Decline and Inter-Regional Job Shifts* (New Brunswick, N. J.: Rutgers University, Center for Urban Policy Research, 1976).

INCOME FLOWS

But it is not sheer numbers of individuals alone that must be considered in the formulation of new social and economic policies for central cities. The pattern of migration, both of population and jobs, is manifested in the drastic changes which have taken place in the incomes recorded by central city residents. Exhibit 26, then, is of crucial importance. *It indicates that, as a function of selective migration coupled with the net decline in population in the brief period from 1970 to 1974, the purchasing power of central city residents declined by $29.6 billion.* People of economic means migrate from the central city; the replacements are considerably less affluent. Thus an enormous dollar gap opens up. Using the somewhat shopworn but still commonly employed 25 percent of the household budget devoted to rent, the income loss translates to a decline of $7.4 billion in central city rent paying capacity. In turn if one were to capitalize this missing flow of "rent" dollars at a nominal "five times the rent roll" rate, a reasonable approximation for older rental housing, a decline of residential valuation of some $37 billion dollars is implied. Neither of these declines is felt in any one year, but cumulatively they *must* result in long-term patterns of shrinkage in the absolute value of central city realty—hence, its tax base—and consequently its capacity to provide services for its inhabitants. The sheer magnitude of the decline requires yet another amplification of this illustration. Assuming housing units valued at $25,000 each, there is a decline within four years in the support available for nearly 1.5 million units, a total equivalent to that encompassed within the entire Philadelphia SMSA. When the central city abandonment problem is viewed via this framework, its wide-ranging presence does not appear surprising.

The ramifications for other economic sectors can also be approximated. If 10 percent of the gross household budget is allocated to food, then about $3.0 billion (.10 x $29.6 billion) in food purchasing is "lost." [10] Since supermarkets currently have average sales of $130 per square foot per year, approximately 23 million square feet ($3.0 billion ÷ $130 per square foot) of food store space can no longer be supported. [11] For example, new suburban supermarkets average 25,000 square feet; the equivalent of 920 such stores (23 million square feet ÷ 25,000 square feet) have lost their economic underpinning.

It is in this sense that earlier in this paper we employed the notion of redundant infrastructures. The translation of income flows to new areas fosters the rapid replication of older facilities. Left behind are the bypassed resources, wasting for lack of an economic rationale. The fractured landscapes of a number of America's cities bear testimony to the pyramiding effects of this phenomenon.

EXHIBIT 26

INCOME IN 1973 OF FAMILIES AND UNRELATED INDIVIDUALS 14 YEARS OLD
AND OVER WHO MIGRATED TO AND FROM CENTRAL CITIES BETWEEN
1970 AND 1974

Subject	Living in Cities in 1970	Moved Out of Cities between 1970 and 1974	Moved to Cities between 1970 and 1974	Net Change between 1970 and 1974
Families (thousands)	16,823	3,363	1,563	−1,800
Mean Income (dollars)	$13,349	$14,169	$12,864	−$1,305
Aggregate Income (billion dollars)	$ 224.6	$ 47.7	$ 20.1	−$ 27.6
Unrelated individuals (thousands)	6,975	1,066	926	−140
Mean Income (dollars)	$ 6,134	$ 7,099	$ 6,092	−$1,007
Aggregate Income (billion dollars)	$ 42.8	$ 7.6	$ 5.6	−$ 2.0
National Total: Aggregate City Income Loss (billion dollars)				−$ 29.6

Implications of Loss

Residential Rental Support Capacity [1] (billion dollars)	−$ 7.4
Residential Valuation Support Capacity [2] (billion dollars)	−$ 37.0
Unsupportable Residential Units [3]	1,480,000

NOTES: 1. 25 percent of total aggregate central city income loss, assuming rent accounts for 25 percent of income.
2. Assuming residential rental property values have a gross rent multiplier of 5.0.
3. Assuming units valued at $25,000.

SOURCE: Income loss secured from Vincent P. Barabba, "The National Setting," in George Sternlieb and James W. Hughes, eds., *Post-Industrial America: Metropolitan Decline and Inter-Regional Job Shifts* (New Brunswick, N.J.: Rutgers University, Center for Urban Policy Research, 1976).

PROCESSES AND DILEMMAS

Many of the processes of change previously discussed also manifest themselves in the urban arena. Additionally, the following changes and effects are of major significance.

1. The central city population and migration losses are intimately tied to the interregional shifts of extant manufacturing activity documented earlier, as well as to the passing of the golden age of manufacturing. These major fountainheads of urban industrial society are rapidly losing their fundamental rationales. The bonds between urban centers and manufacturing activity have been shattered.

2. The lack of replacement functions is perhaps a consequence of the fundamental origins of America's cities. As Wilbur Thompson suggests:

   We did not, for the most part, build great cities in this country; manufacturing firms agglomerated in tight industrial complexes and formed labor pools of half a million workers. That is not the same thing as building great cities. . . . Our great industrial transformation has left us with a great number of overgrown "factory towns," a ramification we have not faced up to.[12]

3. Clearly, the cities' role as incubators of new functions may be an obsolete conceptualization. Perhaps the real problem is not the loss of old industry, but the failure to continuously innovate to more or less replace what they have lost.

4. It is apparent that service and white-collar functions have not been able to compensate sufficiently. Cities have been losing their manufacturing employment just as the rationalization and the automation of paper and information handling has finally come to fruition, limiting effective increases in labor force commensurate with increasing levels of activity.

5. While central city population losses are a major consequence, it is clear the less mobile and less skilled are remaining behind. With manufacturing waning, what is the replacement integrative mechanism? A widening gap is emerging between the capacities of central city residents and the remaining jobs in the urban core. The linkages between central city economic activity and urban residential populations have been repealed.

6. The partial vacuums opening up in central cities are derivatives not only of accelerated out-migrations and declining national fertility rates, but also of the demise in the flow of replacement populations. The ranks of potential rural recruits, whose availability was a function of the agricultural revolution, may have finally been depleted, while the pace of European arrivals has rapidly diminished since the change in the immigration laws in the early 1920s.

7. Moreover, deteriorating physical amenities and vastly reduced scopes of economic activity have made obsolete the image of the city as the place of opportunity—the once fabled promised land. Its once attractive magnetism has been relegated to the history text.

8. In addition to the potential redundancy of urban populations to the nation's economic systems, the major central city question derives from what we call the infrastructure dilemma. On the one hand, the physical plant of central cities was and is predicated on population levels far in excess of current realities. (The New York City subway system stands as a case in point, carrying but 50 percent of the patronage of a decade ago.) Such redundant capacity is not easily reduced in scope, or abrogated, without completely shaking the cities' ecology. At the same time, the economic wherewithal to support and maintain extant facilities is clearly diminishing.

9. On the other hand, one must distinguish between the myth and reality of central city infrastructures. We may decry what appears to be the expensive duplication in growth areas of the same facilities languishing in aging urban centers; however, we must also realize that, in many cases, the older capital plants—sewer and water systems, for example—may be but remnants of a once glorious past, so long neglected that their rehabilitation may be far more costly than starting over again elsewhere.

The Broader Considerations

The problems engendered by the new economic geography of America are escaping the instruments and policies which are being brought to bear. The broad, enduring parameters of growth are changing. Yet we are still responding largely with short-range localized approaches. The data shown here are intended to provide the beginnings of an arena within which the current and future dimensions of American policies must be rethought.

The sheer measure of regional and metropolitan shifts clearly renders obsolete much of our political wisdom and folkway. It is evident that the older political instrumentalities—city, state, and subregional jurisdictions—simply do not have either the scale or the wherewithal which is required. Is the federal government capable of dealing with the problems that have risen? Certainly the pattern of the last several decades has been mostly one of national growth policy de facto, i.e., unanticipated by-products resulting from the shape and direction of government subsidy programs, Department of Defense contracts and the like. Equally obvious has been the failure to provide the de jure equivalent; as witness stands the paucity of results generated by the congressional requirement for an annual report by the president on national growth policy embodied in the 1970 Housing Act—the product comprises but a passive compendium of data.

At the same time there has been a disturbing tendency to meet harsh immediate dilemmas with somewhat hazy future abstractions. Much of the response to the new spatial patterns of American society have invoked the ultimate shadow of energy costs and shortages. Whether it is the desired revitalization of the central city, or the slowing down of metropolitan and regional decentralization, the shade of fuel consciousness is raised. Without minimizing the ultimate realities implicit in such anticipations, over the short to intermediate future, i.e., the next five to ten years, we would question their significance. Even in a longer range context, the ultimate shape of geographic adjustments imposed by energy constraints may be quite different than the conventional wishful thinking would hold, and may not bring about the expected resurgence of older metropolitan-urban forms.

While political incoherence remains a constant, with an uncertain millennialism the major response, increasingly stern challenges to those struggling within the urban context have now emerged—not merely planning for no-growth, but rather for negative growth. In turn, this very real phenomenon requires skills and competences for which we simply have no experience—and even less provision in our training curricula.

Democracy, despite its limitations, has worked well as a system of government and allocation within a growth context. Can it meet the challenge of decline? Of reallocation of resources to shrinking entities? Or can we consciously and publicly face up to planned shrinkage?

These questions must be raised within a society that suddenly has its total national potential under global challenge. The necessity is present. The political will is as yet uncertain.

NOTES

1. Wilbur Thompson, "Economic Processes and Employment Problems in Declining Metropolitan Areas," in George Sternlieb and James W. Hughes, eds., *Post-Industrial America: Metropolitan Decline and Inter-Regional Job Shifts* (New Brunswick, N.J.: Rutgers University, Center for Urban Policy Research, 1976).

2. See: Robert Murray Haig and Roswell C. McCrea, *Major Economic Factors in Metropolitan Growth and Arrangement*, Regional Survey, vol. 1 (New York: Regional Plan of New York and Its Environs, 1927), and Edgar M. Hoover and Raymond Vernon, *Anatomy of a Metropolis* (Cambridge, Mass.: Harvard University Press, 1959).

3. Unpublished data, Rutgers University, Center for Urban Policy Research, Miami Beach Study.

4. Income data obtained from U.S. Department of Commerce, Bureau of Economic Analysis, *Survey of Current Business* (Washington, D.C.: U.S. Government Printing Office, Monthly).

5. The social and cultural predispositions generating America's population flows are described in: Brian J. L. Berry, "The Decline of the Aging Metropolis: Cultural Bases and Social Process," in Sternlieb and Hughes, *Post-Industrial America*, pp. 175-86.

6. Agglomeration refers to standard consolidated areas and standard metropolitan statistical areas.

7. For an elaboration of the analysis, see: U.S. Bureau of the Census, *Current Population Reports*, Series P-25, no. 640, "Estimates of the Population of States with Components of Change: 1970 to 1975" U.S. Government Printing Office, 1976).

8. The concept of resynthesizing metropolitan areas is that of Wilbur Thompson. See: "Epilogue" in Sternlieb and Hughes, *Post-Industrial America*, p. 265.

9. For an analysis of this phenomenon, see: George Sternlieb and Robert W. Lake, "Aging Suburbs and Black Homeownership," *Annals of the American Academy of Political and Social Sciences* 422 (November 1975) 105-17.

10. For household budgetary allocations, see: U.S. Department of Labor, Bureau of Labor Statistics, "Selected Average Weekly Expenditures Classified by Family Characteristics," *Consumer Expenditure Survey Series: Diary Survey 1973*, Report 448-2, 1976.

11. The $130 per square foot per year was secured from: The Urban Land Institute, *Dollars and Cents of Shopping Centers* (Washington, D.C.: The Institute, 1975).

12. Wilbur Thompson, in *Post-Industrial America*, p. 189.

A National Policy Towards Regional Change

W. W. ROSTOW

THIS IS THE FIRST TIME I have spoken in public on the regional problems of the country. As an economic historian I have given a good deal of thought to them and their roots in the longer past. But perhaps my greatest qualification is that I am a loyal son of the Northeast who has been privileged to live and work and travel in the Sunbelt over the past eight years. I understand tolerably well, I trust, not only the problems of New York City, New Haven, and Boston but also those of El Paso, Houston, New Orleans, Memphis, and Atlanta, not to say Austin. I think I can reconstruct with human sympathy, as well as resonable technical comprehension, the attitudes and anxieties of both the North and the South.

In this spirit I shall try to do three things: first, to explain the origins of the present problems and prospects of the major regions; second, to explore briefly the remedies now being suggested in different parts of the country; and finally, to outline the kind of national perspective and policy which would ease the regional problems and permit the country as a whole to go forward in affluence and amity while continuing to improve the quality of our lives.

Problem Origins

The two phenomena to be explained are why the South and Southwest have been narrowing the historic gap in real income per head between the North and the South, and why the future prospects of the South and Southwest appear to be more promising than the prospects of the older industrial regions of the North.

The first phenomenon flows from one of the best established but least well known characteristics of economic growth: the tendency of late comers to modern economic growth to catch up with those who began earlier.

Economic historians have long been aware that, in the early stages of a country's development, regional differences in growth rates and real income are likely to increase. This happens because modern industrial technologies are picked up and applied, sector by sector, in areas endowed either with appropriate resources, location, or with particularly creative entrepreneurs. In the United States, for example, New England led the way with a modern textile industry in the 1820s; Pennsylvania with a modern iron industry in the 1840s and 1950s; Chicago with farm machinery; and later, Detroit with automobiles. The northern regions of a number of countries industrialized before the south: in Britain, the United States, France, Germany, and Italy. Thus Stephen Potter's gamesman's ploy for breaking the flow of pretentious exposition at a cocktail party: 'Ah, but it's different in the south.' Brazil was an interesting exception: São Paulo and Rio in the south led the way, while the Brazilian north, initially committed like the American south to a single crop (sugar), lagged. But with the passage of time and the availability of a diversified pool of unapplied technologies, the lagging regions begin to exploit their opportunities and to catch up. As one analyst of this problem (Jeffery G. Williamson) concluded: "rising regional income disparities and increasing North-South dualism is typical of early development stages, while regional convergence and a disappearance of severe North-South problems is typical of the more mature stages of national growth and development." The regional evolution of the United States conforms to that general proposition.

What has been true within countries has also been true among countries. The familiar cliché that the poor get poorer and the rich get richer is simply not true. Both historical and contemporary evidence suggests the opposite. I have recently reviewed and analyzed that in an article whose subtitle is: "Reflections on Why the Poor Get Richer and Rich Slow Down." For example, the average growth rate in income per capita of Britain, from the beginning of its industrialization in 1783 to 1967, was 1.3 percent per annum; for the United States, for the period 1843 to 1972, 1.8 percent. On the other hand, Japan, which started in 1885, and Russia, starting in 1890, both averaged 2.5 percent. Mexico, starting in 1940, has done even better: 3.4 percent.

The same broad result emerges if one looks at growth rates, in cross section, for the 1960s. The poorest countries (under $100 per capita in 1967 dollars) averaged only 1.7 percent. The rate rises steadily to a peak at about $1,000 per capita, where growth rates were 6.5 percent. The growth rate then declines for the richer countries, with the U.S. averaging in that decade only 3.2 percent.

The two basic reasons for this pattern are, I believe, these: first, the late comers to industrialization have a large backlog of modern technologies to absorb, whereas the more advanced nations must depend on the flow of new technologies, while carrying a heavier weight of old or obsolescent industrial plant; second, as countries (or regions) get richer, they allocate more of their income to services which, in general, do not incorporate technologies of high productivity to the same extent as manufactures.

The relative rise of the Sunbelt flows from the fact that it was late in moving into sustained and diversified industrialization and the modernization of its agriculture; but once the process took hold, the South moved ahead faster than the older industrial areas because it had a larger backlog of technologies to bring to bear. Its more rapid increase in income and accelerated urbanization amplified the process.

In the long sweep of the South's history the turning point clearly came between 1930 and 1940, in the period of recovery from the Great Depression after 1929.

Between 1840 and 1860, on the eve of the Civil War, the real income of the South, relative to the rest of the country, declined, as the North as a whole experienced its first rapid phase of industrialization; but, still, the southern regions stood at about two-thirds the national average in 1860, roughly the same level as the East North Central agricultural states. The southern states lost ground seriously after the Civil War. This was a result not only of wartime destruction and the vicissitudes of Reconstruction but also because of a sharp decline in cotton prices and a slowing down in the expansion of the world's cotton consumption. There was some recovery from the mid-1890s to 1920, as the cotton price improved and some modest industrial development occurred in the South centered on the textile industry. In the 1920s the region again lost ground relatively, as agricultural prices sagged. In 1930 relative income per capita was only about half the national average. From the mid-1930s, however, four decades of sustained relative progress occurred. The states of the Southwest followed a similar path, although their relative income position in 1930 was a bit higher than in other parts of the South.

The rise of the Sunbelt in terms of relative income is, then, a phenomenon some forty years old. It was accompanied by a large flow of black migrants to the North. Between 1940 and 1970, for example, the white population of the South increased by 59 percent, the negro population by only 21 percent. In the Northeast and North Central regions the Negro population more than tripled in these years, and increased more than ten-fold in the West.

The process which brought about this striking movement of the South toward income equality with the rest of the country had these specific features:

1. A remarkable decline in agricultural employment accompanied by the technical modernization of agriculture, including a shift to the West and mechanization of cotton production.

2. A more than doubling of manufacturing employment, with a marked relative shift toward the production of durable as opposed to non-durable goods (e.g., textiles).

3. A large shift of labor to construction as the region's population moved into the cities and suburbs (37 percent of the population in the South was urban in 1940, 65 percent in 1970).

4. A rapid expansion of public and private services, including education. In Texas, for example, the proportion of the population in 1940 in institutions of higher education was 0.6 percent as opposed to the national average of 1.2 percent; in 1970 the proportions were 3.1 percent and 3.4 percent. Much more than the gap in income was narrowed North and South in those thirty years.

In broad terms, then, the structural differences between the South and the rest of the nation were rapidly reduced over the period 1940-1970. It could no longer be said in the old way and to the same extent: "It's different in the South."

As of 1970, the uneven movement of the South toward rough homogeneity in income and structure with the rest of the country was a phenomenon little studied in the North; and, when noted, it was a source of gratification rather than anxiety. In particular, the success of the South in adjusting to the Civil Rights Acts of 1964 and 1965—ending Jim Crow and permitting a rapid increase in voting among southern blacks—was widely, if not universally, regarded as a victory for the nation as a whole in dealing with its oldest and most difficult problem.

Meanwhile, what was happening in the North?

In the 1950s and 1960s the North also moved ahead. It enjoyed higher levels of income per capita than the South, but growth was slower. There was, it is true, some concern about specific problems. In the 1950s, New England was troubled about the decline of the classic industries it had pioneered; for example, textiles and shoes. But the rise of electronics and other new sectors incorporating rapidly elaborating technologies, compensated rather well—a process symbolized by the plants that line Route 128 around Boston. In the Midwest, automobiles and steel faced increasing foreign competition from the second half of the 1950s; and there was a tendency for some industrial plants to grow obsolescent. But the high national growth rates of the 1960s, the rapid expansion of such service industries as education, health, and travel concealed these underlying potential problems. On the other hand, from the explosion in Watts in 1965 and the subsequent difficulties of the inner cities, the nation became conscious that the south to north migration and the universal flight to suburbia had gradually created deep and intractable problems in the North.

Nevertheless, the affluent northern regions, taken as a whole, moved ahead in reasonable comfort, expanding social services at a rate which could only be sustained if regular growth yielded regularly expanding tax revenues.

Then came the fifth Kondratieff upswing.

Over the past several years I have been mildly bewildering various audiences with titles for my talks which suggested that we are in the early phase of a fifth Kondratieff upswing. Who is Kondratieff and what it a Kondratieff cycle?

N. D. Kondratieff was a Russian economist. Writing in the 1920s, he suggested that capitalist economies were subject to long cycles, some forty to fifty years in length. His views were published in the United States in summary in the mid-1930s. They generated considerable professional discussion and debate, but dropped from view in the great boom after World War II. Most contemporary economists vaguely remember having run across his name and ideas in graduate school but have forgotten precisely what it was he said.

Looking back from the mid-1920s, Kondratieff saw 2½ cycles in various statistical series covering prices, wages, interest rates, and other data expressed in monetary terms. He sought but failed to find concurrent long cycles in production indexes. Kondratieff did not develop a theory of long cycles, but he asserted that a coherent explanation must exist. Since he wrote, the cycles he described have continued down to the present.

My own explanation for the phenomena Kondratieff identified centers on shifts in the prices of food and raw materials relative to the prices of manufactures.[1]

The period since the end of 1972 is the fifth time in the past 200 years a rise in the relative prices of basic comodities has occurred; and on each of the other four occasions it has been accompanied by manifestations similar to those we have experienced over the past four years: an accelerated general inflation, an extremely high range of interest rates, pressure on the real wages of industrial labor, pressure on those with relatively fixed incomes, and shifts of income favorable to producers of food as well as energy. The other four occasions occurred in the 1790s, the early 1850s, the second half of the 1890s, and the late 1930s. On each occasion, food and raw material prices then fluctuated in a relatively high range for about a quarter century. Approximately another quarter century followed in which the trends reversed; that is, the prices of basic commodities were relatively cheap, as they were from 1951 to 1972. Each of these periods was, in an important sense, unique, and the trends did not unfold smoothly; but the fact is that the world economy for almost two centuries has been subject to a rough and irregular pattern of long cycles in which periods of about twenty to twenty-five years of high relative prices for food and raw materials gave way to approximately equal phases of relatively cheap food and raw materials.

I am not wedded to the notion that these cycles will continue in the future. But I would guess that the inexorable pressure of excessive population increase in the developing world, the tendency of the poor to spend increases in income disproportionately on food, the rising demand for grain-expensive proteins among the rich, the raw material requirements of a world economy where industrialization is spreading in the southern continents, and the high marginal cost of expanding the non-OPEC energy supply—that these will persist for some time. Given these powerful and sustained forces operating on food, energy, and raw material prices and the costs we shall have to incur to achieve and maintain clean air and water, I believe we are in for a long period when the prices of these basic inputs to the economy will remain relatively high.   Indeed, I would guess that we shall only have a fifth Kondratieff downswing if and when we create a new, cheap (hopefully infinite and nonpolluting) energy source.   As we all know, energy is a critical factor not only in its own right but also because of its role in agriculture and in the extraction of raw materials and, potentially, in rendering economical the conversion of salt water into fresh water.

Down to 1914 the classic response to a Kondratieff upswing was to open new agricultural and raw material producing areas: the American West, Canada, Australia, Argentina, and the Ukraine.   The great movements of international capital during this era were, in substantial part, induced by the price system, combined with new technologies of transport and production, to bring new supplies into the market and to restore balance in the world economy.   In the fourth Kondratieff upswing (say, 1936-1951), the diffusion of new agricultural technologies, rather than the opening of new physical frontiers, reestablished a tolerable balance in food production without much conscious government intervention; although the exploitation of Middle East oil after 1945 ranks, in the field of energy, with the opening up of the American West in agriculture a century earlier.   But in the 1970s and beyond we confront the fifth Kondratieff upswing period in a setting quite different from that of the past.   I wish we could, but we cannot realistically rely to the same extent on the automatic workings of the price system and private capital markets to restore and maintain balance. All over the world, in one way or another, policy toward resources is in the hands of governments or is strongly influenced by governments. At every stage in the effort to restore balance, therefore, public policy will be involved.   We shall have to think and consciously act our way through the fifth Kondratieff upswing.

Now, back to the American regions.   It was the coming of the fifth Kondratieff upswing in 1972-'73 which suddenly converted a relatively benign pattern of regional development into something of a national problem.   This was the case because the relative rise in food and energy prices accelerated the development of a good many Sunbelt states which exported energy and agricultural resources to the rest of the country; while the relative price shift decelerated the already slower rate of expansion in the Northeast and North Central industrial states.   The population shift to the Sunbelt picked up momentum, although about two-thirds of the recent population increase in that region is due to somewhat higher birth rates than in the North. But the fact is that more than half the nation's population increase between 1970 and 1975 was in the South. And the flow of blacks from south to north reversed.

In the sharp recession of 1974-75, unemployment averaged in the latter year over 9 percent in New England, the Middle Atlantic, and East North Central states; 7.9 percent in the South Atlantic states, with Florida, dependent on tourism, as high as 10.7 percent; 6.9 percent in the South Central states. Texas experienced in 1975 only 5.6 percent unemployment. The relatively higher levels of unemployment cut northern tax revenues and increased requirements for compensating social services at precisely the time the tax base was also being weakened by the initial impact on the North of the fifth Kondratieff upswing on real income and the accelerated flow of people to the South.

Thus, the shift in relative prices since the end of 1972 did not create the problems of the Northeast and North Central states; but it converted a slow-moving but livable erosion of their relative position into something of a northern crisis.

The role of the relative price shift in bringing about these changes is underlined by looking beyond the Sunbelt. Between 1970 and 1975 both the agricultural states of the West North Central area and the coal-rich Mountain states also enjoyed a rise in relative prices, a favorable relative shift in income, and lower than average unemployment. The Mountain states, in fact, experienced the highest rate of population increase (16.3 percent) of any of the nation's regions over those five years.

The coming of the fifth Kondratieff upswing, then, hit hard the two northern regions. They had committed themselves to enlarged public and private services at a time when their manufacturing base, with high obsolescence in certain sectors, was decelerating or declining and the rate of population increase was slowing down. The unfavorable shift in the regions' terms of trade, as in Britain, reduced real income at just the time the North confronted unemployment rates about 2 percent higher than those in the South and Southwest. The fiscal problems posed for state and local governments were only in degree less acute than for New York City. Meanwhile, the relative rise in energy and agricultural prices accelerated the flow of population to areas producing these products, widened growth rate differentials, and still further weakened the foundations of the economies in the Northeast and North Central states.

The Suggested Remedies

Now, what about remedies?

As this situation became apparent, the initial reaction of politicians in the North was to seek redress by inducing the federal government to reallocate federal expenditures from South to North. That theme dominated the literature of early 1976 on the subject of regional change. In crude terms the argument was: the rise of the Sunbelt was a product of disproportionate outlays of the federal government financed by northern taxes; now is the time for the South to contribute disproportionately to the rehabilitation of the North. As experts dug into the data on federal tax and expenditure flows, the evidence suggested a less straightforward picture of the past and less simple remedies for the future.

For example, when federal tax contributions are calculated as a proportion of income per capita in the states (rather than on a per capita basis) the relative contribution of the still higher income northern states to federal revenues is much reduced. And there is a good case for measuring taxes against income per capita. On the other hand, when present (inadequate) cost-of-living indexes are applied to the regions, the North-South real income per capita differential is further narrowed. But when the flow of federal grants is systematically correlated with various indicators of economic development in the states, no significant association emerges. When federal expenditures are broken out by categories and measured in terms of outlays per capita in the various states, the Northeast appears to have been drawing more from Washington than the South in defense contracts, welfare programs, and, marginally, retirement programs. The more rapidly urbanizing South acquired somewhat more for highways and sewers, a great deal more in defense salaries due to the location of military bases. The midwestern states, both industrial and agricultural, fared worse than the South in all categories except highways and sewers; but the West (a high income area) far outstripped all other regions in defense contracts and salaries, highways, and sewers, the latter category mainly because of the still expanding interstate highway program in the Mountain states.

The analysis and debate about federal tax flows and expenditures can be expected to become more complex but to remain a lively part of the national political scene. My own view is, quite simply, that the major regional changes in the country have been determined by deep and understandable historical forces. They have been only marginally shaped by the balance of federal tax and expenditure flows. I believe the future of federal policy and outlays in the regions should be determined by the requirements of the several regions, seen in terms of their structural problems and the larger interests of the nation as a whole. It is a wholesome fact that, as analysis of the nation's regional problems has gone forward in 1976-'77, this is the direction of thought and prescription.

When, for example, the Northeast Governors Conference met in Saratoga in November 1976, they did, indeed, point to the apparent imbalance between tax revenues and federal expenditures in which the South and West appear to profit at the expense of the North. But they went beyond to propose measures which would enlarge investment in energy production and conservation, to rehabilitate the region's transport system, and to expand and modernize industrial capacity in areas of particularly severe unemployment. They proposed manpower training and public works programs, exhibiting considerable sensitivity to assure the latter were undertaken in sectors where investment would prove productive over the long run; e.g., transport rehabilitation, solid waste disposal plants, etc. The conference also considered the complex problem of welfare reform on a national basis, but with an understandable emphasis on the extent to which slow growth, the long prior period of south to north migration, and higher than average unemployment since 1973 have converged to make the welfare problems of the Northeast particularly acute.

The institutions and policies, regional and national, do not yet exist to translate these directions of thought into lines of action; but the fundamental issues and remedies being explored are significant and hopeful.

Over the past year similar analyses have been emerging in the North Central states; for example, the studies of the Academy for Contemporary Problems in Columbus, Ohio. The academy has surveyed extensively the structural changes and problems of the whole East North Central region and prescribed in detail for Ohio. Its policy agenda includes special measures to expand local coal production and to reduce energy consumption, a modernization of the transport system, special incentives to stimulate high growth manufacturing and export industries as well as to rehabilitate aging or obsolete plants. As in the Northeast, there is a call for redirected federal tax revenues, a national welfare plan, and intensified regional cooperation between the public and private sectors to stimulate investment in the directions necessary for further development.

The South and Southwest confront what may appear in the North an easier future; but analysis and policy are also increasingly addressed to their serious structural problems. The excellent report of the Task Force on Southern Rural Development, for example, measures the scale and character of poverty in the South relative to the rest of the country. In 1974 there were still 10.8 million poor Southerners, 13.5 million outside the South. Fifty-four percent of the southern poor are rural; only 38 percent are rural outside the South. Evidently, a massive problem of poverty still exists in the rural South roughly matching in scale the more visible urban poverty of the North, but constituting a higher proportion of the total southern population. The recommendations of the task force, notably with respect to retraining and bringing the poor effectively into the working force, are similar to the manpower proposals of the Saratoga program of the Northeast Governors Conference.

As the South and Southwest look to the future, analysts are beginning to perceive a set of investment and policy tasks quite as challenging, in their way, as those in the North and Northeast. For example, the whole irrigated area of the high plains, from northwest Texas to Nebraska, is endangered by the decline of the underground water basin which supplies it. The region produces a significant part of the American agricultural surplus. Large investments in surface water conservation and transfer will be required to preserve it.

On March 31-April 2, 1977, a conference of the Southwest American Assembly was held in Texas on "Capital Needs of the Southwest: The Next Decade." Its agenda would be familiar to analysts in the North, including among the major investment fields: energy and raw materials; plant and equipment for manufacturing; pollution and environmental controls; housing, public facilities, and education.

The challenge to the Sunbelt is, of course, to complete its transition to industrial modernization; to develop its resources in energy and agriculture in both its own interest and that of the nation; to deal with its social problems, under conditions of rapid population increase; and to do all these things while avoiding, to the degree possible, the environmental degradation which marked the urbanization of the North. The problem of the North is to regather momentum by bringing to bear its enormous potentials in technology, finance, and entrepreneurship; to exploit its energy resources in the new price environment; to rehabilitate its transport system in cost-effective ways; and to modernize the industrial sectors which hold greatest promise for the future. This will require a new regional sense of purpose as well as intimate public-private collaboration.

But the central point I would make is this: once the debate shifts from the allocation of federal revenues to the deeper structural problems of the several regions, the possibilities for national policies which would mitigate the tensions between the regions enlarge. I believe an appropriate reallocation of federal revenues would flow naturally from an approach to regional problems in these basic terms.

A National Perspective

This brief survey of regional change and the directions of regional thought about future development is, of course, too simple. It cannot be overemphasized that there are great differences among states and, even, within them. There are special problems and prospects in the Mountain states and Far West, Alaska and Hawaii. But six large, general conclusions stand out.

First, a return to sustained full employment and high growth rates on a national basis would greatly ease the special problems of the northern states by simultaneously reducing welfare requirements and expanding tax revenues. Further, a view of the national situation in terms of the regions strongly reinforces the central argument I have been making up and down the land; namely, that sustained full employment is to be achieved not by unbalancing the federal budget a little more, not by easing monetary policy a bit, but by expanded investment in energy and other resource development and conservation fields combined with outlays to reaccelerate the growth of productivity. Without full employment and rapid growth, it will be exceedingly difficult to sustain our welfare services and deal with our poverty problems, North and South.

Second, economic as well as social and human considerations require serious and sustained efforts to bring into the working force the large number of Americans now trapped in urban and rural poverty in both regions. The nation should look with equal concern at the problem of the central cities and the impoverished margins of life in the southern countryside. We do not yet command the data to measure the scale of the nation's special investment requirements over, say, the next ten years in agriculture, energy, raw materials, the environment, the rehabilitation of obsolescent industrial and transport facilities, research and development, manpower retraining. It seems palpable, however, that they will require us to use our manpower resources to the hilt. Through imaginative policies, stubbornly pursued, we must try to convert into a national asset the human beings now caught up in marginal lives of poverty.

Third, the case for a national energy policy which would both enlarge our resources in all the regions and economize their use is greatly heightened as one observes the differential regional impact of the energy crisis which has had us by the throat since the autumn of 1973. Here, with energy policy, we face the most potentially divisive issue in the nation. I cannot convey to you with sufficient force the depth of the feeling in the southern energy exporting states about some of the attitudes of the North. At one and the same time, the North appears to be demanding both low energy prices and refusing to develop its own energy resources on environmental grounds. This is seen in the South as a straightforward colonial policy of exploitation underlined by the fact that natural gas is much more expensive in producing states than for interstate commerce. That is why the governor of Texas flirts with the idea of a refinery tax and the governor of Louisiana with a cutback in energy production. Some of the western states already have a severance tax on coal production. It would not be difficult to split the nation, yielding an OPEC within it. The only answer is to have the nation as a whole face up to the fact that energy is and will be expensive, that conservation and economy are required of us all, and that the energy potentials of the country as a whole—not merely the South and the West—must be promptly and fully exploited under environmental rules of the game that are firmly settled.

Fourth, we require a national welfare policy which would render more uniform the criteria for public assistance; but this may be somewhat more expensive, and will certainly have to be introduced over, say, a three-to-five-year period. And, once again, such a system will be viable and sustainable only in an environment of full employment and rapid growth.

Fifth, within the states and regions new forms of public-private collaboration will be necessary as well as at the national level. Obviously, there is no way the kinds of problems I have reviewed here can be dealt with by antiseptic devices of fiscal and monetary policy. If we are to mitigate or solve our problems we must deal with particular sectors, regions, cities, and rural areas. We do not have and we do not want a fully planned and directed economy. On the other hand, a public role is inescapable. We have no other course than to learn how to make the public and private sectors work together.

Finally, it seems clear to me, at least, that these problems cannot be dealt with if the states and regions look merely to Washington for salvation. The basic analyses, investment plans, public-private consortia must be developed within the states and regions. Local capital and entrepreneurship must be mobilized; and for this to happen state and local governments may have to alter their taxation systems. I agree with James Howell, senior vice-president of the First National Bank of Boston, who said: ". . . I strongly believe that our region will be better served if we begin the task through self-help programming, leaving to the Federal Government its proper share." The revitalization of the North is a development task; and the firmest lesson of development economics is that it must be rooted in self-help. In the end, however, there is scope for federal assistance in the form of tax incentives, investment capital, manpower retraining programs, and the direction of public service job programs toward areas judged of high priority within states and regions.

Although the creation of state and regional development corporations may have a role, it is likely that a national development bank will be required like the old Reconstruction Finance Corporation. Its authority should extend not only to the fields of energy and energy conservation (where such an institution was proposed to the Congress by the Ford administration) but also to the financing of water development, transport rehabilitation, and other projects judged of high priority national interest. Wherever possible, such a bank should use its authority to guarantee or to marginally subsidize funds raised privately or by state or local governments, rather than engage in full, direct financing.

In addition, it would be wise, in the phase ahead, for both state and federal governments to organize their budgets in ways which would separate out authentic investment outlays from conventional expenditures and transfer payments.

There is a warning to be made about any proposal for an increased government role in the investment process: high standards of priority and productivity must be preserved. The experience of Great Britain and other countries with nationalized industries (which I would oppose) and with government loans to private industry suggests that there is an inherent danger of confusing criteria of productivity and simple job maintenance or creation. The latter can lead to increasing public subsidy and the drawing off of scarce investment resources to low productivity tasks. Public authorities tend to persist with lines of investment, even if of low productivity, because they do not face the competition of the market place and because political vested interests build up around such public ventures. But if I am right, the United States and the other industrialized nations have ample opportunities to generate full employment through high-priority and essential investment tasks. None can afford to compound existing tendencies toward declining rates of productivity increases in the advanced industrial world by committing public funds to essentially wasteful enterprises.

The Future

Now a final question. Do the Northeast and industrial Middle West have a future? As we have seen, their present positions are the result of deeply rooted structural differences which decree a greater relative load of obsolescent industries, a heritage of large past commitments to expensive social services, a large concentration of poor in the central cities reflecting a prior South to North population flow over a protracted period. There are those who have concluded that the North, after a century and a half of leadership, should gracefully decline and surrender economic leadership to the South and Southwest.

I do not share that mood of passive pessimism about the North. For one thing, as the case of Great Britain illustrates, economic decline is not a graceful process. It is painful, socially contentious, and potentially quite ugly in the political moods and problems it generates. Nations or regions which choose to go down in the style to which they have become accustomed find it a difficult or even tragic path to follow. Moreover, I believe it is unnecessary. Surely, the pattern of economic development in the North will have to change. Surely, the North cannot go on doing what it has been doing if it is to cope with the special pressures of the fifth Kondratieff upswing. Surely, the antiseptic, easy devices of fiscal and monetary policy will not cure the ills of the North. But the lesson of economic development in many parts of the world is that it hinges mainly on the human resources available, mobilized around the right tasks. The North commands both the material and human resources for a great revival.

The problems of the North will not be resolved, then, by incantation or by somewhat enlarged flows of federal funds. But there are a good many examples of nations which successfully recaptured momentum after falling behind under the weight of mature industries, with substantial obsolescent plant. Post-1945 France and Belgium accomplished such a transformation as, indeed, did post–World War II New England. The initial assessments of postwar Germany—the economy split in a historically unnatural way, burdened with refugees and great war damage—were exceedingly gloomy. Structural transformations are clearly possible if there is a common will to accomplish them, a sense of direction, and a general environment of rapid economic growth. Only those who live in the North can generate the common will and sense of direction. What the North—and all of us—have the right to demand of Washington are policies which would get the nation as a whole back to full employment and rapid growth. Part of that process will prove to be the regathering of momentum in the North.

NOTE

1. I analyze long cycles in "Kondratieff, Schumpeter, and Kuznets: Trend Periods Revisited," *Journal of Economic History* 35, no. 4 (December 1975): 719-53. A full account of these cycles is included in part 3 of my forthcoming book, *The World Economy: History and Prospect* (Austin: University of Texas Press).

Aging Industries and Cities:
Time and Tides in the Northeast

WILBUR R. THOMPSON

Introduction: Lagging Perception of Reality

ONE OF THE VERY FIRST STEPS to be taken in formulating a strong program of economic redevelopment for the Northeast is for its populace to face up to the basic and persisting nature of industrial relocation and population migration. But one of the problems in facing up to reality is that often we do not even see it. George Sternlieb and James Hughes have made the important point that the shift of economic activity and population from the "frostbelt" to the Sunbelt has been going on for decades, but more dramatic post-war shift of population and industry from central cities to suburbs created so many immediate and pressing economic and social problems that our attention was diverted away from the more subtle interregional movements.

Other "noise" in the system distracted us. First, for a full decade from 1930 to 1940 we were mired in deep depression and then for another five years, from 1940 to 1945, we were fully engaged in all-out

war. The production of consumer durable goods was largely deferred
for fifteen years, products heavily represented in the local industry
mixes of northeastern and midwestern cities. In 1945, flush with victory
and unprecedented amounts of liquid assets (following from the deficit
financing of the war), this fifteen-year backlog demand for consumer
durables was released. The Northeast and Midwest misread this "temporary" post-war surge in the demand for their products as basic and
enduring economic vitality. As we grew at faster than the national
average rate, we lived high, but on borowed time.

Seen from a slightly different perspective, the mass migration from
the rural areas to northeastern and midwestern cities disguised the aging
of these cities and their economies by giving them a temporary trans-
fusion of in-migrants. In due course this parade would end as the farms
emptied out. And the counterpart to this *apparent* strength of northern
cities was the *apparent* weakness of southern rural areas. The end of
southern decline was also in sight, but only to those who could see.
I can remember reading a paper in 1970 or so describing rural industrialization in Arkansas, which I thought of as a novel aberration, and
paid scant attention to this eddy in the mainstream of national growth
and urbanization. Because the number newly employed in manufacturing in these out-of-the-way places was usually only equal, at most,
to the number leaving the farms, there was no dramatic net gain in
employment and population there to capture our attention. But the
hard fact was that those farms *were* emptying out and the thin entering
edge of manufacturing was wedge-shaped. How often of late have I
second guessed my own insensitivity to those early warning signs.

Once again, the rapid rate of natural increase of the post-war period
misled us about the nature of long-run regional trends by favoring colder
places—the existing distribution of population. To the best of my
knowledge, babies are born where their mothers are located—the fathers
may be anyplace. Thus it takes a positive decision for population to
redistribute itself elsewhere. Simple human inertia acts to confirm the
vitality of established places. All in all, there were a host of good
reasons why we were surprised by the sharp reversals in population
trends around 1970.

Disequilibrating Processes and Long Swings

Given then the way in which we missed seeing in the 1960s the early
signs of the 1970s, what can we do now to anticipate what the 1980s
have in store for the Northeast so that we can work with, rather than
blindly oppose, current trends? Too often we try to turn completely

around powerful market forces with relatively weak public policies when the best we could hope to do (within our existing political institutions) is to bend those trends a little and adjust more gracefully to their main thrusts. The authors of the background paper have begun for us the important work of gathering empirical information. I propose to add to this only a few brief remarks about the nature of the interactions between industrial relocation and the urban growth process, in the context of the aging cities of the Northeast.

The challenge, as I see it, is to convince the many parties at interest throughout the region that the events of the past half dozen years are not a transitory aberration but are rather a very deep and persisting trend—or, better, a long swing in relative fortunes. It will be very difficult to formulate good public policy if the Northeast thinks in terms of months or years instead of decades.

I find it instructive to classify the main forces in urban growth into those that tend to be disequilibrating—either cumulative expansionary or cumulative contractionary in nature—and those that tend to be equilibrating—ones that dampen shocks. The concept of a disequilibrating change is as homely as the old adage that "the rich get richer," and equilibrating movements are as familiar as a bouncing ball. At least in its early stages, urban growth tends to be a disequilibrating force; because as growth enlarges city size, the costs of doing business fall, and households, too, find prices lower and selection greater. Bigger *is* better, for a while, and feeds back to generate more growth.

All growth—fast or slow—brings larger size and economies of scale; but a rapid rate of growth brings a construction boom that adds so many new buildings that there is an overall reduction in the average age of capital in that place. In short, faster is newer, and to many (most?) people, newer is prettier. Thus "attractive" cities attract people, and more growth is generated. To this we can add the rapid expansion of the local construction industry as another source of local growth. Thus southern and western towns are not only becoming cities and developing economies of scale in competition with the cities of the East and Midwest, but these places are also "growing" newer because they are growing so rapidly. In sharp contrast, the (historically) older cities of the Northeast are, because of slow growth, becoming (physically) older and too often shabbier.

No place can find the key to *perpetual* youth in rapid growth. A place can continue to have half of its capital stock less than ten years old by continuing to double every ten years (and even then the average age is increasing). But how long can that go on? In time, local growth slows because there are fewer and fewer other places from which to draw it and in part because the great size into which it has cumulated becomes more difficult to arrange in space and manage well. Thus we see in the Northeast the mature stages of the urban growth process where great city size has challenged (and defeated?) our managerial skills and/or overwhelmed our political institutions. We see in the Sunbelt mostly cities entering the stage when bigger is better and faster is newer—a passing stage to be sure, but reckoned in decades not years. The Northeast and Midwest must in part play a waiting game— waiting for the Sunbelt to catch up in size and years. Meanwhile, there is work to be done.

Rearranging Reward Structures: Relocation Allowances

One of the more compelling arguments for educating the broad public of the Northeast that the best estimate of the foreseeable future is that the days of rapid growth, or even any appreciable growth, are over, if that is indeed one's best estimate, is that public policies assisting out-migration become more politically palatable. Local politicians, chambers of commerce, local unions, and most other organized interests have a near-conditioned response to policies such as relocation allowances. They do not intend to preside over the dissolution of their local empires. Clearly, budgets, patronage, profits, and power of all kinds are at stake. Still, if depopulation will come sooner or later, a little contraction sooner that maintains productivity and income levels may eliminate the need for more contraction later. The need for a broad public understanding here is made especially important because various community leaders, such as local politicians, have very short time horizons, and a little bitter medicine now may not be preferable to more later. Their successors can worry about that.

The strongest kind of case can be made for relocation allowances across much of the Northeast and Midwest, especially when they are contrasted with the prevailing inter-regional differentials in public assistance, unemployment compensation, and other transfer payments. Various financial aids to migration could change the reward structure to induce redundant labor to leave the Northeast while the present pattern of much higher transfer payments in this region acts as a strong incentive to stay on with the least excuse. Well worth noting here is the fact that our new Secretary of Labor, Ray Marshall, comes to this critical post from a background rich in the intricacies of structural unemployment and with considerable exposure to Appalachian development problems, where relocation allowances have been a continuing center of attention. If you believe, as I do, that the older manufacturing economies of the Northeast and Midwest are heavily overstocked with lower-middle to middle-skill blue-collar labor, and that much of this work is moving south and west, then you too may see a critical role for relocation allowances to speed and ease the industrial-employment adjustments needed throughout much of this broad area.

An urban area that does come to accept the probability that the local economy cannot support, for the foreseeable future, a population and labor force quite as large as the one it inherited from the past may come to support relocation allowances and other aids to migration for still another reason. Besides reducing the current labor force, net out-migration acts to reduce the local rate of natural increase, because migrants come, much more than porportionately, from the younger and more fertile members of the labor force. In general, local economies throughout the Northeast and Midwest that anticipate a "steady state" condition, perhaps at most, should not try too hard to hold young adults indiscriminately, but rather should help, if not encourage, the migration of those with only a high school education and headed toward semi-skilled work.

Creating New Industries: The Direct Approach

I would like nothing better than to be able to say what you would like to hear from me: the name of a new industry or two that is now about to enter its rapid growth stage, demands high skills (or pays high wages for not-so-high skills) and can therefore afford your high cost structure, industries that have not come to anyone else's attention, and are just waiting to be asked. Or I could exhort you, in keeping with your consultants' advice, to seek high professional services—join the throng.

Still, the Northeast does have the advantage of a headstart and still enjoys a lead in science and technology. But some leads are hard to maintain; catch-up can be relatively easy in something as mobile as ideas. Progress in science and technology may be subject more to equilibrating than to disequilibrating processes. But slowing national growth may bring some important exceptions. The Northeast has in general the nation's strongest private universities and the Midwest hosts the strongest state universities, and these leads may persist longer than usual. As one travels around the country to the new and rising metro-politan areas, one senses the urgency they feel to move onward and upward in science and technology—to close the gap—and the frustration when they are unable to "build" a major new graduate school to support the local development of high-science manufacturing. The advantage that the older, established industrial areas enjoy is that we have, as a nation, probably over-built capacity in higher education and must go slow in adding more. The slowing growth of the nation can act to shore up the foundations of the older areas.

Strong universities and emphasis on science and technology would seem to be especially important to the manufacturing economies of the Northeast and Midwest because, with their high cost structures, these places can not hope to fall heir easily to firms leaving (fleeing?) other areas. The cities of the Carolina Piedmont have grown and can continue for some time to grow by acquiring larger shares of existing (older) industries, but the Northeast and Midwest will need much more to create new—brand new—industries that can pay their high wages and rents. New industries tend to require high skills and are less subject to intense competition, for a while.

The Northeast has an even greater need than the Midwest to be inventive and innovative, following from the fact that this region has been growing slowly for a long time. When fast-growing places slow in growth, they can then turn to the business of making up their lag in local services—they can turn to "import substitution" growth. In the process of filling in the gaps in retail trade and personal services, they can cushion the impact of their sagging export sector. But the manufacturing cities and towns of the Northeast probably do not have much of this work still to do—do not have the many unmet local trade and service needs that arise out of rapid growth. The Midwest has a brief grace period following from its greater post-war boom.

But a purely industrial approach to the redevelopment of the economic base of an aging metropolis, even one emphasizing science and technology, is not nearly enough. Those who plan the redevelopment strategy need to think also in occupational terms. A more comprehensive approach would cross-classify alternative industry mixes against the corresponding occupational mixes to balance the local labor market. To illustrate, manufacturing economies tend to provide a much better range and quality of occupations for males than for females, especially so for those with higher levels of education. I join Prof. Harrison in his skepticism about the value of local subsidies for industry and could come to support these inducements to location only in very special and carefully selected cases. The selective subsidization of industry could be socially beneficial when used to plug a hole in the local occupational mix or to set in motion a long-run chain reaction of industrial development.

Specifically, the acute shortage of good jobs for highly educated women that tends to characterize manufacturing economies might be *efficiently* corrected by subsidizing an activity that generates an unusually large number of professional, technical, or managerial jobs that are already open to females. Such an action would have virtue not only for its own sake, but would also recognize that the chances of recruiting and/or holding a highly educated male depends in important measure on whether his highly educated wife can also find appropriate work. Industrial development aids that seek to balance the local labor market, especially with an eye to long-run economic development as well as current choice, seem to stand well apart from the fool's game of standing ready to subsidize any payroll that will come to town.

Building Better Cities: The Indirect Approach

In lieu of identifying new industries that the Northeast can harness to reverse its current fortunes, I offer instead a little different and somewhat broader framework within which to see and weigh one's developmental options. In addition to seeking new industries, the region could seek to attract and hold talented persons, those who in the long-run create new industries. To the extent that talented persons choose where they would like most to live and, directly or indirectly, force industry and businesses to come to them, the principal line of causation runs from the natural and man-made environment to the economic base of the community, rather than the reverse. Places that lack superior natural environments must then try harder to create superior man-made— physical and social—environments. Thus city-building becomes an integral and critical component of economic development. Those places in the Northeast that lead the way in public safety and justice, responsible and responsive government, and aesthetics and urban amenities will certainly vastly improve their competitive position in the contest for new business and new bases. And new jobs and new tax bases will act in turn to finance that better environment.

This audience does not need to be reminded that building better cities will not be easy. Large, dense populations, more than smaller places, must learn to trade off immediate private satisfactions and comforts for future social benefits—a most "unnatural" behavior. Fortunately for you (if not the nation), your Sunbelt competitors are not building *new* cities; they are building old cities on new sites. The urbanization of the Southwest is little more than a replay of the post-war suburban boom that swept through the Northeast and Midwest, its solemn pledges to avoid the sins of the East, notwithstanding. The old grid patterns of land use are formed from even larger lot sizes, ensuring even longer journeys to work. Again, after almost three decades of unmistakably bad experience with oversize slums, these "new" cities are blithely building equally large concentrations of poor, alienated, and desperate people.

Sunbelt cities are not going to impose a heavy discipline on themselves for their future good as long as raw growth makes the livin' easy. In a hard fight between easy living and the "good life," pick the former. But the Northeast does not have that choice; the nation is not offering you raw growth; you must choose mature development. If you accept the crisis theory of behavior, what you do have going for you in this time of hard choices is desperation.

The cities of the Northeast do have some considerable advantages in the difficult business of building better man-made environments. For example, in the most important work of disciplining the automobile, your pre-auto cities with the narrow twisting streets create intolerable traffic congestion at a much earlier stage than do the straight, wide streets of the post-auto cities. Clearly, the harder it is to use automobiles, the easier it is to persuade citizens to use public transit. But even public transit is not efficient when there are only a half dozen riders on the bus. And so planning and implementing land use patterns that bring travel origins and destinations closer together is likely to be even more fundamental to the building of energy-efficient cities.

Bringing home and work closer together implies more in-town living among the affluent professionals, if one believes, as I do, that central business districts are here to stay, languish a while yet though they may. Again, the Northeast has an advantage over the Midwest because of its many "historic districts." The early impressions of inner city watchers are that historic districts are well ahead of other places as magnets for residential redevelopment of the inner city. Walking around downtown Philadelphia, a Detroiter can not help but feel the power of the national historic district surrounding Independence Hall as a base from which to rebuild the center of that metropolitan area. In the battle of imagery, ongoing work of the city and the National Park Service is overtaking the legacy of W.C. Fields.

Building better cities will surely require forming better local governments. On first impression, the Northeast would seem to be at a serious disadvantage in local governance because this region struggles with the worst political fragmentation. The South and West enjoy in general much easier annexation and have achieved most of the more notable city-county consolidations. But your relative position in local government is not as bad as it seems because easy annexation does not seem to do the trick. To annex suburbs as they attain small city size is at best to play fiscal catch-up, but without ever getting the basic public land planning in place ahead of the private investment. The community is always faced a fait accompli in land use patterns, and invariably one that is very inefficient for the delivery of public services, and usually destructive of the social environment (e.g., segregated residential patterns).

Local government, at its best, would be effective out beyond the built up area—the "urbanized area"—to encompass the full commuting range —the "standard metropolitan area"—and perhaps on beyond that to full watersheds and recreational areas. Local government would, at its best, also be small enough to be responsive and invite political participation. The really fundamental innovations in local government are still ahead and probably lie more in the direction of "two-tier" government. A Northeast that became inventive and innovative in local governance would regain the lead in one very important dimension of the social environment.

Not Everything That Goes Up Has To Come Down

To conclude, I would like to knit together two of these random threads of thought. Net out-migration, assisted perhaps by relocation allowances, might well lead to some appreciable depopulation, but this is far from being synonymous with "decline." Modest population contraction from a large population base is not likely to diminish appreciably the important gains that flowed from growth to that large size. Some examples of the economies and qualities of large scale that would tend to persist, largely undiminished, due in large measure to heavy fixed investments in capital with very long life, are: great universities and museums, and superior transportation and utility systems. Again, in a somewhat different vein, contraction from large size will recreate open space. We may well come to find that open space that is so hard to preserve while "enjoying'" rapid growth will come to hand much more easily under depopulation. Admittedly, the problem will become more that of finding public funds to transform abandoned "open space" into recreational space.

But, all in all, well planned and managed retrenchment from very large size would seem, deductively, to offer as many opportunities as it does problems. And as the Northeast becomes the new cutting edge of American urbanization, logical deduction and disciplined imagination is about all we have to go on. So hang in there, think big, and be patient.

Section II

The Federal Domain and
Regional Preliminaries

Introduction

AFTER THE PANIC OF 1873, the South, finding it more and more difficult to attract and secure retrenching northern capital, turned to the federal treasury as its last remaining hope. As C. Vann Woodward has pointed out, the South pressed forth with arguments railing against the largess showered upon capitalist enterprise in the North:

> A favorite and telling argument . . . was a comparison of Federal expenditures for public works in the North and West with those in the South. Official figures from the Treasury Department provided impressive evidence to support the argument that the South had a legitimate grievance over the distribution of these funds. Of the $103,294,501 spent on public works from 1865 to 1873, the South (the eleven ex-Confederate states, plus Kentucky) received only $9,469,363. The share of New York State alone was $15,688,222, and that of Massachusetts was $6,071,197. . . . These sectional inequalities, according to the argument, were not confined to the period of Reconstruction, but ran back to the beginning of the government.[1]

Despite the compelling rationale for a "new deal," the South had:

> arrived tardily at "The Great Barbecue." She arrived hungry and perhaps a bit greedy and not a little angry at being uninvited—only to find the victuals just about cleaned up. The feasting had been rich and bounteous while it lasted, from about 1865 to 1873, but the South was

155

unfortunately absent during that period. The depression had inaugu-
rated an era of reform, remorse, and morality—moods characteristically
reserved by Americans for hard times. The South, a belated reveler,
arrived in a mood for tippling while the rest of the county was nursing
a hangover.[2]

During this period, the nation had embarked on an era of industrial
urbanization and massed population concentrations. A plausible argument could well be put forth that differential federal spending helped
propel the Northeast as the centerpiece of industrial America by assisting in the creation of a basic infrastructure upon which the evolution
of the early manufacturing city and metropolis hinged.

In analogous fashion, it has been argued that the dominant growth
poles of 1970s America—the maturation of the post-suburban focus of
industrial and residential development—have also been structured by
federal capital facilities investments. However, their trajectories are
now extensively targeted to southern destinations.

As W. W. Rostow noted in the last section, the South's drive to regional parity commenced in the period immediately following the Great
Depression. Beginning with the New Deal programs (such as the Tennessee Valley Authority and rural electrification) and continuing to the
present day through pork barrel legislation (a galaxy of harbor, canal,
and military facilities) and the evolution of the federal capital plant
(the development of the interstate highway system which redefined
accessibility for much of the southern geography), as well as general
program distribution biases (subsidized housing), the South has developed an infrastructure appropriate to the economic parameters of the
balance of the twentieth century. Meanwhile, the Northeast's capital
plant—bereft of federal updating—is in some respects a languishing
remnant of a bypassed age.

It is the belief in the efficacy of this line of reasoning—the power of
public investment to direct the flow of private economic activity—that
has focused considerable attention on the federal role in instigating
and/or exacerbating the Northeast transformation, while concomitantly
emphasizing it as the prime vehicle for amelioration and restoration.

If indeed the Northeast must turn to the federal treasury for reprovi-
sioning its physical capital and hardware and to secure a greater input
of general program resources—and by no means do the papers in this
section fully agree on this point—then success depends on the ability
of the region's federal lawmakers to function effectively in the national
political arena.

The Region's Political Wherewithal

Martin Tolchin, *The New York Times* congressional correspondent, is a daily observer both of the never ending tensions and undercurrents defining Capitol Hill, and of the hitherto obliviousness displayed by the region's legislators to all concerns save immediate political advantage. Emphasizing the discordant notes of the past, and their lingering presence, Tolchin perceives a brief interlude in which it may be possible to arouse and press forth a coherent regional presence.

1. *Using New York's political leadership as a surrogate for the Northeast equivalent, a political milieu is dissected, one in which a congressional delegation is virtually impotent, where local personality conflicts predominate, and where self-serving political behavior is evident to the extreme.*

2. *But since the New York City fiscal crisis and the emergence of the Northeast's economic woes, not only has the New York City delegation been turned around—because the eyes of the city and the country are on it—but also members of the Northeast and the Midwest congressional delegations have united in a Northeast-Midwest Economic Advancement Coalition.*

3. *Their principal focus has been on congressional aid formulas, with instantaneous computer analyses serving to aid the forays toward regional parity. But older biases do not die easily. A kind of "Alice in Wonderland" world of federal grant-in-aid formulas exists, a world in which national objectives are clearly stated—to fight poverty, educate children, and aid mass transit —but the criteria for relief are manipulated to gain maximum support, appease key chairmen, and win approval of important committees.*

4. *The pulling and hauling over formulas is as old as the concept of formula grants, which originated in the 1930s and reflected the serious economic problems of the predominantly rural states. There has been a historic bias in the formula mechanism, which continues to channel a disproportionate amount of aid into the south-eastern states, despite changing national and regional positions.*

5. *Efforts at constructive change confront a basic reality: when it comes to formulas that determine the amount of federal funds to be received by their constituents, most congressmen seem to*

respond to pressures that they believe can determine their political survival. A vote against their own state or district, they fear, can lead to their untimely political demise, even if they believe their action to be in the broader national interest.

6. *But while government yields to various political forces—the goal being the reelection of people in power rather than any particular public benefits—the new coalition does put the public spotlight on 208 members of the House of Representatives. It provides a data base for them, makes them more effective, and more knowledgeable on the implications of all legislation. There is going to be definite public pressure on them to pursue regional interests.*

7. *The entire federal leadership may be of a configuration amenable to responding to a Northeast initiative. A "frostbelt" Speaker— Tip O'Neill of Massachusetts—has assumed position just as the diffusion of congressional power has reached its apogee. The resultant vacuum this evolution has created is ready to be filled by the new Speaker of the House and the Senate majority leader, resurrecting a new power alignment, although not as absolute as in the days of the congressional barons. The Northeast may be in a favorable position to benefit by these events.*

8. *Despite these positive stirrings, and a brightening public spotlight, the fact of deep-seated political ambition cannot be downplayed. In fact, in New York City the deleterious behavior of the past is edging forward again—the same kind of sniping that in the past has been very detrimental to New York and the entire region. When the light of the public is on the political actors, you can bring them together. As soon as that light falters, they are off and running.*

Given Tolchin's pulse reading of the Northeast political organism, long-term consensus may indeed be a tenuous premise for sustained regional commitments. Consequently if any temporary impetus is not to atrophy—induced by adversity, complacency, or inherent instability—innovative institutional arrangements may have to be erected, predicated not on federal income maintenance requirements, but on more substantial investment and redevelopment efforts.

Political Feasibility and Redevelopment Priorities

Paul London, executive director of the New England Congressional Caucus, shifts the focus from general federal support programs and vigorously avows the requirement to grant priority to infrastructure imperatives which have greater potential to generate independent and sustained economic viability. Integral to this task is the molding of an environment enhancing the feasibility of the region's leadership to entertain the very politically risky decisions so vital to the Northeast's long-term future. Advocating a Northeast TVA, London envisions a twenty-first century infrastructure as a concrete objective upon which to target the region's energies and aspirations.

1. *Three keys to a Northeast revival are parity in energy prices, parity in transportation costs, and parity in local taxes.*

2. *Billions could be spent in the Northeast for such programs as urban mass transit, housing, education, public service jobs, and welfare. But if energy, transportation, and local tax costs remain noncompetitive, sustained demand for workers and capital investment will not be generated for the region.*

3. *What the Northeast needs to rise above its present difficulties is a redevelopment effort of the kind which built up the West and South in recent years. The key to such an effort should be a federal commitment to achieve energy and transportation cost parity between the Northeast and other regions of the country.*

4. *The federal government made this kind of commitment to the South and West years ago, and the TVA, Bureau of Reclamation, Corps of Engineers, and highway program investments have made the pledge reality.*

5. *Hence a Northeast TVA appears to be a response vehicle appropriate to the requirements for the balance of the twentieth century. It is incumbent to ensure that the next round of federal investments for internal improvements recognizes the needs of the Northeast. A regional authority of the TVA mode may be the most effective instrumentality for achieving this end.*

6. *It would have at its disposal large federal appropriations in its early years—as national investment programs gradually materialize—as well as revenues and tolls from its various energy and transportation projects. These assets might well provide the main*

impetus for the region to marshall its forces to create a twenty-first century infrastructure.

7. *Its potential functional advantages are of several dimensions.*

   a) *It could pull together separate investments into a coordinated and purposeful whole.*

   b) *Its assets would be less likely to be used for economically sterile income maintenance projects compared to conventional political institutions.*

   c) *It would avoid becoming enmeshed in local politics which would dissipate its resources.*

   d) *It could focus its assets on uniquely tangible investments that lower the cost of doing business in the Northeast, concentrating on the restoration of regional competitiveness.*

8. *This proposed vehicle reflects London's basic sentiments in regard to the task at hand.*

   a) *The region should not dissipate its political capital on short-term expediencies. Long-term restructuring must predominate.*

   b) *The intellectual community has an obligation to recognize the difficult issues politicians face, and make it easier for them to choose the long-term over the short-term—the use of political resources to make the region grow.*

The Intellectual Ambience of the Northeast

Yet the latter presumption must grapple with an ominous, but real, intellectual ambience which, when mutually supportive of a short-range political mentality, has the capacity to stifle and restrict any fundamental restructuring of the region's inherent deficiencies. Roger Starr, former administrator of New York City's Housing and Development Administration, takes to task the predilections of the region's elite opinion molders, generalizes their behavioral patterns to areas experiencing stasis and decline, and contrasts their profiles to those exhibited by their analogs in the growth phase of urban and/or regional evolution.

1. *In the growth phase, the elite are environmentally indifferent, are virtually oblivious to income inequality, are willing to assess to individuals complete responsibility of their own actions, are culturally aggressive (pursuing elite preferences), and are polit-*

ically inert—political institutions are ascribed limited roles for dealing with matters of concern; the political milieu is exceedingly simply.

2. *In the decline phase, the elite have reached a point of exquisite environmental sensitivity, are guilt-ridden over income inequality, exhibit a great reluctance to impose individual responsibility for antisocial actions, are culturally defensive (disdaining advancement of elite initiatives), and are politically insomniac—political action is the vehicle for addressing every dissatisfaction; a political ambience of advanced complexity predominates.*

3. *Starr disdains suggesting which set of attitudes is right and which is wrong. The issue is what they imply—the range of politically feasible opportunity areas—for initiatives and possibilities in each of the two phases of regional growth. But the difference in attitudes does tend to limit what an area can do when it starts on its downward path.*

4. *What these contrasting attitudes may reduce to are simply ambient differences in business climates—the growth territories are probusiness while the Northeast, by and large, is not.*

5. *Priority actions by the Federal government are mandatory. The very first question that it should address is a national growth policy, particularly the underlying concerns of migration incentives and disincentives. Unfortunately, for federal leadership these are subjects as unpleasant as planned shrinkage is to the mayor of New York City.*

6. *The latter issue has been virtually impossible to raise within the New York political and intellectual environment. So instead of relocating people before they burn down their buildings, by default the Neanderthal method of waiting until after the fires to relocate the occupants is imposed.*

7. *The return capacity of the Northeast may ultimately be dependent on regional evolution in the Sunbelt. Even then two priorities stand forth: overcoming fundamental national economic problems; and avoiding interference with the ultimate attractiveness of the areas that are being largely depopulated in older cities by foolishly investing federal largess to secure short-run benefits.*

Consequently, the entire policy and program formulation process must be cognizant of a complex social and political environment—the boundaries and the constraints affecting the feasibility of each and every contemplated response.

Whatever possibility exists to somehow deflect the weight of current trendlines, there are those who question the wisdom of intervention. It is to these reservations that the next paper of this section is addressed.

A Market Perspective

William C. Freund, vice president and chief economist of the New York Stock Exchange, raises several questions as to the ultimate desirability of interceding into a process that will inevitably run its course. Perceiving the likely intervention efforts as dissipating into an amalgam of quotas, tariffs, and subsidies, all serving to reduce national efficiency, productivity, and wealth, Freund stresses the most fruitful policy would be to target aid to those impacted most negatively by the force of decline—the unemployed, the aged, and the habitually abject.

1. *Large-scale efforts to reverse basic economic trends may prove not only unproductive but counterproductive from a national perspective. Shoring up the inefficient through artificial stimuli reduces national productivity and efficiency.*

2. *In short, Freund proposes the unorthodox and perhaps even iconoclastic view that the basic economic trends in the Northeast be allowed to run their courses.*

3. *Nonetheless, there have been important policies, man-made in Washington, which have aggravated the northern loss of population, jobs, and income. The Northeast seems to have been systematically shortchanged by the federal government over the last fifteen years—political pressures favored the South in federal contracts for defense highways, rivers, and canals as well as in the ratios of federal spending to taxes collected.*

4. *In any event, the decline of the Northeast, though exaggerated by discriminatory federal programs, would still have occurred. If we discover, as we probably will, that natural economic forces have played a dominant role in producing the economic decline of the Northeast, then policies designed to counter or reverse these trends will be not only futile but inconsistent with national objectives of economic growth and productivity.*

5. *But the brunt of the burden of slow growth or decline tends to be concentrated upon those groups least able to bear the ad-*

justment. Consequently, there is a need to provide financial assistance to affected workers, their families, and employers. We should not ask the poor, the displaced, and the unemployed to shoulder the hardships of adjusting to the dynamics of economic change. It is for these groups that special intervention is warranted.

Yet there are counter arguments as to whether the efficiency of the social system is maximized by the optimization of the economic sector, as well as to the myth and reality of unfettered market forces underlying the entire process.

Reaffirmation of the Governmental Role

Professors Norman I. Fainstein and Susan S. Fainstein examine the institutional biases and cleavages in the United States which retard explicit national planning in the mode of other major industrialized western nations. Yet the federal role—defined by unanticipated consequences of its actions—proves powerful, setting the parameters of the arena of economic competition, within which state and local governments are immersed. In turn, the actions of the latter serve further to intercede into apparent free market flows.

1. *The United States, unlike the Western European nations, lacks any explicit policy of urban and regional development beyond vague commitments to reducing inequalities among regions and within metropolitan areas. Nevertheless many federal policies have important implications for the distribution of industry and population, despite the frequent failure to take account of their consequences.*

2. *The policies having the most important effects on geographical distribution of resources can be partitioned into five groups.*

   a) Taxation. *The use of the federal tax system to stimulate new investment contributes to industrial mobility.*

   b) Direct government investment. *Both the obvious effects of infrastructure development and their less subtle investment counterparts influence spatial relocation.*

   c) Direct government expenses. *The regional bias in federal expenditures has had cumulative effects and accounts for many of the present difficulties of the Northeast.*

d) Regulation and its absence. *For the most part, subordinate political jurisdictions in the United States are encouraged to attract industries within their borders, and in order to survive, are forced to externalize as many costs as possible.*

e) Subsidies. *The emphasis toward revenue sharing and formula distribution—encouraging local determination for use of federal funds—reduces even further the federal determination of local priorities.*

3. *Federal policy, or a lack thereof, provides the parameters within which local and regional rivalries for prosperous populations and industries take place. While some have tried to justify regional shift as the working out of private market forces, it is difficult to refute the roles played by federal, state, and local political instrumentalities in the overall process.*

4. *This stands in marked contrast to major European countries, which have explicit policies aimed at directing the flow of resources and population to relatively disadvantaged regions.*

5. *These policies are centrally controlled and involve restrictions on investment in developed regions, incentives to growth in designated development areas, and direct governmental investment in productive enterprise and housing as well as subsidization of labor costs.*

6. *Many of the differences stem from the fragmented character of the American state system. This fragmentation appears in the vertical layering of the authority of federalism, as well as horizontally at each level of the federal system. By definition, these attributes make effective governmental planning difficult.*

7. *As a result, any efforts at establishing critical masses of federal resources in particular areas usually dissipate into an allocation of trivial amounts of aid to many areas.*

8. *While it is likely that our present system of regional competition will not be altered to any great extent, the fact that the national government is being forced to take cognizance of the effects of its public investment, taxation, and aid policies provides some reason to be sanguine.*

Despite a number of varying viewpoints then, the papers of this section isolate a number of critical elements which must be considered when specific interventionary mechanisms are proposed. The latter are subject to examination in the following section.

NOTES

1. C. Vann Woodward, *Reunion and Reaction* (Garden City, New York: Doubleday, Anchor Books, 1956), p. 63.
2. *Ibid.*, p. 65

The Federal Arena:
The Northeast's Political Wherewithal

MARTIN TOLCHIN

Introduction

WE SHOULD START WITH WHAT I consider the bottom line and the bottom line is that when one flies into New York City or near New York City, one sees that skyline and all that money pointing up to the heavens. It is difficult to believe that all the people who own all that real estate —the Rockefellers, Madam Chiang, Reverend Moon and people all around the world—are ever going to let that city go down the drain.

When I started covering the New York City fiscal crisis in Washington, the overwhelming feeling was that New York City was going to be left to flounder and hopefully to disappear. But the Rockefellers, the publishing industry, the communicators, the bankers, the unions, locally and nationally, probably even internationally, joined forces and produced the result that was totally unpredicted when New York's mayor first went hat-in-hand to Washington to say, "Save our cities."

The Inequality

Being a New Yorker, I ride the Washington subway almost every morning to get from my office to the Capitol. It is a magnificent subway. It is new, it is gleaming, it is safe. One of the reasons that it is safe is that there is a police officer in every car. There are clusters of police officers at both ends of every station and in the middle; when you take the escalator up to the main landing, there are more officers and then there are a few plainclothesmen near the entrances as you come down. As I ride that subway, I really think—having covered New York and having spent some time in the South Bronx and having ridden in New York subways—what a contrast to the graffiti-ridden, unsafe New York subways. I recall once standing on a station platform at Broadway and 72nd Street and three teenagers came down and began kicking one of the gum machines. There were about two dozen passengers waiting for a train, not one of whom would intervene. I guess it was not only because of the New York idea that you don't interfere, but also because of the real fear that those kids could have been armed.

When one rides the Washington subway, it is galling to realize that New York not only doesn't have these physical facilities, it doesn't even have one patrolman on a train—or didn't when I was there—seldom has one at a station, and rarely has one anywhere in sight because the people who are responsible for that Washington subway also are responsible for telling New York to reduce its number of policemen, its firemen, its park attendants, its physicians, its nurses, its interns, and the hours of its museums. They are telling us to tighten our belts and at the same time are using federal funds, which New Yorkers know can be put to much greater advantage, to do the very things that they criticize us for.

The Problem of Concern

A lot of people question whether cities are really necessary. When I was working in New York, and living in Montclair, New Jersey, which is about fifteen miles due west of New York City, my neighbors there didn't think that Montclair had anything in the world to do with New York City. What happened in New York happened in some other country.

In the same way, members of Congress first perceived that what happened in New York really doesn't have anything to do with Pocatello, Phoenix, Miami, or anywhere else. Of course, America's cities evolved from towns on rivers and harbors where the trading of goods and services was centralized. The towns—Boston, New York, Baltimore, New Orleans, and St. Louis—grew into cities, demanded great public services, roads, sewers, water, mass transit, schools, fire and police protection, and cultural facilities.   Likewise the railroad towns evolved into Chicago, Kansas City, and Denver.   But then came the new technology which made it perfectly feasible for a major industry to locate not on any port but totally inland, because, after all, you don't need to be located on a port when your principal goal is landing a rocket on the moon.   In Houston, NASA is just as close to the moon as New York or Boston.

The new technology—communications and transportation—made it seem as if people no longer had to be in the same place to transact business.   Hence, economic activities flowed out of the cities.   Out of the Northeast cities flowed the middle class, first and foremost, as well as jobs.   As the middle class left, the poor came in.   Because of the politics of the cities and because city politicians wanted to expand their bases, they assisted in that migration of the poor.   They offered welfare facilities, medical care, housing.   They signed up new voters and they created the South Bronxes.

Actually, the South Bronx was directly created by New York City. The Department of Social Services, which decided that the South Bronx was really an ideal place to locate welfare clients, simply concentrated welfare clients in that area and that's how the South Bronx became the South Bronx.

When I was covering City Hall, John Lindsay had a plan to maybe send some of those welfare families into Forest Hills.   The middle-class people there put up a great fight and prevailed.   In retrospect, many of the people who thought it was a great idea to build three twenty-four-story towers for low-income people in the heart of Forest Hills now are delighted that it wasn't built.   The middle class stayed there and continued to be functioning and paying members of New York City society.

The crunch for New York City, of course, came because of the recession and because of the middle-class exodus.   New York City politicians went to Washington and they did not find very much sympathy.   As far as members of Congress and the president were concerned, New York was profligate.   Under special attack was the City University system.   Congressmen said that their constituents had to pay tuition at the University of Wisconsin or the University of Illinois. Why should the federal government subsidize New York City students with free tuition at the City University?

New York City's labor relations also came under very sharp attack, especially pension programs that enabled members of the services to retire at half pay after twenty years.

The Local Leadership Question

In New York City, the Congressional delegation was not of very much help. It's a media-oriented delegation. It has, until last month, totally lacked any clout in the Congress. It's an eighteen-member delegation without a single committee chairman. Last January, Jim Delaney of Queens became chairman of the rules committee and Jack Murphy of Staten Island and Lower Manhattan became chairman of merchant marine fisheries, and that's it.

The reason that New York had no clout, no chairmen, and very few subcommittee chairmen was because New York politicians never regarded Congress as an important place. They regarded it as a stepping stone from which to run for mayor or governor or senator. As a matter of fact, more than half of the present members have run for other office while still holding their congressional spots.

Then, of course, there's the personality conflicts. Eddie Koch still isn't talking to Bella Abzug and neither is Ben Rosenthal. Ben Rosenthal also isn't talking to Herman Badillo. They are media oriented and have a very limited attention span when it comes to staying on one committee. Herman Badillo has just now, just this term, switched from judiciary to banking and currency, which is about the fourth switch that he has made. Ben Rosenthal would have been chairman of the agricultural committee, had he stayed on it instead of jumping to two other committees. In his defense, he says that a twenty-year parity in farm prices is more than he could sustain and he wouldn't have been chairman anyway; he probably would have been in a mental institution.

It's hard for New Yorkers, in any event, to become involved in the day-to-day operations of the Congress, the day-to-day concerns; and this is resented by their colleagues. New Yorkers are also unpopular because they happen to be the champions of unpopular causes, champions of Vietnam, of the inner cities, the poor, blacks, and so forth.

When Mayor Beame and Governor Carey—incidentally, when this started, Governor Carey didn't want any part of this crisis either; he said, "That's happening in New York and doesn't affect the state;" he had to be dragged into it—went to Washington, they found a president who thought he owed nothing at all to New York, to labor, to the cities, and to the blacks. He was extremely inhospitable to even the suggestion of helping New York. He felt that his arguments were that to have the Federal government help New York or any other large city would be precedent setting; once it started with New York, it would have to help Baltimore and help Philadelphia. It would be a violation of the federal-state relationship, although nobody seemed to bring this up when it came to a Lockheed loan. But in retrospect a lot of New Yorkers now give some credence to that argument because, in fact, they feel not only the violation of federal-state relations, but also that they have lost control of their destiny. They are now being run by Washington, primarily, and Albany and an Emergency Financial Control Board.

The president and the conservatives and moderates in Congress also said, "Listen, why should we subsidize inefficiency and why should we subsidize these unions? If, in fact, we help New York out of this crisis, we will absolutely be undermining the bargaining position of city officials all over the United States because then when they sit down with the labor leaders, the labor leaders will say, 'Listen, what are you arguing with? The money we are asking for isn't coming out of your pockets. It's going to be coming out of Uncle Sam's budget.'"

Of course, the prevailing argument from the point of view of Arthur Burns was that such help was inflationary. Fortunately, for New York and for the country, the Democratic congressional leadership saw this as just a beautiful, no-lose campaign issue. They felt that if they made this kind of an issue and the Republicans failed to provide help to New York and New York went bankrupt and the ripple effect that had been predicted actually occurred, then they could have said, "Well, we told you so and this is the result of those insensitive Republicans."

On the other hand, if, as everybody expected at that time, nothing was done and nothing happened, they could say, "Well, at least we were conservative."

Of course, the Democrats are based in the cities. Their constituents are the labor unions, labor people, blacks, and the poor. They seized on this as just an ideal issue. Maybe it was the *Daily News* headline, "Ford to City: Drop Dead," that really turned Washington around. Imagine the President of the United States picking up his *Daily News* and seeing "Ford to City: Drop Dead" and saying, "Is that what I said, especially in an election year?" That probably had a great, great impact.

In retrospect, there are some in Washington who believe that his position on New York City cost him not only New York State but actually the White House. Since the fiscal crisis, not only has the New York City delegation been a turned around delegation, because everybody is looking at it—the eyes of the city and the country are on it—but also members of the Northeast and the Midwest have united in a

Northeast-Midwest Economic Advancement Coalition which consists of 208 members. Their big gripe is that they are not getting their share of anything. They are not getting their share of military appropriations. They are really getting short-changed by congressional formulas.

Aid Formulas and the Congress

Technology has really meant a new day for congressional formuluas. It used to be that when legislation came out, first of all, nobody even knew when it was coming out of a committee and when it was going to be on the floor. This was in the days of Sam Rayburn and very, very closely held information. Today with the modernization of Congress and the use of the computer, print-outs are available literally within hours after the development of any formula. The first thing a member of Congress does is go and look at that print-out and see, "Well, how does my district fare under the new formula compared with how it is doing now and other formulas?" But older biases do not die easily.

THE STRUGGLE

Three years ago, in 1974, ten million chickens were destroyed in Mississippi because they had eaten contaminated feed that had been shipped in a railroad car previously used to transport a pesticide. It was a $6 million disaster for the state's chicken farmers, which the Senate voted to have federally reimbursed.

In March of 1977, those chickens came home to roost. Senators from the industrial Northeast reminded the Senate that they had voted to aid those unfortunate chicken farmers, and expected to vote soon, and gladly, to aid the drought-stricken southwest. But fair was fair, they said, and the industrial Northeast also had legitimate claims on the federal treasury.

The issue arose as the Senate debated legislation to provide $4 billion for public works jobs to ease unemployment. Senator John Durkin, New Hampshire Democrat, had proposed that every state receive a minimum of $30 million, regardless of the extent of its unemployment. Sen. Jacob K. Javits, New York Republican and leader of dozens of similar, ill-fated battles, protested that the Durkin amendment would undermine the purpose of the legislation.

"Let us be perfectly realistic with each other," the senator began. "This is a bill which was entirely designed to help states heavily impacted by unemployment. It is one of the unfortunate parts of our

Senate debates, when we get on a measure of this kind, that people look at what it means for their state instead of what we are trying to do generally for the country."

"We have always said that if that should become the habit, then everything goes down the drain," Senator Javits continued. "We cannot do anything for anybody if we have to compensate Mississippi for losing ten million dead chickens and we have got to find dead chickens elsewhere, even if they do not exist."

Senator Durkin was unphased. "Let's face it, we are talking about money," he said. "There are no great principles involved here." The Durkin amendment was ultimately accepted by the bill's floor managers, including Senator Javits, because they could not afford to lose the votes of senators from twenty-four states that would profit from it.

To broaden the bill's support, the floor managers already had reduced the criteria for the severity of unemployment that would entitle a state to extra relief—from 7.9 to 6.5 percent. At that, the bill's managers staved off an attempt by Sen. H. John Heinz, Pennsylvania Republican, to remove the unemployment criteria altogether, and simply allocate funds on the basis of the number of unemployed in any state, rather than on the basis of severity of unemployment.

It was a classic example of the "Alice in Wonderland" world of federal grant-in-aid formulas, a world in which national objectives are clearly stated—fight poverty, educate children, aid mass transit—but the criteria for relief are manipulated to gain maximum support, appease key chairmen, and win approval of important committees.

THE BIAS AND THE MECHANISM

Who is poor? Who is hungry? Who is unemployed? Who needs mass transit aid? Congressmen eagerly await computer print-outs of proposed definitions, to determine whether the new formulas offered will benefit their constituents.

Since most states do not have large, decaying cities, congressmen from urban areas have been forced to compromise to gain the support of some of their rural colleagues. Those compromises, they fear, have deprived their states of federal funds that were needed and deserved.

"For twenty years I have stood in or almost in this place in comparable struggles," Senator Javits told the Senate. "The result is very apparent. The result is that a great section of the country is slipping, and slipping badly. That section which paid the bill for years for other states is not being given the same consideration in return."

In the same debate, Sen. Abraham Ribicoff described the process of creating the formulas. "Day in and day out on this floor all of us get these sheets of paper, and everybody fiddles around with a formula to find out in the formula whether it will give a dollar more to twenty six estates, and then you become a winner and then the national interest is forgotten."

The pulling and hauling over formulas is as old as the concept of formula grants, which originated in the 1930s and reflected the serious economic problems of the predominantly rural states. The objective was to encourage states to undertake specific programs that Congress and the administration felt were in the national interest. Most of the programs were targeted to the states with the poorest populations.

But who is poor? Most of the federal formulas use a state's per capita income as an index of poverty. This discriminates against New York, however, because it is the home of both the very rich and the very poor, who tend to cancel themselves out in per capita estimates.

"The use of per capita income tended to give a rural bias to the federal formulas and channeled a disproportionate amount of aid into the southeastern states," said Sally W. Swartzmiller, an economist in the New York State budget division. "But to make doubly sure that the funds for maternal and child health, crippled children's services, and child welfare services went into rural areas, the number of rural children and the number of rural live births were counted twice for part of the distribution."

Similarly, federal aid to education is based on children between the ages of five and seventeen in families with incomes below the poverty level. Welfare payments are counted as income, and, in New York City, bring families above the national poverty level, partly because the cost of living is higher in the Northeast than in other sections of the country.

The original revenue sharing bill used as formula factors the lack of plumbing facilities and the number of persons per room. New York senators point out that most buildings without adequate plumbing were in the South, and that lack of heat was a more prevalent problem in the North. Plumbing was dropped as a factor, but overcrowding remains in the formula, defined as a housing unit having 1.01 or more persons per room, a condition far more prevalent in the South than in the North, where families of four in the South Bronx live in rat infested, unheated six-room apartments.

New Yorkers fought a desperately hard, ultimately victorious battle for mass transit aid. To get the legislation through Congress, however, they accepted a formula that was based on population and density, but not riders. Consequently, New York City, with 31 percent of the nation's mass transit riders, has only 15 percent of the funds. The disparity is even greater in federal funding for narcotics programs. New York City has 50 percent of the nation's addicts, but only 7 percent of the funds.

Other factors that often hurt states with large urban areas are those that place a maximum on the amount a state can receive under any program (mass transit maximum is 15 percent of the federal funds), and clauses that guarantee that no state shall receive less than it previously received, despite changed conditions.

AID AND POLITICAL POWER

In the final analysis, formulas reflect an area's political power or lack thereof. One of New York's major problems, for example, has been a divided delegation which, until this year, lacked a single committee chairman, while rural areas had a disproportionate number of chairmen and congressional leaders. The problems of the aging cities of the Northeast and Great Lakes states have led to the creation of a Northeast-Midwest coalition of 208 congressmen who are committed to work together on formulas, but there is not yet any indication that such a coalition will be effective.

The reality is that, when it comes to formulas that determine the amount of federal funds to be received by their constituents, most congressmen seem to be responding to pressures that they believe can determine their political survival. A vote against their own state or district, they say, can lead to their untimely political demise, as in the case of former Sen. James L. Buckley, who attributes his defeat, in part, to his early opposition to federal aid to New York City. "Sure I want to be a broad United States senator, with national concerns," Sen. Howard Metzenbaum, Ohio Democrat, said during the debate on the jobs bill. "But charity begins at home."

Nevertheless, the technology that has hurt the Northeast in many ways is starting to help it, at least in one small way. It was Lud Ashley of Ohio who said, "Listen, you know we're just getting screwed and we have been getting screwed all these years and we are asking for equity and we have the clout to demand it. We have 208 members from these states," although very few people believe that all 208 members would support anything. As a matter of fact, all 18 members from New York City very, very rarely unite on anything.

The Federal Leadership

The other new reality in Washington is that we have now a Sunbelt president, who owes a great deal to the Northeast, and a "frost belt" Speaker. Thomas P. "Tip" O'Neill of Massachusetts, as Speaker, is joined by James Wright of Texas who campaigned for the majority leadership of Congress on a platform of helping the cities, on a platform that he was one of two Texans to vote for fiscal aid to New York, one of something like seven southerners to do so. He has supported mass transit and supported the cities and he actively solicited the help of people in cities.

This is the leadership in the House of Representatives, Tip O'Neill and Jim Wright. The Democratic leadership in the Senate comprises Robert Byrd and Alan Cranston. Maybe it also reflects that in my lifetime the Speakers of the House were Sam Rayburn of Texas, John McCormack of Massachusetts, Carl Albert of Oklahoma, and Tip O'Neill of Massachusetts. One wonders how, with all that Northeast clout in the Speaker's office, the situation had been allowed to deteriorate to the extent that it has.

The Dimensions of Change

The days of the barons are over. The Capitol Hill autocrat, that often cantankerous solon who would take extended vacations rather than convene his committee to consider legislation he regarded with distaste, who would fail to recognize committee members with differing views and advise freshmen that "to get along, go along," has become all but extinct.

Power in Congress, once tightly held by a handful of leaders and chairmen, has become increasingly dispersed. No longer can a few senior members meet over bourbon and branch water to make secret deals that bind their colleagues.

This diffusion, which began in the 1960s, gained impetus during the general assault on institutional authority during the Vietnam War and greatly accelerated with the massive influx of freshmen congressmen in the last four years—159 in the House and 30 in the Senate.

The ouster of three senior House chairmen in 1975, curbs on the powers of House and Senate chairmen, prohibitions against the leadership's ability to surprise opponents by unexpectedly bringing legislation to the floor without notice, the opening of committees to public scrutiny, the initiation of recorded votes, the development of the House Democratic caucus and the steering and policy committee—all have greatly diminished the powers of those who formerly ran the institution.

Such diffusion was unheard of in the era of Speaker Sam Rayburn and Senate Majority Leader Lyndon B. Johnson, who ran their respective institutions with a handful of committee chairmen.

To illustrate how times have changed, the present Speaker, Thomas P. O'Neill, Jr., tells of another freshman in 1953, a midwesterner, who had run afoul of the Justice Department. The midwesterner appealed to Speaker Rayburn, who summoned the attorney general to his office and persuaded him not to press criminal charges. The grateful freshman pledged eternal loyalty to the Speaker, who then told him that, eternity aside, he needed his vote on a controversial bill the following week.

During the intervening weekend, however, the freshman's hometown newspaper charged that he had sold his vote to avoid criminal prosecution. He told Mr. Rayburn of his plight, and the Speaker told him to seat himself in the first row of the chamber. If he needed the freshman's vote, Mr. Rayburn said, he would expect it. If not, he would signal the freshman to vote otherwise, as he eventually did. The freshman heaved a sign of relief only to discover a dozen other legislators, sitting near him in the first row, also looked very relieved.

Those days are gone forever, Speaker O'Neill says, and nearly everyone agrees. "The day is ended when any committee chairman can run his domain like a feudal barony, oblivious to the wishes and sensitivities of other members," said House Majority Leader Jim Wright. "All now have been put on notice that their colleagues will hold them accountable for their stewardship. The office of committee chairman must now be regarded no longer as a right but a privilege, a gift of opportunity bestowed by one's peers, and those who give also can take away."

Procedure affects policy. The obstructive powers of chairmen were often invoked by conservative Democrats in league with likeminded Republicans, and therefore one of the results of the power dispersal has been to make the Congress more hospitable to liberal legislation such as tax reform or a code of ethics.

In the Senate, 59 of the 100 members belong to a new senators group consisting of those who have served for less than eight years and three months, and have played an active role in shaping legislation, including the code of ethics and reorganization bill.

"We've democratized the Senate as never before," said Sen. Adlai E. Stevenson, Illinois Democrat and chief architect of legislation that severely limited the number of committee and subcommittee chairmanships that a senator could hold, thereby diminishing authority and spreading the wealth.

In the Senate, almost each of the sixty-two Democrats hold subcommittee chairmanships, some of them wielding authority previously exerted by chairmen of the full committees. Sen. Daniel P. Moynihan, Democrat from New York who has served only since the beginning of this year, is chairman of the public assistance subcommittee of the finance committee. Similarly, 128 Democrats in the House hold subcommittee chairmanships.

This diffusion of power has occasionally bewildered the Carter administration, as for example when James Schlesinger, the president's energy advisor, sought to consult a senator on the president's energy package. He chose Senator Stevenson, a subcommittee chairman and one of the acknowledged senate experts in the field, thereby offending among other senior members Sen. Henry Jackson, chairman of the interior committee and one of the senate's most powerful members.

Subcommittee chairmen in the House who are acknowledged to be that body's leading experts in their fields include Democrats Thomas L. Ashley of Ohio (housing); Paul O. Rogers of Florida (health); John Dingell of Michigan (energy), and Benjamin Rosenthal of New York (consumer affairs).

Some colleagues believe that the pendulum is beginning to swing, that the diffusion has created a vacuum that will be filled, in part, by the new Speaker and senate majority leader. They believe that Mr. O'Neill, in particular, has already demonstrated that he has the drive and talent to resurrect the power of his office which, even in its diminished state, nevertheless played a key role in the impeachment process and the New York City fiscal crisis, among other measures.

"With this Congress, Democrats in the House have made the judgment that we've gone as far as we could have gone to disperse and diffuse power," said Rep. John Brademas of Indiana, the Democratic Whip. "Any more diffusion, and it would make it difficult for the House to function."

Mr. O'Neill displayed his leadership potential in his House speech on behalf of a code of ethics. "The bull strength that O'Neill demonstrated, and the intelligence, are the qualities of a strong Speaker," said Rep. Richard Bolling of Missouri, the floor manager of the bill and a leading scholar of power in the House.

House Majority leader Wright added, "We probably won't ever again see the monolithic style of leadership asserted by Mr. Rayburn. But Tip has the power to persuade. He can't decide things unilaterally. The emphasis is on persuasion."

"He's got to be a leader," Mr. Wright added.

Conclusion

But government still yields to various political forces, the goal being reelection of the people in power rather than any particular public benefits. Major planning decisions in which the leaders appear to be blindfolded, very carefully weighing the merits of various alternatives, are very often deceiving. There's no way really you can conceal the political implications involved.

In the first place, the Northeast-Midwest coalition does put the spotlight on 208 members of the House of Representatives. It also, incidentally, provides a data base for them. It makes them much more effective, much more knowledgeable of the implications of all legislation, not only as far as their own districts, but as far as the region as a whole. The public is beginning to look at them in that sense and their media orientation—the personality conflicts, the squabbles, and the committee hopping—and they are beginning to feel public pressure, public knowledge that this is how they are perceived and this is one of the reasons they are not esteemed by their colleagues, by and large. There is going to be a political pressure to unite with members so situated in this Northeast-Midwest corridor.

As was suggested before, though it is inconceivable that 208 members of the House are going to vote together on anything, especially on a set of issues, the groundwork has been laid. When various things do come up—such as new formulas typified by mass transportation, public works, and manpower legislation—we are going to see, if not 208 members working together, at least the vast majority of these people voting together. The rest are going to have to explain to their constituents why they are departing from this coalition, which might be a little hard for some of them to do.

There's going to be definite political pressures on them that just may overwhelm their personal needs and personal political ambitions. The same will probably hold true for the relationship between the Congressmen and the governors. One of the real problems, again getting back to New York, is that half the members of that delegation, at any time, are running for mayor or running for governor and, therefore, are almost automatically in an adversary relationship with people they should be working together with for the common good.

Moreover, their real perception of their job, underneath it all, really may be political ambition over everything else. However, again you have the light of the public really being focused on them and it could be very politically disadvantageous for them not to unite.

At this very moment, as a matter of fact, running actively for mayor in the New York delegation is Eddie Koch. We have Herman Badillo who is starting to line up support as well as some talk from Jack Murphy. So it's all starting again. This kind of sniping in the past has been very detrimental to New York and the same is true of the entire region. The moment the spotlight is on them, you can bring them together. As soon as that light falters, they are each off and running.

Revitalizing the Northeast: Making Redevelopment Politically Acceptable

PAUL A. LONDON

Introduction

ACADAMICS AND INTELLECTUALS OFTEN IGNORE the fact that to be effective, ideas for the Northeast must be politically acceptable. As the economic advisor to the New England Congressional Caucus in Washington, I work with twenty-five practicing politicians who often do not see the problems of the Northeast as intellectuals do. Since these politicians are the real decisionmakers, academics and intellectuals have to ask themselves how to fit their ideas to political realities. The real question when we prescribe solutions to regional problems in the Northeast is the political one. Can you sell the idea to representatives from the region? Can it be sold to others?

The Hard Decisions

Politicians obviously face conflicts, choices between what is politically appealing and economically useless, and what is politically difficult but useful. The literature on the Northeast regional problem, unfortunately, avoids dealing with this problem. It focuses on shifts of population, employment, and income, and on subsets of these shifts, such as the transfer of manufacturing jobs or of construction employment.

The Northeast literature goes on to describe some relationships between obsolete political jurisdictions, climate, local tax burdens, slums, race, aging capital plant, and various other features of the Northeast landscape. This descriptive literature is useful but it never quite comes to grips with those issues on which politicians need help, that is on the hotly politicized issues.

The bulk of recent literature on the Northeast is very depressing. Because it "poor mouths" the region, it only makes it easier for a northeastern politician to do what he always did anyway, which was to ask for more federal money for the region. It doesn't tell him what kinds of programs are priority, or suggest a program of economic rejuvenation.

Should our politicians use their political capital to get short-term relief on heating oil this winter or should they go for a long-term energy policy? I think that's an important type of question. Does a northeastern politician go before a committee with a chairman who's from Louisiana and say that the Northeast must have heating oil for poor people this winter or do we say we will discount the short-term in order to save our political capital for something much bigger?

I think the intellectual community has an obligation to recognize that this is the kind of an issue that politicians face and to make it easier for the politician to choose the long-term over the short-term.

The Dissipation of Efforts

Roger Starr, and a few other writers, whom I would characterize as being in the Edward Banfield school, are making it easier for politicians to do what is hard but useful. As I read them, they are saying, "Don't waste your political capital and the region's money on dying neighborhoods and on moribund industry." This position needs to be made politically acceptable in a broader sense.

The broader argument is that less money should be spent on hopeless efforts and that more should be spent on hopeful ones, if we can identify them. Intellectuals and progressives found this argument acceptable when it was made about Vietnam. Vietnam was a rathole, a bad place to pour our money, unimportant to the United States in terms of its overall foreign policy objectives.

Northeast redevelopment is the same sort of problem. There are a lot of ratholes that are politically attractive as places to put our money and we are tempted to pour our money in them rather than saying, "What are the useful things that will give this region a leg up in the next twenty-five years?"

The Energy Dilemma

Energy has long been a case in point. I pick energy because energy is a subject upon which twenty-five New England congresspersons can hope to get a unified position, because New England with some exceptions has basically the same sorts of energy problems. We don't have an upstate-downstate problem. We don't have a Republican-Democratic problem. We have an oil problem. We have an energy problem.

Energy is a very big problem. It is quantifiable, and yet groups in the region and the region's leaders have been unable to agree on the fundamentals of our energy problem. It's an interesting example.

What is the energy problem from a regional perspective as I see it? In a nutshell, the problem is that Northeast consumers, because of federal policy, pay more for energy than the region's competitors, residential and business, in the rest of the country.

Why is this? Data show that we pay the same price for gasoline that the people in Texas pay for gasoline, and the same for heating oil as the people in Texas or Louisiana, plus five percent or so which is the price we pay for normal transportation cost differences. If oil prices are similar, what is the problem? The answer is that our energy problem is almost completely the difference in price between oil and natural gas.

Oil, from 1959 on, was regulated at a price above market levels by the mandatory oil import program, which the Northeast opposed, by and large. Natural gas, on the other hand, was and is regulated well below its world market price by the Federal Power Commission.

This asymmetry in federal policy created a situation where oil using regions like the Northeast pay high prices, much above what would be called a competitive market price, while the Sunbelt, which is a natural gas using region, a quintessential gas using region, gets cheap natural gas. (See Exhibit 1.)

EXHIBIT 1
COMPARISON OF PRIMARY FUEL COSTS TO LARGE INDUSTRIAL USERS
(Cents per million BTU)

Census Region SMSA	January 1960				January 1969				January 1973			
		Fuel Oil				Fuel Oil				Fuel Oil		
	Gas	No.2	No.6	Coal	Gas	No.2	No.6	Coal	Gas	No.2	No.6	Coal
New England Boston, Mass.	109.7	75.0	44.3	—	134.0	83.6	40.9	—	197.7	90.9	84.9	—
Middle Atlantic New York, N.Y.	122.5	77.9	42.4	42.9ᵃ	121.3	82.2	42.1	44.8ᵃ	146.4	89.4	87.0	73.4ᵇ
South Atlantic Charlotte, N.C.	121.1	80.8	—	32.7ᵃ	70.6	91.2	—	42.8ᵃ	81.0	88.7	—	72.0ᶜ
East North Central Chicago, Ill.	63.8	75.0	57.8	32.1ᵃ	56.3	82.9	59.9	36.7ᵃ	80.7	88.7	84.4	50.2ᶜ
East South Central Nashville, Tenn.	48.9	—	—	34.9ᵃ	49.3	—	—	44.8ᵃ	68.9	—	—	73.8ᶜ
West North Central Minneapolis- St. Paul, Minn.	68.2	80.8	59.8	57.1	67.1	82.2	60.6	63.9	76.2	82.9	73.2	96.9
West South Central Houston, Tex.	18.3ᵃ	—	—	—	19.4ᵃ	—	—	—	25.2ᶜ	—	—	—
Mountain Denver, Colo.	11.4	—	—	32.5ᶜ	23.0	—	—	31.5ᵃ	25.6	—	—	37.7ᵃ
Pacific Seattle, Wash.	67.7	82.9	49.9	40.7	65.3	88.0	52.6	53.5	81.6	101.7	77.1	77.4

ᵃ Annual averages.
ᵇ Price for 1971; later price not available.
ᶜ Annual average for 1972.
NOTES: Costs for gas are based on rates for firm gas.

The political point of interest is that while the Northeast correctly opposed the mandatory oil import program which kept oil prices high, it never made the jump to understand that it was not in the region's interest to support low natural gas prices. Many of those who are concerned with the Northeast's regional lag still support, I suspect, low natural gas prices and would roast a politician for opposing this position. It's a wonderful example of a region which is unable to define its own economic interests in a key area.

New England is 85 percent dependent on oil. Texas, which produces oil and gas, uses almost no oil for anything but automobiles. The windfall which goes to Texas manufacturers alone, Texas industry alone, in the low price of natural gas comes to about $4 billion a year.

So natural gas users probably get in the neighborhood of a $20-billion-a-year windfall. It seems to me that from the Northeast's point of view, our interest is to see that the windfall goes to the producers of gas with whom we do not compete, rather than to manufacturers in Texas and Louisiana and Arkansas with whom we do compete. My point is that intellectuals and academics in this region never helped to make that political choice clear.

I can't blame a politician, who has natural gas users in his district, for wanting low prices. I can't blame him for saying, "Well, it's never popular to vote for a high price," but I can blame intellectuals, who have no political stake and who aren't going to lose their jobs, for not helping the politician make a tough choice.

There are other issues of this type. It should have been easier for a politician in the Northeast to vote for deregulation of natural gas or at least for higher prices, but intellectuals in this region didn't make it easier. Many yelled oil company sellout when a politician moved in that direction. Many politicians know that regulation has been terrible for the country, but they are afraid to vote the other way because somebody out there is going to say they sold out to the oil companies.

Focusing on Specifics

Let me make some comments about the new effort to broaden our New England group to set up the CONEG, the northeastern governors group, and move on to a Northeast-Midwest coalition with 208 members instead of 25. In our 25-member New England Congressional Caucus, we have never gotten into upstate-downstate problems where people in Pittsfield, Massachusetts have obvious differences with people in Boston. *Choosing issues is important.* Northeastern regional efforts are going to have great difficulties when they come down to the issues which require political guts. Energy will be one of them.

One of the reasons why the New England Caucus has had some success is because we do know what we are concentrating on. We have worked on oil and managed to "get" $100 million here and $100 million there through various negotiations with the Federal Energy Administration. I won't go into the details of that. I don't think it's absolutely fundamental, but we have had some successes because at least we have focused on a few of the big issues.

I'm not sure that the wider groupings are going to focus on those issues. They may get into formulas on which I believe they will find everybody voting their district and not the region.

The key is that when you start up a group like this, it seems to me you should know what you want. When I first went to work on the Hill, I worked for Senator, now Vice President, Mondale. I remember being struck by his view that when you had a set of hearings, you ought to know what you wanted to come out of the hearings before you started. The analogy is that the Northeast governors or the Northeast-Midwest coalition ought to have specific goals. They ought to have a few substantive, a limited number of substantive objectives.

Consciousness raising on the Northeast-Sunbelt issue is dangerous unless you know what you want to do after you have raised consciousness. I am not sure that we know what step number two is.

The new administration is asking, "What do you want?" We do not seem to be able to tell them. For lack of anything better, we say we want a development bank. We have lots of banks. Is that what we need? We don't have any borrowers. What we need in this area of the country is borrowers, not bankers. We are waiting for people to come and do the investing.

Investment Foci

I began by saying that the key question is what should a politician do. My answer would be that the Northeast should seek major investments in the energy area. Eight hundred billion dollars are going to be spent on energy investment in this country probably in the next ten or fifteen years. We should want a major share of this investment.

What kinds of investment do we want? Let's look first to investments by a TVA-type agency, not to a new bank. I don't think we need more bankers. We have plenty of money. We need borrowers.

As a second point, very similar, we ought to ask: What does a twenty-first century infrastructure for the Northeast look like? Our aim should

be to get the federal government to buy us a twenty-first century infrastructure. We will make jobs along the way building this infrastructure
as we will with energy investment. We should focus on tangible investments that lower the cost of doing business in the Northeast and not
piddle our money out a dollar at a time through little programs that
make people happy a day at a time.

A REGIONAL TVA: SPECIFICS

Many in the Northeast are calling for a New Deal for the region.
It is important to think boldly about this and to lay out a plan which
can succeed. During the Great Depression, the federal government
created the Tennessee Valley Authority (TVA), not merely for river
basin development but also to give the Southeast energy and transportation cost parity with other areas of the country. The TVA may be a
good model for a similar effort in the Northeast.

Three keys to a Northeast revival are parity in energy prices, parity
in transportation costs and parity in local taxes. A TVA for the Northeast can deal with the first two of these basic problems. Before
discussing the outlines of a Northeast TVA, however, it is important to
understand the magnitude of the region's energy and transportation
cost problems.

Energy prices in the Northeast are often twice as high as in the fast-
growing South, Southwest and West. Oil costs $2 per million British
thermal units (BTUs) in New England while contract natural gas,
which fuels most industry in other areas, costs about $1.30 in the
South, $1.06 in the Southwest, and $1.13 in the Mountain states. An
industry in the Mid-Atlantic region pays $1,900 for electricity which
costs its competitors $820 in the Tennessee Valley, $785 in the Southwest, and $855 in the Rockies.

We know less about the transportation disadvantage of the Northeast
than we do about its energy disadvantage. But we do know that goods
are more expensive to move within a crowded eastern urban area than
in a wide open southern or western city. Railroads in the Northeast
have deteriorated badly and there is no unified regional approach to
transportation cost problems.

As a result of these problems, what growth is taking place in the
Northeast is in a limited number of sought after industries, which do
not need much energy, which locate in suburban areas where trucks can
serve them and which can ignore the local tax situation. Billions could
be spent in the Northeast for such programs as urban mass transit,
housing, education, public service jobs, and welfare. But if energy,

transportation and local tax costs remain noncompetitive, sustained demand for workers and capital investment will not be generated in the region.

High energy, transportation and local tax costs have drawn off funds which might otherwise have been spent to redevelop the Northeast's decaying physical plant. At the same time, federal programs over the past forty years have built modern facilities in other regions. Three billion dollars in federal investment built over twenty dams and power-plants in the TVA area, secured the area from floods, and provided it with a 650-mile low-cost transportation system. The Bureau of Reclamation, which operates only in seventeen western states, has spent over $6 billion since 1960 on capital projects, which, in turn, make private investment more attractive. Since 1960, $8.7 billion in Corps of Engineers spending has favored the Sunbelt states. Over $79 billion in federal highway money during the same period has made the wide open spaces of the West and South more attractive for business investment than eastern city centers.

It is too late to give regional balance to the government investment programs of the 1950s and '60s. It is not too late, however, to make sure that the next round of government investment for internal improvements recognizes the needs of the Northeast. This is why the Northeast should review the TVA experience.

What the Northeast needs to rise above its present difficulties is a redevelopment effort of the kind which built up the West and South in recent years. The key to such an effort should be a federal commitment to attempt to achieve energy and transportation cost parity between the Northeast and other regions of the country. The federal government made this kind of commitment to the South and West years ago and TVA, Bureau of Reclamation, Corps of Engineers, and highway program investments have made the pledge reality.

The TVA approach is a good one even though the Northeast has no comparable river system. TVA was built on the foundation of a detailed survey of the resources of the Tennessee Valley region. A similar survey of the energy and transportation resources of the Northeast should be part of the first step in an effort aimed at restoring the region's competitive position. But lest the region be fobbed off with another survey, it should be clear that a survey is not enough.

To be worthwhile, a survey must lead to a plan, as was the case with TVA. The plan should lay out the region's energy and transportation options—Appalachian coal, new coal burning technology, solar, off-shore oil and gas, rail, highway, pipeline, coastal shipping—and suggest a program of development. A vital part of a plan for the Northeast should be the means to carry it out. TVA is a government corporation endowed with extensive powers and resources. It had at its disposal not only large federal appropriations during its early years, but revenues from its huge power projects. Because it was an independent corporation with large assets at its disposal it was able to pursue its aims—navigation, flood control, and power development—without becoming enmeshed in local politics which could have dissipated its resources.

There are other examples of regional "government corporations" such as Mass-Port or the Port Authority of New York and New Jersey. Because of their focused purposes and independent sources of revenue, these government corporations have often been successful. It is possible to imagine a Northeast TVA with federal money to invest, for example, in coal development, pipelines to bring ashore oil and natural gas, new utilities, and modernized transportation facilities. Like TVA it might have independent revenues from power sales and pipeline and transportation tolls. Again, like the TVA it might pay some fees to local governments in lieu of taxes, but its assets would be less likely to be used for economically sterile income maintenance projects than those of most local governments.

Implementing a plan for the Northeast aimed at approximate parity in energy and transportation costs will no doubt require government investments comparable in scale to the investments which the federal government has funneled into projects outside of the Northeast for years. Some of these investments have begun to be made already —for example, in the Northeast freight railroads—just as the government's investment in Muscle Shoals and other Tennessee Valley projects predated the creation of TVA itself. But a TVA approach to the Northeast should pull together separate investments into a coordinated and purposeful whole.

Conclusion

These are two specific suggestions, energy and infrastructure. I look to the TVA and Bureau of Reclamation and Corps of Engineers and say that we want the kinds of things they do. What does a twenty-first century TVA look like and what does a twenty-first century Bureau of Reclamation look like? Let's have such agencies building infrastructure in the Northeast.

Third, there has been a terrible imbalance in military spending in the South. A lot of that spending has been based on unexamined Pentagon policies. If the six states of New England just had an average Pentagon wage and salary disbursement, we would be getting $440 million more a year. That's the difference between what we get now and the National average and we ought to ask whether that has anything to do with this country's military strategy.

What can we do as nonpoliticians to make these things happen? The answer is that we can help create an intellectual climate so that a politician can make a tough vote. We have to give politicians support when they vote against a nice hospital or more short-term aid because we need other things—they should be using their political resources for other things—to make this region grow.

The Intellectual Ambience of Decline

ROGER STARR

Introduction

I WAS VERY MUCH STRUCK by what Wilbur Thompson had to say with respect to continuing disequilibrium, that when a city starts to grow, it continues to grow; when a city starts to lose its growth, that loss of growth itself accelerates and turns into decay. I suggest that the most important controlling factor on what our options are in declining regions has to do with the consciousness or the set of beliefs of the elite.

I was struck also by what Wilbur had to say with respect to the fact that the Northeast continues to have a large number of intelligent, well-educated, energetic, lively leadership types. I agree. My problem is what they are thinking about.

The objective of this paper is to contrast what I take to be the characteristics of the elite in a city that is experiencing disequilibrium toward growth with the characteristics of the elite in a city which is moving in the opposite direction.

Environmental Perspectives

In the first place, in its growth phase, the urban elite is environmentally indifferent. In its shrinkage phase, the elite is environmentally sensitive. I don't know which comes first and for the moment I don't really care.

A useful comparison is the reception of steam vessels in New York harbor in the first or perhaps the second quarter of the nineteenth century with the reception of the Concorde today; the Concorde is being opposed primarily on local and environmental grounds. There may be other very sound grounds for opposing the Concorde and I'm not arguing with those. I'm taking my reading of where the elite in New York stand on this issue, and I find that in great part they are opposed to it because of what it does to the local environment. It makes noise.

I put it to you that the environmental quantum jump between sailing vessels and steam vessels which were greeted here, as I remember it, with open arms, is infinitely greater than the quantum jump between the 747 and the Concorde. I find this an interesting index of what we can do, what our options are in a city in this phase because we have reached a point of exquisite environmental sensitivity.

Compassion

Secondly, in the growth phase of a city when it's moving toward growth disequilibrium, I would say that the elite are marginally compassionate. They are compassionate toward the hardship which they cannot escape looking at. They are compassionate perhaps toward the cook in the kitchen. In the nongrowth declining phase, if you will, of regions and cities the elite are guilt ridden. I don't think any of us can deny that that is the condition in which the elite find themselves today.

Growth Inequality

I would say that in the growth phase the elite are tolerant of and even tend to celebrate growth inequality between persons. The respect and adulation given to the big business leaders in the time of urban growth or in the phase of disequilibrium toward growth is very marked. Our business heroes were very highly regarded. They were adulated, regarded as great servants of the people and while, of course, there tended to be forces in the opposite direction, generally speaking they were treated with immense respect. Today I would say egalitarianism and outrage against growth of inequality between persons—not only from the point of view of their legal position, but the fact of the share of the gross national product that they enjoy—has become characteristic of the urban elite.

Individual Responsibility

I would say that in the period of growth the elite were prepared, fairly or unfairly doesn't matter, but they were prepared to assess individual responsibility and to assert it against those who broke what the elite regarded as a necessary code of urban society. At the present time there's a great reluctance to impose individual responsibility. There's a reluctance to impose even criminal responsibility for criminal acts on the individual person. Environment and other qualities are blamed; when one discusses the nature of the people in poverty, he is accused of saying that he's blaming the victim for poverty. He's blaming the victim for his disorder.

I'm not here to tell you that one of these sets of attitudes is wrong and the other is right. That's not the issue. The issue is what this set of attitudes—which are quite prevalent at the present time—means for the range of options which are politically possible for an area that is in the phase in which these attitudes become dominant.

Cultural Aggressiveness

In the growing up phase, a city or the elite of a city are culturally aggressive. In the declining phase, they are culturally defensive.

Now, I will give you two simple examples of that. A friend of mine, who is connected officially with New York City's cultural (for lack of a better word) establishment, told me recently he was approached by a representative of a very wealthy Houston family who asked him, "Is the Museum of Modern Art for sale?"

My friend expressed disbelief that this question was serious. He said, "Why don't you take some of the paintings that we have in the cellar of the Museum of Modern Art? We haven't got the room for all of them on the wall. I'm sure that the City of New York would be happy to lend them to the City of Houston."

The man said, "I have $250 million from a group of Houston socialites. We want our own museum. Houston needs its own museum with its own art."

I'm only an anecdotal type and if you are waiting for statistics, you've got the wrong fellow. When the Metropolitan Museum was about to build the Temple of Dendur or reconstruct it in Central Park, having brought it over stone by stone from Egypt, and put a wooden fence to keep kids from falling into the excavation, the fence immediately became the number two target for graffiti in New York, number one being the subway cars. On that fence I saw the following graffiti, to which I attach great significance. It said: "Stop building this museum. Only God can make a tree."

The theory being, of course, I suppose, that anybody can paint a Rembrandt.

Culturally, the older cities are on the defensive. When a few million dollars were put into the purchase of *Aristotle Contemplating the Bust of Homer,* the objection was raised that this money should be spent on real live people instead, or on somehow equaling out the cultural level of the ghetto with the central city; it should have been used for making museum trucks which would go around the city displaying works of art so that people could benefit from them.

Once again, I'm not attempting to argue as to which is the correct attitude, if such a question is possible. I'm only saying that one set of attitudes is consistent with the growing phase of an area; the other with the nongrowth phase.

Political Awareness

Finally, in the growing phase, we find that the elite are politically asleep. In the declining phase, they are politically insomniac. Everything becomes a matter of politics. There is no subject too small, no matter, no decision too tiny to escape political interest.

One of the most fascinating things, at least in my city which happens to be New York, has been the proliferation in the last few years of tiny community and neighborhood newspapers whose stock in trade is the politicizing of all kinds of local issues, issues of infinitesimal size. I have said before, but thank goodness not to this audience, that the one good thing about the fiscal crisis in New York City is that when I sit down at a dinner party table, the lady next to me doesn't turn to me and say a sentence beginning with "I don't see why, in the richest city in the world, we can't . . . ." You can fill that in.

I no longer have to listen to that. In any case, it's a statement that her dissatisfactions are to be solved by political action. Whether she wants comfort stations for poodles or whether she wants buses not running in the street in front of her house or whether she wants the new subway line, which perhaps will never be completed, moved to the next block, we don't know; but politics is the vehicle through which this is going to happen.

The politics of growing areas I take to be rather simple. They revert to or they are established on the basic question of who gets what and how. They are simple politics and most people are inert to them.

Now, this difference in the set of attitudes has, I think, limited what an area can do when it starts on its downward path, a path which seems to me is one that stimulates acceleration. Once you are on it, you go faster and faster.

Planned Shrinkage: The Political Reality

Of all people I am asked the question: "Is it politically feasible to consider planned shrinkage?" I would think that that question should answer itself. It certainly isn't politically feasible if you call it planned shrinkage.

I have spent a year thinking up other names for the same thing. I will burden you with only two of them. One is studied negative growth and the other is organic community intensification.

Wilbur Thompson, who doesn't know the number of nights I have sat up reading his *Preface to Urban Economics*, never fails to impress me. He spoke a permanent truth before you when he said there is no transportation economy in running a bus with eight people in it. I would like to repeat that over and over and over again because what happens in the older cities when they lose industry and they lose population is that they are running buses, schools, sanitation wagons, and a great many other expensive municipal commodities or municipal services half full. We cannot provide over the same physical network of services what we used to provide when that network was originally designed for a capacity of ten or twelve million people and now has a clientele which is shrinking.

Our public social policy may limit the speed at which we shrink; but I submit that this is an awesome and terrifying prospect, that a greater and greater percentage of the people living in the larger eastern cities are there only because it's federal social policy to keep them from moving elsewhere where they might have more opportunity at this phase of the cycle to enter into the mainstream of American economic life. In New York it is noticed that welfare stipends are diminishing. They are certainly diminishing relatively because even if they were fixed and are fixed, the general inflation of prices means they buy less as compared with people whose salaries and wages are not fixed; second, we are actually seeing in absolute numbers a steady reduction in the welfare stipend, not without great resistance. Liberal friends, and I have a few in the New York State legislature, tell me that they are astonished by the extent to which the opposition to the governor's proposal to reduce welfare stipends to families on home relief (funded entirely by the City and State of New York, not the AFDC program) has been very much less than was expected. And so is the opposition to his rental allowances which New York City uses in the calculation for stipends for AFDC families as well.

I see no alternative to this process of shrinking; and I suppose what's going to happen is that as cities shrink, they are going to shrink without anybody planning them that way. One of the things that I suppose we should be doing—if we were adventurous social scientists—is to relocate people before they burn their buildings down. If not, we are going to have to use the Neanderthal method of waiting until after they burn their buildings down to relocate them. This is exactly what's going on in a remarkably large section of the City of New York. I find it a very dismal prospect.

Migrational Disincentives

That raises the very real question of how a freely elected government deals with the question of noneconomic growth over a long period of time. Until now, this government has dealt with it by open frontiers and free migration, that is, encouraged migration. Whether or not the blacks, Puerto Ricans, and the aged, who are the greatest victims of the present turndown in our economic process, will be able to avail themselves of the option of migration to parts of the country which are now booming, seems highly problematical. It would be, if I had my choice, a very first question for the federal government to address. But I'm afraid that for the federal government, it is as pleasant a subject as planned shrinkage is to the mayor of the City of New York, because it makes him many enemies, probably one for every friend.

Resource Allocations

Finally, what should be the realities of resource allocation in declining cities? Well, first of all, my hope for the older eastern cities is that their disequilibrium will reverse itself when the disequilibrium with the growing cities of the Southwest begins to reverse itself. I confidently predict—this is Roger Starr's rule of cyclical history—that the children of the people who came to my friend wanting to buy the Museum of

Modern Art will be saying in Houston thirty years from now that what we ought to have is buses to take our works of art, Giacometti no doubt, out to the Chicano section of the city so they can see what normal human being look like.   I have no doubt that the problems that we have in the eastern cities—the structural problems, the problems of consciousness raising or diminishing, or consciousness changing—will occur there. There will come a time when the eastern cities, with adequate land, all sewered, streets, electric light available, with labor that's been reduced to desperation, will look like a promising place in which to undertake economic activities which now people think should only be undertaken in the far west.

Obviously, for this to work out, two things are necessary.   One is that the nation as a whole must solve its fundamental economic problems, which I think are quite serious.   Second, we must not do anything to interfere with the ultimate attractiveness of the areas that are being largely depopulated in the older cities by foolishly investing federal largesse.   But the present government, under the influence of an egalitarian point of view, says things like the first deputy mayor of the City of New York: "No neighborhood in this city can be allowed to die.   They are all precious."   Presumably they are equally precious in the eyes of the city mothers.

Can Quotas, Tariffs, and Subsidies
Save the Northeast?

WILLIAM C. FREUND

Introduction

IN "The New Metropolitan and Regional Realities of America," professors George Sternlieb and James W. Hughes document the pervasive economic malaise of the Northeast relative to the nation in terms of people, jobs, and investments.[1]

During the past fifteen years, employment in the Northeast Region has risen less than 22 percent compared with 70 percent in the South. Manufacturing employment *declined* by 14 percent in the Northeast compared with an expansion of 41 percent in the South. Population as a whole increased some 22 percent in the South, more than double the northern rate. During the most recent five years, population grew less than 1 percent in the Northeast and 8.4 percent in the South. These overwhelmingly favorable statistics for the South were also reflected in per capita incomes. Between 1960 and 1975, per capita income grew 148 percent in the Northeast and 192 percent in the South. These are the facts. The problems exist.

The overwhelming task now is to explain these trends and to develop appropriate policies for dealing with them.

Reasons for the Decline

One of the basic reasons for the dramatic decline of the Northeast economy has been the startling post-war growth in the service industries. Since World War II, nearly the entire growth in employment has been in the services sector. In a recent article, Prof. Eli Ginzberg deplores the widespread failure of policymakers to appreciate this basic trend and to alter their policy prescriptions accordingly.[2] Attempts to develop manpower programs suitable for a predominantly manufacturing economy were doomed to failure as output shifted dramatically to services. Prof. Ginzberg shows that among the goods producing industries, only construction posted any sizable increase. Agricultural employment declined more than half since 1946—from 7.6 million to 3.5 million workers. Mining declined by approximately one-third. Manufacturing recorded a small absolute increase from 16 million to approximately 20 million workers, but in relative terms its share of total employment declined from 27 percent to 21 percent.

This new focus on services—including defense, education, and health—provides the background to one of the most important economic transformations in the United States. The full details and implications of this transformation have not been adequately examined or assessed. Overall, the goods producing industries—agriculture, mining, manufacturing, and construction—provided 45 percent of the jobs in 1948 and only 33 percent in 1974. By contrast, the share of services, including government, transportation, trade, utilities and finance, increased from 55 percent to 67 percent of total employment.

In viewing the services sector, policymakers generally tend to include only those enterprises catering to consumers directly, in the form of medical care, recreation, hairdressing, and the like. But there has also been a large growth in producer services, such as trucking, advertising, law, management consulting, and computer services. These are the support activities upon which basic industry has come to rely.[3]

For our purposes, the important factor to recognize is that many of the producer service industries did not exist when World War II ended. New and rapidly growing, they have become geographically decentralized. They did not shift from one location to another but grew up in new places where population growth was fastest and where the amenities of life made employment most desirable.

There are of course many other reasons for the emergence of new centers of employment opportunities. Our population has become incredibly mobile. To own a car is no longer a mark of distinction. Nearly every family now has four wheels. Remote places have become easily accessible. Along with the automobile has come an enormous public investment in transcontinental highways.

Further, the spread of low-cost air conditioning has made climatic conditions in all regions more homogeneous. It is no longer a burden to live in the Sunbelt during hot and humid summer months.

Professors Sternlieb and Hughes properly emphasize that what started out as the decline of the cities has spread like a cancer and has cast a shadow of decay over the entire industrial north. The suburban growth of the post-war years has now given way to regional and transcontinental expansion.

Contributing to this development has been the arteriosclerosis of the older regions. The aging of capital plant has rendered existing facilities less productive and competitive. The head start of northern industry has become a force of comparative disadvantage. A recent prospectus for the development of the Middle Atlantic region acknowledged that: "Since the economy of the mid-Atlantic region developed earlier than most other regions, key elements of its economic infrastructure were developed around an industrial, transportation/communication and energy technology different from today's and, in certain ways, unsuited to the needs of modern business and industry." [4]

Indeed, there is a kind of vicious circle of decline, with aging plants leading to abandonment, to higher taxes, to less productivity, to higher cost output, and in the end, to further abandonment. Economists have probably tended to overstate the actual migration of industry from north to south. Such migration does not seem to have been an important element in northern economic stagnation. What has happened is that many older firms have had to close and that new enterprises have flourished elsewhere, particularly with the spectacular growth of services. The more hospitable southern climate, the existence of broad tracts of land, low taxes, and low wages provided the initial pull. Population begat industry in a self-reinforcing cycle.

Other factors have also played a part. The relatively high cost of energy in the Northeast has undoubtedly undermined the economic performance of these states. In 1974, for example, the rate per thousand kilowatt hours of energy was 44 percent more in the Northeast than on average in the U.S., and 61 percent more than the average for the U.S. minus the Northeast. [5]

Policy Prescriptions

These trends are well understood. Indeed, their widespread appreciation has led to a new conventional wisdom: namely, that intensive federal, state, and local efforts must be adopted to reverse these trends. Both CONEG, the Coalition of Northeast Governors, as well as the proposed Mid-Atlantic Regional Action Planning Commission, have set as their task to restore the vitality of the old industrial north through new initiatives. From their point of view, such action is necessary and sensible. Governors have an obligation to their own electorate to provide jobs, to stimulate growth, and to ameliorate the hardship of residents within their states. But what may serve the local interest may be inconsistent with national objectives. Large-scale efforts to reverse basic economic trends may prove not only unproductive but counterproductive from a national perspective. Shoring up the inefficient through artificial stimuli reduces national productivity and efficiency. In short, I propose the unorthodox and perhaps even iconoclastic view that basic economic trends in the Northeast should be allowed to run their course.

What has been lacking in the debate on revitalizing the Northeast has been a clear and competent analysis of the extent to which the economic plight of the older industrial region has been due to natural economic forces and the extent to which it has resulted from government intervention.

So far, the presence and intensification of adverse fundamental economic factors have been stressed: aging industrial plants, shifts in population, the growth of services elsewhere, changes in technology, relatively high energy costs, and the vicious fiscal spiral which has been the inevitable outcome of these trends. But in addition to natural economic forces, there have been important policies, man-made in Washington, which have aggravated the northern loss of population, jobs, and incomes. There are no useful estimates of the extent to which the problems of the older Northeast have resulted from basic economic forces and the extent to which they have been triggered by policies adopted in Washington. Unless we know much more than at present about the relative importance of each in quantitative terms, it is impossible to prescribe appropriate national policies to deal with these trends. However, let us review briefly the two major federal policies which undoubtedly have aggravated the plight of the Northeast.

FEDERAL EXPENDITURES

A number of studies have shown that per capita federal spending in the Northeast has been lagging seriously behind expenditures elsewhere in the country. The ratio of federal spending to taxes has favored the South Atlantic Division (in particular Delaware, Maryland, Virginia, the Carolinas, Georgia, and Florida) at the expense of the six New England states and the Middle Atlantic Division of New York, New Jersey, and Pennsylvania.[6] In New Jersey for example, federal spending per person amounted to $1,154 in the full year 1975, compared to $1,412 for the United States as a whole. Moreover, per capita federal taxes collected totalled $1,760, making for a spending-tax relationship of 66 percent.

Clearly, spending and taxing should not always be equal in each and every state, but the Northeast Region seems to have been systematically shortchanged by the federal government over the last fifteen years. In effect, the North has been paying subsidies to the Sunbelt states. It is possible that federal programs were consciously designed to bring the South to a higher level of prosperity through regional income redistribution. But it seems doubtful that any master plan was involved. More likely, political pressures favored the South in federal contracts for defense, highways, rivers, and canals.[7] The whole question of the allocation of federal funds, and the formulas used in various programs to allocate such funds, needs careful review.

WELFARE PAYMENTS

Welfare has been a second major federal program disadvantaging the North. Alabama, for example, provides welfare benefits of about $30 a week for a family of four and receives 75 percent in federal reimbursements. New Jersey on the other hand receives a reimbursement of only 50 percent. This is not the place to examine the extent to which welfare payments are overly generous or miserly. The plight of New York in paying for its welfare costs is well known. From the national viewpoint of policies for dealing with the economic decline of the Northeast, the enormous problem of population flows and income subsidies stemming from welfare payments must be considered.

Comparative Disadvantage

At this point, it is possible to suggest that the decline of the Northeast, though exaggerated by discriminatory federal programs, would have occurred in any event. The importance of declining comparative advantage is a subject which cries out for intense study so that policy makers can distinguish between basic economic forces and man-made Washington policies.

The thrust of these remarks is quite simple. If we discover, as we probably will, that natural economic forces have played a dominant role in producing the economic decline of the Northeast, then policies designed to counter or reverse these trends will not only be futile but inconsistent with national objectives of economic growth and productivity.

The issues we are dealing with here, namely interfering with natural economic forces, are analogous to the economics of international trade. It has been a tenet of liberal economic thought that worldwide prosperity is enhanced by the unrestricted flow of trade. Yet, greater comparative efficiency in one region of the world can cause unemployment in another. Changing imports will displace jobs, cause dislocations, and engender suffering. The tendency is for governments to intervene by imposing tariffs and quotas on imports and to subsidize exports. But generations of economists since Ricardo have deplored such interference in the evolution of natural economic forces. Quotas, tariffs, and subsidies all serve in the long run to lower worldwide standards of living. Current efforts to reverse the industrial plight of the Northeast are akin to policies in the international trade field to preserve jobs in the face of shifting comparative trade advantages.

Populations are particularly immobile across national frontiers and cannot easily respond to job opportunities in other countries. Consequently, the dislocations caused by trade imbalances can create great personal hardships. Our federal government provides aid to industries and workers displaced by the international competition. Here again there is an analogy to regional economics. Although the mobility of population is significantly greater domestically than internationally, the dislocations caused by disparate economic growth in various regions cause hardships. Indeed, the brunt of the burden of slow growth or decline tends to be concentrated upon those income groups least able to bear the adjustment. In other words, the burden of adjustment constitutes a regressive tax. Consequently, there is a need to provide financial assistance to affected workers, their families, and employers. Programs should be developed to assist in the search for new jobs, in training and retraining workers to accept new opportunities, and to meet the expenses of relocating. Moreover, many older persons, in particular, will be unable to seize opportunities elsewhere and will require federal financial aid. It would seem particularly desirable to focus welfare assistance on older persons and incentive programs to retrain and relocate on the young. We should not ask the poor, the displaced, the unemployed to bear the brunt of the burden of adjusting to the dynamics of economic change.

Conclusion

The conclusion is really self-evident. To the extent that the economic decline of the Northeast has been due to federal programs such as defense, transit, and welfare expenditures, these programs need to be carefully reexamined. To the extent that the decline has been due to deep-seated, basic, longer-run economic forces, there should be no intervention in the form of artificial restraints or incentives. The most urgent need now is not to identify but to quantify the relative importance of these two major categories of influences on the economic plight of the Northeast.

Despite the skepticism about the likelihood of any short-term reversal of the basic trends discussed here, we should not believe that the outlook is inevitably gloomy for the long-term. Basic economic forces provide their own self-correction. It was inevitable that the gap between the rich North and the poor South would tend to be closed in an economy where there is free movement af resources. However, as the Sunbelt states enjoy a more rapid expansion, as they catch up with the industrial North in people and incomes, their economic growth too will slow. Wage scales will rise, unions will gain, densities will increase, land costs will mount, taxes will rise, and the process of comparative cost inflation will accelerate. We should have greater confidence in our free market forces to which we tend to pay more adherence in speeches than in regional and national economic policies.

In the closing pages of their paper, professors Sternlieb and Hughes raise the elemental question which should now be reaffirmed. Can we consciously and publicly face up to planned shrinkage where it is appropriate in the light of basic economic trends? Or are we forever to be dedicated to the theme "Revitalizing the Northeast" at any cost? More often than not, the action syndrome produces questionable long-term results.[8]

NOTES

1. Last fall, professors C.L. Jusenius and L.C. Ledebur prepared a paper entitled "A Myth in the Making: The Southern Economic Challenge and Northern Economic Decline." They disputed the conventional wisdom of the decline of the Northeasst and the rise of the Sunbelt. They detected little in the way of migration either of people and jobs. Unfortunately, they

relied solely on data for the period 1970 to 1975. Even during this period, they admit to a faster expansion of the Sunbelt states. But they question whether recent data foreshadow a longer-term trend or whether they show merely a cyclical downturn in the industrialized North occasioned by the most severe recession since World War II. The Sternlieb-Hughes paper puts to rest the feeble attempt by Jusenius and Ledebur to explain away exceedingly disturbing and well-documented trends since 1960.

2. Eli Ginzberg, "The Pluralistic Economy of the U.S.," *Scientific American*, December, 1976, pp. 25-29.

3. "Modern economic growth has been marked by successive shifts in employment from primary industries (agriculture and mining) to secondary industries (manufacturing) and from those to the tertiary sector (services); this latter sector has been subdivided and extended by Daniel Bell to the quantenary sector (exchange and information) and quinary sector (research and government)." Fred Hirsch, *Social Limits to Growth* (Cambridge, Mass.: Harvard University Press, 1976), p. 44.

4. "Mid-Atlantic Economic Development Region; Prospectus and Development," (An application for designation as a Title V Regional Action Planning Commission), February, 1977.

5. Data from *Ibid.*, p. 71. A sharp rise in the cost of energy undoubtedly will encourage a further movement of jobs and households away from older regions to energy-rich states such as Colorado. Texas, and Wyoming. Between 1970 and 1973, urban areas with highest costs of living had a net out-migration while those with the lowest experienced substantial in-migration. (See George Sternlieb and James W. Hughes, *Post-Industrial America: Metropolitan Decline and Inter-Regional Job Shifts*, (New Brunswick, N.J.: Rutgers University, Center for Urban Policy Research, 1975), p. 168.

6. *Ibid.*, p. 83.

7. There have been approximately eight times as many federally supported housing starts in the South as in the Northeast under Section 235 of the Housing Act. In the case of mass transit, one analyst recently noted that New Jersey received a 4-cent subsidy for every mass transit passenger in 1975 and New York 2 cents. But communities with fewer passengers received from 11 cents in Denver to 45 cents in Grand Rapids. The reason is that the funds are distributed on a formula related to population, not to mass transit riders. If the federal total of $300 million in 1975 had been allocated according to the average subsidy available per passenger (10¢ each), the MTA would have received $110 million more in 1975 and New Jersey another $10 million. The political problem is that about 40 percent of the nation's mass transit riders are in New York City. (Michael J. McManus, "Issues Facing the Northeast," Mimeographed (Fund for the City of New York, June, 1976), p. 29.)

8. Sternlieb and Hughes, *Post-Industrial America*, p. 22.

Federal Policy and Spatial Inequality

NORMAN I. FAINSTEIN
SUSAN S. FAINSTEIN

DOES GEOGRAPHY DETERMINE DESTINY? The connection between economic advantage and territory has been a preoccupation of American politics since the Great Compromise of the Constitution. Representatives from different parts of the country have always sought to use government to redress liabilities resulting from location and establish a political process that would benefit their areas. Sectional cleavages have sometimes crosscut class alignments; more often territorial boundaries have been used to enhance the accumulation of wealth through the generation of tax havens, captive low-wage labor pools, artificial scarcity of desirable land, and special subsidies. It is the purpose of this paper to discuss the ways in which national policy has affected sectional and infra-metropolitan imbalances, possible alternative policies, the relation between class and territorial interests, and the politics of geographical distribution.

The Character of Spatial Inequality

Territorial differences, expressed in concentrations of poor people in urban slums and declining rural areas, suburbanization, and movements of the more mobile population and industry to regions with high rates of development, have beset all the industrialized countries. The patterns for mass dislocation were set by the British enclosures of the eighteenth century, Parisian urban renewal of the nineteenth, and the flight of industry to areas offering low wage rates and minimal regulation throughout the period of industrialization.

The basic forces creating large-scale migration have always been the same. Capital can move quickly to areas which offer the most profitability. Some portions of the population are capable of moving with it and benefiting from higher levels of productivity; others are displaced by mechanization and move in hope of jobs or welfare, creating geographical pockets of destitution. The rise of the national conglomerate and the multinational corporation in the twentieth century has vastly increased the magnitude and rapidity of capital flows, which can now be easily achieved through the internal decisions of a single firm or consortium.

Territorial shifts and imbalances are not necessarily undesirable. Aggregate regional statistics for the United States indicate an overall national equalization of income (see Exhibit 1), though the South still lags behind. On the surface such an equalization, combined with the decentralization of industry which has caused it, would seem praiseworthy from an equity standpoint. Unfortunately the costs of dislocation are borne unequally, so that the marginal populations of regions suffering net outflows of jobs and capital are doubly disadvantaged by spatial as well as social status. One impact is revealed by unemployment figures (Exhibit 1). Even though the Northeast maintains an edge in per capita income, it suffers from higher rates of unemployment than the rest of the country because of the withdrawal of investment from the area and consequent negative multiplier effects, as well as because of the characteristics of the populations trapped in the old northern cities. In the United States in the last decade the movement of capital away from the Northeast and Central regions has been reinforced by governmental policies. The populations which have suffered the consequences have been largely uncompensated for their losses.

While attention has recently turned to regional shift, *intra*-metropolitan differences remain as extreme and intractable as ever.[1] Fiscal crisis has reinvigorated the lament over the inner city, as physical and social decay is recorded in the financial ledgers by revenue shortfalls. Certain of the same factors which produced urban-suburban differences, such as lower land costs, greater amenities, new transportation systems, flight

EXHIBIT 1

REGIONAL DISTRIBUTION OF PERSONAL INCOME, UNEMPLOYMENT, AND FEDERAL TAXING AND SPENDING

	Per capita personal income, 1975	Ratio, fed. expends. to tax revenue 1975[a]	Unemployment rate, 1975[b]
REGION AND DIVISION			
Northeast Region	$6,305	.86	10.2
Middle Atlantic[c]		.83	9.7
New England[d]		.96	11.4
North Central Region	$6,011	.76	8.5
East North Central[e]		.70	9.5
West North Central[f]		.94	6.0
South Region	$5,148	1.14	8.3
South Atlantic[g]		1.12	9.3
East South Central[h]		⎱ 1.17	8.2
West South Central[i]		⎰	6.7
West Region	$6,269	1.18	9.2
Mountain[j]		1.30	7.6
Pacific (excludes Hawaii, Alaska)[k]		1.13	9.8
U.S. Total	$5,834	1.00	8.9

NOTES: a. Amount of dollars spent per capita by the federal government divided by the per capita tax contribution.
   b. Rates derived from data supplied by state employment security agencies. Recalculated by region.
   c. New York, New Jersey and Pennsylvania.
   d. Maine, New Hampshire, Vermont, Massachusetts, Rhode Island, Connecticut.
   e. Ohio, Indiana, Illinois, Michigan, Wisconsin.
   f. Minnesota, Iowa, Missouri, Kansas, Nebraska, South Dakota, North Dakota.
   g. Delaware, Maryland, Virginia, West Virginia, North Carolina, South Carolina, Georgia, Florida.
   h. Kentucky, Tennessee, Alabama, Mississippi.
   i. Louisiana, Arkansas, Oklahoma, Texas.
   j. Montana, Idaho, Wyoming, Colorado, Utah, Nevada, Arizona, New Mexico.
   k. California, Oregon, Washington.

SOURCES: George Sternlieb and James W. Hughes, "The New Economic Geography of America," *supra;* "Special Report: Federal Spending: The North's Loss Is the Sunbelt's Gain," *National Journal,* 8 (June 26, 1976), p. 881; *Employment and Training Report of the President,* U.S.G.P.O., 1976, pp. 311-12.

from racial minorities and social disorder, have also contributed to regional migration. As we shall discuss below, federal policies have stimulated the movement of population and employment both within and
among regions.[2]

National Policy and Territorial Development

The United States, unlike the Western European nations, lacks any
explicit policy of urban and regional development beyond a vague commitment to reducing inequalities among regions and within metropolitan
areas. Nevertheless, many federal policies have important implications
for the distribution of industry and population, despite the frequent
failure to take account of their consequences. The kinds of policies
which have the most important effects on geographical distribution of
resources can be summarized under five headings: (1) taxation, (2)
direct governmental investment, (3) direct governmental expenses, (4)
regulation and its absence, and (5) subsidies. Their manifold impacts
will be dealt with only briefly and illustratively here.

TAXATION

The use of the federal tax system to stimulate new investment contributes to industrial mobility. Investment tax credits and fast depreciation write-offs mean that sunk investment can lose its monetary value
well before it exhausts its use value. In other words, tax incentives
often make it irrational for a firm to maintain aging equipment. Instead
it becomes more profitable for the individual firm to jettison the old
in favor of more modern capital goods. Profitability for the individual
firm, however, may result in an aggregate social loss if the cost of new
equipment plus tax relief minus productivity gains exceeds the cost of
operating with old plant (i.e., even if social costs exceed social benefits).
Once firms decide to build new plan, differential wage rates and local
subsidies furnish inducements to change location.

DIRECT GOVERNMENTAL INVESTMENT

In addition to the obvious examples of government investment contributing to population dispersion, such as the development of the interstate highway network, there are more subtle effects. Many commenta-
tors have cited the cheap energy advantages of the western states, even
though these states are far worse off in terms of water supply. The
federal government bears much of the enormous expense of water resource creation in the West, while the user bears only the operating

costs. In fact, without federal investment in massive water resource projects, much of the West would be uninhabitable. Cheap energy itself results only partly from proximity to gas and oil reserves; much of it is attributable to the federal investment in hydroelectric facilities and public ownership of utilities. In contrast, eastern energy consumers must pay much of the price for the development of energy resources as well as the profits of private power companies.

DIRECT GOVERNMENTAL EXPENSES

Here the effects of federal activity have not escaped notice. Congressmen and senators are quick to assess the impact of any federal expenditure program on their region and to compete for contracts and payroll. The northern and central states have largely lost out in this contest, however, as funds, particularly defense contracts and payroll, have flowed to the South and West (Exhibit 1). This regional bias in expenditures has a number of causes, including the seniority system in Congress, southern dominance of the military services, and the inertial effect of past patterns of expenditures. Its impact on capital formation has been cumulative and accounts for many of the Northeast's present difficulties in attracting investment.

REGULATION AND ITS ABSENCE

Federal regulation of interstate commerce and the constitutional prohibition against the levying of import duties by states moderate to some extent the tendency toward local mercantilism. But for the most part subordinate political jurisdictions in the United States are encouraged to attract industries to locate within their borders. Reliance on local property taxes, locally administered; the existence of right-to-work laws; differentials in welfare benefits and service provision levels; local or state subsidies to industries; locally conceived and administered land use statutes; the total absence of national priorities for the location of investment and population; the unimpeded migration of jobs and people—all these factors contribute to inter- and intra-regional differentials. Americans take geographical competition for granted. But as will be discussed below, no invisible hand assures that competition produces a least cost result for the nation as a whole. Rather each jurisdiction, in order to survive, is forced to externalize as many costs as possible— to encourage dependent populations to migrate elsewhere; attract investment even if that investment could be used more productively in another location; keep down local wage rates; discourage unionism. As a result, some areas have a contrived advantage, others become the dumping grounds for social problems, and disadvantaged groups bear the costs while those in protected enclaves reap the benefits. Conservative economists are quick to see the price of federal interference in economic decisionmaking, but reluctant to see it when intervention occurs at state and local levels.

SUBSIDIES

Governmental subsidies take two forms: they can be directed at the suppliers of infrastructure or services (e.g., public housing, worker training programs, hospital construction), or they can assist consumers (e.g., rent allowances, FHA mortgage guarantees, Medicaid). The former mode of subsidy has largely been opposed by liberal economists as inefficient and more directly beneficial to governmental employees who supply services than to needy clients.

Federal subsidies can also be differentiated according to whether they are categorical or general; and whether they are automatic (e.g., Aid to Families with Dependent Children, general revenue sharing) or responsive to specific application (e.g., housing rehabilitation programs, educational innovation). On these dimensions current economic wisdom encourages what are viewed as more efficient market processes through revenue sharing and formula distribution.

The effect of recent trends in federal subsidies is to reduce even further federal determination of locational priorities. Supplier oriented subsidies, categorical grants, and targeted aid, while suffering from some obvious drawbacks, do allow national policymakers scope for national planning. Specific programmatic aid provides federal officials with inducements that are otherwise lacking. In contrast, automatic subsidies additionally stimulate inter-jurisdictional competition. The refusal of advantaged areas to use their funds for low-income housing or mass transit further excludes needy groups from their jurisdictions, thus reinforcing initial advantages. Areas without deprived populations use their funds instead to develop more amenities, thereby increasing property values and becoming even more exclusionary.[3]

OVERALL IMPACT OF GEOGRAPHICAL COMPETITION

Federal policy then, if only by default, provides the parameters within which local and regional rivalries for prosperous populations and industries take place.[4] There are at least three arguments which try to explain the present system: (1) the invisible hand, (2) the natural tendency toward interregional equilibrium, and (3) the demands of international competition. We will discuss each briefly.

The invisible hand. This argument makes an analogy between the competition among firms, as presented in classical economic theory, and that among locations.[5] But the dubious assumptions that permit market economists to deduce an identity between individual and social rationality within the economic system are transparently invalid in the territorial system. The most important one concerns the impact of poor performance. In the market model a bankrupt firm simply disappears —its owners bear the brunt of failure, and consumers benefit from the triumph of the most efficient producers. Massachusetts or Illinois, however, cannot simply vanish, regardless of its inability to increase per capita product or meet the needs of its citizenry. The costs of its maintenance thus continue to be borne by resident populations and the federal government. Moreover, the effect of losing out in the Darwinian struggle is a vicious circle of further losses as employable workers depart, tax base declines, investment goes elsewhere, and the costs of production increase. Cutbacks in services in New York City and other old industrial areas hasten the flight of those able to leave and increase the needs of those who stay.

The tendency toward interregional equilibrium. The claim here is that lagging regions tend to catch up with leading ones because they are not burdened with obsolete plant; they can take advantage of new technologies; and they offer attractions to industry of low wage labor and unexploited resources. These arguments, however, only apply to previously undeveloped areas and offer little hope to those which are declining because their infrastructure is decrepit and their populations dependent. Moreover, the catching up process is often achieved through the expulsion of surplus populations. Because much of southern poverty has moved to the North, while rich northerners now reside south of the Mason Dixon line, the South is deemed to be pulling even with the rest of the country. But, if one's ultimate concern is equity among people rather than places, the mode by which interregional balance is achieved becomes crucial. Regional equalization of per capita income does not necessarily imply equalization among social groups.

Demands of international competition. According to this reasoning, factories must locate where production costs are lowest so that the United States will be able to compete with low-wage or highly capitalized industries abroad. Calculations of competitive advantage, however, usually do not include the overall national costs of production. For example, if a New Jersey firm moves to Texas and reduces its energy bill but causes New Jersey to pay unemployment compensation to its former employees exceeding in amount the energy savings, then the improvement in national competitive position is illusory. Rather the costs of production are shifted. To the extent that moving creates costs external to the firm which are borne by government, national productive efficiency does not increase even though there may be greater private profit. The national cost of these added government expenses will appear either in inflation or higher taxation.

Whether or not decentralization and shifts in production in the United States have created overall gains and greater regional equity is extremely difficult to calculate. Such an accounting requires introducing numerous qualifications into the equation. It is, however, clear that the movements that have taken place have been largely unplanned, while other advanced industrialized nations now have a lengthy history of conscious policy toward investment, migration, land use, and industrial location as well as more generous programs for the maintenance of dependent populations.[6] It should be noted that while some nations (e.g., England) have lagged economically, others (Sweden, Denmark, West Germany) have prospered and exceeded the United States in their rates of economic growth. The United States now stands fourth internationally in per capita gross national product behind Switzerland, Sweden, and Denmark, and barely ahead of Norway and West Germany.[7]

Policies of European Governments

All the major European countries have explicit planning programs aimed at directing the flow of resources and population to relatively disadvantaged regions. These policies are centrally controlled and involve restrictions on investment in developed regions, incentives to growth in designated development areas, and direct governmental investment in productive enterprise and housing as well as subsidization of labor costs. Until recently, designated development areas were in relatively unpopulated locations, since policy was designed to siphon population from the major cities. Now that some of the European countries are beginning to experience shifts of population and employment which threaten the viability of urban areas, programs are being revised to reverse the flows that once were encouraged.

Land use and population migration are controlled through required regional or national planning permission for new residential construction by private developers, public ownership of land, and direct government activity within the large public housing sector. The long waiting time to obtain public housing in most European countries strongly limits residential mobility and contributes to the attractiveness of new towns as housing units become available within them. Restrictions on land development, the small size and low profitability of the private rental market, and confiscatory taxation of speculative gains on land in some countries prevent opportunistic development. In the United States the absence of controls contributes to overinvestment and subsequent economic contraction.

European systems of taxation and finance also limit the private gains which can be reaped from locational advantage. No European country depends heavily on the local property tax; thus, jurisdictions do not, on the one hand, benefit financially from excluding low income residents and, on the other, have little incentive to compete for ratables. In England where there is some reliance on local rates, a national equalization formula compensates areas with low property valuation. European systems of education, with their heavy use of examinations and tracking, do not require middle class parents to live in a homogeneous neighborhood in order to obtain the academic benefits of class stratification for their children.[8]

Central banks, which are the repositories of a large percentage of private savings in Europe and carry on their investment programs in line with national policies, also contribute to the greater ability of those countries to set national priorities. Central bankers are no more likely to accept risk than private ones. But they are not inclined toward speculation; they have sufficient resources to overcome threshold effects; and they can await long-term gains. As a result they are willing to fund enterprises in development areas where front end costs are high and returns are far off.

European policies of regulation and centralized planning have their price. Restrictions on movement clash with individual freedom; bureaucratic clearance procedures are endlessly time consuming; housing shortages continue to be severe; planned communities often produce monotony, inconvenience, and generally inhospitable surroundings. Those policies, however, which keep local and regional jurisdictions from competing to bring in ratables, exclude undesirables, and shelter investments have fewer social costs. While many Americans would regard it as unconscionable if their community did not have the power to entice industry or decide on the package of services it offers its citizens, many Europeans would consider it equally preposterous that such decisions should be made at the local level. The benefits of jurisdictional competition, except to those who live in well-off areas, are doubtful at best, yet this form of competition is the major determinant of the American landscape.

Social Policy

European welfare programs are older and more comprehensive than American ones. They go far to mitigate the effects of capitalist economies on groups which are unable to purchase a decent standard of living and personal security in the private market. Enacted in response to threats from the left, and often under the auspices of social democratic governments, welfare measures have nonetheless been mainly the accomplishments of state bureaucrats.[9] The model remains largely as set by Bismarck. According to one observer:

> It is noteworthy that the great economic reforms of the nineteenth century were not the work of parliaments and political parties but of public servants like Stein and Bismarck. . . . The administrative officialdom adopted the attitude that it represented the interests of the state against the conflicting interests of individuals and groups. In this attitude, which was most fully incorporated in Bismarck, the bureaucracy perpetuated an important aspect of the concept of monarchical absolutism, which was that the prince is the supreme arbiter of the national interest over and above the conflicting claims of his subjects.[10]

Again, uniform national policy prevents local and regional jurisdictions from dumping their externalities onto less fortunate areas. The poor need not be supported by the tax base of the locality in which they reside. Thus, the phenomena of geographical fiscal inequities, the flight of the prosperous from urban areas, differential welfare payments and health care eligibility standards, exclusionary zoning, and overburdened municipal services are either avoided or minimized.

Welfare policies in Europe have largely ceased to make distinctions between deserving and undeserving recipients. Numerous incentives in the form of training programs and subsidies help to return the able-bodied unemployed to the job market. But most programs, such as family allowances, housing subsidies, health services, and old age pensions are designed to provide universal coverage and a minimum benefit regardless of individual contribution. Government intervention in the lives of citizens is accepted, and no one expects that the private market and "trickle down" will remedy the consequences of inequality.

This brief summary of European directions is not intended to show that inequality and uneven development can disappear as a result of governmental intervention in capitalist societies. Nor is it meant to demonstrate that lower class interests prevail in European societies. A number of Marxist critics have made convincing arguments that statism in Europe serves the interests of the business class in maintaining social peace and producing long-term financial gains for the class as a whole.[11] Nevertheless, the well-being of the lower classes is better served when the state acts as their protector, even within the limits of capitalism, than when it does not.[12] The remainder of this paper is devoted to examining the political circumstances which have produced the divergence in the development of the national state in Europe and America and analyzing whether any political forces exist likely to produce changes here more in accordance with the European model.

The Structure of American Government

When someone mentions the state, Americans immediately want to know which one—New Jersey, Mississippi, Texas? We have fifty states but only the vaguest idea of *the* state in the sense well understood by Europeans: the system of administrative, parliamentary, and judicial agencies, along with the army and police, which stands as a sovereign political power apart from, and above, society and economy. Americans do have ideas about "government," however, and these ideas, often very deeply rooted in the national culture, help in part to account for the fragmentation of the American state system and the consequent difficulty of conceptualizing the state as a single entity.

Most thinking about government in this country, especially about the federal government, is oriented in terms of potential dangers. Ideological differences are relatively minor when viewed within the context of cultural assumptions which make most Americans unusually fearful of a strong state. Government, Americans feel, is basically unproductive; it only expropriates resources created in the private economy, wastes many in its cumbersome administration, and redistributes those which remain. It threatens individual freedom and initiative both because it is powerful and because its very largesse leads to a paternalism fostering dependency and low productivity. Most of the symbolism in American political debate centers about how to limit the state, not how to capture it and direct its power.

The reality of the American state system is, in part, completely at odds with these dominant ideas and, in part, very much shaped by them. On the one hand, corporate capitalism depends on government to subsidize private production, and local government relies on the federal fisc for support. But on the other hand, the state itself is prohibited from directly engaging in "profitmaking" activities, and the national government is largely prevented from coordinating and planning the activities it finances. In fact, the single most striking aspect of the American state is its fragmentation. The national government not only controls less of the means of production than any other under similar conditions of advanced capitalism, it also has the least central political control over its own means of administration. This fragmentation appears in the vertical layering of federal authority, as well as horizontally at each level of organization.

THE EXECUTIVE BRANCH

We have no national center of political control. The executive is limited in its ability to formulate and fund programs by the domestic legislative authority of Congress. Thus, the president can make foreign policy, not to mention war, with considerable autonomy, but cannot reorganize the executive departments without congressional approval. In contrast to the ease with which several administrations did as they pleased in Vietnam, it took more than a decade to establish HUD, and even then only at the cost of dropping the original conception of a Department of Urban Affairs.[13]

The overall weakness and fragmentation of the American state is further reflected in the divisions of administrative authority within the executive branch. Many departments and agencies are responsible for elements of what might constitute a national urban program. Commerce, HUD, Labor, HEW—each has its own interest group clientele and its distinct relations with particular committees in Congress. There is no effective cabinet system dependent on party discipline to design and coordinate programs at both the legislative and implementation stages. Tight administrative control is made even more difficult by the absence of a permanent civil service elite to maintain the continuity of state activities in the face of changing elected officials.

CONGRESS

The formal authority vested in Congress provides a check on executive planning of domestic policy, but this veto power is not matched by a congressional ability to itself initiate policy. Congress is particularly handicapped as an institutional source of national urban policy. House members each represent a relatively small territory and depend for reelection on their ability to satisfy the important interests in their districts. While national investment planning requires the establishing of priorities in allocation, the logic of the House has always been to strive for reciprocity, to effect a politics of log-rolling. The executive exacerbates this tendency by using federal allocations to gain compliance from individual congressmen and women. The territorial basis of Senate representation produces a similar—though less acute—dynamic. The fate of the Economic Development Administration (EDA) programs, intended to channel national investment into planned development areas, is typical. Congressional pressure transformed a weak, albeit well-intentioned, effort at establishing critical masses of federal resources in *particular* areas into an allocation of trivial amounts of aid to many areas.[14] The same thing happened to Model Cities.

Spatial inequality *within* congressional districts and, of course, entire states further limits representation of the older cities. Congressmen who directly represent these urban areas constitute a distinct minority. Their power is further diluted by personal and partisan rivalries and the greater turnover of urban representatives in a seniority system of committee chairmanships. The usual disarray of the New York City delegation is a case in point. The only way in which specifically urban interests in diverse regions are united in the legislature is through such lobbies as the National Conference of Mayors and the liberal caucus of the Democratic party. Even so, the urban force is relatively weak and breaks down entirely when regional allocation decisions are involved. The one region which has been consistently represented in Congress is the South.

COURTS

The federal judiciary, the third branch of the national government, is both quite independent of electoral or administrative political control and internally fragmented into district and appellate courts. This judicial government is de facto a source of much national urban policy. Even, however, with the Supreme Court as ultimate arbiter, the individual federal courts make policy without much consistency or concern for the actual effects of rulings rationalized as interpretations of law. The courts have promulgated a series of strikingly inconsistent decisions in recent years which directly affect, among other things, the possibilities of regional planning and governance, the power of localities to exclude undesirable industry and people, and the method of financing public education. Two examples of judicial power and disorganization will suffice. District courts in several states have applied the one-man-one-vote Supreme Court decision to efforts at creating regional govern-ment agencies (council of governments). In doing so they have immersed themselves in a quagmire of clearly political decisions, have been contradictory in their decisions, and, in general, have created a climate of uncertainty inimical to innovation in metropolitan govern-ance.[15]

Consider the irrationality of a second pair of cases. Within a period of two months during the spring of 1977, federal district and appellate courts ruled first that the rights of bondholders precluded further in-volvement of the Port of Authority of New York and New Jersey in mass transit, and second, that environmental protection required New York City to reduce week-day auto traffic 20-50 percent (according to conflicting interpretations) regardless of the economic impact of such a move.[16] The American situation, where separate courts can and do make public policy on this scale, is unique among industrial nations. The aggregate impact of the judicial system is to provide another obstacle to national planning, and further, to block particularly those initiatives which are deemed to conflict with the property rights of individuals.

FEDERALISM

Fragmentation in the central government is reproduced within each of the fifty states and in the loose connections between them and Washington. The federal system amounts to a public marketplace in which the national government tries to affect its citizens by providing inducements to the actual "owners" of the means of public administra-tion: state and local governments.

The national government has, of course, advanced many programs in recent years aimed at targeting resources to particularly deprived localities and social groups, as well as at encouraging planning on both the state and municipal levels. But their impact in reducing spatial inequality has been limited by severe problems of implementation arising from the public marketplace structure of the federal system. By accept-ing the "property rights" of state and local governments, the federal government has limited itself largely to subsidizing those activities which are compatible with local interests. Federal aid programs thus reinforce the very processes they could be checking, whether it is the migration of AFDC families to northern states with relatively generous welfare and Medicaid programs or the concentration of public housing in old central cities.

PARTIES

The character of the American political party system reinforces the mobilization of institutional bias against national planning and welfare programs. Neither the Republican nor the Democratic party is a national entity. Both are rooted locally, and increasingly in candidates' organizations rather than the party hierarchy. As a result, the parties play little role in unifying the federal administration, in aggregating local interests into coherent programs which then structure electoral choices, or in orchestrating the implementation of national policy. Recent empirical evidence shows that an already weak party system is further disintegrating.[17]

Interrelated with these organizational aspects is the narrow ideological spectrum reflected in the parties and American debate about public policy. There is no statist-elitist conservative party in the United States, and no major party resembling even the most mild mannered of the European socialist parties. American political leaders share the cultural assumptions outlined earlier. The party most linked to the business class has no ideology congruent with twentieth century reality: Republicans fall back on laissez faire ideas which would appear curious to their European counterparts. Where the left of the Democratic party differs is in somewhat less fear of national planning and in its greater commitment to using government as a mechanism for equality of opportunity. There is no significant force committed to equality of condition or antagonistic to the values and social relations of capitalism. This party system—and the politics associated with it—is the most immediate "cause" of the underdevelopment of welfare state programs in the United States.

It is also part of a larger set of factors: the parties continuously re-educate the public to dismiss fundamental policy alternatives on the one hand, and they institutionalize underlying class relations on the other. Thus, the forces which confine national planning and welfare policy cannot be described adequately without venturing into the un-American activity of class analysis.

Class Politics

Certain relationships are fundamental to all capitalist economies. The business class controls capital and the process of production; through its market power it makes most decisions with regard to investment and pricing, and is rewarded in the form of profits, rent and interest, as well as in the high wages which go with executive jobs. Yet individual businessmen or firms operate in a more or less competitive situation, the logic of which may be quite narrowly defined and short run—to make a profit for a *particular* company, bank, or department store, not to secure the profit situation and social control of business in general. The business class by itself cannot overcome the anarchy of capitalist competition and fragmentation; in short, it cannot plan *collectively*. For this it requires the state (Marx's "executive committee of the bourgeoisie"). As we have seen, however, there is considerable variation among capitalist nations in state activity of this kind.

Analysts of divergent political persuasions have argued that rational planning of urban development is in the long-run interest of business as a whole; Marxists tend not only to take this for granted but to assume that business, especially big business, will therefore support state planning. Welfare programs, as distinct from planning, are usually interpreted as benefiting business only indirectly in maintaining social peace and aggregate demand. Our task is to account for the relative underdevelopment of planning *and* welfare in the United States, both of which seem highly problematic from the American perspective. Let us consider planning first.

LACK OF BUSINESS SUPPORT FOR NATIONAL PLANNING

One place to begin is with the mentality of the American business class as a social group. Here, two aspects are immediately important. The first is attitudes toward the federal government which must be, after all, the instrumentality of national urban policy and planning. On the whole, business people see government as at best a somewhat hostile force in a free enterprise system, and national government as more dangerous than local.

The second aspect of the mentality of the business class which affects American urban policy involves business orientation to the city itself. Americans, and the upper classes most especially, seem to have less attachment to an urban style of life than other nationalities. American business is relatively indifferent, or even hostile, to urban locations for its firms; as individuals, business people prefer a suburban existence. These locational preferences contribute on the one hand to the exit from urban settings of jobs and population, and on the other to relatively little concern within the business class as a whole over the loss of our urban resources.

It would be misleading, however, to stop at this level of analysis. The business class contains within it divergent economic interests which further explain our difficulties with urban policy and planning. We do have some urban planning in America; we have practically no national and regional planning. There are many efforts at regulation, public capital investment, and the enticement of businesses and people—but all at the local level. The situation is quite varied. In some cities (Pittsburgh, Detroit) a leading business actor has been sufficiently concerned (whether for economic reasons or not) with preserving urban investment to lead efforts at renewal. In other cities (New Haven, Philadelphia) this role has been played by selected officials with strong business support. Often neither route has been followed; businesses have chosen to leave rather than attempt to reshape the urban environment, even in their own image. The particular response seems to be conditioned by a complex interplay of specific business interests, local chauvinism, and, in no small part, individual entrepreneurship. On a micro level, businesses have thus taken some part in rationalizing urban development, but on a regional and national level urban islands of "progress" exist at the expense of resources drawn from other areas which decline even more rapidly as a result.

Beyond this, many business actors have an economic interest which is more apparent and immediate in maintaining spatial segregation and uneven development than in any rationalizing effort. As individual consumers, homeowners, and residents, business people benefit from geographical stratification. As representatives of corporate interests, they may depart from declining areas and thereby avoid the costs of maintaining their aging infrastructures and surplus populations. Landlords may be able to extract monopoly rents from slum districts without investing in improvements in the quality of the housing stock. When profits cease, they walk away. Builders and realtors create the pattern of urban development which government intervention seeks to check. City financial institutions export capital for residential mortgages in suburbs and need worry only about being robbed in the declining neighborhoods of their home offices. And those businesses which *do* have a big stake in preserving the city may be highly competitive, fearful of government, and simply unable to express and enforce a collective interest.

Big business as a whole has not pushed for a national urban program and has, in fact, resisted efforts which directly benefit particular firms and segments of the class.[18] Thus, urban renewal, while shaped to favor business, received relatively little corporate support in Washington and was always a relatively small program with total expenditures to date barely $10 billion. Even more striking, perhaps, was business reluctance to encourage development of the national highway program.

Except for the auto, trucking, and petrochemical interests, there was considerable opposition within the Eisenhower administration to the establishment of the national highway trust fund. Eisenhower himself had to be convinced that inter-city highways were within the scope of the federal government. Advocacy by a few corporate leaders, foundations, and lobbies like the CED for greater state planning and rationalization is the exception on the American business scene, not the rule. Without a strong governmental administrative elite to create and enforce a corporate vision of urban policy within the business class, national planning is replaced by corporate strategies for maximizing the direct interests of each firm in a spatially fragmented environment.

NO CLASS SUPPORT FOR WELFARE PROGRAMS

The limited nature of welfare state activities in the United States can be explained more readily than the absence of planning. The key here lies in both the lack of working class organization and the historically interrelated weakness of the state. The American working class stands deeply divided along racial, ethnic, and communal lines, and largely dominated by a middle-class ideology. Without a significant socialist or labor party committed, in theory at least, both to advancing class solidarity and welfare state measures, it is caught within a politics of status whereby its concerns are focused more on minority group threats than on upper class domination. Moreover, parts of the working class have a stake in preserving the spatial inequalities from which its better-off members benefit as suburban homeowners. It remains tied to the interests of local businesses and their ability to make money and provide jobs. It is highly ambivalent about welfare state programs, supporting those tied to work (Social Security, unemployment insurance) and hostile to those associated, however incorrectly, with "the dole" and minority groups (AFDC).

White working class families who have escaped from the city have a stake in preserving suburban capsulation. The ones who remain attempt even more desperately to maintain the boundaries of their neighborhoods, frequently against the planners who are viewed as representing a combination of business and minority group interests. Trade unions are concerned with keeping their well-established relations with local officials; they have little ideological commitment to greater national planning and insufficient power in Washington to effect legislation which they do claim to support, e.g., national health insurance. In short, then, the disorganized American working class is caught by a system of spatial and class stratification within which it defines its short-run interests in ways that do not threaten the system.

Even given these divisions, however, working class representatives from part of the union establishment and the left wing of the Democratic party stand as the main source of pressure for welfare state measures. But the business class, unthreatened by the spectre of a socialist movement, identifies welfare state programs with radicalism and remains intransigent. The state, already weak in America, cannot advance welfare measures as a national "mediating" solution to the demand of business for profits on the one hand, and those of the working class for socialization of the means of production and equality on the other. The lack of business class support for national urban policy is matched by the lack of working class power to expand welfare state programs. Overall, class politics contribute to the severity of urban development problems in the United States without generating a social force which might advance a solution.

New Directions

Major planning and welfare state initiatives have been taken by the federal government largely during periods of crisis, though the start of programs has by no means assured their permanence. Economic collapse and popular unrest precipitated Social Security and AFDC, both of which later took on a scope never intended by their initiators. Other Depression programs such as WPA and NIRA, however, disappeared quickly. World War II brought national economic planning, but the end of conflict just as rapidly permitted the dismantling of almost the entire set of institutions which had been created. The civil rights movement and ghetto rebellion produced a climate of urgency which contributed to the establishment of OEO, yet within a decade the priorities of Vietnam and the Republican opposition turned most innovative programs aimed at mobilizing inner city resources into empty shells. While crises have generated limited and tentative response, the "normal" situation has spawned even fewer initiatives. Assuming continuity in past American patterns, we can ask what is likely to be done about the spatial inequality and uneven development now evident to observers with quite different politics.

Intra-metropolitan inequality is supported by fundamental institutional and class arrangements in a way that regional disparity is not. The two problems, while mutually reenforcing, do not require the same magnitude of effort from the national government to be significantly mitigated and should be considered separately. Simply put, there can be no great reduction in city-suburban disparities and improvement in the life of the urban poor without major innovations in national planning and welfare programs—and these are unlikely.

The last decade produced two approaches which might have furthered metropolitan equity. The first was to pump resources into central cities —either directly, through such spatially defined programs as public housing, urban renewal, community action and Model Cities; or indirectly, through AFDC, Medicaid, aid to education, and similar programs targeted to populations concentrated in urban core areas. The second was to redistribute metropolitan resources by moving people or capital—efforts at open housing and bussing or prohibiting redlining are obvious examples.

The impact of all these programs has been limited. The national government has never funded programs of the first kind at a level high enough to rebuild the cities or reduce relative income disparities; those of the second kind have generated a zero sum politics among city neighborhoods and metropolitan localities—witness the enormous conflict associated with metropolitan school integration. In spite of national concern, and not all of it merely symbolic, there has been almost no improvement in the relative position of central cities or their trapped populations in the last ten years.

Two kinds of crises might force renewed attention to old central cities. The first is rebellion. We saw that in the sixties, and it may come again. But for the time being minority groups have ceased to constitute a major political force. Part of the reason for this stems from the policies of city governments to quiet unrest through social expenditures. These very activities have produced the second sudden deterioration in the urban scene—fiscal crisis. So far, however, the imminent fiscal collapse of New York and other cities has not caused the national government to expand its planning and welfare roles. Rather, it has become a test to see how much urban social services could be cut back without producing popular explosions. The answer has been quite a bit.

New York City was made into an example of how local governments must strive to keep public needs in line with local revenues. Robert Gerard, former (Republican) assistant secretary responsible for overseeing U.S. treasury loans to New York, put the matter bluntly:

> If we say to New York that we will lend it money to finance an operating deficit in the current budget, we are saying, "Spend what you need to spend, and if your revenues won't cover it, we'll roll the presses to make up the difference." That's honoring the principle of federalism, which is

noninterference in local fiscal decision-making. But if we find that unacceptable, and I fear that it is, then . . . national government policies would determine local priorities. That to me is as unacceptable as turning the printing presses over to the mayors and governors. Is it ever necessary for the federal government to fund deficit spending at the state or local levels? I conclude that it is not.[19]

New York City was "saved," then, only through delegation of public authority to the business community, because its bankruptcy would have hurt capital. William Proxmire, Democratic chairman of the Senate Banking Committee explains:

I saw it as a national problem. If New York went bankrupt it would be an absolute nightmare. . . . The effect on the banking system would have been serious . . . because the banks are so heavily invested in municipals, and all municipals would have been in trouble. The Federal Reserve would have really been busy.[20]

The Carter administration has been more responsive than Nixon-Ford to big city interests. It, however, has made no movement toward national planning of urban development. Its only welfare state initiative has been to propose reform of AFDC but not increase fiscal support for the program. The Democratic coalition represented by the Carter presidency is not likely to overhaul the fragmented governmental structures and class arrangements that reproduce intra-regional inequality. Liberal Democrats will push for more public service employment and change in federal aid formulas, but avoid entirely the underlying structures created by segmented labor markets and fiscal encapsulation. Thus, Henry Reuss, in a recent publication of his House Subcommittee on the City, interestingly entitled "Toward a National Urban Policy," assures us that "despite adversity, the American city *does* seem to have a future." But he dismisses the idea of a "massive Washington-centered" program like the Marshall Plan, and leaves to state and local governments the responsibility for conserving neighborhoods, land use controls, reforming political institutions, and reducing suburb-city fiscal disparities.[21]

There is reason to be more sanguine about the problems of inter-regional uneven development. The discovery of regional shift and the relative decline of the Northeast and Midwest came as a shock to political leaders partly because their attention has long been focused on intra-regional inequality—on how to keep social costs bottled up in central cities. Suddenly, "us" and "them" were in the same ship— at least to some extent. But the ship has two classes of accommodations, and the life boats are on the upper deck.

Inequality and political structure need not be attacked to revitalize the Northeast suburbs. The national government can have a relatively significant policy impact simply by taking greater cognizance of the effects of its own public investment (power, water), taxation, and aid activities. Here, then, there is more hope, though we can expect little movement toward national planning solutions. Instead, we will maintain our present system of regional competition, state economic development programs, and the like. Besides a possible redirection of federal policies which have contributed to the problem, we may see new initiatives along the lines of a regional development bank for the Northeast (an idea attractive to important segments of the financial community) and perhaps also some new energy and transportation programs.

The Northeast and Midwest may, therefore, be revitalized under this administration, but the festering problems of American urbanization will continue to worsen. If anything, the gap will widen between America and the European welfare/planning states in their ability to control urban conditions. American backwardness does not result from lack of knowledge ar example. As we have briefly recounted, European countries have presented us with many policy models. To be sure, those countries have not always been effective in implementing policies limiting urban malaise. Nevertheless, the United States is alone among advanced industrial nations in allowing capitalist accumulation to proceed largely outside the confines of national governmental planning and welfare measures. The explanation for American divergence lies in the uniqueness of the political system. There is no political force to demand a coherent national urban and regional policy, even one which would only require the short-term discipline of business interests to assure their long-run aims. Nor is there the basis for such a force. The future then is one of continued social inequality and uneven development, devoid of the comfort that we are still the richest country on earth.

NOTES

1. See Richard Child Hill, "Separate and Unequal: Governmental Inequality in the Metropolis," *American Political Science Review* 68 (December 1974): 1,557-68.

2. See esp. Roger E. Alcaly and David Mermelstein, eds., *The Fiscal Crisis of American Cities* (New York: Vintage, 1977) for a number of enlightening discussions of the underlying causes and important consequences of fiscal crisis and uneven development.

3. See David Harvey, "Class-Monopoly Rent, Finance Capital and the Urban Revolution," in Stephen Gale and Eric G. Moore, eds., *The Manipulated City* (Chicago: Maaroufa Press, 1975), pp. 145-67.

4. See Ann R. Markusen, "Class and Urban Social Expenditures: A Local Theory of the State," *Kapitalistate,* nos. 4-5 (Summer 1976): 50-65.

5. Charles M. Tiebout, "A Pure Theory of Local Expenditures," *Journal of Political Economy* 64 (October 1956): 416-24.

6. See James L. Sundquist, *Dispersing Population: What America Can Learn from Europe* (Washington: Brookings Institution, 1957) for an excellent study of European locational policies. For a comparison of the post-tax, post-transfer income distributions of the OECD countries, see Malcolm Sawyer, "Income Distribution in OECD Countries," *Occasional Studies* (OECD), July 1976.

7. U.S. Bureau of the Census, *Statistical Abstract of the United States: 1976* (97th edition), Washington, D.C.: U.S.G.P.O., 1976, p. 877. Supporters of the view that there is a necessary tradeoff between welfare and economic development tend to dismiss the Scandinavian countries as anomalous cases, distinguished by small size and ethnic homogeneity. If, however, one calculates the per capita GNP for the three Scandinavian countries, the Benelux countries, and West Germany together, one comes out with a result of $6,822 (1975 dollars) per capita for an aggregate population of 102.9 million—only a little less than the $7,099 per capita figure for the U.S.

8. The present British policy of eliminating the grammar school and replacing it with a comprehensive high school attended by all students within a district may change this pattern in the United Kingdom. The tradeoff here in terms of democracy and equity is ironic.

9. See Hugh Heclo, *Modern Social Policies: England and Sweden* (New Haven: Yaye University Press, 1974); Gaston V. Rimlinger, *Welfare Policy and Industrialization in Europe, America, and Russia* (New York: John Wiley, 1971).

10. Rimlinger, *Welfare Policy,* p. 92.

11. Ralph Miliband, *The State in Capitalist Society* (New York: Basic Books, 1969); James O'Connor, *The Fiscal Crisis of The State* (New York: St. Martin's, 1973); William Goldsmith, "Marxism and National Urban Policy," paper presented at the Northeast meeting of the Association of American Collegiate Schools of Planning, New Brunswick, N.J., October 1976; David Harvey, *Social Justice and the City* (Baltimore: Johns Hopkins, 1973).

12. See Paul Adams, "The Political Economy of the 'Welfare State': Social Control or Social Wage," Mimeographed, Graduate School of Social Work, University of Texas at Austin, August 1976; George W. Carey, "Land Tenure, Speculation, and the State of the Aging Metropolis," *The Geographical Review* 66 (July 1976): 253-65.

13. Mark I. Gelfand, *A Nation of Cities* (New York: Oxford University Press, 1975), chap. 9. Maurice Stans, Director of the Bureau of the Budget, may have been overly alarmed by the danger of such a department when he declared in a 1960 confidential memo: "It would be unfortunate if any department should develop, as a policy, a pattern of direct national-local relationships at the expense of the state governments, and thus provide a focal

point for interest groups rallying in support of additional federal expenditure" (p. 273).

14. Sar A. Levitan and Joyce K. Zickler, *Too Little But Not Too Late* (Lexington, Mass.: Lexington Books, 1976).

15. See, for example, *Salyer v. Tulare*, 410 U.S. 719 (1973) and *Locklear v. North Carolina*, 514 F.2d 1152 (4th Cir. 1975).

16. *United States Trust Co. v. New Jersey*, 97 S. Ct. 1505 (1977); *New York Times*, 6 July 1977.

17. Walter Dean Burnham, "American Politics in the 1970's: Beyond Party?" in William Chambers and Walter Dean Burnham, eds., *The American Party Systems* (New York: Oxford University Press, 1974); Gerald Pomper, *Voters' Choice* (New York: Dodd, Mead and Company, 1975).

18. Gelfand, *A Nation of Cities*, chap. 6.

19. *Fiscal Observer* (Center for New York City Affairs, New School for Social Research), pilot issue, 1977, p. 7.

20. *Fiscal Observer* 1, no. 1 (June 1977), p. 11.

21. U.S. House of Representatives, Committee on Banking, Finance, and Urban Affairs, Subcommittee on the City, *Toward a National Urban Policy*, April 1977, p. 133.

Section III

The Pressure Points and
Interventionary Mechanisms

Introduction

It is not Surprising that the Initial Attempts at structuring north-eastern policy responses have been to invoke the example of the central city. There are several reasons for this, principally clustering about the difficulty of adjusting to a regional conceptual framework. The inertia of older conventions is understandable; the dominant public policy experience with decline in the United States has been constrained and bound to the urban locus. And even within these settings, the policy evolution has been toward decentralization, with actions targeted to ever reduced scales of application. Even the drive toward metropolitan area planning has succeeded in just a few locales. Notwithstanding the contemporary Appalachian endeavors, the primary limitation has been the historic lack of coherent regional development policies in this country. As D. Quinn Mills observes:

> We have a history letting regional development go where it will. . . . We are virtually the only major industrialized country that does. If one spends time in Europe, one observes a range of policies that attempt to cushion the impact of market forces on different regions. It is interesting to speculate on why that is. It is reasonably clear why the French do it. Consider the coal mining regions of Lorraine. The French did not allow that area to degenerate into an Appalachia because the French periodically fight a war with Germany over that region; they are not prepared to have it disaffected politically from the country as a whole.

231

> The French internal situation is far less stable than our own. There is great concern about the communist party and the other parties of the left. For that reason, the French government has not been prepared to let pockets of political and social dissatisfaction to develop on a geographic basis.

Drawing contrasts to the United States, Mills points out that we have no external neighbors who constitute any threat to our peripheral areas. There is scant likelihood that, if New England is permitted to decline economically, its dissatisfaction can precipitate invasion from Canada. And, since our internal political processes are very stable compared to most western nations, major areas of poverty and political turmoil can develop without greatly affecting the nation's overall foundation. It is for these reasons, Mills concludes, that we have historically devoted very little attention to explicit regional development policies, with the exception of permitting growth as an escape valve.

We find ourselves struggling to uncover workable mechanisms and strategies which give some promise of "through-put"—of being able to deliver substantive results—on a regional partition. Yet the current acknowledgment of regional necessities takes place in a virtual vacuum of philosophy and methodology. In the preceding section, select prerequisites for a regional agenda were stressed—such as transregional infrastructure development and modifications in the trajectories of federal spending flows—predicated on their linkage to the broader determinants of decline. The latter also imply actions to be initiated by the region's internal political echelons. But an equally important focus of concern is the competitiveness of the Northeast and Midwest as a setting for conducting economic activity.

The primary reference framework centers on the factors entering into the locational decisionmaking process of individual business firms and enterprises. To a substantial degree, these variables also help define the attributes of the region's business environments—the direct costs of real estate, construction, labor, utilities, energy, transportation, and taxation; the physical parameters of functional operation, such as the basic requirements for space, communications, and external economies; and other less quantifiable preferences and strictures, typified by such concerns as image, prestige, lifestyle, environmental setting, and security. Certainly there are wide variations across any regional area; yet the Northeast and Midwest states do share common scores on several of these factors. And one of the more important of these, at least as gauged by the level of concern placed upon it, is the question of taxation and allied tax reduction mechanisms.

The Tax Incentive Question

It is difficult to segregate the myth and reality of taxation as it impinges upon the locational rationales of modern economic enterprise. Nonetheless, it is essential to distinguish the impacts associated with local business incentive initiatives, and to isolate the likely significance of such actions. This exacting task is undertaken by professors Bennett Harrison and Sandra Kanter, who make persuasive arguments that the payoffs for such extended efforts may indeed be very meager.

1. *The belief in the efficacy of business incentive policies rests on their apparent plausibility: if one state jurisdiction reduces the relative costs of doing business compared to others, then firms will find it a more attractive environment for doing business.*

2. *However, it is the contention of Harrison and Kanter that business incentives do not produce new output or jobs, but that they do have real costs in the form of foregone tax revenues which do have valuable alternative uses.*

3. *The entire discussion cannot continue on a popularized abstract plane. It must be specified by establishing organizational partitions through which the key questions and assumptions can be efficiently approached.*

4. *A preliminary distinction has to be made: the levels of activity of profit-making firms (any legislation's target) depend not only on the costs of doing business (the legislation's objective), but also on the existence of markets for the output of those firms. Changes in relative costs, in the absence of changes in demand (or potential sales), are not sufficient to induce changes in output and employment.*

   a) *At the state level, business tax incentives do little to stimulate the demand for locally produced output.*

   b) *There may be some level of business incentive so great that the resulting cost reduction would stimulate increases in output and employment. But the larger the incentive, the greater the foregone revenue to the state; hence the establishment of incentives large enough to insure employment increases is constrained by political limitations as to their acceptable magnitudes.*

    c) The range of incentives between the "floor" established by industry parameters, and the "ceiling" set by political feasibility, is probably too narrow to make incentives effective policy instruments for job creation.

5. *Furthermore, one must distinguish between apparent and actual cost changes. What appears to be a significant tax or financing concession may dissipate markedly as it works its way down the corporate balance sheet; the end result may be a marginal alteration of the total costs of doing business. Since expansion and relocation decisions are assumed to be a function of relative total costs in different places, it follows that business incentives are unlikely to make much difference.*

6. *Intertwined with the latter assertions are the importance of threshold effects: unless price, cost, and other "environmental" conditions change by more than some minimum amount in a given period of time, the firm will probably choose to ignore these changes, since the very act of adjusting to them imposes very real costs. Marginal adjustments in the cost of debt finance or in certain tax rates stand little chance of affecting a major decision unless a firm is at or near the threshold.*

7. *Perhaps the most important differentiation which must be made in analyzing incentive mechanisms is between short-run impacts and policies—increasing the levels of plant utilization—and their long-run equivalents—inducing plant relocations, expansions of existing firms, and the formation of new activities (start-ups).*

8. *The short run is that planning period during which the physical plant is essentially fixed; what is variable is the level of activity within the plant. Again the discussion must be further refined, disaggregating firms into "competitive" and "oligopolistic" categories, each of which exhibits unique behaviors.*

    a) Competitive industries are forced by the existence of their competitors to sell their output at the going price, regardless of their production costs. Hence any reduction in costs will induce at least some response in the output-employment decision. But such industries have the least desirable jobs as a consequence of their competitiveness—jobs paying the lowest wages and offering the worst working conditions.

b) Oligopolistic firms (the generic term for a range of conditions whose limiting case is outright monopoly) exist in industrial environments defined by small numbers of large producers. Their main characteristic is some degree of "market power," i.e., in their search for maximum profits, they have the ability to set prices as well as output levels. Cost changes, it is asserted, will have a smaller impact on the output and employment decisions of oligopolistic industries since they are relatively free to protect profit margins by passing costs on to consumers. Any savings derived through incentive provisions will probably be treated as windfall profits. Hence the better types of jobs are relatively insulated from business incentive policies.

9. *The long run is that planning period wherein the physical plant is variable—and changes occur by virtue of new start-ups, expansions, and relocations. Again the demand for output is construed as the most important consideration; exclusively "cost-side" policies are unlikely to be sufficient to induce investment activity that would not have taken place in the absence of the incentive.*

a) In long-run decisionmaking, the availability and cost of capital are equally important as other cost savings (tax payments) created by incentive packages.

b) Briefly, concentrated (oligopolistic) industries do not need tax and interest rate incentives as much as the more competitive sector; consequently the latter may be more likely to take advantage of them—the same conclusion reached for the short-run scenario.

c) Moreover, concentrated industries are better able to reshape their environment, vis-à-vis more competitive industries, to reduce uncertainties (e.g., labor unrest, future sales, etc.). But if competitive industries face greater uncertainties, then they are less likely to invest, i.e., to take advantage of state business incentives.

10. *Additionally, a significant amount of plant relocation out of the United States altogether may be the result of the absorption of what were previously locally owned businesses into multinational corporations or conglomerates that choose locations on the bases of international costs, federal tax policies, and overseas political conditions.*

11. *Long distance moves also tend to be made in* clusters, *whereby certain industries are interdependent* (agglomerated). *If one moves, its complement must follow suit; conversely, the latter cannot move, whatever the business incentive, if the former does not (remains in place).*

12. *One of the consequences that any subsidy mechanism risks is* tax incentive displacement, *i.e., a firm receiving a tax (or financing) benefit may have acted as it did in the absence of the incentive by employing internal resources. Hence the subsidies may displace, rather than complement, the effect of local resources. The result is that the net job creation impact is usually less than the "intended" effect.*

13. *It is also recognized that* inter-regional *(long distance) and* intra-regional *relocations involve very different kinds of decisions. Regions are probably selected by broad, qualitative criteria such as resource availability, unionization, transportation facilities, and so forth. Once a region has been selected, the choice of a particular state jurisdiction may well rest on incremental cost differences—such as those engendered by incentive provisions. While the state granting the subsidy may benefit, clearly the region as a whole has foregone revenues, since the industry in question would have located there in any case.*

14. *Finally, the entire incentive struggle is viewed as taking place within a broader historical frame of assymetric irreversible economic growth completely ignored by conventional economic analysis. When capital (or systems of physical capital, like neighborhoods and regions) becomes less profitable to employ, those who control the process of production begin to abandon it; it is this disinvestment process which explains much of the secular decline in the economic fortunes of the older industrial belt. Despite business incentives, given this larger historical context, the idea of restoring the older regions' "comparative advantage" loses validity.*

The conclusions of Harrison and Kanter are not unique, and are rapidly gaining widespread recognition and acceptance. Yet within the Northeast, there are ominous tax burdens which realistically must have an adverse effect on industrial location. Nowhere is this better emphasized than the case of New York City.

The New York City Temporary Commission on City Finances, finding that the city's economy has lost over 500,000, or one half, of its manufacturing jobs from 1950 to 1975, sought to identify the impact of local taxation on this decline. The positive relationships they uncovered are not surprising, because the parameters of this industrial sector in New York fall within the "impact band" suggested by Harrison and Kanter.

1. *Unlike the city's nonmanufacturing sector, its manufacturing activities are particularly sensitive to local tax rates. Two-thirds of the city's manufacturing firms employ 20 persons or fewer, and 85 percent of the firms employ fewer than 50 persons.*

2. *New York City's tax structure places a particularly heavy burden on firms of this marginal size. In addition to basic property taxes, manufacturers are subject to a bewildering variety of general sales and occupancy taxes and specific business gross receipts or income taxes.*

3. *In general, the tax structure has been modified more for political than economic reasons. Legislative histories and contemporary literature offer little enlightenment as to the economic arguments used in support of the evolution and maturation of the extant tax package.*

4. *Comparative analyses of tax liability in different political jurisdictions shows that New York City imposes forbidding barriers to manufacturing activity.*

5. *As a result of extensive quantitative analysis of the linkage of taxation to employment, the rationale is developed for a whole series of changes in the structure of manufacturing taxation.*

While the proposed changes are presented in depth in this volume—changes which do not appear unreasonable in light of present burdens—the extensive analyses deriving these conclusions have been omitted due to space limitations. Nonetheless, it should be reiterated that while a *significant causal linkage* may be established between taxation levels and employment decline, it is a far more hazardous proposition to forecast the *reversal* of the momentum of decline by altering a single parameter of the overall decisionmaking process.

Consequently, business taxation and incentives may be prerequisite to a broader package of response stimulii, but by themselves offer few prospects for substantive impact. Furthermore, as stressed previously, they have the potential to precipitate harsh intra-regional competition for a finite level of economic activity. Their use may have to be judicious and constrained, with some degree of consistency across jurisdictional boundaries. Their most valid utilization may be to operationalize strategies designed to retain existing facilities.

The Labor Force Dimensions

For the most part, a major input into the operating cost balance sheet—and therefore a consequential input into locational decisionmaking—of any economic enterprise is that of labor. While much homage has been paid to the positive attributes of the southern work force, as compared to its northern counterparts, interregional differentials are not susceptible to precise quantification. Wage rate accounts, the standard measuring sticks, only partially reveal the variations between North and South. And even then, the gaps appear insufficient to precipitate substantial job growth variations. Indeed, it is not wage rates in the North which are prohibitive, but less tangible factors such as labor force attitudes, manifested in work rules and unionization, which provide inhibitors to operating efficiency. Whatever the exploitive capacity of private business, these negative attributes, as perceived by the latter sector, may be the legacy of an aging industrial region, one which adds impetus to the very process of aging.

D. Quinn Mills, professor of business administration and labor relations at the Harvard Business School, focuses on the broader dimensions of the labor force question and stresses the following elements.

> 1. *Overall average hourly earnings in the New England and Middle Atlantic states over the last twenty-five years have declined relatively toward the national average. The Northeast now holds a smaller advantage with respect to average hourly earnings than it used to have in reference to the balance of the nation. This, of course, reflects the growth in service jobs and the decline in manufacturing jobs in the region.*

> 2. *Average hourly earnings in the manufacturing sector of the Northeast have also experienced relative declines toward the national average over the last twenty-five years. This reflects the strong shift of higher wage manufacturing industries away from the Northeast.*

> 3. *In examining the specific wage rate data it is difficult to see the pressure of wage rates in general on the location of manufac-*

turing industries, or for that matter, other kinds of industries, except to some degree in New York.

4. In general in the United States, wage rates are higher in the West than they are in the Northeast. In the last several years, the wage rates of the North Central states have also exceeded those of the Northeast. Only in the South are they substantially lower. Consequently wage rates per se may not be as important a factor, internal to the United States, as initially envisioned.

5. While the Northeast is not a particularly highly unionized area of the country—with the exception of New York—the South is markedly less so (the West is the most highly unionized).

6. Whatever the consequences, the unionization factor, and its attendant by-products, weighs heavily in business decisions about the location of capital investment. Hence this element in and of itself may be much more significant as a policy variable.

7. Individual tax burdens are also highly relevant. The impact of local taxation on the personal fisc of high income decision-makers may be of more significance than taxation's impact on the corporate balance sheet. Ominously, New York fares extremely poorly on this index.

The policy implications of these observations are, at best, problematic. With Congress rejecting the so-called common situs picketing bill that would have allowed various unions on a construction site to walk out if a single one struck—which raises significant doubt as to the repeal of federal legislation permitting states to pass right-to-work laws—it appears that unions will find it increasingly difficult to recapture once unionized jobs as they flock to the South. Hence interregional variations will probably persist for the forseeable future, undermining any anticipation of regional equalization. What appears mandatory, then, are greater public efforts at fostering accommodation between labor and management *presently*.

As events in New York City have recently shown, only when relocation or termination decisions reach "irreversible thresholds" has labor offered significant concessions. Waiting until the pain of nonaction precipitates response is a strategy which offers scant prospects for affecting foregone decisions. While early warning mechanisms and greater lead times may not always be utilized for effective policy-making, increasing vigilance and initiatives by public instrumentalities may, at worst, be able to salvage some residuum of potential job losses.

The Energy Question

In comparison to the latter concern, the subject area of energy is more susceptible to rigorous quantitative analyses. The energy disadvantages of the Northeast—both supply and cost—are etched deeply on the financial ledgers of any energy-dependent business enterprise. While it is possible to conceive of long-range technological thrusts to counter these limitations, it is apparent that the resolution of the region's energy problems are closely bound to complex political strictures. The Mid-Atlantic Economic Development Region, a proposed Title V Regional Action Planning Commission, has provided a baseline reference document delineating the reality and scope of the energy dilemma.

1. *The lack of readily available and usable energy supplies within the region has had, and will continue to have, a negative impact upon economic development because of the flow of dollars out of the region to pay for imported energy and because of lost investment and industrial expansion caused by higher energy prices, relative to the rest of the nation.*

2. *Since 76 percent of the total energy use of the mid-Atlantic states comprises petroleum and natural gas, they must import almost all the energy they consume.*

3. *In 1972, $7 billion were expended by the Northeast to pay for petroleum and natural gas. By 1975, nearly three times as much, about $20.7 billion, was expended. These moneys were paid either to oil and gas producing regions of this nation or foreign countries.*

4. *The current national solutions to the energy-dependency problem may have the same effect on the Northeast, i.e., a continued drain on the capital of the Northeast, since the major energy investments and projects will accrue to the western parts of the country.*

5. *The locational problems of energy supply, i.e., the regions' lack of existing resources, have been compounded by additional problems which have limited exploration and utilization of available resources. Most of these center about public environmental resistance.*

6. *But it is difficult to ask for cheap energy and the resulting benefits from other states while being unwilling to accept the costs of locating facilities in the northeastern states.*

7. *Conservation—the more efficient use of energy—is suggested as a politically feasible strategy for the Northeast, one which can affect the outflow of energy dollars from the region. However, the anticipated saving of $1 billion may represent less than 5 percent of the capital drain.*

8. *Alternative approaches, although less appealing politically, would include the greater use of eastern coal, outer continental shelf exploration and development, and the resolution of the problems of the nuclear fuel cycle.*

The parameters of the energy matrix enveloping the Northeast, then, appear to imply the requirements for long-term innovative technology, painful readjustments, political confrontations, and energyenvironmental tradeoffs. As with the preceding factors, it is difficult to rectify in the short term the precedents set—the pyramiding effect of previous decisions—over a very long period of time.

The Capital Resource Question

Are capital limitations or availability the key to the regional problem? Certainly this hypothesis underlies the various suggestions which would lead to a new Reconstruction Finance Corporation or energy bank— or any of the many special regional development financing institutions that have been promoted. John G. Heimann, now comptroller of the currency, basically takes issue with this approach. In its place he proposes a reform of the financial institutions in place. The key then becomes subsidies and insurance to aim the flow of capital to foster societal goals.

1. *The bulk of the Northeast Region's capital supplies is located in New York City and New York State.*

   a. *New York State, with approximately 8.5 percent of the nation's population and 9.5 percent of its personal disposable income, has within its borders financial institutions with about 20 percent of its personal disposable income, has within its borders financial institutions with about 20 percent of the total commercial banking assets of the nation (more than $200 billion), 20 percent of the thrift assets (about $70 billion), 70 percent of the foreign bank deposits residing in this nation ($30 billion) and the control of 20 to 30 percent of the retirement systems ($40 billion).*

2. *This capital cannot be mandated for the purposes of local problem solving; such a requirement is probably unconstitutional. Moreover, it cannot be forced into local investments since it is private capital, the capital of individuals who have chosen those intermediaries in which to store their capital.*

3. *The intermediaries can be divided into two types of savings systems.*

   a. Deposit thrift institutions *(commercial banks, savings banks, savings and loan associations, credit unions, etc.) have as their fundamental characteristic control by the public: all of us put money in and take it out. It is the individual depositors' choice; it is short-term money for the most part.*

   b. Contract thrift institutions *(long-term thrift entities such as life insurance companies and retirement systems) are not controlled by the saver to the extent of the deposit thrift institutions. Long-term contractual agreements are prevalent; it is long-term money.*

4. *These systems are subject to the most extraordinary pastiche of regulatory and supervisory controls at both federal and state levels. Often these regulators tend to compete, not by being more stringent, but by attempting to keep their constituents. There is no uniform, national control over these systems.*

5. *Attempts to restructure the system when problems arise prove difficult, since a whole host of vested interests is confronted, whose privileges and functions may be subject to reordering and change. The federal government usually tries to circumvent, rather than face, such problems by creating or extrapolating the activities of a broad diversity of government agencies and authorities, leaving the financial institutions in their archaic splender.*

6. *Consequently, before any regional effort is formulated, the problem fundamentally must be solved on a national basis; the infrastructure of our financial system is no longer rational; a basic restructuring of the financial institutions and the regulatory authorities that control them is required on a national scale.*

7. *Within this context, it still must be recognized that local capital cannot be applied to local problems through mandate or taxation. Since capital can be shifted rapidly, punitive taxation of financial institutions only hastens their exodus.*

8. *Incentives may have to be created to induce financial institutions to invest in certain socially desirable activities. Such incentives need to prevent excess risk and provide competitive rates of return so that the managers do not run the risk of being sued by those whose money they manage.*

9. *The only way to assure a supply of local capital for urban regional investment growth (infrastructure building) is by making sure that capital is protected. The risks that are being taken must be commensurate with the rates of return. Increasingly the measuring stick of risk-return is not merely national, but international.*

Additional Concerns

The purpose of this section is not to replicate a text on locational decisionmaking, but to illustrate the very real difficulties the region faces as it attempts to confront a process of shift—one with substantial lead time and momentum—through minor alterations of singular factors. A range of other variables deserve similar study and elaboration, but ever present space limitations make the task prohibitive. What should be emphasized, however, is the increasingly "soft" nature of locational decisionmaking as we proceed further into the era of spatial homogenization. The importance of image, of attitude, and of receptivity cannot be overemphasized in this context. As the Northeast increasingly became characterized as a hostile environment for doing business over the last decade, the perception of the South as a backwater was remarkably transformed into *the* place to set up shop. Whatever the realities of the cost-benefit matrix, the major difficulty the Northeast and Midwest may have to surmount is the label *anti-business* which slowly pyramided into prominence as the 1960s came to a close.

One dimension, unfortunately, which has become linked to this image is welfare. Whatever merits of social beneficence it represents, it is a negative symbol to private enterprise. While the region cannot, and probably should not, modify its broader welfare philosophy, it is readily apparent the welfare cost burdens to the region's jurisdictions have escalated as their economic support structures weakened. It is this concern that the final paper of this section addresses.

The Welfare Dilemma

Professor Sar A. Levitan, director of the Center for Social Policy Studies at George Washington University, extends the consistent theme of this section—complexity. Welfare policy was quickly isolated as a prominent concern when the region's leadership initially proposed remedial measures. Yet as analyses proceeded, the logic of preliminary anticipations was undermined, and the efficacy of early "solutions" came under question. Consequently, it is important to review the baseline parameters of the welfare system as they have currently evolved.

1. *Welfare reform may invariably take the format of a zero sum game, involving an inter-regional "struggle" in general pitting the Northeast versus the South over some $40 billion of program resources.*

2. *Five major programs are usually associated with public welfare, with average benefits in the Northeast far exceeding those of the South:*

   a) Medicaid *monthly benefits stand at $185 in the Northeast compared to $105 in the South. In the former area, the state share comprises 49 percent; in the latter, 39 percent.*

   b) Aid to Families with Dependent Children (AFDC) *provides average monthly benefits of $96 in the Northeast while the South's equivalent stands at $42. While southern states contribute 33 percent of this total, the northern states contribute 49 percent.*

   c) Supplemental Security Income (SSI) *monthly benefits average $134 in Northeast as compared to $95 in the South.*

   d) Food Stamps *show little inter-regional variation.*

   e) General Assistance *is purely state aid, with the northeastern monthly average benefit standing at $108; the southern equivalent is $71.*

3. *Despite these varying support levels, the South, with 32 percent of the total national population, has 43 percent of the national populace with incomes below the poverty level. More than 16 percent of the South's populace are below the poverty level compared to 10 percent in the Northeast.*

4. *In 1976, the constituent states of the Northeast expended approximately $12 billion helping the poor compared to $8.7 billion in the South. With 61 percent fewer poor persons, the northeastern jurisdictions spent three times as much per individual.*

5. *The traditional arguments of northeastern partisans is that the region's generosity is not rewarded by the federal government. The southern states actually receive 8 percent more federal funds to support their poor, while paying only 20 percent of the total bill compared to the Northeast's footing 46 percent of the total cost.*

6. *Yet this argument may be misleading, since it ignores the fact that the federal government spends more than double (108 percent) the amount for each poor person in the Northeast as compared to the South.*

7. *And with per capita income in the South 20 percent lower than the Northeast, southerners already allocate 15 percent of their income to state and local governments compared to 18 percent in the Northeast. Given the lower income in the South and the presumed virtues of progressive taxation it would hardly seem equitable to raise the tax level in the South (if it were politically feasible) above what it is presently.*

These are realities which complicate the development of proposals for the federal government to assume the bulk of welfare cost burdens. As long as per capita incomes remain higher in the Northeast, the region will continue to assume proportionally greater shares of federal taxation. Hence tax dollars flowing out of the Northeast to pay for a restructured welfare system could well exceed the additional resources that the region would ostensibly secure, and given the impetus of institutional complexities in this context, and their potential role in perpetuating established functional patterns, the revitalization effect of welfare shifts remains questionable.

Further Discussion

It is frustrating indeed not to be able to pinpoint or suggest definitive measures for countering a process of substantial inertia. The paucity of recommendations is a sad tribute to a growing maturity gained since the time of the initial forays against central city decline—the present realization that the phenomena are much more complex than were envisioned in decades past, and that verbiage promising immediate solutions is pure exhortation. The papers of this section lend credence to this observation, as well as to the complex nature of the reality facing the state of the art of policy analysis and development.

What we tend to find are more and more dilemmas as we probe ever deeper into the question of what is to be done. Several in particular stand forth clearly.

1. The art of predicting the full results of policy decisions is still in its infancy. The unexpected may outweigh the nominal goals.

2. The alteration of factors presumed to be causal may not be able to induce a reversal of the process in question.

3. Modifications necessary to continue functioning in decline environments may act as accelerators to the very process of decline, e.g., the Northeast may have to relax environmental standards to secure industry and energy, yet environment is one of the principal lures of the Sunbelt.

4. If alterations are made which do deliver substantive results, it is possible that the latter may in turn precipitate a resurgence of the local behavior that initiated the problem in the first place.

Moreover, as will be stressed in the following section, regionalism on the scale presumed here—while valid for such broad concerns as infrastructure and energy thresholds—may not coincide with some of the more troubling phenomena gripping the nation. Within all the regions of the country there are visible schisms. In the Northeast, for example, certain territories are intimately tied into the operational economic system of the late twentieth century, while other areas are virtually external to it—for example, the South Bronx may be assuming the socioeconomic contours of an undeveloped country. The South's drive to modernization also reflects the same bimodal tendencies—territorial stretches of poverty and of primitive condition coexist with burgeoning networks of economic viability. While the aging industrial regions' problems appear more severe, many potent concerns are endemic to subsectors within multiple regions. Hence our interpretive paradigm cannot completely jetison all but the regional perspective. Given the limited nature of the opportunities stressed in this section, the filling of the national void—of developing truly national development policies —may well be a key condition to regional and intra-regional problems alike. Indeed the common traumas may well have more general political force—and thus be more open to national resolution.

The Political Economy of State "Job-Creation" Business Incentives

BENNETT HARRISON
SANDRA KANTER

ALMOST WITHOUT EXCEPTION, state government officials across the country advocate the use of incentives to the business sector to stimulate additional production and the derived demand for labor. This is popularly known as *job creation*.

These policies include tax credits and "forgivenesses," the provision of capital raised by the flotation of tax exempt bonds, low-interest loans, and state guarantees of loans or mortgages written by private sector lenders. Nearly every state in the union provides *some* mix of these business incentives. One way or the other, all are designed to reduce firms' (fixed or operating) costs of doing business in the state providing the incentives, relative to other states. It is hoped that this will induce expansions or new investments and a consequent growth in employment.

Perhaps the widespread use of these policies is explained by the fact that state governments have so little power to affect their local economies, officials feel compelled to do *something*, and local taxes and bonding *are* subject to deliberate policy manipulation at the state level. Perhaps it is because these officials—by virtue of campaign financing vulnerability, prior employment in business, or even blood relation—are simply serving the class interests of the business sector, which sees such incentives as yet another source of windfall profits. These pieces of an explanation of the ubiquity of business incentive job creation policy in the U.S. are important and need to be developed further.

The most benign explanation is that state officials genuinely *believe* in the efficacy of business incentive policies. A perusal of statehouse hearings and staff reports on the various pieces of legislation makes this understandable, for no aspect of economic policy has been more poorly argued and documented, yet so uniformly (and warmly) supported by special interest lobbyists. If "everyone" believes that business incentives are a "good thing," and there is virtually no articulated criticism accessible to politicians, then perhaps it is no wonder that the prescription is believed. Besides, it *sounds* perfectly plausible: if one state reduces the relative costs of doing business, viz-à-vis other states, surely firms will find that a more attractive environment for doing business.

It may *sound* "right." But there are a host of reasons, many of them growing out of even elementary standard economic theory, why the kinds of incentives that most states usually promulgate are unlikely to significantly affect output or employment. And there is a growing empirical literature—spotty though it may be—which provides little or no evidence that these incentives make much if any difference. Some of this research was in fact published (mostly in the early 1960s), although not in a form that made it readily accessible to elected officials and their staffs.

It is our contention that these business incentives do *not* produce new output or jobs, but that they *do* have real costs in the form of foregone tax revenues which *do* have valuable alternative uses. It is also possible that some of these incentives raise the price that state governments and less privileged private investors have to pay for borrowing capital from the private sector. Because they cost taxpayers money but do not produce much (if any) new employment, these business incentives constitute a regressive redistribution of income from workers-consumers-taxpayers to the core of the business community. The objective of this paper is to articulate, and to statistically document insofar as possible, the case against business incentives as an effective approach to state economic development.

The policy implications are then straightforward: repeal the existing legislation, pass national laws that make it harder for states to deploy these "weapons," and commit the resulting public savings to direct public investment in the production of socially useful goods and services, with the consequent creation of new jobs at decent pay.

In the next section, we describe the range of tax and other business incentive policies currently in use. This is followed by a theoretical exploration of the *expected* operation and impacts of state job creation business incentives. Next we present a review and evaluation of the existing empirical work on the subject, describing *actual* outcomes. A concluding section will begin to raise some political-economic explanations for why such a thoroughly unproven policy as this continues to be so widely endorsed.

State Business Incentives

The history of state subsidies to business is almost as old as the Constitution. Some of the earliest programs of financial aid to business occurred in the Commonwealth of Massachusetts when, in the late seventeen hundreds, the state government authorized bounties or outright gifts of money to producers of hemp, flax, and glass to encourage production of these goods. The commonwealth also offered to reduce the taxes of brewers who produced over one hundred barrels of beer annually.

Today, while there are almost as many variations as there are political jurisdictions, we can observe four basic types of business incentives available in different states around the country.[1] The oldest and most important of the incentives are property tax concessions. Twelve states and Puerto Rico have legislation which permits cities and towns, counties, or the state itself to exempt part or all of business property from property taxation for a specified period of time.[2] Puerto Rico has probably the most liberal tax incentive law, exempting a manufacturer of a product which was not produced there before the year 1947 from paying either property *or* income taxes for a period of up to twenty-five years. Three states provide similar, though smaller, directly administered tax concessions to new industry.[3] The remaining nine states give their local counties or municipalities permission to enter into agreements with businesses abating them from some or all of their local property tax payments.

Four states—Alabama, Mississippi, Georgia, and North Dakota—exempt new and/or expanding industries from local ad valorem taxes on tangible property for a stipulated period of time. North Dakota and two other states, New York and Massachusetts, also give tax credits to businesses for expanding their employment. Firms new to North Dakota, for example, may receive a tax credit of up to 1 percent of their annual

gross wage and salary expenditures for a period of up to three years.
New York and Massachusetts, on the other hand, use tax credits far
more selectively. The former permits firms expanding in low income
areas to qualify for an income tax credit. The latter gives income tax
credits to businesses that employ people who had been on welfare or
drawing unemployment compensation.

Four states have legislation permitting some form of investment tax
credit.[4] Firms may take a certain percentage of the cost of acquiring
buildings, structures, machinery and equipment as a tax credit and reduce
their total state tax bill by the amount of the credit, which varies from
state to state. New York allows manufacturing firms a tax credit equal
to 2 per cent of the cost of new buildings, equipment, and facilities.
Manufactures in West Virginia may receive a credit equal to 10 per cent
of the cost of new production facilities for a period of ten years.

Another business incentive is the loan guarantee. Thirteen states
guarantee commercial loans.[5] Ten out of the thirteen have organized
industrial finance authorities specifically authorized to guarantee, on behalf of the state, the repayment of some or all of a mortgage or loan
made by a conventional market source on an industrial facility.[6] New
Hampshire, the originator of the program, has a relatively modest policy
and insures the portion of a loan in excess of 50 per cent of the value of
the piece of property or in excess of 65 per cent of a loan made for
machinery and equipment. At the other end of the spectrum, Rhode
Island guarantees up to 90 per cent of the cost of plant construction.
Most states charge firms a fee of 1-3 per cent of the outstanding loan
for administrative costs.

A number of states issue industrial development bonds. There are
two kinds. Thirteen states permit localities to float general obligation
bonds, whose payments are guaranteed by the full faith and credit of
the state or municipality.[7] Forty-three states permit revenue bonds to
be issued which are paid solely from the proceeds of the project and
do not become the obligation of any government.[8] Both types can be
used to finance the construction of industrial development or sports
facilities, convention or trade show buildings, docks, wharves, airports,
parking lots and garages, sewage or solid waste disposal plants, and
air or water pollution equipment. Income accruing to the holders of
both general obligation and revenue bonds is generally exempt from
federal taxation. It is this federal tax exemption which increases the
real financial yield (and therefore the attractiveness) of the bonds, and
enables the issuing public jurisdictions to offer slightly below-market
rates of interest.

Finally, over thirty states have state-chartered credit corporations which make loans to businesses unable to obtain long- and short-term financing in the conventional capital markets. The corporations issue stock to banks, insurance companies, and other private parties and are often exempt from paying state taxes on their income.[9]

Theoretical Analysis

Popular—and legislative—discussions about business incentives to create jobs are invariably couched in simplistic and highly general terms, e.g. "cut *taxes* and get *businesses* to create new *jobs*." But which taxes (and by what amounts)? What kinds of businesses? And which sorts of jobs? Is the policy targeted at firms considering expansion at a given location, at plant relocation, or at new start-ups altogether? Presumably, the levels of activity of profit-making firms (who are the constituency for this type of legislation) depend not only on the *costs* of doing business, but also on the existence of *markets* for the output of those firms. What sorts of biases are introduced by the assumption—implicit in all incentive programs—that changes in relative costs, with no changes in potential sales, are sufficient to induce changes in output and employment? These are just some of the theoretical complexities that are usually left out of the popular discussions of this subject.

With such a maze of variables with which to contend, how shall we proceed? An organization of the analysis into two parts seems useful. First, we will consider the differences between short-run (plant activity-increasing) policies. Then we will examine some general problems with business incentives that seem to apply in both the short and the long run.

SHORT-RUN JOB CREATION THROUGH
INCREASING LEVELS OF PLANT UTILIZATION

To the economist, the *short run* is that planning period during which physical plant is essentially fixed (or given). What is variable (at least to some extent) is the level of activity at which that plant (or office, or hamburger stand) is operated. In particular, how much labor is being employed, in combination with other resources, to produce output? And—more to the immediate point—how is the managerial decision to increase or decrease employment in that plant affected by changes in costs, especially tax and (bond or loan) interest costs?

Even in pure theory, the answer depends crucially on whether the firm we are studying is in a competitive or an oligopolistic industry. T-shirt

factories and barber shops behave differently than automobile manufacturers and large department stores. If the industry is reasonably
competitive, then firms are forced by the existence of their competitors
to sell their output at the going price, regardless of their costs of production; under such conditions, they will try to produce and sell as much
as possible, subject to the constraints of given physical capacity, access
to finance capital, etc. *Any* reduction in costs will induce at least some
change in the output-employment decision.[10] Job creation business incentives in effect reduce the cost to the firm of each additional worker
hired.[11] This is apparently the picture of decisionmaking in the firm that
the advocates of job creation tax incentives have in mind (or are
peddling).[12]

Perhaps it is worth reviewing the structural characteristics necessary
for having an economy of reasonably "perfect" (or free market) competition. First, and most important of all, no firm can be so powerful that
it is able to directly influence the price at which it can sell its output,
or the prices it must pay for the hiring of labor or capital. The maximum
output of any one firm in a competitive industry must be too small to
be able to supply the entire market (in contrast, for example, to the
situation in any regional telephone industry). Entrepreneurs must be
able (and willing) to easily acquire the capital with which to enter an
industry if it appears profitable to do so, and firms that are not efficiently
managed *must* go under (or, in one of those delightful euphemisms of
economic theory, exit from the industry), with no help from the government or anyone else; without such discipline, inefficiency would
spread throughout the system. Labor must be highly mobile, across
occupations (skills) and locations, and firms may not actively discrimin-
ate among different kinds of workers on any criterion other than productivity. It must be possible to attribute each and every dollar of
extra output produced to the partial contribution of a "unit" of labor or
capital, so that hiring can be conducted in accordance with the relationship between wages and other "factor prices" and these "marginal pro-
ductivities;" without this condition, labor and capital will not move about
in ways that are supportive of profit-maximization (the presumed objective of all perfectly competitive firms). The production process must
not generate nontrivial pollutants (or, for that matter, such external
economies as upgraded labor skills) as a joint product or unintended side
effect, or else those critical factor prices will not accurately reflect the
marginal contributions of labor and capital to production of the *intended*
good (or service). And so on.

The history of capitalism is a history of the continual transformation
of the economy from one in which at least *some* aspects of competition

were prevalent to one dominated by large corporations, possessing great economic and political power. Nearly every one of those assumptions underlying the textbook theory of competition no longer holds—and many of them (such as the presumed frictionless labor mobility) *never* held in the real world. Not even in the set of small firms are these conditions always satisfied (although size *is* one important measure of the extent of potential economic and political power). For example, many family firms hire and fire workers, remain open or closed for more or less of the year, and decide whether or not to get out of the business and re-invest their capital in (say) Middle Eastern oil, according to considerations that often go beyond pecuniary profit, such as a strong family tradition of association with the product or location.

Firms in industries characterized by a relatively smaller number of producers are called *oligopolists* (the generic term for a range of possibilities whose limiting case is outright monopoly). Their main characteristic is some degree of market power, defined as the ability to set prices as well as output levels, in their search for maximum profits. The thing which permits this price-making power is the real or manufactured differentiation of their product-service from one another, whether by virtue of style differences (Chevy Novas vs. Plymouth Satellites) or locational monopolies (the electric company in New York City cannot compete with the one in Boston). The greater the extent to which price increases do *not* drive an oligopolist's customers away from it and to a competitor, the greater the extent of that market power.[13] Firms with substantial market power can protect their profit margins when costs increase, by passing at least part of these costs along to their customers in the form of higher prices (they may also, when costs increase, pass them along at a *markup*, thereby gaining a windfall profit). And when costs fall, at least part of those savings get captured in the form of wind-fall profits, i.e. they need *not* be entirely passed along to customers as lower product (or service) prices.

It follows that declining costs will have a relatively smaller impact on the output and employment decisions of an oligopolist than of a competitor. In particular, a reduction in incremental labor costs resulting from a tax or capital subsidy of the sort in which we are interested will increase potential profitability and therefore output levels only slightly. At best, with flexible technology—the ability to recombine labor and capital in varying amounts, more or less continuously—the additional labor needed will therefore be small. If the technology is less flexible, with factor proportions rigid in the short run (whether because labor is hired at discrete periods, and on fixed duration contracts, or because additional amounts of labor cannot continuously be added to a given machine in a corner of the plant), then the tax incentive may well produce no extra employment at all. Occasional endorsements of incremental tax or wage subsidies by orthodox economists ignore these institutional facts of life under modern industrial capitalism. Their prescriptions are based upon a naïve incrementalist view of the world.

In recent years, a huge literature has developed on the rules of thumb by which oligopolists (and even small firms facing less than perfectly competitive conditions) make output and employment decisions, e.g., when faced with uncertainty about prices and other market conditions. This literature, which is now standard fare in even the most conservative business schools, stresses the importance of threshold effects: unless price, cost, and other "environmental" conditions change by more than some minimum amount in a given period of time, the firm will probably choose to ignore those changes, since the very act of adjusting to them would have real costs. Thus, for example, if business taxes fall by a small amount (perhaps for each additional unit of labor hired), the firm may not react *at all*. The extra revenue accruing to the firm from tax incentives that are granted whether the firm increases its hiring or not, as in the case of reduced excise taxes on existing machinery, would then be treated by the firm as windfall profits.

Peter Bearse, formerly the executive director of the council of economic advisors to the governor of New Jersey, discusses the role of these so-called "indivisibilities" in the decisionmaking process:

> Decisions can be arrayed in a hierarchy—from minor allocation decisions of the type described by textbook economic theory to major "all or nothing" decisions like the decision to move or build a plant. Major decisions are subject to thresholds and long gestation periods. Marginal adjustments in the cost of debt finance or in certain tax rates do not stand a chance of affecting a major decision unless a firm is at or near a threshold; and even then, several other factors are also operative. . . . It is a question of probabilities—the odds that a given policy can have an intended effect. I claim that the concept of an adaptive, sequential decision-making process subject to thresholds makes the efficacy of current policies look very dubious.[14]

If even oligopolistic firms can capture larger shares of their respective markets—if they think they can sell more output—then of course they will consider increasing the level of utilization of their existing capacity (and, if that is still insufficient, they may expand that capacity, i.e., build additional plant). In other words, expanded demand for the goods and services being produced will induce increases in output and therefore employment. But at the state level, *business* tax incentives do virtually nothing to stimulate the demand for goods and services (although *consumer* income tax deductions or credits *may* do so). Whether or not there is any way that a single state government can significantly stimulate the demand for *locally produced* output is debatable. But cost-side business incentives are certainly not a substitute for such demand stimulation policies.

In principle, there must be *some* level of business incentive so great that the resulting cost reduction *would*—at least over time—induce a significant increase in output and employment within at least some private firms. But (and we will develop this point later) the larger the incentives, the greater the foregone revenue which could otherwise have been used to finance, e.g., state social services, repayment of interest on the state's bonded debt, etc. There are, therefore, *political* limits to the feasible magnitude of the business incentives. It is quite possible that the range of operational incentives—between some "floor" set by the behavioral rules of thumb used by oligopolistic decisionmakers, and a "ceiling" set by the politically unacceptable opportunity costs of the foregone tax revenue—is too narrow to make this an effective policy instrument for job creation.

Finally, we may return to the competitive-oligopolistic distinction to ask: What *kinds* of jobs get "created" if and when (some firms *do* respond to the introduction of tax incentives by increasing output and employment? According to the dual labor market literature and its antecedents,[15] the jobs in those industries which most closely approximate the competitive ideal type will in general pay lower wages, offer worse (or at least less amply capitalized) working conditions, provide less stable (full-year and/or full-week) employment, and make it more difficult for labor to organize in order to protect its class interests. Yet our theoretical analysis leads us to expect that it is precisely these most competitive firms which are *most* likely to respond to an incremental job creation incentive. Thus, business incentives appear to be policy instruments which—if they work at all—are most likely to boost the sector of the economy with the least desirable jobs, while providing windfall profits to the segment of the business community that least needs them.

With respect to the likely impact of job creation business incentives on short-run, capacity-utilization decisions concerning output and employment, we concluded that economic theory does not predict that the lowering of cost curves via tax or capital subsidies in one state will unambiguously lead to increases in the levels of local output and employment. In fact, we have discovered many structural reasons for expecting that such incentives, set at politically feasible levels, will either have no effect at all or will be concentrated in the segment of the economy paying the lowest wages and offering the worst working conditions.

LONG-RUN JOB CREATION:
INVESTMENT IN NEW START-UPS OR PLANT EXPANSIONS

Economic theory has probably met with its least amount of predictive success in trying to understand the dynamics of the investment decision. But one thing *is* clear: the decision to invest turns not only (or even primarily) on the cost of capital—which can be subsidized through various investment tax credits and other incentives—but also on expectations about the likely returns to that investment in the form of sales. Almost anything that a government can do to reduce the uncertainty about sales is more likely to successfully induce businesspeople to go ahead and invest (build or expand the plant) than any other kind of public action —including the granting of incentives.

Once again, therefore, the demand for output is an important consideration; exclusively cost-side policies are unlikely to be sufficient to induce investment activity that would not have taken place anyway, in the absence of the incentive. This is perhaps most clearly seen in the conventional benefit-cost analysis by which economists describe and study investment decisions. According to one common formulation of this profit-oriented calculus, businesspersons will invest in a given activity if the discount rate r that just equates the expected stream of project costs to the expected stream of project benefits over an expected project lifetime of T years, i.e.,

$$\sum_{t=1}^{T \text{ yrs}} \frac{C_t}{(1+r)^t} = \sum_{t=1}^{T \text{ yrs}} \frac{B_t}{(1+r)^t}$$

is greater than the rate of return available on any other investment of no lesser risk (such as the interest rate on long-term government bonds). (Σ indicates summation of all the annual ratios from year one through year T). Clearly, investment incentives such as those often deployed by states as part of their economic development programs *will* affect this calculation (lower Cs imply higher rates of return, and therefore a greater probability that the investment *will* occur). But benefits (sales) count, too, and it is impossible to say *a priori* which is more important. What *is* certain is that, if the benefit stream is very uncertain, even large cost subsidies may not be sufficient to induce investors to "do their thing."

Orthodox theory is silent on the question of who has access to capital for investment in the first place. Most treatments seem to assume that capital is ubiquitous (for a price), so that if it *pays* an investor to borrow the capital in order to build or expand his or her facilities(because the expected rate of return is higher than that available from other applications of the funds), the borrowing-investing will in fact take place.[16] But it seems to us (although there are few empirical studies outside the housing field) that this critical resource is by no means ubiquitous, nor is it easily available to all those who want to get into business (blacks, women, entrepreneurs working in low-income communities, and non-profit developers have an especially difficult time getting capital at *any* price, and since the New York City debacle, state and local governments may be in the same category). A particular problem concerns the debt-to-equity capital mix. Business lacking sufficient equity (or frontend) capital—the kind that requires the borrower to pay the lender (usually the stockholder) a share of the profits if *and when* there are any profits—face high probabilities of failure (or of inability to grow), because of their indebtedness (the interest on a loan must usually being to be paid back immediately, whether there are profits or not). Equity capital is especially hard to obtain for the various potential investors cited previously.[17]

It is the smallest firms, with the poorest track records and the least powerful small investors or groups, perhaps with no track record at all, who find it most difficult to borrow. Large firms with good credit ratings (those oligopolists we noted earlier) have less trouble raising their own capital, whether externally or through their own retained earnings. But if the investing-lending of private banks (or of state economic development authorities) is conditioned upon the credit-worthiness of the borrower, then the normal operation of the capital markets will work to channel ever more financial resources to the oligopolists, exacerbating the relative (and sometimes absolute) scarcity of finance capital for the more competitive segment of the market. But that in turn will increase the gap between the two segments still further.

The upshot of all this is that the concentrated industries do not *need* tax and interest rate incentives as much as the more competitive industries, and so it is the latter who are more likely to take advantage of them—a conclusion similar to the one about the kinds of firms that might *actually* create new jobs in response to the policies being discussed. On the other hand, the concentrated industries can probably better reshape their environment to reduce the uncertainty of future sales (and other factors, e.g., the likelihood of labor unrest) than can the more competitive industries. But if the latter face relatively greater uncertainty, then they are *less* likely to invest, i.e., to take advantage of state business incentives.

The conclusion, then, is as before: pure economic theory is ambiguous in predicting the likely impact of state business incentives on job creation through private investment. This even extends to the national level, at least in terms of tax credits or tax cuts. The Brookings Institution's economists conducted a series of econometric evaluations of the impact of the 1962 federal investment tax credit, designed to stimulate the business sector's demand for capital goods and therefore, albeit indirectly, the demand for labor. Half the studies concluded that the credit worked; but half concluded that it did not affect output and employment at all.[18] And the U.S. Congressional Budget Office estimates that a $1 billion national corporate and personal income tax cut would—over the twenty-four months following its inception—create fewer jobs, have a smaller impact on the unemployment rate, and return fewer savings to the federal treasury (in the form of welfare and unemployment compensation payments made unnecessary) than any alternative job creation policy also costing $1 billion (public service employment, countercyclical revenue sharing, accelerated public works, or increased across-the-board government purchases).[19]

LONG-RUN JOB CREATION: PLANT RELOCATION

From the speeches of elected and appointed officials, and the terminology used by newspaper editorial writers, it would seem that the way in which most nonbusinesspersons *expect* new jobs to be created in a state economy over time is through the relocation into the state of plants that had been closed down elsewhere, or through the decision of multiplant (maybe even multinational) firms to build their next new plants in the state.

In addition to the kinds of factors already discussed, actual physical relocation involves some additional considerations. There is also a new policy instrument involved: industrial *recruiting*. States hire advertising agencies or management consultants to place ads and "hustle up" new business. Visiting company representatives are wined and dined and shown around the state. All of this costs money—sometimes a great deal of it.

Starting up a new business has its own fixed costs. But relocating a plant from one site (let alone *state*) to another may be even more expensive, since the old plant must be scrapped or sold, possibly at a loss. This alone should lead us to expect firms to be reluctant to undertake such relocations.

When other locations (outside the state, perhaps outside the country) are involved a state government's already paper-thin control over the situation is reduced even further. A state may be able to affect the local costs of doing business elsewhere. If a company is satisfied with its plant in one state, incremental cost reductions in another state are most unlikely to induce an expensive relocation.

Although the hypothesis has not been well researched, it seems plausible that a significant amount of plant relocation *out* of the United States altogether is the result of absorption of what were previously locally-owned businesses into multinational corporations or conglomerates that choose locations on the basis of *international* comparative costs, federal tax policies, and overseas political conditions. Obviously there is little that an American state government can (or should want to) do to emulate, for instance, the labor policies of Korea or Taiwan.

Urban and regional economists are remarkably united in their belief that inter-regional (long-distance) and intra-regional relocations involve very different kinds of decisions. Regions (it is believed) are selected by broad, qualitative criteria such as the availability of basic resources, adequate transportation access, and (although it is seldom put so bluntly) a politically passive labor force. Once a region (or state) has been selected, the choice of a particular location *within* that region may well turn on incremental cost differences—although inter-jurisdictional (intra-state) *tax* differences are unlikely to be significant factors, since the state taxes will be uniform over all such jurisdictions.[20]

Some economists have discovered that many long-distance moves are made in *clusters*. For example, if a firm in industry x moves from location A to location B, and if x and industry y are agglomerated (meaning that there are technological or market processes that link them together, such as a unit-cost saving tendency to share similar kinds of labor or infrastructure), then one or another firm in industry y may move to B, too. On the other hand, if x does *not* move, then y may not be movable, either, no matter how large the business incentive offered by region B, or how intensive the recruiting effort.[21]

A game-theoretic analysis of the interstate plant relocation process suggests that expensive recruitment and incentive policies may be quite irrational. Improving one's business environment (for example, by building industrial parks, cleaning up the rivers, or training the labor force) makes sense for a state;[22] to the extent that when other states try to compete by similar policies within their own boundaries, everyone benefits. But a recruited relocation is piracy, and the state that was "ripped off" will probably try to retaliate. The net effect turns on the fact that for each recruitable plant, this competition among the states is a zero sum game. Only one prize can be won, while there are many players (in the words of one standard textbook writer: "Such a game therefore can only *redistribute*, but never *create*, the object of payoff" [23]). All states incur costs; certainly the costs of engaging in recruiting, but perhaps also the foregone tax revenues if other firms that would have immigrated anyway claim eligibility for relocation tax incentives. But only one player can win; *n-1* must lose. It follows that, for each player, the *expected* net payoff must *at best* be very small, and is almost certainly *negative*. Perhaps the reason why the players (i.e. the government officials who legislate and administer these policies) seem so positive about them is that they are incorrectly focusing on the potential benefits but ignoring the probable losses.

There is another aspect of the phenomenon of plant relocation which suggests that states may sometimes be better off *without* those new plants —however they are induced to come. If the company brings part or all of its labor force with it, the new families will place an increasing burden on the social services, housing, and labor markets of the receiving state. And the net effect on the local unemployment rate will obviously be smaller than was envisioned when the legislature passed the recruiting or tax incentive measures in the first place. Perhaps only the skilled labor force is relocated, in which case the only local job creation occurs in the unskilled, low-wage segment of the labor market. Only recently have state and local planners begun to look carefully at the expected impact of new plants on environmental quality and maintenance costs; under many circumstances, these, too, could more than offset the job creation and tax benefits accruing to the state from industrial recruiting.

Thus, we conclude that not even in the case of actual physical plant relocations does economic theory unambiguously predict a positive return to state business incentive or recruitment policies. And even where such policies *are* successful, the attracted plants may overload the environment into which they have been brought, leaving the state in a worse position than before.

THREE CRUCIAL OVERRIDING ISSUES

Whether the new jobs are to be created through increased utilization of existing plant, through new investment in local start-ups or plant expansions, or (ultimately) through actual physical plant relocations, and whether it is competitive or oligopolistic industries that are the explicit or implicit targets of job creation tax incentive policies, there are three crucial overriding issues that have not been discussed so far in this paper. When we consider them, we will have completed our theoretical analysis of the problem, and can turn to the empirical data.

Apparent vs. actual corporate savings. In Massachusetts (for example), a manufacturing or research and development (R&D) firm is allowed to credit, against its annual excise tax liability, 3 percent of the cost of new investment in buildings, machinery, or other equipment. This may seem like quite a large tax incentive to expand or relocate in Massachusetts. Presumably the commonwealth's legislature intended it as such.

But let us look more closely, from the perspective of a company's own accounting office. Suppose a large export-oriented manufacturing concern undertakes a new investment of $800,000. Because its *federal* tax liability rises by about 48¢ for each dollar of *state* tax forgiveness (we'll assume half, to simplify the math), the net savings to the firm will be only

$$\left(\begin{array}{l} \text{value of the new} \\ \text{deductible investment} \end{array} \times \begin{array}{l} \text{state tax} \\ \text{credit rate} \end{array} - \begin{array}{l} \text{increased federal} \\ \text{tax liability} \end{array} \right)$$

$$= \left(\begin{array}{l} \text{value of the new} \\ \text{deductible investment} \end{array} \times \begin{array}{l} \text{state tax} \\ \text{credit rate} \end{array} \times \begin{array}{l} \text{1—corporate federal} \\ \text{tax rate} \end{array} \right)$$

or $= (\$800,000 \times 0.03 \times 0.5) = \$12,000.$

If state and local taxes for this firm total $200,000, and if (as we will show in the next section of the paper) state and local taxes average about 1–3 percent of total costs in the commonwealth, then estimated total costs for this firm are about ($200,000/.03 =) $6.7 million. Then the $12,000 tax savings amounts to only (12,000/6,700,000 =) 0.18 percent of the total costs of doing business.

Alternatively, consider the commonwealth's Employment Opportunity Incentive program, which permits a firm to take a $500 income tax credit for each new full-time worker it hires off the welfare or unemployment rolls in excess of normal growth (currently set—far too high, we might add—at 3 percent per annum, by regulation). Suppose that our hypothetical company were to hire 100 such workers. Then the net savings to the company would *not* be 100 x $500 = $50,000 (as the legislature probably imagined), but rather

$$100 \times 0.5 \times \$500 = \$25,000$$

which (on the earlier assumptions) amounts to only (25,000/6,700,000 =) 0.37 percent—*less than one-half of one per cent*—of the total costs of doing business.

Apparent corporate savings from these state tax incentives are therefore always twice as large as the actual savings seen by the firms' accountants. And the orders of magnitude of the savings are such that they represent a truly insignificant proportion of total costs. Since expansion or relocation decisions are assumed—even by the advocates of these policies—to be a function of relative *total* costs in different places, it follows that these (and similar) state business incentives are unlikely to make much difference. And since nearly all of the states follow one another in legislating one after another of these incentives, even the *absolute* savings differentials from one state to another are by and large meaningless.

Displacement, or maintenance of effort. Employment and training planners have for several years administered federal grants to state and local governments (for public service job creation) and to private corporations (for wage subsidies for the hard-core unemployed). Often, especially over time, the grant recipients (or prime sponsors) use the transferred funds to finance activities that they would probably have undertaken anyway, in the absence of the grant, with local (or internal) resources. The federal grants partly displace, rather than fully complement, those local resources. The result is that the net job creation impact is usually less than the gross (or intended) impact.

State business incentives may encounter the same problem. It is difficult to prove that a firm taking a tax credit would not have acted as it did, even in the absence of the incentive. The *only* foolproof way around this is to give grants, loans, or tax credits exclusively to *new projects*, created expressly for the purposes defined by the grant or credit legislation. Subsidization of existing entities, whether they be private firms or local governments, always runs the risk that displacement will occur. In the empirical section of this paper, we will show that—in Massachusetts and Connecticut, at least—tax incentive displacement may have been very serious indeed.[24]

The opportunity costs of the tax incentives. Finally, we need to confront the popular belief that—apart from the administrative costs (which are generally small)—these various business incentives are essentially costless. In fact, tax incentives force the state to *forego tax revenue,* the revenue which *would have* been collected in the absence of the policy. Those foregone revenues had other productive uses, and it is the goods and services which those foregone revenues *could* have purchased that constitute the real (social or opportunity) cost of the tax incentives.[25] How many ways can a state spend its money? On housing, health, transportation, its own job creation via public employment—or in the form of personal income tax relief. Economic planners need to closely examine the goods and services that are foregone as a consequence of the implementation of business tax incentives.

Both the additional job-creating investment activity of private firms and the additional spending by state government will have multiplier effects within the state (averaging, we think, about $1.25 to $1.50 of total additional income for each $1 of new spending[26]). But if we are correct that tax incentives do not induce firms to undertake investment activity that they would not have undertaken in the absence of the incentives, while the foregone revenues could have financed new state spending, then the net multiplier effect of these state tax incentives would be *negative;* a $1 tax incentive *removes* 25–50¢ from the economy. Even if firms *do* undertake at least some new investment in connection with the incentives, both the timing and the mix (by sector, location, race, sex, and skill composition of the extra labor demanded) are sure to vary between private investment and public spending. Good economic planning requires a much closer examination of these differences than anyone has ever undertaken, to see what *kinds* of jobs the state tax incentives create, even when they are working efficiently.

Finally, while mortgage guarantees, loans, and industrial development bonds do not reduce the amount of taxes that accrue to state governments, there may also be important opportunity costs associated with these types of incentives as well. Banks have a finite amount of savings at any one time and have to allocate their investments among different kinds of bonds and loans. To the extent that government guarantees of mortgages, and the tax exemptions on industrial development bonds, make these more attractive holdings for banks than other investments, additional funds will be placed in government-backed instruments. The interest rate charged for more risky loans, private bonds, and residential mortgages could, in turn, be increased to reflect a reduction in supply of funds made available for conventional private sector activities by the banks.

Therefore, tax deductible bonds may (for example) make public energy a bit less expensive than privately produced energy, by making a public energy corporation's bonds more attractive to private lenders. But this in turn may make it harder for a state low-income housing development corporation—or a new privately owned fish processing company—to meet its needs.

A Survey of the Evidence

Government agencies and independent researchers have, since the 1950s, attempted to measure the relative impact of business incentives on industrial location or expansion. By contrast, not until recently have serious attempts been made to measure the opportunity costs of such incentives, and then (to our knowledge) only in one state. Finally, we may inquire about the relative *size* of the business costs (mainly taxes) which these incentives are designed to reduce; are they *large* enough to matter? And how many plants actually *do* move from one state to another over time?

Although the number of published studies and reports on the subject turns out to be substantial, the quality of the material is very poor.[27] Inadequate attention has been paid to controlling for differences in regional conditions, point in the business cycle, or financial condition of the companies involved in the various incentive programs. The benefit-cost type studies invariably commit the basic fallacy of comparing before-the-program and after-the-program conditions and attributing changed conditions to the program, when in fact what is called for is a comparison of "after" conditions *with and without* the program. If the findings from these various studies were sharply at odds with one another about the effectiveness of state business incentives, then we would probably be unable to draw even weak conclusions because of our inability to say with any assurance which studies were "better" than others, or to compare different studies.

But that turns out *not* to be a problem. With a very few exceptions, the empirical literature fails to reveal significant plant relocation or expansion resulting from (or even just correlated with) interstate differentials in state business incentives. We do not say that such incentives never have any effect (or that they cannot have an effect), only that the literature does not show an effect to be *typical* or *sizable*.

SURVEY RESEARCH ON THE IMPACT OF BUSINESS INCENTIVES

Many surveys have been conducted of firms either expanding their facilities in a particular location or region or moving into that area. Those employers asked to volunteer the factors that mattered in their decision seldom mentioned such things as state and local taxes or the availability of subsidized credit. When taxes (or credits) were specified by the interviewer, the proportion of respondents checking them off usually rose to between 5 and 15 percent. But when the latter surveys went on to ask the respondent to indicate whether these factors were critical or not, few considered them as such. In most cases, access to markets, labor costs, and the availability of physical space were the paramount locational considerations.

One of the earliest such surveys was conducted in 1950 by the Survey Research Center of the University of Michigan.[28] Only 9 percent of the 188 plants moving into Michigan were under the control of managers who felt that state's tax benefits to be an important consideration in the move. A Regional Plan Association study of firms moving plants *out* of New York City between 1947 to 1955 concluded that 15 percent of the moves were related to inter-regional tax differentials.[29] A questionnaire was mailed to firms expanding or relocating into seven southern states in the late 1950s; 11 percent of the respondents checked local taxes as a factor, but in only 2 percent of the cases was that factor called critical.[30]

One particularly careful study was conducted at the Stanford Research Institute in 1964 by Robert Spiegelman.[31] He analyzed the locational behavior of one of the more footloose industries: precision instrument manufacturing. More than one-half of the forty-five firms in the study considered inter-regional tax differentials relevant, but only one called them the most important factor. Thirteen percent of the firms in a mid-1960s survey of industrial migration into Texas considered taxes to be one determinant of their decision.[32]

A national mail survey conducted by the U.S. Department of Commerce in 1972, covering 2,900 companies in high-growth industries across the country, revealed that fully 78 percent considered tax incentives or "holidays" to be relevant to their locational decisions.[33] But only 8 percent rated such incentives as critical.

There is, of course, no way of knowing who answers these mail questionnaires. Is it a public relations staffer in the company? A lower level manager saying what he (or she) thinks is going on (or should be going on)? In 1974, in order to make company responses more precise, personal in-depth interviews were conducted in two New England states: Massachusetts and Connecticut. Executives of fifteen Massachusetts companies were sampled by two legislative staffers from the pool of companies that had applied for and received state job creation tax credits, fourteen of them for alleged expansion in excess of normal growth, and one for relocation in to the Commonwealth. Every single interview yielded the same result: the company took actions according to its own plans, *then* learned about the existence of the tax credits and applied for them (often at the explicit *urging* of the state bureaucrats in charge of the program).[34]   An independent set of interviews with Connecticut businesspersons participating in that state's business incentive programs produced identical results.[35]   In these cases, at least, the causality is unmistakable: the availability of the incentives did *not* produce business behavior that would not have occurred otherwise.   Instead, the incentives functioned as a windfall for the companies—at the expense of the taxpayers.

CORRELATIONS OF INTERSTATE BUSINESS TAX DIFFERENTIALS WITH INTERSTATE EMPLOYMENT GROWTH (OR UNEMPLOYMENT) RATES

One way to deal with the inherently subjective nature of the survey approach ("Mr. Businessman, do taxes matter to you?" "Of course they do.") is to compare states with high and low business taxes, to see whether or not they vary systematically in the growth of jobs—which is, after all, the ultimate alleged payoff to business incentive policies. In this literature, the results so far have been uniformly negative.

C.C. Bloom correlated growth in manufacturing employment with per capita state and local tax collections among all the states, for the period 1939–53 and the period 1947–53.[36]   In neither case was there a statistically significant relationship.   The first of the multiple equation state econometric models, describing the growth of the Michigan economy between 1947 and 1953, showed no significant relationship between state and local taxes and employment growth over time.[37]   A nonprofit citizens' organization, the Pennsylvania Economy League, rank ordered eleven states in 1971 according to the burden of state and local taxation on ten specific industries.   We find no systematic correlation between this rank ordering and the state unemployment rates; in fact, the lowest unemployment state (Indiana) was consistently found to be among the very *highest* tax burden states for most of the industries.[38]   Finally, a 300-equation econometric model of the Massachusetts economy, describing the period 1950 to 1972, has been constructed by Anne Friedlander, George Treysz, and Richard Tresch.   For fifteen of sixteen major industries studied, there was no statistically significant relationship between quarter-to-quarter changes in Massachusetts's share of national employment and changes in the ratio of Massachusetts business taxes to the average for all states (actually, this conclusion is inferred rather than read directly from the model, since taxes were folded into a composite index of capital costs).[39]

THE OPPORTUNITY COSTS OF BUSINESS INCENTIVES

There are two kinds of real opportunity costs associated with the various business incentives under study. The tax revenues that governments (especially the federal government) must forego when tax related subsidies or credits (what Harvard lawyer Stanley Surrey calls "tax expenditures") are legislated *could* have been used to purchase goods and services, thus putting people to work. Some quantitative estimates have been made of these costs. The second type is more difficult, both to define and to measure. Applying the limited bonding capacity of a state government to certain purposes (such as financing infrastructure for private firms) may make it more difficult for other public purposes (or even other private firms) to acquire capital on the same terms. The attendant displacement (or increased cost) of development elsewhere in the economy also constitutes an opportunity cost of the bonding program.

Surrey estimates that, in fiscal year 1968, the federal income tax deduction of the interest on state and municipal bonds cost the U.S. Treasury about $1.8 billion.[40] More recent figures calculated by the U.S. Office of Management and Budget for FY 1976 show that foregone federal revenues amounted to nearly $4.8 billion that year, with three-fourths of that accruing to corporations and only one-quarter to private individuals.[41]

In 1975, at the request of State Senator William Bulger, the then Massachusetts Commissioner of Taxation, Nicholas Metaxas, prepared an estimate of the annual revenue loss associated with that state's comprehensive business subsidy package known as "Mass Incentives." His unpublished results are as follows:

3 percent Tax Credit. Massachusetts manufacturing and research and development firms may take a 3 percent tax credit for the purchase of buildings and machinery. The Commissioner estimated that the state lost $18 million in fiscal year 1974 from this incentive.

Corporate Roll Back. Firms are entitled under this provision of the law to roll back a proportion of their tax on tangible property and net worth. The roll back cost Massachusetts taxpayers between $20 to $25 million in fiscal year 1974.

Payroll Factor Freeze. The payroll factor freeze is a formula limiting the tax liability of a corporation expanding its payroll from one year to another. The cost of the program in 1973 was $500,000. No estimates were made for fiscal year 1974 and we will assume that the amount of foregone revenue has remained at the level of $500,000.

Sales Tax Exemption. Businesses do not have to pay a sales tax on the purchases they make of materials, fuel, and machinery. The exemption cost Massachusetts taxpayers $25 million in fiscal year 1974.

The $500 Tax Credit.   Firms that have increased the size of their work force by at least 3 per cent in any one year may claim a $500 tax credit for each individual hired who had previously been on welfare, unemployment compensation, receiving veterans benefits or in a manpower training program.   The Commissioner of Corporations and Taxation could not estimate the loss of revenue from the $500 tax credit because the bill was enacted late in 1973, and firms had not filed for credit that year.   Edward Moscovitch, then Deputy Commissioner of Administration and Finance of the Commonwealth, projected the cost of the program to be between $9 and $12 million annually for the state.   The loss seems vastly overstated for a declining economy like Massachusetts and we will reduce that figure to $2 million.

The Commissioner was not able to estimate the cost of the four remaining subsidies in the "Mass Incentives" package.   They include provisions exempting corporate personal property from local taxation, limiting corporate taxes to a percentage of business activity conducted in the state, providing for a carryover of a tax loss for five years, and permitting a firm that leased a plant from a publicly owned development corporation to receive a 3 percent investment credit.

The Commonwealth thus sustained a loss of about $65–$70 million in foregone revenues through the implementation of six out of ten tax incentives in fiscal year 1974.   It is our guess that calculations performed for the other four incentives, especially the local personal property tax exemption, might well have brought the cost to over $100 million per annum.

No estimate of the "capital rationing" (or crowding) problem has ever been made, but the problem deserves our attention nonetheless.   In recent years, banks have come to hold almost two-thirds of all state and local industrial development bonds.   Banks are very unstable customers; they tend to purchase tax exempt bonds when money is easy and they have met their obligations of a legally required reserve and satisfied the loan needs of their customers.   When money becomes tight, banks will often raise net free reserves by selling or at least reducing the proportion of state and local securities held by them.   State and local governments wishing to finance their capital projects in periods when banks are reducing their portfolio of state and local bonds have two choices: they can either offer to pay high interest rates on the bonds to attract other investors or, where possible, finance their project with short-term notes.   But financing with short-term notes requires paying frequent and substantial underwriting charges which, when added to the already high interest rates, increases the taxpayers' burden.   In addition, short-term notes are only a temporary solution to a serious economic problem and are not themselves marketable when banks' free reserves are extremely limited.

RELATIVE SCALE OF THE BASE
AGAINST WHICH THE INCENTIVES ARE APPLIED

Most of the business incentives we have studied, whatever their particular thrust (labor subsidies, investment credits, etc.), transfer the subsidy by reducing a company's tax burden. How important *are* state and local taxes as a percentage of the typical firm's cost of doing business? If this ratio is very small, then the application of even a large rate of subsidy to such a small base cannot possibly yield significant absolute or relative savings to most firms.

The empirical literature is remarkably in agreement on this subject. State and local taxes are consistently estimated at from 0.5 percent to 3 percent of value added and from 2 percent to at most 4 percent of sales (none of the studies measured taxes in relation to business *costs* per se.) A 1954 study in New York showed state and local taxes to be 1 percent of value added.[42] In a 1958 calculation for Michigan, the ratio of state taxes to value added [43] was under 1 percent. A study of the Washington State economy in 1963 found taxes as a percent of value added to range from 0.93 percent in the food industry to a high of 2.73 percent in fabricated metals.[44] Recently, the Federal Reserve Bank of Boston estimated that the average U.S. business paid 4.4 percent of its income to state and local governments.[45] Since corporate and unincorporated business income averages about one-eighth of value added, this translates into an average ratio of state and local taxes to value added of about six-tenths of 1 percent.

Perhaps even more important is the 1961 finding of J.A. Stockfish for the California Economic Development Agency that state and local taxes as a percentage of stockholders' equity varied among selected industries over seventeen states within a very narrow range: 3.9 percent (fabricated metals) to 6.4 percent (apparel).[46]

Remember that a major objective of these various incentives is to impact relocation: to attract companies planning to make a *physical move* from one state to another. Evidence now exists that the incidence of such relocations is actually very small in the U.S.—whatever causes it. Between December 1969 and December 1972, according to an MIT-Harvard Joint Center for Urban Studies report using Dun and Bradstreet credit-rating data on all manufacturing and most nonmanufacturing firms in the country,[47] only about 0.3 percent of the jobs added to the economy and only about 0.2 percent of the jobs lost to the economy were in plants that made interstate moves. In no state was the share of net job change in moving plants ever greater than 0.5 percent. This was, of course, a recessionary period, and forthcoming data through 1973 may show increased movement of plants. Nevertheless, this first empirical estimate of the size of the "game" which all these states have been trying to capture surely gives the analyst some food for thought.

Conclusions and Speculations

Our research indicates that neither conventional economic theory, nor the (admittedly limited) empirical evidence, provide much support for the popular belief that states can significantly affect industrial expansion, relocation, or start-up with the kind of incremental incentives they have been using. Yet the policies continue to be used—even when officials *admit* that they are unlikely to create jobs. What can explain this apparent inconsistency? Is it just a stubbornly irrational attachment to an outworn conventional wisdom? Or does the ubiquity of these business incentives suggest that they have some definite function, after all, one which conventional economic analysis cannot grasp?

Although work on this question has only just begun, we think that political-economic analysis does indeed suggest some systematic explanations for the existence of state business incentive policies. In this concluding section, we present a sketch of these explanations, returning to our earlier short run vs. long run expositional approach.

THE SHORT RUN STRUGGLE OVER TAXES AND PROFITS

The continuing struggle between capitalists and workers over access to and control over capital—and therefore over the distribution of the national income—is the central concern of radical political economists. That struggle is taking place in every institution of American life. Why, then, should it surprise anyone that it occurs as well at the statehouse?

In order to reproduce the system, governments must tax the business sector to help finance the production and delivery of public goods and services which effectively redistribute real income from capitalists to workers. Not surprisingly, capitalists are constantly trying to resist this redistribution, and to reverse it wherever possible. To assist them in this process, business firms employ paid lobbyists (as, of course, do the organized labor and consumer groups as well). But firms can also count on the assistance of many of the officials of the government agencies administering the many programs that affect business, and the legislators who vote upon them.[48] Where direct reductions in business taxes are politically unattainable, argues James Dumont, capitalists and their "friends at court" must seek the same redistribution to profits by the "back door."[49] Tax and capital subsidies that do not require serious additional effort on the part of the companies serve this purpose admirably. The "manifest function" of state business incentives may be to create jobs, but the "latent function" is to increase profits at the expense of workers-consumers.

Some capitalists are remarkably frank about this. One representative of Jobs for Massachusetts, a prominent business lobbying group, told Dumont that he would prefer an outright cut in the state's corporate income tax rate, but since the former was hard to obtain, "tax incentives will have to do." Another lobbyist, who led the successful struggle for passage of the Massachusetts $500 job creation tax credit, admitted to us that his organization fully intended the credit to be a "gift" to companies, to "compensate" for the state's high tax rates.

It seems, therefore, that there may be some truth to the belief of some state officials that "business incentives serve to communicate the impression that the government is 'pro-business,'" an impression thought to be necessary for creating a positive climate for investment. Moreover, from the perspective of this theory, it should not be surprising that capitalists are now beginning to redirect their assault from business taxes to state personal income taxes, arguing that high personal rates discourage executives from wanting to live (and therefore to locate their businesses) in such places. The particular cost of doing business is less important to businesspersons, we think, than their continuing attempts to use the government to increase their income at workers' expense.

LONG RUN ECONOMIC GROWTH AND THE POWER SHIFT

The day-to-day struggles described above are taking place, we think, within a broader historical frame which conventional economic analysis almost completely ignores.

Capitalist economic growth is by nature assymetric and unbalanced, following a process which some have described as "uneven development."[50] When capital (or systems of physical capital, like neighborhoods and even whole regions) becomes less profitable to employ, those who control the process of production begin to abandon it, in a kind of industrial emulation of the profligate slash-and-burn agriculture practiced by some traditional cultures. Those who are left behind are increasingly thrown upon the mercy of the public sector, to be supported by the taxpayers.

Bearse argues that uneven development explains much of the secular decline in the economic fortunes of the older industrial belt of the U.S.

As markets, capital, and even new research and development shift their loci from the older region (with New York City as its political center) to the "newer" South and Southwest (with Texas as the potential new "capital"), the older places undergo secular deterioration.   There is some evidence that the business incentives are in fact most readily available in these older areas.   But—seen in this larger historical context— the idea of restoring the older areas comparative advantage seems ludicrous.   Besides, the new region can still afford to forego, e.g., high taxes, given the relatively lower standard of living that is consistent with its "reproduction" at this stage of its development.   As public cost of reproduction rises over time, taxes and other costs of doing business will rise in the South and the West, too.   But there is no reason to think that firms will then turn around and repopulate New England.   Capitalist economic development is simply not that smoothly reversible.

This shifting of the center of economic activity away from the Northeast and North Central parts of the country (a shift which goes a long way in explaining the current fiscal crisis of the older cities and states) has been supported and consciously promoted by the federal government, ever since the end of World War II.   Public investments in infrastructure, military production contracts, new bank charters have all been awarded increasingly to southern and southeastern capitalists, often at the expense of capitalists in the older regions (especially New York). In this context, state incentives to business in lagging areas are formally equivalent to welfare grants, serving at best to ease the pain associated with what for many business operations is becoming chronic poverty.

CONCLUSION: DEVELOPMENT AND DEPENDENCY

The conventional theory of local economic development is centered around the concept of the industry producing for export, thereby employing local workers and purchasing locally produced goods and (especially) services. Who owns and controls that exporting activity, and especially whether that ownership-control is absentee, is pretty much ignored by this conventional wisdom. Because the payoff to capturing (or growing) such export-base activity is believed to be so high, states and local governments engage in a ferocious competition for the thousand or so new plants built in this country each year. Among the major weapons in the arsenal of these protagonists are the business incentives we have been studying in this paper.

We have concluded that there is neither theoretical nor empirical support for the belief that interstate business incentive differentials make an important difference to the decisions of firms with respect to relocation, expansion, or start-up of new facilities. We have, in this last part of the paper, also speculated about some political-historical explanations of the continued deployment of what seem to be such ineffective instruments of policy. It remains to make the argument that, even if the incentive approach *were* successful, it would be misplaced.

The kind of economic development based upon the implantation of "foreign" capital into a state or other political community produces the same kind of dependency and unbalanced economic growth here in the rihc United States as it has always done in the poor Third World. New plants that are foreign-controlled impose enormous infrastructure costs on a community, import much of their labor (especially at the level of the "good jobs"), often house their highest paid workers outside the taxing jurisdiction where the plant is situated, and then—after all the effort expended to get them in the first place—they often move away again to some other place when the local inducements run out.

But, writes development planner Barry Stein,

> There is an alternative. The true aim of economic development must be the self-renewing community based on creation of a capability for continuing local action and a degree of self-reliance. This emphatically doesn't mean . . . self-sufficiency; that is both inappropriate and impossible in practice. . . . This approach to local development differs from more conventional ones in three critical ways. First, it creates an ongoing institutional capacity within the community to act on its own behalf, rather than to be "acted on." Second, criteria for evaluating alternative development options are related to increasing the community's retention and breadth of distribution of benefits created, and its control over its own affairs, rather than to increasing per capita income, employment per se, etc. Third, economic activities are oriented as much as is feasible toward replacement of imported goods and services by locally-produced ones.[51]

It is the planning and financing of such community based and/or local, publicly owned enterprises which should be getting the lion's share of the resources generated by state and local (and federal) taxes. The present economic development applications of such resources are, we are convinced, going largely to windfall profits for the business sector. Surely, that is at best a waste of scarce resources, and at worst a politically inequitable approach to the problem of regional economic decline.

NOTES

1. The compilation of business incentives by states in these pages is based on material found in New York State Department of Commerce, *The Use of Public Funds or Credit in Industrial Location,* Research Bulletin No. 6, 1974.

2. The states are Hawaii, Kentucky, Louisiana, Maryland, Michigan, Montana, New York, Oklahoma, Rhode Island, South Carolina, South Dakota, and Vermont.

3. Hawaii, Louisiana, and Montana have statewide programs.

4. The four states are Massachusetts, New York, Rhode Island, and West Virginia.

5. They include California, Connecticut, Delaware, Hawaii, Indiana, Maine, Maryland, Mississippi, New Hampshire, North Dakota, Ohio, Rhode Island, and Vermont.

6. California, Hawaii, and Mississippi have similar programs but not under the aegis of an industrial authority.

7. They are Alabama, Arkansas, Hawaii, Kentucky, Louisiana, Maryland, Massachusetts, Mississippi, Missouri, North Dakota, Oklahoma, Tennessee, and Washington.

8. States authorizing revenue bonds are Alabama, Arizona, Arkansas, Colorado, Florida, Georgia, Hawaii, Illinois, Indiana, Iowa, Kansas, Kentucky, Louisiana, Maine, Maryland, Massachusetts, Michigan, Minnesota, Mississippi, Missouri, Montana, Nebraska, Nevada, New Mexico, New York, North Carolina, North Dakota, Ohio, Oklahoma, Oregon, Pennsylvania, Rhode Island, South Dakota, South Carolina, Tennessee, Texas, Utah, Vermont, Virginia, Washington, West Virginia, Wisconsin, and Wyoming.

9. State-chartered credit corporations are located in Alaska, Arkansas, Connecticut, Florida, Iowa, Kansas, Kentucky, Maine, Maryland, Massachusetts, Mississippi, Missouri, Montana, Nebraska, New Hampshire, New Jersey, New York, North Carolina, North Dakota, Pennsylvania, Rhode Island, South Carolina, South Dakota, Texas, Utah, Vermont, Virginia, Washington, West Virginia, and Wyoming.

10. Actually, some of these business incentives reduced the *fixed* rather than the *variable* costs of firms, and therefore are largely irrelevant to short-run, capacity-utilization decisions.

11. In economics textbook jargon, the marginal cost curve shifts to the right (downward), indicating that profits would now be maximized at a higher level of production—and therefore at a higher level of employment.

12. Even in this simplest of cases, it's not as simple as the text makes it sound. In fact, many of the tax incentives do not reduce the cost to the firm of the labor already employed, but only of any *additional* labor hired, usually "over and above normal growth." In such cases, the overall effect on the costs of even a "perfectly competitive" firm would be even smaller.

13. In technical jargon, the more inelastic the firm's product demand curve, with respect to price, the greater the firm's oligopoly power.

14. Peter Bearse, "Government as Innovator: A New Paradigm for State Economic Developers Policy," *The New England Journal of Business and Economics,* 1976, no. 2, pp. 44-45.

15. Cf. Richard Edwards, et al., *Labor Market Segmentation* (Lexington, Mass.: D.C. Heath, 1974); David M. Gordon, *Theories of Poverty and Underemployment* (Lexington, Mass.: D.C. Heath, 1972); Bennett Harrison, *Education, Training, and the Urban Ghetto* (Baltimore: Johns Hopkins Press, 1972), ch. 5.

16. Cf. Mahlon Strazheim, "An Introduction and Overview of Regional Money Capital Markets," in *Essays in Regional Economics*, John F. Kain and John R. Meyer, eds. (Cambridge, Mass.: Harvard, 1971).

17. Belden Daniels, "There Is No Equity," mimeographed (Cambridge, Mass.: Center for Community Economic Development, 1973, mimeo).

18. Gary Fromm, ed., *Tax Incentives and Capital Spending* (Washington, D.C.: Brookings Institution, 1969).

19. U.S. Congressional Budget Office, *Temporary Measures to Stimulate Employment* (Washington, D.C.: Government Printing Office, 1975).

20. Thus, for example, 1961 interviews with 239 business executives who had located plants in Michigan revealed that, although one-half considered interstate tax differentials a significant factor in their decision, only *two* of the respondents thought that taxes affected their choice of a particular site *within* the state. See Eva Mueller and Jamis Morgan, "Location Decisions of Manufacturers," in *Locational Analysis for Manufacturing*, Gerald Karaska and David Bramhall, eds. (Cambridge, Mass.: MIT, 1969).

This is not the place to undertake a study of the literature on intra-regional, e.g., central city to suburban, plant relocation. One important technical issue in that literature is the trade-off between internal economies of scale (reductions in unit operating costs as the scale of operation increases, at a given location) and external agglomeration economies. Oligopolies can internalize many of the latter—they can hoard their own labor, and buy their own photocopy machines—which makes them increasingly footloose, at least within some broad market area where their customers are located. Small and generally more competitive firms continue to depend more on interaction with their neighbors. It follows that intra-regional cost (including tax) variations are likely to have more influence on oligopolists than on competitive firms, while public policies designed to expand agglomeration economies (such as industrial park development) will probably be more important to competitive firms than to large oligopolies.

A second important issue concerns the capacity of electronic communication to reduce the importance of physical proximity of one firm to another. Firms interact via exchanges of information and products-resources. The greater the relative importance of the former type of exchange among two or more firms, the greater the potential extent to which electronic communication may vitiate agglomeration.

21. J. Bergsman, P. Greenston, R. Healy, "The Agglomeration Process in Urban Growth," *Urban Studies*, 1972, no. 3, pp. 263-88.

22. Except perhaps to the extent that there is a net overbuilding of industrial park—or shopping center—capacity, something which may well have occurred in the U.S. We can't tell for sure, since the two recessions since 1970 have obscured the structural effect by reducing demand.

23. Alpha Chiang, *Fundamental Methods of Mathematical Economics*, (New York: McGraw-Hill, 1974), p. 743.

24. Advocates of tax incentive policies argue that, even *if* they only redistribute a constant total of resources (from place to place, or sector to sector), by affecting the *timing* of private investment, they can influence economic growth. This is a plausible hypothesis—thoroughly untested. Of course, had the tax revenues not been foregone, the *state* could have spent funds earlier as well.

25. The definitive studies are those of Stanley Surrey. Cf. his "Tax Incentives as a Device for Implementing Government Policy," *Harvard Law Review*, 1970, no. 4, pp. 705-38 and "Federal Income Tax Reforms: Replacing Tax Expenditures with Direct Governing Assistance," *Harvard Law Review*, 1970, no. 2, pp. 352-408.

26. This is consistent both with an econometric estimate recently published by George Treysz and Anne Friedlaender, and with the fact that a state multiplier must be smaller than the corresponding *national* multiplier since the former economy is more open (has greater leakage from the flow of internal spending) than the latter economy. The U.S. 18–24 month income multiplier is generally thought to be about 2.0, according to the builders of the various large national econometric models. See Treysz, et al., "An Overview of a Quarterly Econometric Model of Massachusetts and its Fiscal Structure," *New England Journal of Business and Economics*, 1976, no. 1, pp. 57-72.

27. A good, although rather old, summary of much of the literature can be found in John Due, "Studies of State-Local Tax Influences in Location of Industry," *National Tax Journal*, 1961, no. 2, pp. 163-73.

28. University of Michigan, *Industrial Mobility in Michigan* (Ann Arbor: University of Michigan, 1950).

29. A. K. Campbell, "Taxes and Industrial Location within the New York Metropolitan Region," *National Tax Journal*, 1958, no. 10, pp. 195-218. A more recent study of firms moving facilities out of New York State shows a much greater sensitivity to taxes as a cost of doing business, with half of the respondents indicating taxes to be one factor in their relocation decision. There is, of course, no way to be certain that taxes—or any other particular factor—*really* mattered (or were the critical factor that tipped the balance). It is possible that managers mention taxes either because discussion of taxes is "in the air"—certainly the case in New York in recent years—or because it is hoped that such mentions will induce states to lower business taxes—a self-fulfilling prophecy which does indeed occur in many places. The more recent research was done by the Legislative Commission on Expenditure Review, State of New York, in 1974.

30. Thomas Berginand and William Eagan, "Industrial Aid Bonds: A Device for Attracting Industry," *Municipal Finance*, 1961, no. 47.

31. Robert Spiegelman, "Location Characteristics in Footloose Industries," *Land Economics*, 1964, no. 84, pp. 79-86.

32. Thomas McMillan, "Why Manufacturers Choose Plant Locations," *Land Economics*, 1965, no. 41, pp. 239-46.

33. U.S. Department of Commerce, *Industrial Location Determinants* (Washington, D.C.: U.S. Government Printing Office, 1975). Research done on the State of Massachusetts by Margaret Dewar, a doctoral candidate in urban studies at M.I.T., reveals that another common incentive, the industrial

revenue bond, is equally ineffective in affecting business location decisions. Personal interviews with fourteen business executives from firms that had used the bonds showed that a lack of space or other type of inefficiency in an existing plant were the most important reasons behind the decision to move or expand. Only three of the fourteen managers who were questioned voluntarily cited revenue bonds as influencing the choice of a site within a region. Further, the bonds were never a factor in a firm's choice between regions. Margaret Dewar, "Effects of Industrial Revenue Bonds on Firms' Decisions," **Ph.D.** dissertation M.I.T., Dept. of Urban Studies and Planning, 1977.

34. The results of the interviews are contained in a memo written by David Knisely and Jeffrey Simon to Massachusetts State Senators Allan R. McKinnon and William Bulger in 1974.

35. James Dumont, "*State Economic Development: Massachusetts and Connecticut,*" mimeographed (Cambridge, Mass.: Harvard University, 1975).

36. C. C. Bloom, *State and Local Tax Differentials,* (Iowa City: Iowa State University, 1955).

37. W. R. Thompson and John Mattola, *State Industrial Development* (Detroit: Wayne University Press, 1959).

38. For a comparison of state and local taxes on ten representative industries using Pennsylvania Economy League data see Bennett Harrison, *The Economic Development of Massachusetts,* (Boston: Joint Committee on Commerce and Labor, 1974), p. 19.

39. Treysz, et al., *An Overview,* pp. 57-72.

40. Surrey, "Tax Incentives" p. 710.

41. United States Senate, Committee on the Budget, *Tax Expenditures,* (Washington, D.C.: Government Printing Office, 1976), p. 151.

42. A. K. Campbell, "Taxation and Industrial Location," in *Comparative Total Tax Loads of Selected Manufacturers,* D. Soule, ed., (Lexington: University of Kentucky, 1960).

43. Michigan Tax Study, *Staff Papers,* (Lansing: State Press, 1958).

44. Washington State Department of Commerce and Economic Development, *Industrial Loads in Competing States,* (Olympia: State Press, 1963).

45. This estimate for 1973 breaks down into 0.9 percent going to pay corporate income taxes, 1.9 percent for property taxes, 0.8 percent for unemployment compensation contributions and 0.8 percent for other business taxes. Robert Eisenmenger, et al., *Options for Fiscal Structure Reform in Massachusetts,* Federal Reserve Bank of Boston, Research Report 57, March 1975, p. 19.

46. J. A. Stockfish, *A Study of California's Tax Treatment of Manufacturing Industry* (Sacramento: California Economic Development Agency, 1961).

47. David Birch, et al., "Components of Employment Change for Metropolitan and Rural Areas in the United States by Industry Group, 1970-1972," Working Paper no. 8, Joint Center for Urban Studies of MIT and Harvard (September 1975).

48. Bearse, "Government as Innovator," observes that some capitalists are better organized than others to engage in this struggle. Thus "it should be no surprise to anyone that development programs are biased towards estab-

lished industry, larger firms, low-risk debt finance and manufacturing. Any stroll through state legislative chambers will show that these are the better organized, articulate political interests."

49. James Dumont, "State Economic Development," p. 57.

50. Friedrich Engels, for example, described the process of growth in a capitalistic society as a vicious circle with "overproduction, glutting of the market, crises every ten years. . . ." Cf., Engels' *Socialism: Utopian and Scientific* (New York: International Publishers, 1935). Other authors including Joseph Schumpeter and Gunnar Myrdal, have considered the spatial consequences behind one aspect of this "vicious circle." Schumpeter observes that "If the industry of a country is financed by another country and if a wave of prosperity sweeps over the latter, which offers capital more profitable than it has found hitherto in the former country, then there will exist a tendency to withdraw capital from its previous investments. If this happens quickly and inconsiderately it can result in a crisis in the first country. . . . Obviously this can happen . . . also between different parts of one country. . . ." See Joseph Schumpeter, *The Theory of Economic Development* (Cambridge: Harvard University, 1934), p. 221. Also see Gunnar Myrdal, *Economic Theory and Under-Developed Regions* (London: Duckworth and Co., 1957), especially chap. 3, "The Drift Towards Regional Economic Inequalities in a Country."

51. Barry Stein, *Size, Efficiency, and Community Enterprise* (Cambridge, Mass.: Center for Community Economic Development, 1974), p. 86.

Taxation and Manufacturing in New York City

*THE TEMPORARY COMMISSION
ON CITY FINANCES*

Summary

The Temporary Commission on City Finances finds that:

1. The economy of New York City is deteriorating rapidly. In the 1970-1975 period, 470,000 jobs were lost, 200,000 more jobs than were gained in the 1950-1970 period. Until the local private economy is stabilized, the local public economy will continue to be depressed.

2. The major weakness in the city's economy has been in manufacturing. Between 1950 and 1975, over 500,000, or one-half, of the city's manufacturing jobs were lost. So widespread is the manufacturing decline that employment in each of the twenty-one major industrial groups within the manufacturing sector declined by more than 20 percent during the 1970-1975 period.

3. While the commission recognizes that the transformation from a manufacturing-oriented to a service-oriented economy is both inevitable and desirable, it concludes that an attempt must be made to retain, and possibly even expand, the city's manufacturing base. This is

necessary for a variety of reasons, including the need to halt job losses, reduce attendant budgetary pressures, and provide employment and mobility opportunities to members of the resident labor force who cannot find employment opportunities in other areas of the city's economy.

4. Unlike the city's nonmanufacturing sector, manufacturing activities are particularly sensitive to local tax rates. Various business tax increases since 1966 have had a particularly negative effect on manufacturing activity in New York City.

5. The reduction of manufacturing taxes proposed in this report would both halt the city's rapid decline in manufacturing employment and result in sharply increased tax revenues for the city of New York.

6. While the commission's proposals may cost the city as much as $90 million within the first two years of implementation, by the end of the third year that entire amount will have been recovered. If the city does not act, it stands to lose as much revenue *annually* within three years as a result of the continued decline in manufacturing activity as it would cost to implement the proposals in the first place without gaining any of the benefits their implementation will bring about.

The Temporary Commission on City Finances therefore recommends that the following measures be enacted simultaneously:

1. The general corporation (business income) tax as it applies to manufacturers should be reduced from 10.05 percent to 5 percent.

2. The 4 percent sales tax on the purchase of machinery, equipment, fuel, and utilities should be eliminated.

3. A 5 percent investment credit against the general corporation (business income) tax should be instituted for the purchase of new manufacturing machinery, equipment, and structures.

4. The commercial rent occupancy tax should be reduced from its present effective rate of almost 7.5 percent to a flat 2.5 percent on all rentals in excess of $1,000 per annum.

5. The exemptions from the property tax for newly constructed manufacturing facilities provided under the recently enacted Padovan-Steingut legislation should be increased to 95 percent of the assessed value added to the property, declining by 5 percent annually over nineteen years from the present 50 percent exemption which declines by 5 percent annually over ten years.

The Temporary Commission on City Finances also recommends that consideration be given to the elimination of the costs associated with the administration of the general occupancy tax by combining it with the commercial rent occupancy tax. The revenue level could be maintained by raising the rate of the commercial rent occupancy tax to the extent necessary above 2.5 percent to achieve this result.

Because these recommendations are designed to be interactive, their implementation on a partial or piecemeal basis will have little significant effect. Moreover, the confidence of those on whom the success or failure of these proposals ultimately depends, the manufacturers themselves, is unlikely to be inspired by anything less than a substantial effort to ease the tax disadvantages their New York City location imposes on them. Consequently, the commission strongly urges that these recommendations be implemented together.

The Role of Manufacturing in New York City's Economy

The economy of New York City is deteriorating rapidly. Between 1970 and 1975, the city lost 470,000 jobs, a decline of more than 12 percent. Every sector of the private economy contracted during the 1970-1975 period, including the two sectors—services and finance, insurance, and real estate—that had emerged as bright spots after 1950. Only one sector, government, grew between 1970 and 1975, but even government employment has shrunk in the last year.

The city's public economy will not stabilize until its private economy stabilizes. Declining private employment complicates municipal finances by depressing revenues and increasing expenditures. In turn, cutbacks in the public sector exacerbate the contraction of the private sector, at least in the short run, by reducing the amount of money injected into the local private economy.

Within the past year, several initiatives have been taken by the city of New York to protect its declining economic base, including the elimination of the bond transfer tax, the estate tax, and a tax on marketmakers in the securities industry. While these tax reforms were significant with respect to specific competitive problems, none can be considered a major stimulant to the city's economy.

Of course, the city's ability to stimulate the private economy through tax reduction is limited by the need to maintain sufficient revenues to finance the city's day-to-day operations. However, the rapid pace and broad scope of the decline in the private economy, plus the dependence of the city government on the private economy, suggest that New York City's long-term developmental interests would be served by increased efforts to reduce taxes selectively, even if this results in increased pressure for expenditure control in the short term.

THE DECLINE OF MANUFACTURING: 1950-1975

In the past twenty-five years, the economy of New York City has experienced several profound changes. Perhaps the most significant change was the dramatic decline of the economy during the 1970-1975 period. As Exhibit 1 shows, total employment increased gradually during the 1950-1970 period, gaining 276,600 jobs, an 8 percent increase. In the 1970-1975 period, however, the local economy experienced a severe contraction, losing 468,900 (12.5 percent) of its jobs. Thus jobs lost exceeded by almost 200,000 the number of jobs added during the preceding twenty years, resulting in an overall employment decline of 5.5 percent in the entire twenty-five-year period.

Between 1970 and 1975 every industrial sector declined, including services and finance, insurance, and real estate, and some declined precipitously: contract construction, 29.3 percent; transportation and public utilities, 17 percent; wholesale and retail trade, 13.6 percent; and manufacturing, 31.1 percent. The losses in the services and finance, insurance, and real estate sectors were smaller than elsewhere—1.9 percent and 8.1 percent, respectively—but contrasted sharply with the rapid growth each sector experienced in the 1950s and 1960s.

The composition of the city's economy also changed substantially in the 1950-1975 period. One important change was the continual expansion of the public sector (Exhibit 2). In 1950 city, state, and federal employees accounted for 10.8 percent of the total work force in New York City. By 1975, government employees represented 17.5 percent of all workers. The vast majority of government workers in New York City are employees of the city of New York, over 75 percent in 1975. While separate employment breakdowns for each level of government are not available prior to 1970, the bulk of the increase in government employment is represented by employees of the city of New York. Since at least 1960, federal employment in New York City has declined. As Exhibit 1 shows, government employment rose 52.8 percent in the 1950-1975 period, a larger percentage increase than any recorded in the private sector. During the 1960-1970 period, increases in government employment accounted for 74.9 percent of the total employment increase in New York City, an indication that the local economy was in serious, if not widely recognized, trouble prior to 1970.

A closely-related compositional change was the growth of the city's private service economy which gained 263,000 jobs in the twenty-five-year period, a 51.8 percent increase. As Exhibit 3 shows, private service jobs jumped from 14.6 percent of total employment in 1950 to 23.5 per-

EXHIBIT 1

EMPLOYMENT BY INDUSTRY IN NEW YORK CITY:
1950, 1960, 1970, 1975

(employment figures in thousands; parentheses denote a decline)

	1950	1960	1970	1975	Employment Change 1970-1975	Percentage Change 1970-1975	Employment Change 1950-1975	Percentage Change 1950-1975
Contract Construction	123.0	125.3	110.1	77.9	(32.2)	(29.3)	(45.1)	(36.7)
Transportation and Public Utilities	331.5	318.1	323.3	268.4	(54.9)	(17.0)	(63.1)	(19.0)
Wholesale and Retail Trade	754.8	744.8	735.5	635.3	(100.2)	(13.6)	(109.5)	(15.8)
Finance, Insurance, and Real Estate	336.2	386.0	459.6	422.1	(37.5)	(8.1)	85.9	25.6
Services	507.7	607.3	785.4	770.7	(14.7)	(1.9)	263.0	51.8
Manufacturing	1038.9	946.8	766.2	527.8	(238.4)	(31.1)	(511.1)	(49.2)
Government	374.4	408.2	562.8	572.1	9.3	1.7	197.7	52.8
Mining	1.7	1.9	1.9	1.5	(0.4)	(21.1)	(0.2)	(11.8)
Total Employment	3468.2	3538.4	3744.8	3275.9	(468.9)	(12.5)	(192.3)	(5.5)

SOURCES: Data for 1950-1974 are from U.S. Department of Labor, Bureau of Labor Statistics, *Employment and Earnings: States and Areas, 1939-1974* (1975), pp. 500-510; data for 1975 are from New York State Department of Labor, *Employment Review* (May 1976), pp. 36-38.

EXHIBIT 2

PUBLIC AND PRIVATE EMPLOYMENT IN NEW YORK CITY:
1950, 1960, 1970, 1975

(employment figures in thousands)

	1950	Per-centage	1960	Per-centage	1970	Per-centage	1975	Per-centage
Total Employment	3468.2	100.0%	3538.4	100.0%	3744.8	100.0%	3275.9	100.0%
Total Private Employment	3093.8	89.2	3130.2	88.5	3182.0	85.0	2703.8	82.5
Total Public Employment	374.4	10.8	408.2	11.5	562.8	15.0	572.1	17.5
Federal	N.A.		116.4	3.3	107.5	2.9	91.4	2.8
State	N.A.		N.A.		40.9	1.1	47.9	1.5
Local [1]	N.A.		N.A.		414.5	11.1	432.8	13.2

NOTE: 1. Local government data include certain employees, such as transit workers, who are not officially counted by the city of New York as city employees.

SOURCE: Computed from data in Exhibit 1.

cent in 1975. Since government is a service, the combined public-private service share (excluding finance, insurance, and real estate) rose from 25.4 percent in 1950 to 41 percent in 1975. The shares of total employment represented by other sectors did not change appreciably in the 1950-1975 period with the exception of manufacturing: contract construction declined from 3.5 percent to 2.4 percent; transportation and public utilities fell from 9.6 percent to 8.2 percent; wholesale and retail trade dropped from 21.8 percent to 19.4 percent; and finance, insurance, and real estate grew from 9.7 percent to 12.9 percent, the only growth sector other than services and government.

The third significant compositional change in the local economy since 1950 has been the huge manufacturing decline. In 1950 manufacturing employed twice as many persons as the private service sector and almost three times the number of government workers, but service employment by 1970 and government employment by 1975 had both exceeded manufacturing employment (Exhibit 1). In 1975, manufacturing jobs accounted for only 16.1 percent of total employment, down from 30 percent in 1950 (Exhibit 3).

EXHIBIT 3

INDUSTRY EMPLOYMENT SHARES IN NEW YORK CITY:
1950, 1960, 1970, 1975

	1950	1960	1970	1975
Contract Construction	3.5%	3.5%	2.9%	2.4%
Transportation and Public Utilities	9.6	9.0	8.6	8.2
Wholesale and Retail Trade	21.8	21.0	19.6	19.4
Finance, Insurance, and Real Estate	9.7	10.9	12.3	12.9
Services	14.6	17.2	21.0	23.5
Manufacturing	30.0	26.8	20.5	16.1
Government	10.8	11.5	15.0	17.5
Mining	0.0	0.1	0.1	0.0

SOURCE: Computed from data in Exhibit 1.

While the overall record of the local economy, on balance, is poor, the picture for manufacturing is particularly dismal. Exhibit 4 breaks down manufacturing employment in the twenty-one major manufacturing categories between 1950 and 1975. Several important trends within the manufacturing sector emerge from the data in Exhibits 4 to 7.

EXHIBIT 4

Manufacturing Employment by Industry in New York City: 1950, 1960, 1970, 1975 (employment figures in thousands; parentheses denote a decline)

	1950	1960	1970	1975	Employment Change 1970-1975	Percentage Change 1970-1975	Employment Change 1950-1975	Percentage Change 1950-1975
Ordnance	N.A.	4.2	0.9	0.0	(0.9)	(100.0)	—	—
Lumber and Wood Products	7.2	6.0	5.2	3.4	(1.8)	(34.6)	(3.8)	(52.7)
Furniture and Fixtures	22.6	17.7	16.3	11.0	(5.3)	(32.5)	(11.6)	(51.3)
Stone, Clay, and Glass Products	12.4	11.3	7.6	5.2	(2.4)	(31.5)	(7.2)	(58.0)
Primary Metal Industries	14.4	13.4	12.4	8.8	(3.6)	(29.0)	(5.6)	(38.8)
Fabricated Metal Products	N.A.	44.4	34.8	23.6	(11.2)	(32.1)	—	—
Nonelectrical Machinery	31.8	35.2	25.9	16.6	(9.3)	(35.9)	(15.2)	(47.7)
Electrical Equipment	52.6	60.3	45.4	29.9	(15.5)	(34.1)	(22.7)	(33.1)
Transportation Equipment	14.9	11.7	8.7	5.2	(3.5)	(40.2)	(9.7)	(65.1)
Instruments and Related Products	26.1	24.2	20.4	13.0	(7.4)	(36.2)	(13.1)	(50.1)

EXHIBIT 4 (continued)

Food and Related Products	98.3	81.6	56.6	37.3	(19.3)	(34.0)	(61.0)	(62.0)
Tobacco Products	4.0	2.7	2.9	2.3	(0.6)	(20.6)	(1.7)	(42.5)
Textile Mill Products	38.5	36.1	32.2	25.1	(7.1)	(22.0)	(13.4)	(34.8)
Apparel and Other Textile Products	340.7	267.4	203.9	142.1	(61.8)	(30.3)	(198.6)	(58.2)
Paper and Allied Products	28.5	30.2	23.9	16.0	(7.9)	(33.0)	(12.5)	(43.8)
Printing and Publishing	119.2	127.2	120.8	91.8	(29.0)	(24.0)	(27.4)	(22.9)
Chemicals and Allied Products	42.3	45.9	40.3	27.8	(12.5)	(31.0)	(14.5)	(34.2)
Petroleum Refining and Products	8.2	9.9	7.7	5.6	(2.1)	(27.2)	(2.6)	(31.7)
Rubber and Misc. Plastics	10.8	10.5	10.6	6.8	(3.8)	(35.8)	(4.0)	(37.0)
Leather and Leather Products	37.4	31.6	26.7	14.2	(12.5)	(46.8)	(23.2)	(62.0)
Misc. Manufacturing	80.6	75.1	62.9	42.1	(20.8)	(33.0)	(38.5)	(47.7)
Total Manufacturing Employment[1]	1,038.9	946.8	766.2	527.8	(238.4)	(31.1)	(511.1)	(49.2)

NOTE: 1. Columns may not add to total employment because of rounding or unavailability of data.
SOURCES: Data for 1950-1974 are from U.S. Department of Labor, Bureau of Labor Statistics, *Employment and Earnings: States and Areas, 1939-1974* (1975), pp. 500-510; data for 1975 are from New York State Department of Labor, *Employment Review* (May 1976), pp. 36-38.

First, the apparel industry, the city's single most important source of manufacturing jobs, accounted for almost 40 percent of the total job loss in manufacturing between 1950 and 1975; manufacturing's overall decline, 58.2 percent, was exceeded by only the much smaller leather and transportation equipment industries.

Second, not one industrial group within the manufacturing sector was able to avoid a major contraction in the past twenty-five years. While a few industries grew moderately between 1950 and 1960—petroleum products, nonelectric machinery, and electrical equipment each grew more than 10 percent in the 1950s—only two industries, tobacco as well as rubber and miscellaneous products, experienced any growth whatsoever during the 1960s. Between 1970 and 1975, employment in every manufacturing industry in New York City decreased by more than 20 percent. For the 1950-1975 period the city's printing and publishing industry stands out as the strongest performer. Employment in that industry declined the least amount, 22.9 percent.

Third, and perhaps most significant, is the extremely high rate of employment decline since 1970. Between 1950 and 1960, manufacturing employment declined from 1,038,900 to 946,800, an average annual rate of decline of 0.9 percent. In the 1960s, the number of manufacturing jobs fell from 946,800 to 766,200. This amounted to an average annual rate of employment loss of 2.1 percent, more than twice the 1950-1960 rate. In the 1970-1975 period, however, 238,400 more manufacturing jobs disappeared, reducing total manufacturing employment to 527,800 in 1975. During this five-year period, the annual rate of manufacturing job loss was 7.2 percent, about three-and-one half times the rate during the 1960s and eight times the 1950-1960 rate.

The overall decline in manufacturing employment has been accompanied by a large decline in the number of manufacturing businesses in New York City (Exhibit 5). Pre-1960 data on the number of manufacturing firms are not available, but between 1960 and 1974, the number of firms fell 37.4 percent, from almost 36,000 to about 22,500. The rate of firm loss was almost identical to the rate of employment loss in the same period. Overall, the average firm size, by employment, increased slightly in the 1960-1974 period from 25.8 to 26.8 employees.

The city's manufacturing businesses, like the city's nonmanufacturing firms, are relatively small employers. Two-thirds of the city's manufacturing firms employ twenty persons or fewer, and 85 percent of the firms employ fewer than fifty persons.[1] While Exhibit 5 shows that average firm size has not changed appreciably, at least since 1960, the mix of production workers and nonproduction workers has changed. The share

EXHIBIT 5

NUMBER OF MANUFACTURING FIRMS AND
AVERAGE EMPLOYMENT OF FIRMS IN NEW YORK CITY:
1960-1974

Year	Number of Firms	Average Number of Employees
1960	35,918	25.8
1961	34,970	26.3
1962	33,839	26.7
1963	33,216	26.4
1964	32,184	26.7
1965	31,328	27.4
1966	30,810	27.9
1967	29,446	28.6
1968	28,311	29.4
1969	27,549	29.8
1970	26,279	29.0
1971	25,138	30.2
1972	24,221	27.9
1973	22,366	29.1
1974	22,492	26.8

SOURCE: Computed from data in New York State, Department of Labor, *Employment Review* (May 1976).

of workers engaged directly in the production process has declined steadily, while the share of administrative or managerial employees has increased.[2] This reflects a tendency existent in other businesses as well, to retain front-office operations in New York City that are dependent on close proximity to other businesses like printing, advertising, and banking, while decentralizing production and related activities that are not so closely tied to other New York City businesses.

The decline of manufacturing has had a depressing effect on manufacturing wages in New York City. This, coupled with high inflation rates, has actually reduced real earnings in manufacturing over the past decade (Exhibit 6). In 1967 dollars, average manufacturing wages for production workers were $5,431 in 1975 compared to $5,437 in 1966.

As Exhibit 7 shows, wages in other industrial sectors, including the public sector, generally are higher and have grown much faster than in

EXHIBIT 6

AVERAGE YEARLY EARNINGS OF MANUFACTURING EMPLOYEES IN
NEW YORK CITY IN CURRENT AND CONSTANT DOLLARS:
1950-1975

Year	Average Yearly Earnings	Earnings in 1967 Dollars
1950	$3,070	$4,311
1951	3,283	4,291
1952	3,408	4,386
1953	3,508	4,486
1954	3,579	4,547
1955	3,735	4,776
1956	3,893	4,903
1957	4,019	4,901
1958	4,142	4,902
1959	4,318	5,044
1960	4,387	5,025
1961	4,529	5,141
1962	4,673	5,227
1963	4,797	5,254
1964	4,953	5,337
1965	5,090	5,397
1966	5,301	5,437
1967	5,543	5,543
1968	5,631	5,631
1969	5,609	5,609
1970	6,595	5,542
1971	7,060	5,607
1972	7,528	5,729
1973	7,962	5,700
1974	8,418	5,138
1975	9,048	5,431

SOURCES: Computed from data in U.S., Department of Labor, Bureau of Labor Statistics, *Employment and Earnings: States and Areas, 1939-1974* (1975); and New York State, Department of Labor, *Employment Review* (May 1976).

manufacturing. The demand for labor reflects the demand for the goods and services labor produces. Wages in those sectors of the city's economy where employment has grown most rapidly (or declined most slowly), generally have increased more than in the slower-growing or declining sectors.

EXHIBIT 7

WAGE INCREASES OF SELECTED EMPLOYEES IN
NEW YORK CITY: 1954-1974

Employee Category	Percentage Increase 1954-1974	Annual Average Rate of Increase 1954-1974
Sanitationman	229.8%	6.2%
Teacher (minimum)	223.3	6.0
Patrolman	223.2	6.0
Staff Nurse	220.4	6.0
Subway Porter	214.5	5.9
Construction	211.4	5.8
Caseworker	197.8	5.6
Telephone & Telegraph	183.5	5.4
Teacher (maximum)	164.3	5.0
Wholesale Trade	153.7	4.8
Engineer	153.4	4.8
Banking	151.9	4.7
Clerk	137.0	4.4
Manufacturing	136.9	4.4
Retail Trade	117.7	4.0

SOURCE: Economic Development Council of New York City, Inc., *Reducing the 1975-76 Budget Gap in New York City* (August 1975), Table 3.

Exhibit 7 shows the percentage increase in pay for selected private and public employee groups during the 1954-1974 period. Nine of the fifteen groups are specific public employee titles. Salaries for the private sector groups are aggregated, that is, they cover average pay for all workers in the industries. The comparison, then, focuses on wage changes rather than wage levels which are distorted by the merging of multi-occupational wages in the private sector.

With this caveat in mind, the data in Exhibit 7 are instructive, pointing up the fact indicated earlier that manufacturing wages have lagged behind other wages during the period of manufacturing's decline in

New York City. The 136.9 percent increase in manufacturing wages trailed all other categories except retail trade wages, which rose 117.7 percent in the period. Various public employee groups headed the list with twenty-year wage gains in the 215-230 percent range. Construction wages managed to increase at relatively high rates despite the substantial shrinkage in the construction industry shown in Exhibit 1.

SUMMARY

The decline of the city's manufacturing base is now three decades advanced. Despite the extent of this decline, the city government must make every effort to preserve manufacturing, as well as, of course, other industrial sectors. The city government has several policy levers with which it can affect, positively and negatively, economic development. Tax policy is one such lever. The following section describes the broad range of taxes levied on the city's manufacturing firms and the competitive problems they cause.

If, as suggested in this report, the city of New York's tax policies have contributed substantially to the decline of manufacturing in New York City, lower taxes on manufacturing should, *ceteris paribus,* contribute to the retention of manufacturing. Other environmental factors than taxes may once again begin to contribute to rather than work against the city's manufacturing base. The city's large and increasingly under utilized labor force remains a substantial if largely potential asset. Labor costs in other areas of the country, where demand for labor is stronger than in New York City, over time should rise relative to New York City. Also, space for manufacturing now is opening up in New York City. The exodus of people and businesses, the creation of industrial parks, and even the destruction of housing and commercial buildings in certain areas of the city suggest that the space requirements for manufacturing will improve in the future. Other problems, like the city's unusually high energy costs, continue to work against the economy in general and manufacturing in particular.

That improvements in local variables like taxes, labor, and space will prove sufficient to counteract the forces that continue to work against manufacturing in New York City cannot be guaranteed, the empirical evidence in this report strongly suggests that manufacturing in New York City can be stabilized. What is clear, however, is that to continue to do nothing to attempt to restore stability in the city's manufacturing sector will have devastating consequences. In this sense, the future of manufacturing in New York City is like the future of the city itself.

The Taxation of Manufacturing in New York City

Manufacturers located in New York are subject to a variety of state taxes including those on income, highway use, and sales. In addition they must pay property taxes to the localities in which they are located. While other states may have lower rates of business taxation per se, they often create effective aggregate tax burdens that exceed New York's tax burden. In addition, manufacturers in some other states are subject to local personal property taxes that frequently include taxation on machinery or inventories. New York State localities currently tax only real property and recently have been authorized to adopt the increasingly popular economic development policy of property tax abatements. On the whole, New York State is a reasonably hospitable location for manufacturing, at least with respect to taxes.

New York City's tax structure, however, places a particularly heavy burden on local manufacturing, greatly reducing whatever advantages are created by the state's tax system. For example, New York City is one of only a few cities in the United States that imposes a business income tax. Furthermore, the city's business income tax rate, presently 10.05 percent, is higher by a wide margin than that of any other city in the country. The city's sales tax, which applies to machinery used in manufacturing, creates an additional burden, as do the taxes on commercial rent, occupancy, leaded gasoline, commercial motor vehicles, and a variety of other miscellaneous taxes and fees.

This section analyzes the various taxes affecting manufacturing in New York City. First a brief history of the development of taxes affecting manufacturing is presented. This is followed by a comparative analysis of the effective tax burden on manufacturing. Finally, the structure of local taxation is examined in the context of the commission's recommendations.

HISTORICAL OVERVIEW

Manufacturers in New York City are subject to both local real property taxes and to a variety of business taxes. The aggregate property tax burden on manufacturers should be proportional to the full market [3] value of manufacturing holdings in the city. The effective tax rate should be equal to that of all other classes of property. In reality, a de facto classified assessment system exists in New York City. Data from New York State's Board of Equalization and Assessment indicate clearly that manufacturing property has been consistently overassessed relative to other classes of property, and is therefore subject to a higher effective tax rate. Abatements or reassessments generally have been unavailable to manufacturers.

In addition to the basic property taxes, manufacturers are subject to a variety of general sales and occupancy taxes and specific business gross receipts or income taxes. A summary of the imposition and modification of the major nonproperty taxes of significance to manufacturers is presented below:

—1934 City general business (gross receipts) tax imposed at a rate of 1/20 of one percent of gross receipts.
—1934 City sales tax enacted at a rate of 2 percent.
—1935 Gross receipts tax rate doubled to 1/10 of 1 percent.
—1941 Gross receipts tax halved to 1/20 of 1 percent.
—1941 City sales tax halved to 1 percent.
—1946 Gross receipts tax doubled to 1/10 of 1 percent.
—1946 City sales tax doubled to 2 percent.
—1948 Gross receipts tax doubled again to 1/5 of 1 percent.
—1951 City sales tax increased to 3 percent.
—1955 Gross receipts tax increased to 1/4 of 1 percent.
—1959 Gross receipts tax increased to 2/5 of 1 percent.
—1960 Commercial motor vehicle tax imposed.
—1963 City sales tax increased to 4 percent.
—1963 City commercial rent occupancy tax imposed at 5 percent.
—1965 City sales tax decreased to 3 percent.
—1965 State sales tax imposed at 2 percent, exempting machinery, equipment, fuel, and utilities.
—1966 Gross receipts tax replaced with the general corporation (business income) tax at 5.5 percent.
—1970 City commercial rent occupancy tax increased to 7.5 percent.
—1971 General corporation (business income) tax increased to 6.7 percent.
—1974 City sales tax increased to 4 percent.
—1975 General corporation (business income) tax increased to 10.05 percent.

In general, the tax structure has been modified more for political than economic reasons. Legislative histories and contemporary literature offer little enlightenment as to the economic arguments used in support of the various tax changes.

The switch in 1966 to a corporate income tax, however, did in fact reflect legitimate problems created by the gross receipts tax for certain commercial sectors other than manufacturing. Taxes based on gross receipts tend to hit hardest those industries with small profit margins. Narrow margins are generally associated with incipient business failures, industrial sectors with cyclically low profits, or firms with relatively little capital investment. As the apparel industry and wholesale sectors operate with narrow margins on large revenues, they were particularly disadvantaged by the gross receipts tax. Firms such as manufacturers that are capital intensive and add significant value to their product are relatively favored by a gross receipts tax. By 1965 widespread dissatisfaction in the apparel industry had generated sufficient public pressure to promote a radical change in the tax structure.

In 1965 Mayor Robert F. Wagner, Jr., established the first Temporary Commission on City Finances, commonly known as the Schwulst Commission, which recommended that the gross receipts tax be replaced either by a gross margins (value-added) or a net income tax.[4] The commission expressed a mild preference for the former.[5]

The new Lindsay administration's 1966 legislative tax program did not, however, include the value-added tax option preferred by the Schwulst Commission. Instead, it proposed a system of business net income taxes similar to the state's corporation franchise tax, financial corporation tax, and unincorporated business tax that was adopted. The city's new business income tax rate was set at 5.5 percent in 1966, raised to 6.7 percent in 1971, and to 10.05 percent in 1975. During the same period, the state's general corporation tax rate rose from 4.5 percent to 10 percent with an additional 20 percent surcharge on precredit tax liability.

The city and state have made minor modifications to reduce the effective tax burden on certain new investments. However, these slight modifications have not appreciably mitigated the disastrous effect the switch from the gross receipts to the net income basis for taxation has had on manufacturing.

A COMPARATIVE ANALYSIS OF NEW YORK TAXATION OF MANUFACTURING

The wide range of taxes used by states and localities makes direct comparison of effective tax burdens difficult. Beyond basic differences in the structure of state and local tax systems (that is, the presence or absence of a particular tax) there exists wide diversity in the imposition of taxes. For example, Washington State is constitutionally barred from taxing income; Wyoming has a bank excise tax but no corporate income tax; New York taxes corporate incomes, banks, and personal income. Each state has distinct definitions of tax bases, and many states also have tax credit programs to promote industrial development. This diversity makes accurate comparison of tax liabilities difficult at best.

Further complicating a comparative analysis is the role of personal preferences. Some analysts of locational choice have tended to assign a determinant significance to private motives. They believe that nonbusiness taxes and other environmental factors are responsible for the relocation of business outside New York. The commission believes that nonbusiness taxes and other environmental factors generally become relevant only in marginal cases.[6]

A comparison of tax liabilities for some sample locations clearly demonstrates the tax disadvantages of operating in New York City. For illustrative purposes, assume a hypothetical company, the Sisyphus Corporation, is contemplating locating in one of five possible places: New York City; White Plains, New York; Groton, Connecticut; Parsippany, New Jersey; and Honey Creek, Indiana. The company's general characteristics are as follows:

Net Sales		$10,000,000
Net Income		1,000,000
Total Assets		16,500,000
Total Liabilities		10,500,000
Net Worth		6,000,000
Fixed Assets		10,000,000
Total Real Property		3,000,000
Land	$ 500,000	
Building	2,500,000	
Total Personal Property		$ 7,000,000
manufacturing equipment	$6,000,000	
nonmanufacturing equipemnt	1,000,000	
Inventory		$ 1,500,000
Salaries		2,000,000

Assume further that:

1. In the first year of operation all assets will be newly acquired or contracted
2. The manufacturing operation will be strictly intrastate
3. There will be no pollution control equipment
4. All motor vehicles will be leased.

Given this information and certain qualifying assumptions,[7] the relative costs of any given location can be estimated. Exhibit 8 displays the results of such a calculation. While certainly far from precise, these estimated tax liabilities do illustrate the variation in tax structures. For example, excluding potential sales and use taxes, the tax liability for White Plains, New York is approximately 23 percent greater than it is for Honey Creek, Indiana. If sales and use taxes are included, the difference increases to 32 percent. More startling, however, is the difference between New York City and White Plains, where the basic difference amounts to 40 percent. If sales and use taxes are included, the difference between New York City and White Plains comes to 114 percent.

Viewed from another perspective, New York State is a relatively hospitable location for manufacturing, but New York City imposes forbidding barriers. Exhibit 9 presents the estimated tax burden per manufacturing employee. This crude index [8] is derived by allocating business and property taxes between manufacturing and nonmanufacturing functions, and where applicable, adding sales taxes on manufacturing employees to yield an estimate of manufacturing tax burden per employee.

New York State is tied for eighth place with Massachusetts at a per capita rate of $535. While certainly higher than many states (Georgia $179; Texas $127; Ohio $189), New York's rate is not excessive when compared to Connecticut ($719) and New Jersey ($858). However, when the effective tax burden is calculated for a manufacturer located in New York City, it becomes clear that there are formidable obstacles. The effective tax burden in New York City is $237, which when added to the state tax burden, brings the city's per capita manufacturing tax burden to $772, the third highest in the group. Only the states of Washington and California have higher effective tax rates.

It is also interesting to note that states with disproportionately high effective tax burdens have disproportionately small ratios of manufacturing employment to total employment. For example, Washington, which is 77 percent above the mean effective tax burden, is 31 percent below the mean ratio of manufacturing to total employment; California, which is 63 percent above the mean tax, is 21 percent below the mean employment ratio. Conversely, some of the states with the lowest effective tax rates have the highest ratio of manufacturing employment to total employment. Michigan is 25 percent below the mean effective tax rate and 20 percent above the mean employment ratio; South Carolina is 57 percent below the mean effective tax rate and 30 percent above the mean employment ratio. New York City is 54 percent above the mean effective tax rate and 51 percent below the mean employment ratio.

While these comparisons are helpful, they can be misleading because taxes are only one component (albeit, an important one) in any corporate locational decision. Locational decisions, like any other rational economic calculation, are based on market conditions. The locational market has many suppliers (local jurisdictions) offering a good (loca-

EXHIBIT 8

COMPARATIVE ANALYSIS OF POTENTIAL LOCATION COSTS OF THE SISYPHUS COMPANY

	New York City	White Plains, N.Y.	Connecticut	Pennsylvania	New Jersey	Indiana
Federal Taxable Income	$1,000,000	$1,000,000	$1,000,000	$1,000,000	$1,000,000	$1,000,000
Adjustments	+190,000	+90,000			+75,000	+150,000
Local Taxable Income	1,190,000	1,090,000	1,000,000	1,000,000	1,075,000	1,150,000
Estimated Corporation Income Tax	120,000	109,000	100,000	95,000	80,000	42,500[1]
Net Worth Tax—Connecticut			186			
New Jersey					12,000	
Capital Stock Tax—Pennsylvania				24,000		
Supplemental Income Tax—Indiana						27,500
Total Local Income Tax	120,000	109,000	100,186	119,000	92,000	70,000
Real Property Value	3,000,000	3,000,000	3,000,000	3,000,000	3,000,000	3,000,000
Equalization Rate	0.4755	0.3813	0.7000	0.5000	0.7328	0.3333
Assessed Value	1,426,000	1,144,000	2,100,000	1,500,000	2,200,000	366,000
Adjustments					+100,000	+100,000
Estimated Tax	125,000	124,000	90,000	120,000	106,000	27,000
Personal Property Value			7,000,000		7,000,000	7,000,000
Equalization Rate			0.7000		0.5000	0.3333
Assessed Value			4,144,000		3,500,000	933,000
Adjustments			−1,080,000			0.4000
Estimated Tax			178,000		46,000	69,000
Inventory Tax—Indiana						24,000

EXHIBIT 8 (continued)

	New York City	White Plains, N.Y.	Connecticut	Pennsylvania	New Jersey	Indiana
Commercial Rent Tax— New York City	90,000[2]					
Total Local Property Tax	125,000	124,000	268,000	120,000	152,000	120,000
Sales and Use Taxes[3]	320,000	70,000	280,000	60,000	350,000	40,000
Summary						
Income Taxes[4]	$ 202,000[4]	$ 98,000	$ 100,168	$ 119,000	$ 92,000	$ 70,000
Property	125,000	124,000	268,000	120,000	152,000	120,000
Basic Tax Liability	327,000	222,000	368,186	239,000	244,000	190,000
Sales and Use Taxes	320,000	70,000	280,000	60,000	350,000	40,000
Potential Tax Liability	647,000[5]	292,000	648,186	299,000	594,000	230,000
Net Tax After Federal Deductibility	336,440[6]	157,560	337,056	155,480	308,880	119,600

NOTES: 1. Tax liability equal to greater of gross income tax or adjusted gross income tax.
2. Applies only to leased property and is mutually exclusive with property taxes.
3. Applies to initial purchases of personal property not otherwise exempted.
4. Combined New York City and New York State taxes.
5. For a local manufacturer who leased instead of owned property, the total basic tax liability would be $292,000 and the potential tax liability would be $612,000.
6. Denotes net state and local tax liability after their deductibility from federal taxes has been calculated.

SOURCE: Staff computations.

EXHIBIT 9

COMPARISON OF THE EFFECTIVE TAX BURDENS ON MANUFACTURING FIRMS IN SELECTED STATES: 1972

State	Total Number of Firms	Number of Firms With More than 20 Employees	Employment (in thousands)		Estimated Effective Tax Burden Per Manufacturing Employee
			Manufacturing	Total	
Alabama	4,986	1,630	322.6	1,065	$453
California	35,713	11,160	1,544.3	7,229	818
Connecticut	5,835	2,229	398.9	1,186	719
Georgia	7,622	2,657	466.7	1,671	179
Massachusetts	10,780	4,161	625.1	2,267	535
Illinois	18,638	7,358	1,306.0	4,283	663
Michigan	14,863	5,031	1,075.9	3,024	374
Minnesota	5,699	1,929	302.6	1,351	394
New Jersey	15,065	5,912	834.6	2,666	858
New York	38,360	13,008	1,681.2	7,022	535
North Carolina	8,632	3,795	744.0	1,847	487
Ohio	16,396	6,491	1,346.0	3,934	189
Pennsylvania	18,396	8,069	1,416.6	4,371	545
South Carolina	3,719	1,442	354.4	919	214
Tennessee	5,647	2,292	467.8	1,450	677
Texas	14,431	4,798	731.5	3,882	127
Washington	5,343	1,460	224.7	1,100	888
Wisconsin	7,849	2,864	501.0	1,577	370
New York City	24,312	8,011	757.3	5,192	237
New York City plus New York State					772

SOURCES: Computed by the staff from data in U.S., Department of Commerce, Bureau of the Census, *State Tax Collections, 1973* (1974); U.S., Department of Commerce, Bureau of the Census, *Government Finances in 1972-1973* (1974); U.S., Department of Commerce, Bureau of the Census, *Census of Manufacturers, 1972* (1973); U.S., Department of Commerce, Bureau of the Census, *County Business Patterns* (1973); and U.S., Advisory Commission on Intergovernment Relations, *The Property Tax in Changing Environments: Selected State Studies* (March 1974).

tion) for a price (the effective tax burden). The consumer shops around to find the particular type of location that satisfies his needs for an acceptable price. These needs include raw materials; access to efficient, reliable and cost-effective transportation; a labor force sufficiently trained and employable at competitive wage rates; a local economy that provides at reasonable costs those goods and services necessary to conduct business; and, finally, an environment that meets the social, professional, and personal needs of the employees, particularly management. Obviously, the value of one particular attribute may vary in different situations. For example, a company locating in North Carolina may find that low wage rates compensate for higher transportation costs. On the other hand, a firm located in New York City may find that the wide diversity of services locally available and immediate access to a concentrated mass market compensate for higher wage rates. In each case, the particular characteristics of the company will determine the price it will pay for a given location.[9]

MANUFACTURING TAXES IN NEW YORK CITY AND THE COMMISSION'S RECOMMENDATIONS

The structure of a local tax system is to a great extent controlled by the nature of the state tax system. If the city attempts to tax beyond the basic boundaries established by the state's structure, it risks the flight of local businesses. To fully understand the tax issues confronting the city, a basic knowledge of the state's tax system is required.

State Taxation of Manufacturing. States should consider business tax policy and personal income tax policy separately. Unlike the federal situation, the bulk of any state's manufacturing is owned by "foreign" [10] companies, that is, industries or corporations located outside the state whose stockholders are spread around the country. In most situations the influence of one state tax on the allocation of capital to business is minimal. Federal income tax considerations are far more important than state (or local) considerations for planning purposes. A state that taxes business income is restrained only by the competitiveness of its aggregate tax burden and policy goals relating to economic development.

In general, most states adhere to the basic outline of the federal income tax as it applies to business income. This reduces taxpayer compliance costs and eases local enforcement problems. New York State's system of business income taxation is broadly similar to that of the federal government. One major difference, however, is the state's unincorporated business tax which is designed to tax income from other than corporate business enterprises.

One area unique to state and local taxation is the allocation of interstate business income. The problem has been substantially resolved elsewhere through widespread use of the "Massachusetts allocation formula" which determines the allocation of business income on the basis of the extent of property holdings, payrolls, and sales in any given state. Constant refinement of the definitions used in the formula is carried on through the courts. Presently, New York State allocates business income on the basis of a formula involving sales by destination, payrolls, and property.[11]

New York State imposes a franchise tax [12] (general business income tax) determined by one of the following methods (whichever is greatest):

a. 10 percent on allocated entire net income
b. 1.78 mills on each dollar of allocated business and investment capital
c. 10 percent on an allocated income and salaries basis
d. $250.

The optional methods of determination are designed to reduce tax avoidance by adapting the tax structure to various organizational business forms. There is, in addition, a tax on subsidiary capital. The third method listed above (c) may be of greater concern to some smaller, closely held corporations while new firms may be most concerned with the minimum tax. The first method, net income, will be most pertinent to manufacturers.[13]

Over the last fifteen years, the state has instituted a system of tax credits and income deductions [14] to reduce the effective state tax rate on new investments. The patchwork construction of the tax law has, however, left some weaknesses. For example, a 2 percent investment credit produces lesser benefits for a long-lived asset than it does for a short-lived asset. A second area of concern is the lack of distinction between investments in facilities subject to property taxation. Presumably, a somewhat larger credit is necessary for taxed property. Third, there is the problem of delays and mistakes inherent in the discretionary process necessary to obtain the depressed area employment credit. This creates uncertainty and increases compliance costs, reducing the value of the credit. Finally, the consistent discrimination against leased property used in production would appear to frustrate the intent of the credit and to penalize certain new businesses.

The state unincorporated business tax is applied to noncorporate manufacturing enterprises at a rate of 4 percent on a tax base that is roughly similar to that of the corporation franchise tax.[15] The major difference between the two taxes is a specific deduction for "reasonable compensation of the proprietors" that is found only in the former. Most of the other deductions and credits discussed above also apply to the unincorporated business tax.[16]

City Taxation of Manufacturing. New York City's business income tax system is similar to the state's except that it has retained the state's double depreciation for production facilities instead of having moved to an investment credit.[17] The city's general corporation tax rate is currently 10.05 percent, and its unincorporated business tax is 4 percent. The city's taxes also perpetuate the state's systemic discrimination against leased equipment and facilities and the double taxation of retained earnings of "Subchapter S" corporations.[18] The commission recommends that the city reduce the rate of its general corporation tax to 5 percent for manufacturers. This rate is approximately equal to the effective rate prior to 1966 under the gross receipts tax.

The city has been unwise in failing to implement an investment credit, for the present deduction does not adequately balance the effective tax on the investment. In principle, a credit should be related to the present value of the stream of depreciation deductions.[19] To neutralize the taxation of investment, the commission recommends a 5 percent investment credit against the general corporation tax for the purchase of new manufacturing machinery, equipment, and structures.

The same credit system would apply under the unincorporated business tax, but at a proportionately lower level. The investment credit also should be available either to the owner or the user of leased property. If the owner elects to take the credit, it should be applied at the lower effective rate of either the unincorporated business tax or the general corporation tax.

Manufacturers also are subject to both city and state sales taxes on some purchases. Office supplies, parts, and materials not physically incorporated into their final products are subject to the combined 8 percent sales tax. Machinery, equipment, fuel, and utilities used in the production process, however, are subject only to the city's 4 percent tax.[20] The sales tax on machinery is also a form of investment taxation which makes New York a less attractive location. The commission recommends that the city move to conform to the state's exemption of manufacturing purchases by eliminating the 4 percent sales tax the city presently levies on machinery, equipment, fuel, and utilities.

Manufacturers who rent property in New York City for use in production, warehousing, or administration must pay a commercial rent occupancy tax based on annual rental. The tax rate is determined by a graduated schedule based on aggregate annual rentals and ranges from 2.5 percent for annual rentals of $2,499 or less to 7.5 percent for annual rentals of $11,000 or more. In addition, manufacturers renting space must pay the general occupancy tax of between $2 and $12 a year.[21]

Exhibit 10 displays the combined effect of these two taxes. Because the rate structure is not smoothly graduated, it tends to encourage the manipulation of long-term lease payments to minimize commercial rent occupancy tax. The commission recommends that the commercial rent

EXHIBIT 10

Occupancy Taxes in New York City: 1976

Annual Rent	Commercial Rent-Occupancy Tax	General Occupancy Tax	Total	Occupancy Taxes as Percentage of Annual Rent
$ 0- 1,000	$ 0- 25	$ 2	$ 2- 27	-2.7%
$ 1,001- 2,000	25- 50	4	29- 54	2.9-2.7
$ 2,001- 2,499	50- 62	6	56- 68	2.8-2.7
$ 2,500- 3,000	125-150	6	131-156	5.2
$ 3,001- 4,000	150-200	8	158-208	5.3-5.2
$ 4,001- 5,000	200-250	10	200-260	5.3-5.2
$ 5,001- 7,999	312-500	12	324-512	6.5-6.4
$ 8,000-10,999	560-770	12	572-782	7.6-7.5
$11,000 +	825	12	837	7.6-7.5

Source: The City of New York, *Administrative Code of the City of New York*, sections E 46-5.0 and L 46-2.0.

occupancy tax be modified to impose a single flat rate tax of 2.5 percent on all rentals in excess of $1,000 per annum. The minimum rental would eliminate many small returns, reducing administrative costs. In this connection, the Temporary Commission on City Finances also recommends that consideration be given to the elimination of the costs associated with the administration of the general occupancy tax by combining it with the commercial rent occupancy tax. The revenue level could be maintained by raising the rate of the commercial rent occupancy tax to the extent necessary above 2.5 percent to achieve this result.

Manufacturers bear the burden of property taxes whether they own or rent, and are often obligated to pay all property taxes. The level of property taxes in fact often plays a more significant role in investment decisions than local income considerations. Unfortunately, the constitutionally prescribed method for the determination of local debt limits and taxing authority is dependent upon property tax values. To offer direct relief to the manufacturing sector risks reducing both debt limit and taxing authority. Notwithstanding the risks, the extreme sensitivity of manufacturing to property taxes requires some form of abatement in addition to other tax relief.

The recently enacted city law providing for the creation of an Industrial and Commercial Incentive Board to grant sliding scale exemptions from the property tax for newly constructed and reconstructed commercial and industrial buildings acknowledges the barrier the property tax structure presents to new construction, and seeks to deal with it. Authorized by the Padovan-Steingut Bill passed during the legislature's spring term, the local law permits the exemption of a declining portion of the difference between the assessed value of newly constructed or reconstructed commercial or industrial property before and after that construction is completed. For reconstructed buildings the initial exemption is 95 percent of the value added to the building diminished by 5 percent annually over nineteen years. Newly constructed buildings receive a 50 percent exemption that declines by 5 percent per annum over ten years.

While the distinction between newly constructed and reconstructed buildings was probably embodied in the legislation to provide short-run incentives to reduce the supply of excess space presently available in the city's older buildings, it would be preferable for the city to equalize the exemptions in order to avoid discriminating against new construction. Larger manufacturing operations require specialized facilities that are expensive to build, difficult to finance, and greatly increase the assessed value of the property once they are built. Because property taxes imposed on the value of new buildings add another substantial element of cost to such undertakings, the 50 percent exemption declining over ten years will not in most cases provide an adequate incentive to manufacturers to build new plants in New York City. Because the city is gaining no revenue at present from the construction of new manufacturing plants (none are being built) it will cost nothing in the short run and add to property tax revenue in the long run if exemptions are provided for new construction equal to those which are provided for reconstruction. The commission therefore recommends that the exemptions for newly constructed manufacturing facilities be increased to 95 percent declining by 5 percent annually over nineteen years.

The commission also urges that the procedure for applying for and granting the exemptions be made as simple and direct as possible. Bureaucratic red tape and the importance of influence in expediting discretionary decisions are two of the major drawbacks to doing business in New York City. Any delay or uncertainty caused by the city's procedure for granting exemptions will undermine the incentive offered by the exemptions to invest in manufacturing.

NOTES

1. The city of New York, Department of City Planning, Economic Planning and Development Division, "Strategies for Economic Recovery," preliminary draft, unpaginated.

2. See State Study Commission for New York City, *New York City: Economic Base and Fiscal Capacity* (New York: State Study Commission for New York City, 1973), pp. 1, 20-21.

3. *Full market value* means fair market value or an approximation based on capitalized income.

4. Dick Netzer, ed., *Financing Government in New York City* (New York: Graduate School of Public Administration, New York University, 1966), pp. 495-555.

5. Ibid., p. 69.

6. The argument that factors other than business taxes cause relocations basically begs the issue. Management's action is restrained by the implicity profit motivation of the stockholders. In other words, management can justify a move only if it can prove a long-run increase in anticipated net income. If a company can do better in another location merely because of a tax difference, then it clearly implies that the effective tax burden in New York it too high. The point at which management's private preferences can legitimately play a role is the point at which taxes outweigh the advantages of New York City. Then, and only then, can management exercise its prerogatives in choosing a relocation site. It is clear that management's prerogatives exist only under a condition of uncompetitive taxation. It is a flawed syllogism to argue that personal preferences, not taxes, are the determinant factors in plant location. The role of the former must of necessity be a result of the latter.

7. These qualifying assumptions are: (a) all sales and use taxes represent initial investment and exclude recurring or annual tax costs related to the purchase of taxable goods and services; (b) the value of real property is constant despite anticipated fluctuations of land values and construction costs; (c) property values are derived from official equalization ratios despite the possibility of discriminatory fractional assessment.

8. This procedure yields only a crude estimate, for there are a number of problems. First, allocating business and property taxes to manufacturing and nonmanufacturing depends upon a ratio that can be only approximated. Second, data sources are not entirely compatible. Revenue data were taken from U.S., Department of Commerce, Bureau of the Census, *State Tax Collections in 1973* and U.S., Department of Commerce, Bureau of the Census, *Government Finances in 1972-1973.* Data on employment were derived from the *Census of Manufacturers 1972* and *County Business Patterns.* Finally, the allocation of property taxes was done using 1966 ratios taken from *The Property Tax in a Changing Environment: Selected State Studies* (Advisory Commission on Intergovernmental Relations).

The equation used to estimate the tax burden per manufacturing employee has the form:

$$\text{Effective Tax Burden} = \frac{(\text{Property Taxes}) \, R_1 + \text{Corp. Income Tax } R_2 + \text{Sales Tax}}{\text{Manufacturing Employment}}$$

where R_1 equals commercial ratio and where R_2 equals a ratio of manufacturing employment to total employment. An equal amount for sales tax was added only in those states where manufacturing equipment is taxed. In the case of New York City, property taxes were added directly to the numerator without multiplying by R. This was possible due to the availability of more refined tax data.

9. Uncertainty plays an important part in these calculations. Predicting an uncertain future requires the business planner to weigh the probability of an event and the potential benefit to be accrued. A small but assured benefit is often preferable to a large but highly uncertain reward. When considering tax matters this implies that potential credibility is important. That is, a relatively attractive tax structure may be ignored if the locality has a history of heavy taxation. On the other hand, a stable and reliable political environment may compensate for other local deficiencies.

10. The word *foreign* refers to those industries or corporations located outside the state while *domestic* refers to those located in the state.

11. In its classical version, all three factors were weighted equally, with sales being determined by point of origin, destination, or some combination thereof. New York State presently weighs sales by destination most heavily (50 percent) and considers property and payroll to a lesser extent (both 25 percent). This weighting reflects New York's changing role as a net importer of manufactured goods. The emphasis upon sales by destination tends to favor exporting domestic manufacturers who are very sensitive to taxation while slightly increasing the burden of the more resilient local service industries.

12. New York State, Tax Law § 210 (1)(a)(1).

13. This report does not deal with either the taxation on investment income (interest, dividends, etc.) or subsidiary capital. These important issues are more properly considered with an analysis on the effects of business taxation on office as opposed to manufacturing employment.

14. During the 1960s, a series of special deductions and credits were introduced to reduce the effective tax rate on certain investments. In the

1963-1968 period, taxpayers were permitted to deduct twice the amount of annual depreciation permitted by their federal return for investments made in New York up to the value of the asset (Tax Law § 210(3)(d)(1)). In 1963, businesses were allowed to deduct as expense items investments in research and development facilities located in New York when used in the "experimental or laboratory sense" (Tax Law § 210(3)(d)(2)). Two years later, similar treatment was permitted for industrial waste treatment facilities and air pollution control facilities (Tax Law § 208(9)(g)). In 1969, the double depreciation of production facilities was replaced by a 2 percent investment credit (Tax Law § 210(12)). A special tax credit for investment in qualified facilities in depressed areas was established in 1968 (Tax Law § 210 (11)). Finally, in 1976, an additional amount equal to 50 percent of the investment credit was made available for each of three years if the firm's New York employment rises slightly each year (Tax Law § 210 (12A)).

15. New York State has not, however, implemented any provision for federal Subchapter S corporations. Corporations having elected Subchapter S status for federal purposes are thus liable for the state's corporation franchise tax. In addition, any remaining income becomes a personal income tax liability of the shareholders whether or not retained by the corporation. A more rational approach would involve the state's taxing only the individual's share of dividends paid.

16. Curiously, the credits apply at the same rate despite the significantly lower tax rate.

17. There are also several other minor differences in credits and deductions. See Wilbur R. Thompson, *A Preface to Urban Economics* (Baltimore: Johns Hopkins Press, 1965), chap. 1.

18. See Fred Durr, *The Urban Economy* (Scranton: Intext Educational Publishers, 1971), p. 194.

19. The credit in theory should compensate for the effects of discounting future depreciation deductions. Such a credit would be equal to the tax rate times one minus the present value of the sum of depreciation deductions. This approach would create a sliding scale of investment credit depending upon the continuance of the double depreciation, the presence of property taxation, and the useful life of the asset. For example, an asset not subject to property taxes with a useful life of five years or less (with double depreciation) should receive no investment credit. A similar asset with a useful life of ten years should receive a credit of approximately 2.3 percent, while an asset with a 50-year life would be eligible for a credit of almost 6.5 percent. Assets subject to property taxation would receive slightly greater credits.

20. New York State, Tax Law § 1115(a)(12) and § 1115(c).

21. The general occupancy tax was, until recently, the only local tax specifically earmarked. The proceeds are reserved for housing authority subsidies and expenses (including debt service) associated with certain housing and urban renewal projects excluded from the city's general debt limit. The New York State Constitution (Art. 18 § 4) requires the city "to levy annually a tax or taxes other than *ad valorem* tax on real estate" to cover excluded debt associated with housing. It appears there is some question about the precision of the city's compliance with the constitutional provisions.

The Aging Industrial Legacy:
Labor Force and Wage Rates

D. QUINN MILLS

Introduction

THE OBJECTIVE OF THIS PAPER is to review wages, the labor market, and productivity in the northeastern states as they have developed over time and as they relate to the basic problem of the revitalization of the northeastern economy. It is apparent, at least to a limited extent, that equilibrating forces of the nature that Dr. Freund described are already evident in the data with respect to wage rates, earnings, and the labor market in the Northeast Region. These will be described subsequently.

The basic question that we have to consider is not simply whether or not there are policy initiatives that can be taken which give some promise of revitalizing the Northeast's economy. Equally important, if the economy is somehow stimulated, is the question: will it tend to be choked off by a resurgency of the same kinds of behavior that created the problem in the first place? This is a very serious and a very real issue.

It is extremely difficult to generalize about the Northeast. New York is quite different from New Jersey; Pennsylvania is special in many ways; Massachusetts could not be more different from New Hampshire and, in fact, each state exists in the form that it does because they are adjacent to each other and to a substantial degree they are a reaction to each other.

As a consequence, generalizations in this area, especially with respect to the labor market, are somewhat hazardous. Nonetheless, if we are talking about the Northeast, there's no other method than to recognize the problem by noting exceptions as we proceed.

The Informational Base

Since this is an important concern of considerable complexity, we should begin by briefly reviewing what kind of information is available about wage rates and productivity. Four specific comments are warranted. First, the information on population, employment, income levels and earnings is reasonably good for the Northeast, for its various states, and for many of its metropolitan areas. It's reasonably good for the nation as a whole. We have in the United States probably the best set of national statistics that exist anywhere in the world about such matters.

Second, information on unemployment by states and subareas exists, but it is imperfect and possibly, in may instances, erroneous. Nevertheless, the national unemployment statistics are also among the best in the world. They are not perfect, and there are certain problems with them that are well known; they are developed via statistical sampling and are reasonably good.

Third, information on wage rates (in contrast to that on income levels and earnings) is extremely spotty. What data we have are very interesting; some of them will be cited subsequently, but they are the result of very few surveys. There are no comprehensive data available on wage rates.

Fourth, information on productivity in states and areas is absolutely nonexistent, to the best of my ability to determine. Some agencies in various state governments and some academic researchers have periodically set out to create such data, but no one has done it in any comprehensive and reliable form. When we talk about productivity figures, we talk in statistical and factual darkness to a substantial degree.

Empirical Analysis: The Implications

The analysis of the extant data will be summarized in a series of points. They add up to an interesting picture which is somewhat different from what we would initially envision.

First, projections that are available make it reasonably clear that until 1980, over the next three or four years, both the New England and the Middle Atlantic divisions will continue to lose their historical share of manufacturing industries. That does not necessarily mean for all states an absolute decline in manufacturing jobs; but the projections are for a continued decline in the Northeast's relative role in manufacturing. This is especially true in the higher wage, higher income manufacturing industries, but it is also true to a lesser degree in lower wage industries (Exhibit 1).

Second, in the Middle Atlantic and New England states over the last twenty-five years or so, there has been a disproportionate decline in manufacturing employment and in construction employment. Services have grown disproportionately (the proportion, in all cases, is in reference to the national average). Government employment is below the national average in the region as a whole and it has grown about the same rate as in the nation as a whole (Exhibit 2).

The state of New York is a pronounced exception to some of those generalizations. The drop in construction and manufacturing employment is much more pronounced in New York than in the region as a whole. Its growth in government employment is much more pronounced.

Third, average hourly earnings in the New England and Mideast states over the last twenty-five years have declined relatively toward the national average. This is not to say that they declined in absolute terms, of course. Wages in the country and average hourly earnings have grown substantially with inflation, and there have been increases in real earnings as well. However, earnings have declined relative to the national average. To put it another way, the Northeast Region now holds a smaller advantage with respect to average hourly earnings than it used to have with respect to the balance of the nation. This, of course, reflects the growth in service jobs and the decline in manufacturing jobs in the region (Exhibit 3).

Average hourly earnings in manufacturing in the northeastern states —this is manufacturing alone—have also declined over the last twenty-five years relative to the national average. This reflects the strong shift of higher wage manufacturing industries away from the Northeast (Exhibit 4).

EXHIBIT 1

NEW ENGLAND AND MIDDLE ATLANTIC DIVISIONS:
SELECTED MANUFACTURING INDUSTRIES
PERCENTAGE SHARE OF UNITED STATES TOTAL
1969 AND 1980

Manufacturing Industry	Average Hourly Earnings (1975)	Division			
		New England		Middle Atlantic	
		1969	1980	1969	1980
Higher Wage					
Motor Vehicles	$6.47	.94%	.87%	10.84%	10.02%
Transportation Equipment (except motor vehicles)	5.99	11.63	9.56	13.13	12.77
Petroleum Refining	6.40	.71	1.58	23.91	23.62
Primary Metals	6.18	4.12	3.17	30.79	26.55
Fabricated Metals	5.04	8.65	8.90	18.52	16.43
Chemicals	5.35	3.52	3.93	32.49	30.75
Machinery (except electrical)	5.36	8.14	6.69	21.36	17.61
Medium Wage					
Electrical Machinery	4.58	9.02	8.48	25.47	19.61
Paper	4.98	10.25	9.15	22.05	19.44
Lower Wage					
Textiles	3.39	9.66	5.94	18.73	15.84
Apparel	3.18	5.40	4.63	45.42	32.94
Lumber and Furniture	4.00	4.57	4.01	11.87	9.42

SOURCE: D.H. Garnick, "Northeast States in Context of Nation," paper delivered at the Harvard and M.I.T. Joint Center for Urban Studies, January 19, 1977 (U.S. Department of Commerce data).

Fourth, it is important to examine wage rates per se. This information is little enough known in the academic and broader spheres of our society to require considerably more analysis. Pay levels or wage levels disaggregated by occupation in the Northeast show a mixed picture.

EXHIBIT 2

Industrial Employment as a Percentage of Total Nonagricultural Employment Selected Areas: 1950 and 1975

Area	Construction		Manufacturing		Trade		Service		Government	
	1950	1975	1950	1975	1950	1975	1950	1975	1950	1975
U.S. Total	5.2	4.5	33.7	23.8	20.8	22.0	11.9	18.2	13.3	19.2
New England										
New England Division	4.4	3.6	43.9	27.9	19.3	21.7	10.5	20.1	11.4	16.1
Massachusetts	4.2	3.4	40.8	25.5	20.9	22.7	10.9	21.8	12.0	15.8
New Hampshire	4.1	4.5	47.1	29.0	17.1	21.9	11.1	19.4	11.8	16.3
Mideast										
New York	4.14	2.98	34.3	20.7	20.4	20.6	13.2	21.2	11.7	19.5
Delaware	8.8	6.66	42.6	29.4	17.3	20.5	9.9	16.4	8.6	16.9
New Jersey	4.9	3.41	45.7	27.6	16.5	22.1	10.1	17.6	10.3	17.6
Pennsylvania	4.4	1.05	38.7	30.3	17.8	20.2	10.7	18.1	9.3	15.6
Maryland	3.4	6.45	42.9	16.1	18.9	25.0	10.0	20.0	14.7	21.2

NOTE: The Mideast classification is that of the Bureau of Economic Analysis, U.S. Department of Commerce.
SOURCE: U.S. Bureau of Labor Statistics.

EXHIBIT 3

AVERAGE HOURLY EARNINGS, PRIVATE NONAGRICULTURAL EMPLOYMENT
NORTHEAST STATES AS A PERCENTAGE OF NATIONAL AVERAGE
1950, 1960, and 1975

Area	1975	1960	1950
U.S. Total	100	100	100
New England			
Connecticut	105	111	107
Vermont	89	88	90
Massachusetts	98	100	103
Maine	83	84	89
Rhode Island	84	89	96
New Hampshire	87	84	90
Mideast			
New York	108	110	114
New Jersey	108	113	113
Pennsylvania	109	110	107
Delaware	111	110	106
Maryland	110	108	102

SOURCE: U. S. Bureau of Labor Statistics.

New York City rates have risen substantially relative to the nation over the past fifteen years or so. The Boston rates are mixed in their relationships. They have risen for office and clerical occupations, as well as for skilled labor occupations, but they have fallen for unskilled occupations. Philadelphia, in contrast, has demonstrated slight decreases in skilled labor rates, but slight increases in the other categories. We are speaking now of cities because the data are for cities. It's impossible to obtain comparable data for states.

Some further examples are informative. In 1960-1961 in the City of New York, office and clerical wage levels were about 2 percent above the national level; by 1973-1974, they expanded to 8 percent above the national level. Skilled labor wage rates averaged 2 percent below the national level in 1960-1961 in New York City. In 1973-1974, they moved to the national average. Unskilled workers in manufacturing plants, in 1960-1961 in New York City, had rates which averaged 3 percent above

EXHIBIT 4

AVERAGE HOURLY EARNINGS OF PRODUCTION WORKERS
ON MANUFACTURING PAYROLLS, NORTHEAST STATES AS PERCENTAGE
OF NATIONAL AVERAGE: 1950, 1960 and 1975

Area	1975	1960	1950
U.S. Total	100	100	100
New England			
Connecticut	100	102	100
Vermont	84	81	84
Massachusetts	92	92	95
Maine	79	78	82
Rhode Island	79	83	88
New Hampshire	82	78	84
Mideast			
New York	102	102	109
New Jersey	102	104	104
Pennsylvania	103	102	99
Delaware	105	102	98
Maryland	104	100	94

SOURCE: U. S. Bureau of Labor Statistics.

the national level; by 1973-1974, they were 15 percent above the national parameter.

Boston has a very different pattern. In 1960-1961, office and clerical jobs were 7 percent below the national average. In 1973-1974, they moved to 1 percent below the national level. Skilled maintenance jobs in Boston in 1960-1961 were 6 percent below the national average, and by 1973-1974 were 3 percent below the national average. Unskilled labor in plants has been noted a great deal in discussions of the Northeast. In 1960-1961 in the Boston area, unskilled labor wage rates were 3 percent below the national average, and by 1973-1974 had fallen to 9 percent below the national average (Exhibit 5).

It is difficult, in examining these data, to see the pressure of wage rates in general on the location of manufacturing industries or, for that matter, other kinds of industries, except to some degree in the New York City area. Now, that is not to say that in certain industries that pressure

EXHIBIT 5

PAY RELATIVES BY SELECTED OCCUPATION, MAJOR CITIES
ALL INDUSTRIES: 1960-1961, 1963-1964, 1973-1974

Area	Occupation		
	Office-Clerical	Skilled Maintenance	Unskilled Plant
United States	100	100	100
Boston			
1960-1961	93	94	97
1963-1964	93	94	97
1973-1974	99	97	91
New York City			
1960-1961	102	98	103
1963-1964	103	101	106
1973-1974	108	100	115
Philadelphia			
1960-1961	95	98	101
1963-1964	96	99	102
1973-1974	97	97	103

SOURCES: 1960-1961: Toivo P. Kanninen, "Wage Differences among Labor Markets," *Monthly Labor Review*, 85, no. 6, pp. 614-20.
1963-1964: Kenneth J. Hoffman, "Metropolitan Area Pay Differences," *Monthly Labor Review*, 88, no. 4, pp. 407-12.
1973-1974: S. E. Baldwin and R. S. Daski, "Occupational Pay Differences among Metropolitan Areas," *Monthly Labor Review*, 99, no. 5, pp. 29-35.

does not exist.   For example, textile wage rates in New England are substantially above those of the nonunionized companies of the South. But across the broad range of manufacturing activities, the Northeast has been losing manufacturing jobs and relative positions substantially at a time when, with some few exceptions—New York City being the major one—its wage increases have not been above the national average.

There are many ways to interpret these findings.   Those who wish to assert that the market works perfectly—because the Northeast Region is losing manufacturing jobs, therefore, its wage rates are declining relative to the national average—may do so. After the fact, there may seem to be some evidence of that, but that is not what we often recognize as the causal connection. In scrutinizing the data, it is very difficult to find those wage rates in the Northeast that drive firms to move to other regions of the country.

Fifth, in general in the United States, wage rates are higher in the West than they are in the northeastern states. They have come to be higher in recent years in the North Central states—Ohio, Michigan, Illinois, for example—than they are in the Northeast. In the South, especially in the Southeast and to some degree the Southwest, wage rates remain substantially lower.

This differs considerably, of course, by industry. In 1974, office clerical jobs in the major cities of the Northeast averaged 1 percent below the national average. In the West they were at the national average. In the South they were 8 percent below the national average. Skilled maintenance rates were 5 percent below the national average in the Northeast; 3 percent above in the West; 3 percent above in the North Central states; and 8 percent below in the South. Unskilled plant jobs were 4 percent below the national average in the Northeast Region; 10 percent above in the North Central states; 6 percent above in the West; and 25 percent below in the South (Exhibit 6).

EXHIBIT 6

Pay Relatives, by Selected Occupation by Region: 1974

Geographic Region	Occupation			
	Office Clerical	Electronic Data Processing	Skilled Maintenance	Unskilled Plant
Northeast	99	97	95	96
North Central	98	96	103	110
South	92	93	92	75
West	99	100	103	106

Note: All metropolitan areas combined equal 100.
Source: S. E. Baldwin and R. S. Daski, "Occupational Pay Differences among Metropolitan Areas," *Monthly Labor Review,* 99, no. 5, p. 32.

If you look at the rate structure, however, in most jobs, the Northeast as a whole is not the highest wage sector of the American regions. It follows behind the West and North Central states while the South tends to have a substantial advantage in terms of much lower rates.

Further detail can be gleaned from the statistics relating to construction activity. Wage rates in this sector were initially compiled during the wage control program of a few years ago and the Labor Department has continued to collect them. Thus, we have, not earnings data, but good solid wage rates nationally for construction. In 1976, construction wage rates in the United States on average rose 7.3 percent. In the Northeast Region, they increased by only 4.7 percent, while they grew by about 10 percent in the West. *The equilibrating mechanisms that reflect the lack of employment in construction in the Northeast are showing up.*

The above changes are indicative of a longer term trend encompassing actual rates. For example, we can evaluate a major industrial construction rate over time. The rate for pipefitters (members of the United Association) in San Francisco in 1965 was $5.76; at the same time, the New York City rate was $5.93, which exceeded the San Francisco rate by 17 cents. As of 19 December 1976, the rate in San Francisco was $17.73 while the rate in New York City was $14.25—this is indicative of a rather substantial relative movement.

Overall building trade rates can also be compared. In 1960, the average building trade rates in San Francisco were $3.74 while in New York City they stood at $4.26, about a 52-cent differential in favor of New York City. At the end of 1975 (the 1976 data are not yet available) the San Francisco rates were $12.88, while in New York they were $12.56. San Francisco has moved ahead.

Here one observes the market operating. But an interesting question is the following: If construction recovers in the Northeast—if we see a substantial amount of additional capital investment in the Northeast and a lot of construction employment—what will happen to those wage rates? An initial guess is that the New York rates will rise very rapidly until the historic differentials with the West Coast are reestablished.

What procedures, what mechanisms, what processes in the society might cause something different to happen seems to me is the essence of the problem of the revitalization of the Northeast.

Adjacent Concerns

Let us turn to other matters. Unemployment rates remain abnormally high in the Northeast. They had not been particularly bad during the 1960s, but the position of the region has deteriorated rapidly the last several years.

UNIONIZATION

The Northeast as a whole is not a particularly highly unionized area of the country. The West is more highly unionized. The South is less unionized than the Northeast, but much less so than the West. New York State, an exception to the Northeast pattern, is a substantially unionized state, much more so than the other parts of the Northeast Region.[1]

It happens—perhaps it shouldn't, but it does—that there continues to be in our country a substantial element of business decisions about the location of plants and capital investment which involves the attempt to avoid unions. This element is separate and independent of the question of the economics associated with unionization, certainly to the extent that one can evaluate wage rates or labor costs.

One of the interesting things I do and where I make my living is teaching at the Harvard Business School. I teach executive programs, so I see five hundred to six hundred executives from major American firms each year, sometimes more than that. One of the things I like to do in class when I have a case that deals with a unionization campaign —these are people that calculate the cost of everything and anything to see what they should do or shouldn't do—is to ask them what they think of this union campaign: Should they oppose it? Evaluate it? What will they do? Fifty percent of them say they will oppose it. "On what basis?" I say. "Have you calculated the costs, the benefits of that?"

Absolutely not. I say, "How do you know you want to oppose it? Do you hold it as a matter of faith that a union has to be more expensive and should not be dealt with?" They hold it as a faith.

The Europeans have the opposite point of view. When the unions campaign, they calculate the benefits and go whichever way is sensible; but this is not the case with the American business community. That continues, I think, to be a situation that may be inappropriate, but unfortunately it is real.

The fact that particularly the State of New York is as heavily unionized as it is does constitute a major problem for the location of plants and equipment in that area, independent of the costs involved. Perhaps this will change over time, and perhaps it won't. But it is not going to change very fast, it can be assured, with respect to the South.

PER CAPITA PERSONAL INCOME

Per capita personal income has declined relative to the national level over the last twenty-five years for the entire Northeast Region. While it is still generally ahead of the national average, it is falling toward it and doing so especially dramatically in New York, Pennsylvania, and Massachusetts. Pennsylvania is already at the national average in terms of per capita personal income (Exhibit 7).

EXHIBIT 7

PER CAPITA PERSONAL INCOME BY STATE AND DIVISION AS
PERCENTAGE OF NATIONAL AVERAGE: 1975 AND 1960

Area	1975	1960
United States	100	100
New England	103	109
Connecticut	118	127
Maine	81	83
Massachusetts	103	110
New Hampshire	90	96
Rhode Island	98	99
Vermont	84	83
Mideast	108	115
Delaware	114	125
Maryland	109	105
New Jersey	113	122
New York	111	123
Pennsylvania	100	102

SOURCE: Bureau of the Census.

TAX BURDENS

Tax burdens also deserve a brief analysis. The latest statistics available on the relative burden of state and local taxes show that the burden is especially high in the Northeast, and also that taxes are generally less regressive. If you will, taxes are more progressive there than the tax structures elsewhere.

In New York State, the combination of state and local taxes for a high-income family appear to be double the national average as a percent of the income of high-income families (Exhibit 8). We can be certain that industrial and business decisionmakers are not unaware of this fact either.

EXHIBIT 8

TAX BURDEN (STATE & LOCAL TAXES) AS A PERCENTAGE OF 1974 INCOME
FAMILY OF FOUR AT VARIOUS INCOME LEVELS

	Income Level				Index of Regressivity
Area	$5,000	$10,000	$25,000	$50,000	
United States	11.5	8.9	8.1	7.7	1.62
New England					
Connecticut	18.4	12.3	9.8	7.6	2.42
Maine	13.6	9.7	8.3	7.8	1.74
Massachusetts	16.0	13.9	13.0	11.6	1.38
New Hampshire	12.3	8.2	6.4	5.1	2.41
Rhode Island	14.3	10.5	9.3	8.8	1.63
Vermont	11.9	10.4	10.0	11.0	1.08
Mideast					
Delaware	9.8	8.3	9.5	8.6	1.14
Maryland	13.9	12.8	11.9	11.7	1.19
New Jersey	20.5	14.4	11.6	9.6	2.14
New York	11.6	10.6	11.5	15.0	.77
Pennsylvania	12.5	11.5	9.9	8.9	1.40

SOURCE: Stephen E. Lile, "Family Tax Burden Differences among the States," *State Government*, Winter 1976.

This completes the rather complicated picture that the data indicate about developments in the Northeast with respect to wages and labor costs. However, two more general points should be raised.

Regional Development Policy

The first centers about regional development policies in the United States generally. Historically, we have a history of letting regional development go where it will. In the 1820s, New England was virtually depopulated by the moving of its farmers out toward the then western states such as Illinois and Ohio. More recently the Appalachian situation has replicated the same phenomenon, as people left the coal mining areas for the employment in Detroit and other cities.

We have a history of ignoring the human problems involved with such changes as we let the market operate. We are virtually the only major industrialized country that does. If one spends time in Europe, one observes a range of policies that attempt to cushion the impact of market forces on different regions. It is interesting to speculate about why that is. It is reasonably clear why the French do it. Consider the coal mining regions of Lorraine. The French did not allow that area to degenerate into an Appalachia because the French periodically fight a war with Germany over that region; consequently they are not prepared to have it disaffected politically from the country as a whole. The French internal political situation is far less stable than our own. There is great concern about the Communist party and the other parties of the left. For that reason, the French government has not been prepared to let pockets of political and social dissatisfaction develop on a geographic basis.

Contrast that with the United States. We have no external neighbors who constitute any threat to our peripheral areas. There is no likelihood that New England, if it is left to decline economically, can become a hotbed or an invitation to invasion by Canadians. Quite the contrary, we can be assured. Similarly, our internal political processes are very stable with respect to most of the countries of the western world. Major areas of poverty, dissatisfaction, unhappiness, and political turmoil can develop without affecting the nation's overall stability in any substantial way (although they might affect which of our two political parties is elected, or whatever). Therefore, we devote very little attention to these kinds of matters.

Mobility Restrictions

Perhaps many people believe this has been a reasonable policy. Let the market forces operate; let them go where they will over a period of time. But it has become an increasingly difficult policy for two reasons. First of all, it was always based on the proposition that other regions of the country could develop at will and at whatever speed people and industry moved into them. That is no longer the case. The environmental situation is such that we no longer have a country where unlimited movement to the growing regions can be allowed to occur.

Second, we have developed over the past thirty or forty years a whole series of social welfare programs—unemployment compensation, welfare, etc.—which regardless of how the financial burdens are distributed, find themselves acting to hold the population in the areas in which it now exists. So we have created for ourselves a society in which we now have much more restraint on movement of population than we used to. To what degree are we prepared to adopt policies which have the function of smoothing these kinds of transitions in our economy?

Conclusion

Now, the art of public policymaking is not to develop policies that rigidify the current situation and keep us in the business of supporting and maintaining inefficient industries and subsidizing employment in marginal activities and operations. The art of public policy is to identify what the future will look like, what the country wants it to look alike, what industries will develop and grow, and through affirmative public policy to support and cushion the development. If you will, public policy should ease the birth pangs of the future in our various regions. Thus, it is apparent that if we were to debate the question of whether or not the federal government should have a policy with respect to growth and development in the regions, the answer is clearly yes. To say that we will simply tolerate the unfettered operation of market forces is, at this time, unreasonable. The question is what types of policies are appropriate and how are the analytical skills in government developed to deal with those matters.

NOTES

1. U. S. Department of Labor, Bureau of Labor Statistics, *Directory of National Unions and Employee Associations* (Washington, D.C.: Government Printing Office, 1974).

Energy Realities

MID-ATLANTIC ECONOMIC DEVELOPMENT REGION

Introduction

THE STATES OF THE MID-ATLANTIC REGION share a common geography, climate, and culture. They have played a central role in shaping the economic development of this nation: in agriculture, forestry, mining, trade, transportation, urbanization, manufacturing, finance, service, and energy production and generation. This region provided, in abundant measure, the food, fuel, machinery, and technical expertise necessary to the successful development of this nation. Unfortunately, as the resources of the region have been depleted, or no longer usable, industry has moved elsewhere to locations which provide greater incentives and opportunity for economic growth. Depletion of natural resources alone has not caused the decline in the economic growth of the mid-Atlantic region; the reasons are much more complex. However, the lack of indigenous resources and/or the relative high costs of such resources are certainly among the major causes of this economic decline.

Among the resources which are not readily available and usable in the mid-Atlantic states, are energy supplies. Thus, these states also have in common a dependence upon other regions of the nation and the rest of the world for most of their energy supplies. This dependence upon others for energy supplies is common to New England as well. Hence, the entire Northeast region of the nation, to a considerable degree, is an importer of energy. The lack of readily available and usable energy supplies within the region has had, and will continue to have, a negative impact upon economic development because of the flow of dollars out of the region to pay for imported energy, and because of lost investment and industrial expansion caused by higher energy prices, relative to the rest of the nation.

Understanding the differences among regions is important to the formulation of a national energy policy since those states and regions importing energy may have different viewpoints on issues such as price, cost, and availability than the states and regions exporting energy. The national debate on the various issues which must be resolved in formulating a national energy policy would benefit from serious and systematic study of regional energy problems. Such a study would focus national energy policy debates more clearly upon the needs of people in different parts of the country.

The importation, in increasing amounts, of most of the energy supplies required by this region, especially of oil, has brought problems of rapidly increasing energy costs and unreliability of supplies. The rapid increase in costs has caused economic hardship to the region's residents and an increased flow of wealth out of the region. Coupled with the unreliability of energy supplies, escalating energy costs have reduced the region's ability to attract new industries and to provide more jobs. Ironically, this increased dependence on foreign fuel occurs despite the fact that the mid-Atlantic region has abundant existing energy resources (coal) and potential new energy resources (gas and oil from the outer continental shelf). Indeed, the mid-Atlantic states also have the potential to reduce the demand for additional supplies of energy by conservation measures and by exploring the feasibility of renewable energy sources. This region must learn to make better use of existing energy resources as well as work toward the development of new sources of energy at reasonable cost.

Energy and the Economy

The economic performance of the mid-Atlantic states and the entire Northeast has lagged behind that of the rest of the country for some time. This economic misfortune is especially evident in the manufacturing sector. Using 1960 levels as a base, Exhibit 1 presents employment growth indices for the region and for the rest of the country for the years 1960 to 1973.

EXHIBIT 1

Trends in Manufacturing Employment, 1960-1973

Year	Northeast	Rest of U.S.	Total
1960	1.00	1.00	1.00
1961	.97	.98	.97
1962	.98	1.01	1.00
1963	.97	1.03	1.01
1964	.97	1.05	1.02
1965	1.00	1.11	1.07
1966	1.04	1.18	1.13
1967	1.04	1.21	1.15
1968	1.04	1.23	1.16
1969	1.05	1.27	1.19
1970	1.00	1.21	1.13
1971	.93	1.17	1.08
1972	.93	1.32	1.18
1973	.96	1.39	1.23

Source: U.S. Bureau of the Census *Annual Survey of Manufacturers*, 1973.

As the exhibit shows, manufacturing employment in the Northeast region of the country, which includes the mid-Atlantic states, has been relatively stable for nearly the last fifteen years. During the same time, manufacturing employment in the rest of the country has risen by about 40 percent.

The total employment picture is similar to that for manufacturing: the entire Northeast, including the mid-Atlantic states, has fallen behind the rest of the country in employment and growth since 1960 and has suffered more during the recent recession. For example, during the ten-year period from 1960-1970 when the nation experienced an employment growth of slightly more than 30 percent, the mid-Atlantic states had a growth rate of 20 percent. However, during the recent recessionary period from 1970-1975, when the nation had an employment growth rate of 8.6 percent, the mid-Atlantic states had a decline of –0.6 percent. The mid-Atlantic states' relative decline has been the result of a complex set of factors. Costs of doing business, including state and local taxes, energy, land and labor, impair the region's competitive position. Thus, energy supply and price are not the *only* cause of the region's current economic difficulties but an improved supply of less costly energy may be an important solution.

Costs

Energy costs among the New England and mid-Atlantic states vary considerably as shown in Exhibit 2.

EXHIBIT 2

RELATIVE COST OF ENERGY CONSUMED BY MANUFACTURERS, 1974
PER 1,000 KILOWATT-HOURS (U.S. = 100.0%)

Area	Total	Purchased Fuels	Purchased Electricity
Maine	141.5%	184.0%	109.7%
New Hampshire	164.5	179.5	139.8
Vermont	191.5	171.5	159.6
Massachusetts	187.7	168.6	190.7
Rhode Island	197.1	175.9	173.0
Connecticut	201.2	185.5	180.6
New York	140.9	143.5	109.5
New Jersey	162.9	165.0	166.3
Pennsylvania	123.0	128.7	130.2
Maryland	185.9	182.8	165.4
Delaware	140.1	141.1	145.8
Northeast	144.4	146.8	138.3
U.S. minus Northeast	89.9	86.4	91.2
Total U.S.	100.0%	100.0%	100.0%
U.S. (actual)	$ 4.96	$ 3.31	$13.80

SOURCE: U.S. Department of Commerce, *Annual Survey of Manufacturers*, 1974 "Fuels and Electric Energy Consumed," 1976.

EXHIBIT 3

PURCHASED FUELS AND ELECTRIC
ENERGY CONSUMED IN MANUFACTURING, 1974

Area	Kilowatt-Hours Equivalent (billions)	Total Cost (million dollars)	Cost per 1,000 Kilowatt-Hour Equivalent	Index U.S. = 100
United States	3924.7	19461.9	4.95	100
Northeast	658.4	4695.3	7.13	144
U.S.—excluding Northeast	3266.3	14766.6	4.52	91
North Central	1143.6	5899.4	5.16	104
South	1698.1	6960.8	4.10	83
West	421.0	1906.5	4.53	92
New England ⎫ Northeast	116.2	1039.5	8.95	181
Mid-Atlantic ⎭	542.2	3655.8	6.74	136
East N. Central ⎫ North Central	928.7	5013.3	5.40	109
West N. Central ⎭	214.9	886.1	4.12	83
South Atlantic ⎫ South	487.8	2990.3	6.13	124
East S. Central ⎬ South	317.7	1545.4	4.86	98
West S. Central ⎭	892.6	2425.1	2.72	55
Mountain ⎫ West	104.9	397.6	3.79	77
Pacific ⎭	316.1	1508.9	4.77	96

SOURCE: U.S. Department of Commerce, *Annual Survey of Manufacturers*, 1974 "Fuels and Electric Energy Consumed," 1976.

Despite the differences among states in the Northeast, it is apparent that the mid-Atlantic states and the entire Northeast pay more for energy than the rest of the nation. The sources of energy available for use, as well as national policies contribute substantially to this high cost. Exhibit 3 describes the cost of 1,000 kilowatt-hour equivalents of energy consumed in manufacturing for the year 1974 for all regions of the nation.

Unfortunately, the problem of relative cost differentials among regions is widening. Exhibit 4 shows the cost of 1,000 kilowatt-hour equivalents of energy consumed in manufacturing for the years 1971 and 1974.

As these exhibits demonstrate, the mid-Atlantic states pay a relatively high price for energy. These high prices seem to have contributed to the out-migration of energy intensive industry, and as a result, the mid-Atlantic states must specialize in attracting manufacturing and service industries which are less energy intensive.

The increase in energy expenditures also means that available moneys must be used to maintain—not expand—industrial activity and jobs. Energy costs have thus become a much more important cost of manufacturing, and this importance has been rising rapidly. Recent increases in energy expenditures have broken a long trend of relatively declining energy costs as a percent of value added. The cost of purchased fuels and electric energy decreased from 4.6 percent of value added in 1950 to 2.8 in 1969. Yet, from 1973 to 1974, the cost of purchased fuels and electric energy increased 43 percent in absolute terms and 32 percent in cost relative to value added. Thus, the mid-Atlantic states are at a disadvantage in attracting manufacturing and other activities due to energy prices which are both higher than other regions and which become increasingly important as a cost of manufacturing. Finally, the increasing rate of the regional difference means that an existing economic problem is growing more severe.

Supply

The entire Northeast including the mid-Atlantic region has little natural energy readily available and usable. Given the geography and geology of the region, there is no uranium, very little natural gas, relatively small amounts of hydroelectric power, and little petroleum remains. At the moment, coal is either difficult to extract or costly to burn. For example, in 1966, New England utilities burned 10 million tons of coal. In 1973, 1.3 million tons were burned. Our new national environmental statutes and regulations contribute to this increased cost and decreased use.

EXHIBIT 4

Cost Per 1,000 Kilowatt-Hour, by State; Ranked by 1974; 1974 and 1971

			Cost per 1,000 Kilowatt-hour Equivalents		
Rank	State	% of Average Cost	1974 (dollars)	1971 (dollars)	1974/ 1971 relative
1	Texas	52	2.59	1.29	2.01
2	Wyoming	53	2.61	1.66	1.57
3	Louisiana	55	2.74	1.22	2.25
4	Montana	56	2.78	2.21	1.26
5	Oklahoma	57	2.85	1.67	1.71
6	Kansas	61	3.03	2.04	1.49
7	Utah	68	3.39	2.07	1.64
8	North Dakota	71	3.53	2.68	1.32
9	Washington	73	3.61	2.61	1.38
10	Nebraska	74	3.65	2.49	1.47
11	New Mexico	75	3.73	2.29	1.63
12	Colorado	76	3.78	2.13	1.77
13	Arkansas	78	3.87	2.16	1.79
14	Mississippi	79	3.91	2.12	1.84
15	Iowa	83	4.11	2.47	1.66
16	Idaho	86	4.25	2.99	1.42
17	Oregon	87	4.32	2.95	1.46
18	West Virginia	89	4.40	2.28	1.93
19	Missouri	92	4.55	3.05	1.49
20	Arizona	94	4.66	2.83	1.65
21	Tennessee	95	4.69	3.01	1.56
22	Minnesota	97	4.79	3.18	1.51
23	Alabama	99	4.91	2.64	1.86
X	United States	100	4.96	2.74	1.81
24	Indiana	100	4.98	2.91	1.71
25	Alaska	103	5.10	2.31	2.21

		% of Average Cost	Cost per 1,000 Kilowatt-hour Equivalents		
Rank	State		1974 (dollars)	1971 (dollars)	1974/ 1971 relative
26	Nevada	104	5.18	2.44	2.12
27	Wisconsin	105	5.23	3.28	1.59
28	California	106	5.27	2.97	1.77
29	Illinois	107	5.31	3.25	1.63
30	Ohio	110	5.46	3.03	1.80
31	Georgia	113	5.58	3.08	1.81
32	Kentucky	114	5.64	3.66	1.54
33	Michigan	118	5.85	3.49	1.68
34	Pennsylvania	123	6.10	3.06	1.99
35	Virginia	123	6.10	2.91	2.10
36	South Carolina	125	6.22	3.17	1.96
37	Florida	127	6.32	2.94	2.15
38	South Dakota	135	6.69	3.33	2.01
39	North Carolina	139	6.87	3.38	2.03
40	Maryland	140	6.95	3.45	2.01
41	New York	141	6.99	4.00	1.75
42	Maine	142	7.02	2.73	2.57
43	Hawaii	143	7.09	3.48	2.04
44	New Jersey	163	8.08	3.76	2.15
45	New Hampshire	165	8.16	3.70	2.21
46	Delaware	186	9.22	3.78	2.44
47	Massachusetts	188	9.31	4.32	2.15
48	Vermont	192	9.50	4.44	2.14
49	Rhode Island	197	9.78	3.91	2.48
50	Connecticut	201	9.98	4.27	2.34
51	District of Columbia	241	11.95	5.22	2.29

SOURCE: See Exhibit 2.

Exhibit 5 shows energy use in the Northeast and mid-Atlantic regions by type of fuel for the year 1972.

EXHIBIT 5

Type of Fuel Used—by Percent, 1972

Area	Coal	Petroleum	Natural Gas	Hydro & Nuclear
Mid-Atlantic	19.9	57.1	18.9	4.1
Northeast	15.6	63.4	16.6	4.3
United States	17.3	45.7	32.1	4.9

Source: U.S. Bureau of Mines.

The consequences of our position are clear. The mid-Atlantic states must import almost all the energy they consume since 76 percent of our total energy comes from petroleum and natural gas. As a region we secure our energy either from other sections of this nation or from foreign suppliers. Our primary source of power comes from petroleum, an energy source with a high cost and with a high dependency on unstable international agreements.

In 1972, $7 billion were expended by the Northeast to pay for petroleum and natural gas. In 1975, nearly three times as much, about $20.7 billion, was expended. These moneys were paid either to oil and gas producing regions of this nation or to foreign countries. It is clear that in the near future, this trend will continue as oil and gas prices continue to rise.

The higher crude oil prices resulting from the recent decision of the Organization of Petroleum Exporting Countries will impact sharply on the Northeast economy. Exhibit 6 presents four possible scenarios.

The current national solutions to the energy dependency problem may have the same effect on the Northeast, i.e., a continued drain on the capital of the Northeast. The new domestic energy resource projects anticipated by the Energy Research and Development Administration (ERDA) and other federal agencies represent large investments by the nation, but the majority of these projects will be located in the western parts of the country.

Available evidence suggests that the coal industry may be moving westward. Oil shale development, use of synthetic fuels, and the creation of large solar thermal stations and geothermal sites, all of which

EXHIBIT 6

TOTAL ANNUAL IMPACT ON NORTHEAST ECONOMY
(in millions of dollars lost)

Study	Case 1	Case 2	Case 3	Case 4
New England	80.0	330.0	457.0	577.0
New Jersey	80.2	363.4	505.3	643.7
New York	37.1	155.5	214.2	273.2
Pennsylvania	47.5	179.8	246.8	312.0
Total	244.8	1,028.7	1,424.3	1,805.9

NOTES: 1. Base case—Domestic "composite" price increase of 10 percent.
2. OPEC increase of 10 percent and domestic "composite" price increase of 10 percent.
3. OPEC increase of 15 percent and domestic "composite" price increase of 10 percent.
4. OPEC increase of 20 percent and domestic "composite" price increase of 10 percent.

represent massive investments, are being considered for the western part of the country. In some instances, the decision is based upon the location of the resource, but evidence further suggests that this movement may in part be influenced by federal policy. Alaskan oil and gas development is an excellent example of this phenomenon. Not only has the oil and gas development been a catalyst to substantial investment in Alaska, but the resulting oil and gas will likely be shipped to the continental United States via the West Coast. This additional supply of oil (and in the case of gas, possibly to the Midwest), could provide a 500,000 barrel per day oil surplus in the West once the Alaskan oil begins to flow at its maximum rate of production.

These national energy development investments, both present and future, will encourage substantial private investments and employment growth in the West. The capital for the primary and the secondary investments will in large part be generated in the East and invested in the West. Unless there is a countervailing force, the mid-Atlantic states will not only witness a steady drain of money to finance their purchases of energy, but will also witness a greater drain of investment capital and attendant jobs out of the region.

Current trends are not encouraging. National energy consumption is increasing. So is dependency upon foreign energy sources. Unfortunately, as national energy usage has increased so has the energy use of the mid Atlantic states, which now account for 17 percent of the nation's total energy consumption. Interestingly, the per capita energy consumption of the northeastern states as shown in Exhibit 7 is significantly below the national rate due primarily to a significant difference in energy use by the industrial sector. The greater residential and commercial use of energy by the northeastern states is probably due to differences in climate. A basic fact regarding consumption, however, is that the northeastern states are not relatively extravagant users of energy. In fact, they fall below the national average.

The mid-Atlantic states, as part of the Northeast Region are in a precarious position due to our dependence upon oil and natural gas, especially imported oil, as shown in Exhibits 8 and 9. Among the states in the region, however, New York and New Jersey, for example, are much more dependent upon oil than Pennsylvania where there is extensive use of coal. Nonetheless, sixty-three percent of the mid-Atlantic region's total energy in 1973 came from petroleum and seventy-four percent of that amount was imported. Unfortunately, both our dependence on oil and, in particular, our reliance on foreign oil are increasing.

The locational problems of energy supply, i.e. the region's lack of existing resources, have been compounded by additional problems which have limited exploration and utilization of available energy resources. These include the following:

Air pollution, endangering public health, has greatly reduced the use of coal, especially for electric power generation. This is especially troublesome since use of eastern coal would reduce the flow of wealth out of the region. Various attempts to develop a solution which does not endanger public health and which also permits the use of eastern coal have been underfunded by federal research grants.

Siting of electric power plants, especially those involving nuclear fueled facilities, has been difficult in some states and nearly impossible in others. This has led to slow growth in electric power capacity. This potential problem has been reduced or masked by the recent decline in demand resulting from the economic recession and by energy conservation measures.

Recovery of Lake Erie natural gas in a manner similar to existing gas production on the Canadian side has been thwarted.

Oil and gas exploration of the Atlantic outer continental shelf, while presenting environmental dangers, also represents potential energy supplies for the Northeast. The continuing debate between the federal government and the state governments protecting the interests of their citizens, has caused delays of this activity.

Public resistance to the siting of energy facilities, especially nuclear facilities, has greatly reduced our bargaining position in the national

EXHIBIT 7

COMPARISON OF NORTHEAST AND U.S. ENERGY USE
BY SECTOR AND PER CAPITA—1972

Sector	Northeast Region			United States		
	Consumption (10^{15} BTU)	% of Total	per capita (10^6 BTU)	Consumption (10^{15} BTU)	% of Total	per capita (10^6 BTU)
Residential	3.32	23	61	10.64	16	51
Commercial	1.72	12	31	5.88	9	28
Industrial	2.95	21	54	21.76	32	105
Transportation	3.90	27	71	16.52	24	79
Electric[a] Utility	2.52	17	46	12.80	19	61
Total	14.41	100	263	67.60	100	324

NOTE: a. Taken as energy used to generate electricity less electric energy
delivered to the consuming sectors.

SOURCE: U.S. Bureau of the Mines: Mineral Yearbook and Mineral Industry
Surveys.

EXHIBIT 8

COMPARISON OF NORTHEAST AND U.S. RESOURCE
CONSUMPTION BY TYPE—1972
(10^{15} BTU)

Resource	Northeast Region		United States	
	Consumption	% of Total	Consumption	% of Total
Oil	9.83	63	32.97	45
Gas	2.82	18	23.12	32
Coal	2.64	17	12.60	18
Hydro	0.17	1	2.89	4
Nuclear	0.15	1	0.58	1
Total	15.61	100	72.16	100

SOURCE: See Exhibit 7.

EXHIBIT 9

SUMMARY OF ENERGY SUPPLY BY ORIGIN
AND FUEL TYPE, NORTHEAST REGION 1972

(10^{12} BTU)

Fuel	Within Region		Outside Region		Foreign Imports		Total	
	Quantity	% of Total	Quantity	% of Total	Quantity	% of Total	Quantity	% of Total
Crude Oil	22.57	1	647.83	25	1,880.71	74	2,551.11	100
Refined Petroleum Products	2,385.60	27	2,875.00	31	3,890.00	42	9,150.60	100
Coal	1,763.37	67	876.00	33	—	—	2,639.39	100
Natural Gas	85.00	3	2,535.65	96	16.87	1	2,637.52	100

SOURCE: See Exhibit 7.

energy debate. It is difficult to ask for cheap energy and the resulting benefits from other states while being unwilling to accept the costs of locating facilities in the states of our region.

Transmission of electric power from Canada, a likely new source of imported energy, has been delayed by resistance to high voltage transmission lines.

Potentially useful joint ventures between eastern Canada and the eastern U.S. have been hindered by national interests and resistance by utilities.

The rapid increase in the cost of capital has greatly changed the capital market. The access of utilities to financing during a period of increasing capital requirements has been reduced. These new capital market situations have changed the basic cost equation by which utilities make construction decisions.

These problems are, in large measure, inherent by-products of a pluralistic society changing from an economy based upon abundant and low-cost energy with high pollution to an economy based upon scarce and high-cost energy with minimal environmental hazard. The stresses and strains accompanying this change cannot be entirely eliminated, but they can be reduced through careful management and selection of the correct policies. Unfortunately, the potential long-term effects of higher-priced energy on our economy and society are not well understood. This is especially true because the specific effects of relative differentials in energy prices upon regional employment patterns are not known. However, we do know that high-priced energy has increased public concern and debate on energy issues. High-cost energy has also caused fuel costs to be a much more significant factor in residential and industrial decisions, especially decisions on site location.

There are some problems which are not symptomatic of a changing economic system. These must be dealt with in a decisive manner by national and regional policy action. For example, the federal research and development (R&D) programs as administered by ERDA and others do not emphasize mid-Atlantic solutions to mid-Atlantic energy problems. Four billion dollars on oil shale development would not appear to have anywhere near the benefit to the nation, especially the mid-Atlantic, as four billion dollars allocated to energy development from renewable resources or to redevelopment of the eastern coal industry. Exhibit 10 demonstrates a regional bias in energy R&D funding which is particularly discouraging, given the relationships of energy deficiency by region.

The current national approach to increased production through increased prices has not been tempered by a strong national effort and commitment to energy conservation. Conservation, the best short-term

EXHIBIT 10

ERDA Grants—Fiscal 1977

Area	ERDA 77	Proportional Share	Deficit
Maine	$ 180,000	$ 27,975,043	$ 27,795,043
New Hampshire	129,000	22,022,906	21,893,906
Vermont	106,000	13,094,701	12,988,701
Massachusetts	28,199,000	165,469,408	137,270,408
Rhode Island	1,292,000	27,975,043	26,683,043
Connecticut	12,143,000	88,091,627	75,948,627
New Jersey	219,269,000	524,978,483	305,709,483
New York	90,657,000	210,110,436	119,453,436
Pennsylvania	247,288,000	340,462,236	93,174,236
Total	$599,263,000	$1,421,370,000	$822,107,000

Source: Federal Regional Council, Region 2; based on 1972 population.

program for the mid-Atlantic states and the nation, has not received the necessary emphasis.

Demand

As we all know, the demand for energy is increasing. However, the various experts disagree greatly on the future projection of demand due primarily to disagreements over the price elasticity of energy demand by sector and the feasibility of significant energy saving shifts in industrial processes. The Brookhaven National Laboratory's (BNL) regional energy studies group, with an ERDA grant, has produced a series of projections on the energy future of the Northeast. According to BNL's figures, if we continue our present patterns of energy consumption and growth for the next twenty-five years (an unlikely scenario), our oil imports will double, use of the nuclear power will multiply thirty-fold, and the use of coal will more than double. If energy costs were to increase at an annual rate of 10 percent, gross energy costs for the region would increase from about $20 billion in 1975 to $70 billion in 1985. Fortunately, trends are not destiny, especially if public policy can influence the course of the economy and society.

The current U.S. consumption of energy is a by-product of our previous low-cost energy economy. We are the most energy intensive culture in the world. According to the Federal Energy Administration (FEA), West Germany, the country most analogous to the U.S. in industrialization and standard of living, uses only half as much energy per capita as does the United States. As stated by the FEA, "Energy use per capita for transportation is only one-fourth that of the United States, for residential space heating (climate correct) only one-half, for other residential uses only one-fourth and for industrial uses 59 percent. . . . This large disparity in energy use between the two countries suggests that continued economic growth and improvement in the standard of living in the United States should be possible without a proportionate increase in energy consumption."

Obviously, a serious program of energy conservation should have a significant impact upon energy demand. Unfortunately, too many people imagine a strong conservation program would mean a Draconian regime of no cars, no air conditioning, inadequate heat, and omnipresent governmental regulators since most people do not know what greater energy efficiencies can bring. Below is a list of some of the commercial conservation projects now in progress. The savings cited are recorded and not theoretical.

> Two 1,200 square-foot homes in Benton, Arkansas are being heated and cooled at the cost of $10.74 per month, a third of the normal cost of a home that size, according to Fred Clark of the Arkansas Power and Light Company. These homes are less expensive to construct than FHA minimum property standard homes and are now being built by commercial contractors in forty-one states.
>
> The Washington Natural Gas Company in Seattle offers for sale an energy conservation package which saves customers an average of 65 percent of their heating bill. WNG guarantees the package, which consists of ceiling and wall insulation, a night setback thermostat, and a pilotless furnace, and is making a handsome profit on their installations. In eighteen months, WNG has insulated enough homes to free up gas for 60,000 new gas heated homes.
>
> A complex of garden apartments in Twin Rivers, New Jersey has been carefully inspected and retrofitted. The first round of improvements cut energy use 25 percent; the second round is expected to save another 25 percent.
>
> The Exxon building in New York City has reduced energy consumption by 36 percent with no substantial capital investment.
>
> The General Services Administration, the operations service of the federal government, reduced energy use in government buildings by 30 percent nationwide during 1974 with no significant capital investment.
>
> The Chesebrough-Ponds factory in Clinton, Connecticut, reduced energy consumption by 30 percent through improved maintenance.
>
> In the service territory of a single New York electric utility, the replacement of half of the room air conditioners to be sold in the next

five years with units twice as efficient, which are available in the same appliance stores as the standard efficiency units, would eliminate the need for $125 million dollars worth of new generating plant capacity. The additional cost of the efficient unit would total about $30 million, which the individual consumers would recoup in electricity bill savings in a few years.

There are dozens of cars on the market, in all price and luxury ranges, which are more than twice as efficient as the average for cars in America today.

The Raytheon Corporation used 46 percent less fuel oil nationwide in May, 1974 than in May, 1973, due to better maintenance and operation.

There are numerous electric generating plants now in operation, utility-sized in Europe and smaller scale in the United States, which use anywhere from 67 to 160 percent more of the energy available in the fuel they burn than does the average U.S. utility plant. This is done by making careful use of waste heat of the plants, which we normally discharge up to smokestacks or back into the rivers or lakes that provide the cooling water for the plant.

Through an aggressive energy planning conservation program the region could increase the efficiency of energy use in all sectors. It need not involve changing lifestyles or imposing hardships. More than any other available course of action, energy conservation can reduce the outflow of energy dollars from the region, moderate upward pressure on the cost of goods and services within the region, slow the regional trend of increasing reliance on foreign oil, buy time to develop alternative energy supply technologies, and assist the region in maintaining a healthful environment. Without doubt, the region would benefit by reducing the capital outflow. Further, any reasonable program would be designed to be cost effective for end users.

The redevelopment of this region could be spurred if energy was utilized more efficiently. This region's energy supply problems give us a special stake in implementing an effective conservation program.

This can be done in two ways: Congress and the administration must be urged to authorize and appropriate funds to support conservation at a level commensurate with its value to the region; and the region itself must establish mechanisms to take advantage of federal program funds and to initiate regionally based conservation efforts.

Through both the Energy Policy and Conservation Act and the Energy Conservation and Production Act, Congress has set forth the rudiments for a comprehensive energy conservation effort. These two bills contain several broad-ranging provisions:

Two separate state energy conservation programs, one aimed at direct conservation implementation, and one aimed at conservation education and consumer protection.

Two hundred million dollars in energy conservation demonstrations over three years for HUD to develop a wide variety of financial incentives to induce homeowners to install energy conserving materials or alternative energy systems.

A program to set forth national energy conservation building codes.

A $2 billion program of loan guarantees for energy conservation initiatives for industrial and commercial users.

Weatherization programs for low-income residences for which $200 million has been authorized for three years.

Strict consumption standards for new automobiles.

A strong energy conservation program could save the mid-Atlantic states nearly $1 billion a year.

In addition, however, the region should develop waste recovery programs (resources recovery). Such programs could result in energy and material conservation and environmental enhancement. Such programs would also benefit the economic development of the region because of new jobs directly generated to construct resource recovery plants and because of the multiplier effects of secondary and tertiary employment.

The Issues

The overriding concern for the mid-Atlantic states is their higher energy costs which are a strong disincentive to economic development. These higher costs are in part attributable to existing available resources on which the region must rely and in part attributable to existing national policies. The following specific issues are important to the mid-Atlantic region in order to attain lower cost energy and more available supplies.

COAL

An obvious boom to the mid-Atlantic region would be the greatly increased use of eastern coal to fuel the region and the nation. Indeed, eastern coal would appear to be a major element of any national solution to critical dependence upon foreign sources of oil. However, federal R&D budgets must be redirected to overcome technical problems such as desulfurization and more head electric power production. A major new industrial opportunity for the mid-Atlantic region would be the development of a coal gasification industry. Various federal proposals could be shaped to launch this industry.

Aside from technical and environmental problems which must be solved, the eastern coal industry also has institutionalized problems that retard investment. New economic development organizations and financing mechanisms appear necessary to overcome such problems.

ENERGY CONSERVATION

Due to their high energy costs, the mid-Atlantic states will benefit greatly from a strong national energy conservation effort. There is a need for a greater emphasis by Congress and federal agencies upon energy conservation programs such as those called for by the Energy Policy and Conservation Act of 1975, and the Energy Conservation and Production Act of 1976. Also, there is a need for greater emphasis by the Energy Research and Development Authority on energy conservation such as the preparation of a comprehensive energy conservation R&D program. The region might also benefit from regional implementation of various energy efficiency standards such as building codes, lighting standards, and appliance standards.

DEREGULATION OF NATURAL GAS

The natural gas price structure and allocation mechanisms are changing and will continue to change. The mid-Atlantic states must make certain that their interests are served by changes to federal policy. Also, wasteful natural gas consumption by other states, such as use of natural gas for utility boiler fuel, should be curtailed.

OUTER CONTINENTAL SHELF EXPLORATION AND DEVELOPMENT

A potential source of energy for the entire Northeast is the outer continental shelf, with recent exploration reports having been encouraging. However, the states must make certain that they receive their rightful share of both the product and revenues. The environmental and social costs associated with outer continental shelf development should be borne by the federal government and oil and gas producers.

ALASKAN OIL AND GAS ALLOCATION

The delivery system for Alaskan oil could be a major regional economic issue which the mid-Atlantic region must address. Also, the route selection, time table and allocation of Alaskan natural gas is likely to have even greater regional economic impact.

STRATEGIC PETROLEUM RESERVES

The Energy Conservation and Production Act of 1976 called for the establishment of strategic petroleum reserves for the nation, regions, and industries. FEA's recent plan for such strategic reserves does not contain regional petroleum reserves. This could become a serious economic problem for the states of this region by exacerbating the already existing problems of energy supply and cost. Furthermore, construction of regional storage facilities would be of great assistance to this region by providing jobs for unemployment workers.

NUCLEAR FUEL CYCLE

Resolution of the health, safety, and security issues of the nuclear fuel cycle at the national level is an important energy issue to this region since much of the proposed electric power capacity is based upon nuclear fuel. Unless these health, safety, and security issues can be satisfactorily addressed, development of additional nuclear power generation will be increasingly difficult.

Conclusion

By traditional standards the mid-Atlantic states have fallen behind the rest of the nation in economic performance. This is partly due to shifts in the national economy which have put older industrial areas of the country at a disadvantage, and partly the result of other factors, including escalating energy costs and the uncertainty of energy supply. Future industrial expansion will continue to be impacted by energy costs and supply.

The mid-Atlantic states' dependence upon imported fuel (almost entirely so in the case of New York and New Jersey) to supply the energy necessary to maintain its industries, commercial activities, and lifestyles makes this region extremely vulnerable to short-term disruption and long-term declines in supplies. This region is a precursor of the nation's growing dependence upon others for energy supplies. That fact should lead to a greater national concern about the energy problems which the mid-Atlantic region faces today, since the rest of the nation is likely to face them in the future and will benefit from solutions developed for this region.

The national energy problem includes two basic elements:

(1) how to avoid or minimize dependence upon other nations for critical energy supplies; and

(2) how to move from an oil/natural gas economy to an economy fueled by other sources over the next two to three decades.

The mid-Atlantic states have a large stake in the solutions to both elements. However, solutions to the latter provide an opportunity for the mid-Atlantic states to improve their economic position in the long run by leading the way in developing a new energy economy. The need for the region to act in the best manner possible is great since the future of our region's economy will, to a significant extent, depend upon the energy development steps we and the nation choose. This region can devise constructive contributions, not only to reduce foreign energy dependence, but also to encourage the development of new industries based upon a new energy economy.

The states of the mid-Atlantic region have been placed at a relative disadvantage by existing national energy policies. The states share common energy problems and can benefit from a comprehensive regional approach to solutions. Thus, the mid-Atlantic states have a mutual interest in working toward changing federal energy policies to better reflect, and be responsive to, the particular energy needs of the region. National energy policy must be designed in a manner which is sensitive to the economic climate and potential of the region, and which provides for equitable energy costs, as related to other areas of the nation.

Capital Supplies and Regional Growth

JOHN G. HEIMANN

IN DISCUSSING LOCAL CAPITAL supplies and urban regional growth, I think we should begin by examining the notion that rational man can be translated to the rational corporation. I am going to assume that means we have also extended the concept to a rational financial system, because one can hardly talk about rational capital supplies and urban regional growth without talking about the system.

The Supply Parameters

I would just like to begin by noting some statistics. What is the capital supply here in the Northeast? If you permit me to be parochial, I would like to concentrate specifically on New York State and New York City, the principal capital market of the western world, where the bulk of the regional supply is located. New York State, with approximately 8.5 percent of the population of the country and 9.5 percent of the personal disposable income, has within its borders and its financial institutions about 20 percent of the total commercial banking assets of the nation, something in excess of $200 billion; 20 percent of the thrift assets, meaning savings banks and savings and loan institutions, approximately $70 billion; approximately 70 percent of the foreign bank assets residing in this nation, that's some $30 billion; and the control over about 20-30 percent, through the banking system, of the retirement systems of the nation, perhaps another $40 billion.

New York and the Northeast have been capital exporters for many years, certainly since the time of the Civil War. After the British stopped financing the U.S., it was the Northeast which financed first the U.S. and then the rest of the world.

The Utilization

There is a capital supply. The questions are: Is it local? Generated locally? Available locally? Can it be moved locally? Invested locally? And then, how can it be used to help, assist, or in any way aid, shape, or form urban regional growth? I don't think I need to stress that every time there is an urban problem, somebody, somewhere, gets up and designs a system which mandates the use of local savings or local capital for local solutions to local problems.

This idea happens periodically. The question is, if it's such a good idea, why hasn't it been accomplished? The answer is, it's probably unconstitutional.

The real reason is that all capital, in this nation at least, is private. Now, that's very hard for a lot of people to really come to grips with and comprehend. It's not the bank's capital, and not the retirement system's capital. It's not the life insurance company's capital. It's the capital of the individuals who have chosen those intermediaries in which they store their capital. In effect, these individuals have asked someone else to invest their capital for them. I think that's important for us all to recognize, because this will be at the crux of the financial problem in the nation when it comes to guaranteeing long-term fixed income investments for social purposes.

The System

There are two kinds of savings systems: deposit thrift institutions and contract thrift institutions, and they are worlds apart. Let me try to explain them, because any financing system for housing, hospitals, or urban growth has to depend on these two systems. Unless we understand the differences, we will be designing, as we have in the past, intermediary functions that don't work or, if they do work, work at such an extraordinarily high cost that they are actually counterproductive.

The deposit thrift systems are the commercial banks and savings banks and the savings and loan associations and their smaller but rapidly growing brethren, the credit unions. The critical factor about the deposit thrift institutions is that all of us put money in and take it out. It is our choice, the individual depositors', whether it's a corporation in a commercial bank or an individual in the local savings and loan. We make the decision to put the money in and we take it out. It is short-term money.

The long-term thrift entities, if you will, are the so-called contract thrift institutions, for the lack of any better name. Those are the life insurance companies and the retirement systems. With the life insurance company, you have a forced savings plan. You put it in, pay the premium, and while you can withdraw some of it by drawing against it, that's not a widespread practice. With retirement systems, which have been the fastest growing thrift entities in the United States, you can't take your money out. Somebody else may put it in for you, depending on your contractual agreement with your employer. That money is invested for you and under a set of circumstances that are clearly prescribed, you receive benefits from it upon retirement or upon disability. There are a variety of ways and times when you get your money out, but you, the individual saver whose money it is, cannot withdraw the funds.

Therefore, the two distinctions that have to be made before we get down to how we solve some of these problems are: (1) the public savers control the money going in and going out of the deposit thrift institutions, and (2) in the contract thrift institutions, the sums are not controlled by the saver to the same exent.

THE OBJECTIVES

Now, those are the systems. You look across the board and you say, "Well, now, what is each component supposed to do?" The commercial banks are supposed to finance industry and consumer short-term loans. Their whole structure is predicated on short-term deposits or short-term investments, i.e., short-term loans to small industries and consumers. Thus, the liability side and the asset side are both short-term and the result is a perfectly sensible, prudent, and workable system.

The savings institutions, on the other hand, were designed to consume short-term investments and deposits, but because of the society in which we live, it was assumed that those short-term deposits were, in fact, long-term deposits. Therefore, the structure of our mortgage home finance market has been basically predicated upon the thrift institutions providing long-term capital with their source of funds being short-term deposits. That worked superbly well, by the way, for about 150 years up until 1965 or 1966 or 1959, depending on which date you want to pick. However, its working well was necessarily based on a society in which the rates of inflation were relatively modest and consistent.

As you know, the life insurance companies have always posited themselves as long-term investors. Their source of supply of funds has been fairly consistent and can be quantified and calculated. They have historically financed not the short-term sectors of the marketplace but the long-term business sectors and the real estate market, although less so in recent years.

Retirement systems, the new baby on the block, so to speak, and the biggest of the babies, have really had no basic investment philosophy concerning long-term investment policies. The retirement systems can either increase the benefits for the beneficiary through a successful investment policy or, on the flip side of that coin, reduce the contribution from the employer.

Now, when you look at it, you may say, "Well, that's our saving system." I tell you that's the bulk of our savings in this nation; it represents some ninety-odd percent. Individuals have savings that they themselves invest in stocks and bonds, but we are talking about where the ballgame really is.

The Controls

How is this controlled? How does government look at it? How does the whole thing work? Who in government and at what level has anything to say about the operations of these institutions? When we talk about local capital supplies and urban regional growth, we are presupposing somebody will get something, i.e., capital will be made available to do something which is deemed to be good. I'm not evaluating the result—it is deemed to be good.

What we have is the most extraordinary pastiche of regulatory and supervisory controls over the savings of the American people. Let me run through these controls category by category, without trying to make a value judgment about them. A commercial bank is controlled and/or regulated and/or supervised by the Federal Reserve Board, if it is a member of the Federal Reserve System; by the comptroller of the currency if it is a national bank; by the state superintendent of banks if it is a state bank. There's no duplication there. It's one or the other. The Federal Deposit Insurance Corporation (FDIC) affects the commercial banking system regardless of category.

Since commercial banks are all publicly held or virtually all publicly held, the sale of their securities is subject to the anti-fraud provisions of the federal securities laws.

The federal savings and loan institutions are controlled by the Federal Loan Bank Board and its insurance partner, the Federal Savings and Loan Insurance Corporation (FSLIC). State savings institutions are controlled by the state superintendent of banks. Both also have a relationship with the FDIC.

If they are publicly held, which some savings and loans are, the SEC, of course, has a voice and, as always, the IRS.

The large source of capital controlled by the life insurance companies is not controlled or supervised or regulated on a national basis at all. Supervision and review of life insurance companies is done by the state superintendents of insurance. We have no federal overview of the life insurance companies, or, I may add, the property and casualty companies, though they are a somewhat different category.

Finally, the retirement systems, in my humble opinion, have no regulation whatsoever, except something rather weak, completely misunderstood, and probably badly thought through, the federal law called ERISA, the Employees Retirement Income Security Act. So the systems through which capital flows have various levels of regulation and supervision, some national, some not. Often, as Dr. Arthur Burns noted sometime ago, these regulators tend to compete. Regulators don't usually compete by being more stringent. They tend to compete by attempting to keep their constituents—you've got to keep the work in the shop.

This type of competing is somewhat like the fellow heckling the third baseman and the third baseman gets so upset, he throws down his glove and says, "If you think you can do better, you come down and play this position." The heckler says, "You bum," walks in and picks up the glove. The first ball that comes at him is a very easy fly and he misses. The second ball is a soft grounder and he fumbles it. The third ball just dribbles up to him and he fumbles it, too. The third baseman is standing there with a smirk on his face and the guy playing turns around and says, "Well, you really made a mess of this position."

We have a system which I think is really a mess. How have we tried to fix it? What techniques have been applied by government to get around the fact that there is no uniform control over these capital systems nationally, or locally for that matter? There are all kinds of techniques, but let me give you two. One has been used nationally and the other has been used by the New York State.

Starting in 1965 and 1966, the first great credit crunch, it became eminently clear that the savings thrift institutions were going to face an extraordinary drain on their deposits because people pulled their money out for higher rates of return somewhere else. That's called disintermediation. Most of us probably acted in this very sensible manner.

In order to prevent, or at least ameliorate, disintermediation, the thrift savings institutions need to do something in the way of restructuring. Obviously, restructuring the financial institutions attacks a whole host of vested interests. When you restructure, you must reorder privileges and functions by taking away from one set of savings institutions and giving to another. This means that somebody is giving and somebody is taking and nobody likes to do that in a capitalistic system.

Rather than face the problem, the federal government sought to circumvent it by creating or extrapolating the activities of a whole host of federal government agencies and authorities to intermediate into the mortgage market to make sure an adequate flow of funds to the thrift institutions continued. At year-end 1965, the federal government and its agencies and authorities owned 3 percent of the total residential mortgage debt of the nation. At year-end 1975, ten years later, the federal government and its agencies owned 14 percent of the total residential debt of the nation. In other words, rather than facing the problem, the federal government just created another intermediary to solve it, leaving the financial institutions in their archaic splendor just as they were and just as they remain today.

How did they do that? Of course, they had to compete in the open market for money. They sold bonds. There's no point in going through the whole history. A lot of studies have been done on it by the Federal Reserve Board and others. It's clear that this intermediary increased the cost of money, and since we really are dealing in international money markets rather than a domestic money market, the end result was a stabilization in the flow of funds to the mortgage market, to be sure, but at substantially increased costs.

The State of New York, faced with these problems, could not follow the federal model. So the State of New York came up with another extraordinary concept of how to get around it. It's known as borrowing. Former Governor Nelson Rockefeller invented the next best thing to the Federal Reserve Board's ability to print money and that was the moral obligation bond. It's the closest thing to it.

At the end of the decade, New York State, with 8.5 percent of the nation's population, and 9.5 percent of the disposable personal income, had about 18 percent of the state and local debt nationwide; 46 percent of the short-term state and local debt of the nation; and over 25 percent, 26.7 percent to be exact, of the nonguaranteed—read the words *moral obligation*—debt of the nation. The state of New York intermediated by borrowing. The federal government intermediated by borrowing, but through different forms of intermediaries.

Guidelines for Change

Apparently we are living in a society where the ultimate fiscal resource of our government has not been the right to tax, but rather the right to borrow. The question is: What do we do about it? If we don't solve the problem fundamentally on a national basis, the Northeast region or any other region may suffer enormously in the ensuing years because the infrastructure of our financial system is no longer rational.

Now, I would like to suggest that it is the responsibility of the Northeast to attack this problem, because all national problems tend to increase at a geometric rather than an arithmetic rate when you have a crucial region that is going, so to speak, down hill. We tried to do something about this problem in the Northeast last year. The banking commissioners of the five Northeastern states all got together and said, let us adopt the program that had been passed in the committee of the House of Representatives and in the Senate, the so-called Financial Institutions Reform Act. I don't need to go into detail, but the plan was that the financial institutions in the Northeast could take this proposal that had been thought out by the Congress and many study groups and apply it regionally to see if it worked. The Northeast, or any other region in the country, could then set a pattern that would perhaps make constructive changes.

The idea was, of course, shot down because we do believe that in this country all laws (financial, economic, whatever) apply equally across the umpteen millions of square miles and millions of people and a trillion dollar plus GNP.

The fact, of course, is that it didn't get a chance to work and I'm afraid it would not have worked on a regional basis. Therefore, *step number one,* in my opinion, is a true restructuring of the financial institutions and the regulatory authorities that control them on a national basis, not just for the Northeast. It is absolutely mandatory for the Northeast, but equally as important for the country as a whole. Of course, their problems will come after ours have either been blown up or perhaps solved.

Step two is to recognize, within that revised structure and even today, that local capital cannot be applied to local problems through mandate or taxation. I may add I'm a liberal Democrat. I have to tell the financial community that since capital can be moved anywhere that is profitable, punitive taxation of financial institutions only hastens the exodus of those financial institutions, because it's perfectly feasible, possible, and plausible for them to exit.

This involves a question of incentives to financial institutions to invest in certain socially desirable activities. This has been the history of this country. We have never mandated capital. We have decentralized capital. I think that will work and we should continue that formula. I believe it is perfectly possible to create in the Northeast the kinds of programs that would give local capital an incentive to stay at home. These programs need to prevent excess risk and provide competitive rates of return so that the managers don't run the risk of being sued by those whose money they manage. In the State of New York, an attempt is being made to create programs to provide incentives for capital investment in the so-called redlined areas of urban centers.

The only way to assure a supply of local capital for urban regional investment growth is by making sure that capital is protected. The risks that are being taken must be commensurate with the rates of return available anywhere else in the free world for the same degree of risk. The creation of that type of an incentive and a risk insurance system for local capital investment is probably one of New York State's most important goals for the next year. By local capital, I'm not talking about entrepreneurial capital, which is a different subject, but the long-term fixed income needed for housing, sewer systems, building and equipping plants which provide employment opportunities, and so on.

Finally, I would like to make one other comment on the subject of tax concessions and incentives. I believe very much in tax concessions for economic development, but I do not feel that tax concessions and incentives are really helpful in promoting social purposes by creating a subsidy to reduce the operating costs. I think that one of the things we have to do, if we are looking to private capital to finance our activities, is to rearrange not only the incentives to private capital, but also the forms of subsidies that are paid. The subsidy system as well as the financial system must be restructured. Historically, at least in the housing and development area, our subsidies have been given to institutions and to intermediaries, but not to the recipient, the so-called ultimate recipient of the grant, the benefit the social purpose.

Our financial institutions are already being rearranged by the market place. Our task is to first, redesign subsidy incentive programs to attract private capital, and second, to make sure those subsidies and incentives flow to those whom we wish to receive them at the lowest possible cost.

The Welfare Question

SAR A. LEVITAN

THE GOAL OF THIS COLLECTION of essays is to move the focus of debate over the problems of the Northeast from the descriptive realm to the prescriptive. But before attempting to explore where we are going, we have to have an understanding of where we are.

The framework for analysis in defining the problems and posing solutions is that of a zero sum game, involving an inter-regional struggle pitting region against region. The decline of the Northeast gives the impetus for growth in the South and West. Hence, many of the strategies for coping with the problems of the Northeast are premised on reallocating fixed resources, and inter-regionl comparisons are a must. In line with this framework, this paper focuses on the relative welfare positions of the Northeast and the South.

The Five Welfare Programs and Poverty

Five major programs are usually associated with public welfare: Medicaid, Aid to Families with Dependent Children (AFDC), food stamps, supplemental security income (SSI), and general assistance. We are talking about a bundle of some $40 billion of various welfare programs and the question is, if we are talking about a zero sum game, how do you distribute the benefits so the Northeast would get a little more and, I suppose, the South would get a little less?

Medicaid and *AFDC* are programs in aid of the poor, with benefit levels set by states and matching support from the federal government at a rate of one federal dollar matched to every local dollar for states with a high per capita income, to more than $3.50 in federal dollars to every local dollar in states with a low per capita income.

The wide differentials in federal aid notwithstanding, average benefits in the Northeast exceed those in the South:

	Monthly benefit
Medicaid	$185 in Northeast
	$105 in South
AFDC	$ 96 in Northeast
	$ 42 in South

	State share
Medicaid	49% in Northeast
	39% in South
AFDC	49% in Northeast
	33% in South

Supplemental security income, which is a program of cash benefits to the elderly, blind, and disabled, guarantees a minimum federal benefit level. Largely because of the varying levels of state support, benefits are $134 a month to each recipient in the Northeast compared to $95 a month in the South.

Food stamps is a federal program, with benefits varying very little. But *general assistance* is purely state aid. These benefits vary between $108 per month for recipients in the Northeast to $71 per month for recipients in the South; four states in the South offer no general assistance.

There is also more participation in welfare programs among the poor in the Northeast than in the South. For example, about 60 percent of the persons in poverty in the Northeast participate in AFDC, compared to fewer than 30 percent in the South. (Participation rates among AFDC eligibles alone is of course higher—but figures here are representative of the differential.) This is due to lower need standards in most southern states. The average state-determined need for the Northeast states is $337 per month for a family of four, while the average for the southern states is $188, with the lowest at $60 and fourteen of the seventeen southern states determining the level of need for a family of four to be below $250. This means a sizable portion of the poor population in southern states is earning income above state determined need levels and is therefore ineligible to participate. Regional cost of living differences alone do not explain the difference. In 1976 the low level cost of living for a family of four living in the Northeast was calculated to be only about 6 percent higher than for a similar family in the South.

Not only are the individuals in poverty or on the edge of poverty worse off in the South (and less likely to be eligible for the smaller benefits) but the number of persons in poverty is larger. The South with only 32 percent of the total national population has 43 percent of the persons in poverty living there. More than 16 percent of the persons in the South are in poverty. In contrast, only 10 percent of the Northeast population is in poverty—only the midwestern region has a smaller proportion of its population in poverty. There are also more nearly poor persons in the south. In 1975 the per capita income in the South was $5,149. In the North it was 22 percent higher, at more than $6,300.

The Welfare Burden

But much of the present concern over the plight of the Northeast is not centered on how the poor fare but how well the region is capable of handling—among other things—the needs of the poor. Again the inter-regional comparisons are inevitable. In 1976 the northeastern states spent a total of nearly $12 billion helping the poor compared to $8.7 billion in the South. With 61 percent fewer poor persons, the northeastern states spent three times as much per individual. The traditional argument of partisans is that the northeastern generosity toward the poor is not rewarded by the federal government. The southern states actually receive 8 percent *more* federal funds to support their poor and pay only 20 percent of the total bill for the poor compared to 46 percent of the bill footed by the northeastern states. But this line of argument is misleading. It ignores the fact that the federal government spent 108 percent more in the Northeast for every poor person than in the Southeast. Furthermore, the ability of the southern states to pay above what it pays now is not clear. With southerners earning about 20 percent less than their northern cousins, they already have 15 percent of their income going to state and local governments compared to 18 percent in the Northeast. Given the lower income in the southern states and the presumed virtue of progressive taxation, it would hardly seem equitable to raise the tax level (if it were possible) above what it is now.

Today, the welfare problem is not one that can be neatly characterized in regional terms. The Northeast pays a relatively heavier portion than the southern states, but largely because it is able to pay more (and that is reflected in the AFDC-Medicaid formulas) and because northeastern states choose to be more generous. The benefit is that the plight of the poor is not quite as serious in the Northeast as it is in the South.

But much of the concern today is for the future—and rightfully so. The trend in the North is toward a growing welfare load and a declining tax base. Welfare benefits are good and jobs are not expanding. The concern naturally is for avoiding the point where the generosity of the Northeast becomes its tragic flaw, leading to its downfall. There is also a concern for eliminating inter-regional differentials that encourage migration of welfare recipients to the Northeast. But the solution is not going to be found playing the zero sum game, pitting the South against the Northeast. New reallocation strategies will help ameliorate the problem, but only a commitment for *new* resources will ultimately solve it.

Who Should Pay?

The typical Yankee solution is to increase the federal percentage match for the joint programs for the states with higher per capita incomes. This could relieve the northeastern states of some of their welfare burden, although it would not help southern states (and the poor persons there) very much.

The popular panacea making the rounds today is to federalize the welfare system, imposing a uniform set of standards and benefit levels. This would simplify some aspects of the problem but complicate other aspects. It would obviously improve conditions for the poor in the South. But if new benefit levels were not as high as current levels in some northeastern states, the poor there might suffer a relative decline in income unless "hold harmless" provisions were included. However, since even the most generous benefits are not raising the income level of most recipients to even the poverty level, cuts would be difficult to make. The drawback, of course, starts with costs. Reasonable uniform benefit levels could easily double or triple welfare costs, taking into account increased eligibility and higher benefits in the current low benefit states. Cost of living differentials for various areas would have to be computed—that in itself would pose a serious administrative problem. But perhaps the greatest complication of standardizing benefits to the northeastern level would be that such a move would drive up the cost of labor in the South. The combined inflationary effect of increasing welfare benefits and higher labor costs could adversely affect southern employment, and rising unemployment in the South is no way to improve the national economy.

In short, raising benefits across the board to reduce inter-regional differentials is not a sound approach, whether it is done with increased federal assistance or a complete federal takeover. Other measures are necessary.

More Than Zero Sum Game

A major factor contributing to the welfare problem in the Northeast is, paradoxically, poverty and generally lower incomes in the South. A pool of skilled workers, unorganized and working for less than their northern cousins, has attracted industrial growth from the North like any good equilibrium model would predict. But many unskilled and unemployable persons unable to latch on to the accelerating southern gravy train have left for the Northeast where relief is more comprehensive and benefits are more generous.

I'm not at all satisfied with the status quo, and I'm not throwing up my hands in despair. There are steps that can be taken. Whatever is done, it will have its costs. I know of no social solution that does not create new problems. Part of the solution for the Northeast will be to encourage strategies that raise income in the South and bring southern standards up to northern standards. One option is a unionization drive in the South that would help raise labor costs closer to the northern levels. Only 16 percent of the southern labor force is unionized compared to 31 percent for the northeastern labor force. Right-to-work laws appear to be a barrier. More than half of the southern states have them, (nine out of seventeen) contributing no doubt to the lowest state unionization rates in the country. Ray Marshall, the new Secretary of Labor, has indicated that he favors repeal of section 14(b) of the Taft Hartley Act which permits the state right-to-work laws.

Another solution would be to raise the minimum wage (and enforce it) and enforce the Walsh-Healy Act, the law that requires contractors with the federal government to pay the prevailing wage.

The Northeast most definitely has problems. Employment is growing very slowly in some states and is actually falling in others. The burgeoning welfare bill in the Northeast is aggravating the problems. But equalizing benefits in the South is not much of a solution; we cannot put the burden on the welfare system. At least with respect to welfare problems, any permanent solutions will have to include strategies for improving earnings in the South and enabling southern states to improve their own welfare systems.

APPENDIX
WELFARE PARAMETERS

DISTRIBUTION OF THE POPULATION

	Total 1975 Population (thousands)	Percent of National Population	Estimated 1975 Poverty Population (thousands)	Percent in Poverty	Percent of National Poverty Population
Northeast	49,461	23	4,949	10	19
South	68,115	32	11,159	16.4	43

SOURCE: *National Journal* 8 January 1976.

REGIONAL INCOME

1970	Income (billion dollars)	Population (thousands)	Per Capita Income	Percent Change 1970-1975
Northeast	$217.9	49,000	$4,447	—
South	$215.7	62,798	$3,435	—
1975				
Northeast	$311.8	49,461	$6,304	42
South	$350.7	68,115	$5,149	50

SOURCES: *National Journal* 8 January 1976 and *U. S. Statistical Abstract*, 1976.

TOTAL WELFARE SPENDING IN FISCAL 1976: AFDC, MEDICAID, SSI, FOOD STAMPS, AND GENERAL AID

	Total Spending (millions)	Federal Spending (millions)	Total Spending Per Poor Individual	Federal Spending Per Poor Individual
Northeast	$11,990	$6,441	$2,428	$1,302
South	$ 8,750	$6,985	$ 784	$ 625

SOURCE: *National Journal* 8 January 1976.

REGIONAL SPENDING IN 1975: STATE AND LOCAL EXPENDITURES
(selected categories)

Category		Percent of Total Spending	Per Capita Expenditure	Per Capita Expenditure as Percentage of Per Capita Income
		Northeast		
Welfare	$ 8,141	14.6	$165	2.6
Highways	$ 4,319	7.7	$ 87	1.4
Education	$19,246	34.5	$389	6.2
Health and Hospitals	$ 4,835	8.7	$ 98	1.6

Total expenditures $55.8 billion, portion of per capita income going to state and local government 17.5%.

Category		Percent of Total Spending	Per Capita Expenditure	Per Capita Expenditure as Percentage of Per Capita Income
		South		
Welfare	$ 5,013	9.6	$ 74	1.4
Highways	$ 6,544	12.5	$ 96	1.9
Education	$20,562	39.2	$302	5.9
Health and Hospitals	$ 4,793	9.1	$ 70	1.4

Total expenditures $52.4 billion, portion of per capita income going to state and local government 15.0%.

SOURCE: *U. S. Statistical Abstract*, 1976.

Section IV

The Local Response

Introduction

REGIONAL DYNAMICS CAN SERVE consciously or otherwise as a rationalization for avoiding the problems of the central city. It is all too easy for both ominous visions of a regional miasma and the converse, the quests for effective regional policy responses, to dominate our thinking to the detriment of other standing imperatives. Struggling with the very concept of a twenty-first century infrastructure—a capital plant responding to both the prerequisites to economic viability in the future and the emerging spatial formats of American society—and envisioning new public instrumentalities to operationalize a set of regional specifics make it possible to underplay the significance of the adjustments required by the aging and shrinking central cities of the Northeast.

Whether or not the region copes effectively with its long-term difficulties—which may imply a smoothing of the transition rather than a dramatic renaissance—it is apparent that its urban centers will continue to contract in size, function, and economic role. It is essential, therefore, to provide an overview of the more prominent policy constraints bounding local political institutions, bounds which must be heeded regardless of any greater regional eventuality.

Central cities, despite the unrelenting momentum of decentralization and dispersion, continue to have unique attributes which can serve as leverage to maintain important, but limited, functional roles. Certainly, regional vitality will serve to enhance the feasibility of these potentials. But this frank admission is a far cry from the expectations weaned from the historic past. At best, our older urban concentrations will fade into an extended constellation of activity centers characteristic of a dispersed metropolis. To confront this evolution directly and to attempt substantial alterations in its course may prove futile and even harmful in the long run. Given the wherewithal and capacity of singular jurisdictions, a more fruitful approach may well be to tailor responses to the forces in motion, adjusting to their main thrust; limited deflections, at best, probably define the realm of the feasible. What this implies, then, are explicit policies facing up to contraction with the objective of reconcentrating extant resources.

Evidence of this reduction in status has pyramided over the course of the decade of the 1970s.

1. Between 1970 and 1976, the central cities of the 243 standard metropolitan statistical areas (as defined in 1970) lost 2.1 million people, 3.4 percent of their 1970 population totals.
2. These same central cities lost 4.6 million persons and gained only 2.7 million through internal migration during the one-year period between March 1975 and March 1976.
3. In both long-term and short-term perspectives, the absolute population declines of selected cities of the industrialized tier of northern states have been precipitous. Exhibit 1 details the losses for both the 1950 to 1976 and 1970 to 1976 periods; in most cases, the long-term declines have accelerated markedly in the present decade.

The historical momentum and current reality of contraction, then, is substantial; for local leadership to refute its presence is to succumb to the most tenuous rationales of political expediency.

The transition to lesser planes of activity leaves many cities with infrastructures and service systems of a scale appropriate not to their reduced status but to the heritage of a much more substantial past. The market—both the remaining populace and resident economic activity—is not sufficient to fully utilize the capacity that exists, nor can it provide the fiscal resources to support it. An appropriate policy track appears to be an overall strategy of contraction, within which extant viability is reconcentrated into distinct focal points or enclaves. This latter concept—areas of critical mass—may permit the survival, and even growth, of CBD activities, for example, that are enhanced by density and interdependency, the traditional attributes of urban places. If spread too thinly, their declining impact can be visibly dissipated. Regrouped into interdependent packages, their very rationale may be

EXHIBIT 1

POPULATION CHANGE, SELECTED CITIES: 1950 TO 1975

CITY	1950[1]	1970[2]	1975[3]	Change: 1950-1975		Change: 1970-1975	
				Number	Percent	Number	Percent
Boston	801,444	641,071	636,725	-164,719	-20.6	- 4,346	- 0.7
Buffalo	580,132	462,768	407,160	-172,972	-29.8	- 55,068	-12.0
Chicago	3,620,962	3,366,957	3,099,391	-521,571	-14.4	-267,566	- 7.9
Cincinnati	503,998	452,524	412,564	- 51,474	-10.2	- 39,960	- 8.8
Cleveland	914,808	750,903	638,793	-276,015	-30.2	-112,110	-14.9
Detroit	1,849,568	1,511,482	1,335,085	-514,483	-27.8	-176,397	-11.7
Minneapolis	521,718	434,400	378,112	-143,606	-27.5	- 56,288	-13.0
New York City	7,891,957	7,894,862	7,481,613	-410,344	- 5.2	-413,249	- 5.2
Newark	438,776	382,417	339,568	- 99,208	-22.6	- 42,849	-11.2
Philadelphia	2,071,605	1,948,609	1,815,808	-255,797	-12.3	-132,801	- 6.8
Pittsburgh	676,806	520,117	458,651	-218,155	-32.2	- 61,466	-11.8
St. Louis	856,796	622,236	524,964	-331,832	-38.7	- 97,272	-15.6

NOTES: 1. April 1, 1950 census.
2. April 1, 1970 census.
3. July 1, 1975 population estimate.

SOURCES: U.S. Bureau of the Census. *County and City Data Book, 1956* (A Statistical Abstract Supplement). U.S. Government Printing Office, Washington, D.C., 1957.
U.S. Bureau of the Census. *County and City Data Book, 1967* (A Statistical Abstract Supplement). U.S. Government Printing Office, Washington, D.C., 1967.
U.S. Bureau of the Census, Census of Population: 1970, Vol. 1, CHARACTERISTICS OF THE POPULATION, Part 1, United States Summary—Section 1, U.S. Government Printing Office, Washington, D.C., 1973.
U.S. Bureau of the Census, Current Population Reports: *Population Estimates and Projections*, Series P-25 (various state report numbers), U.S. Government Printing Office, Washington, D.C., 1977.

emphasized, while allowing municipal resources to be more effectively targeted.

Similarly, the residential dimension may be amenable to analogous policies. Thinned out areas do not tend to replicate the advantages of low density suburbia, but become a hostile presence on the urban landscape. A recompaction, pivoting on unique attributes—historic districts and other areas endowed with special urban qualities—may indeed foster more satisfactory residential environments.

Certainly, the implementation and operationalization of such strategies can prove to be a task of considerable complexity. Conflicts of interest will abound. There will be continual confrontations of competing claims, all possessing some measure of validity, as to what constitutes the public interest of the city or sectors of its populace. There will be no easy resolutions, since there are often no simple rights and wrongs. Yet some measure of detached rationality may be injected into the policy debate. As in the case of the regional analog, an essential preliminary is to counter lingering misconceptions obscuring recognition of the basic parameters of change.

Persistent Fiscal Delusions

Norman Krumholz, director of the Cleveland City Planning Commission, and his associate, Janice Cogger, outline a set of persistent fiscal delusions which help avoid coming to grips with the basic problem.

1. *The first delusion is that the process of declining population and falling jobs can be reversed in the near future, and that the older industrial city can be restored to what it once was.*

2. *A variant of this delusion is that the energy crisis will cause a recentralization of the population. Thus we will all be using public transit and moving back to the central city.*

3. *Such local development incentives as tax abatements, land writedowns, and industrial revenue bonds will have a significant impact upon the location of business and industry. Even more probably, the competition between states and among localities to attract new investment may result in something akin to a gasoline price war.*

4. *Another major delusion is that the fiscal distress in our older cities is cyclical, brought on largely by recession. Despite the recovery, the fiscal crisis in our older cities continues.*

5. *Finally, in this brief litany, is the expectation that the federal government is going to bail the older cities out of all their difficulties. Some help may be forthcoming, but not enough to solve all the cities' economic problems.*

Basically, the days of plenty are past, the era of tough choices is at hand, and we will be better able to deal with our problems if we put aside our delusions and face reality.

The Opportunities

Krumholz and Cogger then raise the questions: what is to be done given the current fiscal distress of the older industrial cities and the prospects that the future situation may be worse, not better? What are the opportunity areas? In short, the management of stasis and decline offers many opportunities to enable cities to provide a reasonable level of service while their fiscal resources decline and they grow smaller. Such activities can be classified into four categories:

Imposition of Restraints: *The avoidance of committing resources to projects offering few returns while consuming scarce public resources.*

Creative Investment Proposals. *The search for opportunities to invest limited resources toward programs and projects which will generate long-term savings, make existing systems operate more efficiently, and channel private resources toward the fulfillment of public objectives.*

Policies for Constructive Shrinkage. *The divestiture of certain responsibilities conceived in a more affluent past, and the acceptance of new ones.*

Strengthening Community Organizations. *Facilitating the effectiveness of turf-based organizations having the potential to maintain residential focal points as the basis for future neighborhood survival.*

In essence, all of these opportunity areas centralize about the concept of planned shrinkage—the rational management of decline.

Planned Shrinkage

It is this very idea which has become closely identified with Roger Starr, former administrator of New York City's Housing and Development Administration. Immersed in the city's fiscal, economic, and social crises, Starr was probably the first public voice to suggest the concept of planned shrinkage, and thus quickly became embroiled in heated controversy. Whatever the magnitude of the reaction, it is difficult to refute the logic of his contentions.

1. *The central fact of New York City's financial crisis is that the city government does not receive enough wealth to sustain the city at the levels to which its citizens have been accustomed. Two familiar remedies exist: economic development, which will increase tax revenues and reduce the financial requirements of the needy, and appeals to Washington for a greater flow of federal support payments.*

2. *The potential for success in these two endeavors is limited. The virtual disappearance of New York's manufacturing base and the but slightly loosened purse strings in Washington, despite a new administration, lend credence to this assumption. Hence a third approach—accept the fact that the city's population is going to shrink and cut back on city services accordingly, realizing considerable savings in the process.*

3. *The city cannot survive if the pattern of its costs remains the same for the smaller population as it was for the larger.*

4. *The resulting planned shrinkage strategy is premised on the following assumptions.*
   a) *Consistent density is a necessary part of building or block survival. Social cohesion is impossible in sparsely populated areas.*
   b) *Large parts of New York City are virtually dead, yet the city must supply services to the few survivors.*
   c) *Equally important, the city can provide services much more efficiently to fully populated areas.*
   d) *Consequently, if the city is to survive with a smaller population, the population must be encouraged to concentrate in the sections that remain alive.*
   e) *The role of the city planner is not to originate the trend of abandonment, but to observe and use it so that public investment will be hoarded for those areas where it will sustain life.*
   f) *The vacated areas can be cleared, parcels assembled, and the tracts eventually reused, if the city does not succumb to pressures for immediate disposal.*

5. *The time to begin planning for a smaller population is now, not after doomsday has come. Yet one cannot underestimate the fears engendered by this notion of growing smaller in a social milieu in*

*which growing bigger has been the hope of those who have not
had a fair share.*

6. *Essentially, planned shrinkage is a recognition that the golden door
to full participation in American life and the American economy
is no longer to be found in New York City (and by inference, the
bulk of the cities of the Northeast).*

The political feasibility and will to implement this approach in New
York City is questionable. Is it feasible elsewhere?

The Coping Environments

Gurney Breckenfeld, member of the board of editors, *Fortune* magazine, provides a journalistic overview of those urban areas that have
been coping, with apparent success, with the transition to a diminished
role in American society.

1. *Despite claims to the contrary, a large infusion of funds is not what
our ailing cities need most. States and localities, mostly the latter,
will receive some $70 billion this year in federal aid. That already
amounts to a Marshall Plan in monetary magnitude, though obviously not in coherence.*

2. *In some ways, this largess, as in the past, will make urban problems
worse instead of better. A new dose of federal aid probably would
deflect mayor and cities from their first task—difficult but not impossible—of adjusting to shrinking populations and economies.*

3. *Most cities lack the skilled, tough, farsighted public leadership
necessary for the long, sustained effort that might, in time, revitalize
them. Under these circumstances, more federal aid would merely
postpone the inevitable day of fiscal reckoning.*

4. *Yet two cities in the troubled Northeast—Pittsburgh and Baltimore
—demonstrate, that with the right kind of local leadership, fiscal
disaster can be avoided.*

5. *Pittsburgh has been guided by the mayoral philosophy that diminishing population levels—the city has lost one-third of its 1950
population total—should permit a reduction in the municipal workforce. Despite furious objections, city employment has been pared
by 30 percent, while still maintaining acceptable levels of public
service to the remaining population.*

6. *Baltimore, afflicted with the same panoply of urban ills and declines plaguing Pittsburgh, has made a significant comeback—physically and psychologically. Two decades of intelligent teamwork between local officials and private business leaders as well as a private, non-profit urban renewal vehicle have made this turnaround possible.*

7. *Again, tight management has been central to the Baltimore experience—long-standing fiscal limits on borrowing and workforce reductions congruent to population declines served as major policy guidelines.*

8. *The great lesson of Pittsburgh and Baltimore is that it is possible for cities to shrink successfully. The real tragedy of our ailing cities is not their shrinkage, some of it unavoidable, but the fact that they have hastened their own decline by a senseless kind of economic warfare against themselves. At many turns perverse incentives created by government have given individuals and companies a self-interest in doing what's bad for the community.*

9. *A great deal of modesty is in order about any new initiatives to relieve urban problems. We know a lot less about cities and how they tick than we were sure we knew fifteen years ago.*

The learning curve is often a difficult one to ascend. Yet the shock-waves emanating from the New York fiscal crisis have prompted leaders in many cities to reexamine old assumptions. Slowly the outlines of regional and urban transition are beginning to be recognized, with the realization that contraction is chronic, not transient. We appear to be embarking on a period of time when planned shrinkage can be considered on its merits, and not on its perverse connotations.

The Challenge of Contracting Municipalities

NORMAN KRUMHOLZ AND JANICE COGGER

TRYING TO EXAMINE MUNICIPAL FINANCE, limited revenues, and a useful role for city planners in a context of constraints is a heavy assignment, so we must plunge right into it. However, I first want to assure you that whereas most speakers or writers approach subjects in a partial and prejudiced way, I am going to approach it in a completely impartial, unbiased, and objective manner. There is some bad news and some good news. On one hand, the financial problems confronting our older, industrial cities are probably more profound than we generally care to admit. On the other hand, the opportunities for planners to help such cities and their people grow older gracefully are much greater than we often realize. The bad news will be examined first, which can be outlined as a set of persistent fiscal delusions.

Persistent Fiscal Delusions

The first delusion is that the process of declining population and falling jobs can be reversed in the near future, and that the older industrial city can be restored to what it once was. In Cleveland (and, I might add, in New York, Detroit, Pittsburgh, St. Louis, etc.) no public pronouncement is complete without a prescription for "saving the city." What is meant by salvation is rarely specified, but it is not merely avoiding bankruptcy. The pleasant stabilization of the tax-exempt bond market in the last eighteen months has allayed that fear. The concern is with attracting population and employment back to the city and restoring it to its state of former greatness. In my judgment, that is a delusion.

The reality is that the job and population losses incurred by such cities has been a reflection of extraordinarily powerful social and economic tastes and the general improvement in our standard of living. Increasingly, they are also a reflection of changes in the national economy. I do *not* believe that the trends resulting from such structural change will be reversed within the foreseeable future.

A variant of this delusion is that the energy crisis will cause a recentralization of the population. We will all be using public transit and moving back to the central city. You can forget it. Even if a tax of 25¢ per gallon were placed on gasoline, the average suburban family would save only $250 per year by moving back to the city. That is hardly enough to influence choices in residential location. What is happening to date is quite the opposite. Typically, Americans have responded to the energy crisis *not* by reducing their use of automobiles but by accelerating it. Vehicle registration figures have skyrocketed in the 1970s far faster than in the 1950s and 1960s. By the year 2000 there may be more vehicles in the U.S. than people. There are already more vehicles than registered drivers.

A second fiscal delusion is that such local development incentives as tax abatements, land write-downs, and industrial revenue bonds will have a *significant* impact upon the location of business and industry. It seems to me that the competition between states and among localities to attract new investment may result in something similar to a gasoline price war. The incentives being offered by various jurisdictions will tend to cancel each other out. The only likely effect will be to increase the expected rate of return on private capital. The best approach may not be the attempt to attract the new, but to hold on to what you have got.

Another major delusion is that the fiscal distress in our older cities is cyclical, brought on largely by recession. There is no doubt that the national recession deepened and accelerated the cities' economic problems by putting pressure on city budgets, but we must be candid on where we stand in that cycle. The country is ending its second year of economic recovery. State and local income tax collections were up 20 percent between the fourth quarter of 1975 and the fourth quarter of 1976. Still, the fiscal crisis in our older cities continues.

Finally, in this brief litany of delusions, is the expectation that the federal government is going to bail the older cities out of all their difficulties. More assistance may be expected from the Carter administration, but this added assistance will likely be in the form of job and health programs as well as some additional block grant money, but this cannot be enough to solve all the cities' economic problems.

In sum, the older industrial cities will probably continue to lose population and employment, though at a slower rate than during the last two decades. The costs of delivering services and maintaining the infrastructure will *not* decline in proportion to declining municipal tax resources. Few of the infrastructure costs of urban growth are easily reversible into economies of shrinkage. These cities will become increasingly dependent upon transfer payments merely to maintain basic services. In other words, the days of plenty are past, the era of tough choices is at hand, and we will be better able to deal with our problems if we put aside our delusions and face reality.

The Opportunities: Planning Activities

Now, what are central city planners to do given the current fiscal distress of the older industrial cities and the prospects that the future situation may be worse, not better? What are the opportunities? (Some people have called the opportunities in our cities "insurmountable opportunities.") The need for a comprehensive theory of planning dealing with stasis and decline has frequently been cited in recent planning literature. Such a theory cannot be supplied here. What *can* be supplied are some examples, drawn from my eight years as planning director in Cleveland, of how planners can work to make public policy more responsive to the needs of the cities and their residents. In my experience, the management of stasis and decline offers planners many opportunities to engage in useful, interesting, and productive work aimed at enabling cities to provide a reasonable level of service while their fiscal resources decline and they grow smaller.

The activities might be classified into four categories: (1) the imposition of restraints, (2) creative investment proposals, (3) policies for constructive shrinkage, and (4) strengthening community organizations. In many respects, many of these activities are more closely related to management than to any traditional notion of planning. And, as you will see, political participation plays a major role in these operations.

The first category is the *imposition of restraints*. In Cleveland, hardly a month goes by without headlines proclaiming a new scheme to "turn the city around." Some of these amount to little more than urban decoration—a mall, a fountain, a plaza—while others involve proposals for major residential, commercial, or industrial development. All promise to attract jobs and people back to the city; all demand a massive infusion of public funds on the front end.

During the past few years, the planning staff has reviewed dozens of such proposals. We have routinely asked the overriding questions: Who gets? Who pays? In those cases where our analysis has indicated that the public costs would likely outweigh the public benefits, or where the benefits were likely to accrue to those least in need of public support, we have frequently and publicly opposed the commitment of public funds to the projects. It is well understood that public officials are under substantial pressure to accept promises of progress at face value. When the headlines say "$350 Million Project Proposed to Save City" we all know it is so, don't we? Our opposition to such projects, then, has frequently embroiled us in heated political debate. Needless to say, we have often failed to halt the expenditure of public funds on these projects. What we *have* done is to gain some public acceptance for the notion that the city and its residents should expect something in return, some *quid pro quo*, for granting subsidies—a startling concept to those who view public funds primarily as a way to take all the private risk out of what used to be called private enterprise.

Arguing against the commitment of resources to projects which offer few returns implies that there are alternative investments which the city should be making. That leads to the second category: developing *creative investment proposals*.

In this operation, we continually seek opportunities to direct the city's resources toward programs and projects which will result in long-term savings, which will make existing systems work more efficiently, or which will direct private resources toward the fulfillment of public objectives. Our activities in this area have taken a number of forms.

In one example, members of the planning staff worked with the city's division of waste collection and disposal for over three years in order to improve its management capacity. By reorganizing collection procedures, reassigning manpower, and spending the division's capital resources on cost-saving equipment, the city is now realizing a saving of several million dollars a year. When we began working with the waste division, its staff lacked any planning or analytical capabilities whatever. Now, the division head (a former garbage collector) talks about picking up garbage heuristically.

In another example, we have been working closely with the city's community development department (the city's CDBG agency) to develop policies and programs for the expenditure of community development block grant funds. As part of this continuing effort, we have convinced the mayor to call the leaders of Cleveland's commercial banks and savings and loan corporations together to form a reinvestment task force. The group's first assignment has been to develop a program for leveraging the city's rehabilitation funds. It has taken over six months, but at last, the city and the lenders are close to agreement, on a program which will leverage the city's funds by a factor of approximately five to one.

Two points should be clear from these examples. First, our proposals for ways in which the city should invest its resources are very modest and, in many ways, not as politically appealing as the proposals we seek to restrain. We do not promise to walk on water; we do not promise to rebuild Cleveland; we promise only to help the city program its resources in meaningful ways. Second, efforts to influence the investment of the city's resources involve time-consuming commitments. It is not enough for planners to articulate broad policy statements, or to prepare capital improvement programs, or to testify at budget hearings, and let it go at that. More is needed. We have found it essential to work closely and over long periods with operating departments to develop and help implement specific program and project ideas.

The third category, *policies for constructive shrinkage*, involves recognition of the fact that as the population and economic base of the city decline, it may have to divest itself of certain responsibilities and accept some new ones.

In recent years, the Cleveland planning staff has played an active role in negotiating the terms and conditions under which the city has transferred both its port facilities and its transit system to countywide authorities. We are currently working out an agreement whereby Cleveland's two large lakefront parks will be transferred to the State of Ohio. As its resources decline and the costs of providing services increase, it may be in the city's interest to transfer certain facilities and activities to other entities which can draw upon a broader base for their financial support. However, we do not believe that such transfers are automatically nor unconditionally in the best interests of the city and its residents. Rather, we work within a principle that prior to such transfers, the city should obtain reimbursement for its past investments and/or guarantees of improved service for its residents—especially those Cleveland residents who need help the most.

The negotiations over the transfer of the ailing Cleveland Transit System to the regional transit authority provide an excellent example. The negotiations took almost five months. They could have been completed in a much shorter time had be accepted the position proposed by the other parties to the negotiations—the downtown business community, the local transit bureaucracy, and the representatives of the suburbs. These "worthies" assumed that Cleveland would benefit by merely "unloading" our $70 million system without prior service and fare guarantees—especially to our transit-dependent population. It was our position that the city should obtain firm guarantees of reduced fares and improved service before agreeing to the transfer. After prolonged conflict we obtained our guarantees. While they were somewhat less than we had hoped for, they were infinitely more than our people would have received had we not been prepared with a well-defined position and a willingness to fight for it.

At the same time the planning staff was working to get the city *out* of the transit business, we were working to get it *into* the land banking business. Our analysis of tax delinquency in the city of Cleveland had revealed that in some areas more than 25 percent of the parcels were tax delinquent. The city was incurring costs for the demolition of abandoned buildings and the maintenance of vacant lots with no prospects for reimbursement. The tax foreclosure process was no longer working to recapture delinquent taxes nor to return properties to productive uses. With the help of a foundation grant which enabled us to hire real estate and legal consultants, and after almost four years of research and lobbying, we drafted, and the Ohio legislature passed in 1976, a bill which will allow cities to take title to and land bank tax delinquent land. We have no illusions that there will be an immediate market for most of the land which the city will obtain through this process. What the new process will do is provide owners with some incentive to pay taxes and assessments on properties they wish to retain, reduce land speculation, and allow the city to gradually assemble developable parcels at little or no cost.

My fourth category of work planners can do to help their cities grow older gracefully is *strengthening community organizations*. This should not be mistaken for what is generally discussed under the heading *citizen participation*. A distinguishing characteristic of the groups with which we work most closely is that they do not wait to be consulted about our plans. They have plans of their own.

The community organizing movement is relatively new to Cleveland. During the past three years, strong, turf based organizations have been developed in two neighborhoods and are currently in the process of being developed in several others. These groups have professional staff and are capable of dealing with a broad range of issues.

We initially began working with these groups because we shared common agendas on certain specific issues. Beyond that, we respect their ability to follow through on issues, to consistently "turn out the troops," and to capture substantial media coverage. Accordingly, we have been devoting increasingly more staff time to helping these groups develop their own agendas.

Why do we view these groups as allies? The answer is simple. They provide a countervailing political force to the incessant demands by downtown interests for capital improvements. They may have a major, long-term beneficial impact upon the efficient delivery of public services to the city's neighborhoods. They frequently argue that neighborhood considerations are more important than regional considerations. They often insist that more grandiose programs must be set aside in favor of basic needs. And we frequently agree on all points.

Conclusion

Well, what is it these examples and comments suggest that might be of some interest to other central city planners.

To begin, these examples provide a model of a planning operation that has largely rejected the notion of working toward grandiose highly improbable futures. Rather, it has come to grips in a long-term, highly political way, with things it can and should be doing—working to overcome or ameliorate the very real urban problems of poor cities, poor neighborhoods, and poor people. It seems to me that if planners seriously want to improve conditions in our cities, we must understand that the challenge requires much more than our traditional responses. Planners are likely to address a problem only in terms of their own professional skills, and then stop. We perform our regressions, or develop our designs, or execute our analyses; we identify alternative recommendations. Whe then represent them as lucidly and persuasively as we can to our planning commission—and then we stop. We fear that what lies beyond is politics which is dangerous.

That is not enough if we seriously intend to affect outcomes. Neither planners nor planning commissions decide public policy issues—politicians and service bureaucracies do. Those who propose ends and who say they care about future conditions must come to care about means as well. We must be prepared to spend some time and take some risks in the political arena in order to improve city conditions. Planners who are serious about their work must understand that both decisionmaking and implementation are processes, not acts, and that both require their protracted and energetic participation. If we are willing to go this route, planners may yet play a major role in making their cities more manageable and their neighborhoods more livable.

Making New York Smaller

ROGER STARR

EVERY NEW YORK CITY commissioner who lived through the first days of the city's financial crisis—from the shutting off of bank credit in early 1975 to the approval of the federal loan near the end of the year— remembers it as the time when the future was hidden behind the doomsday of the next payroll date, or the next call from City Hall setting a quota of new firings.

Winning respite from the biweekly payroll crises by establishing the Municipal Assistance Corporation, the Emergency Financial Control Board, and the U.S. Treasury loan was a monumental achievement of which the governor, the mayor, and their assistants, and counselors can be proud. A helpless debtor with as many dependents as New York City would have been an enormous problem for the federal courts. Nobody knows if they could have managed it without social upheaval and fiscal chaos.

The net effect of New York City's legally required three-year fiscal plan has been to melt all of the little doomsdays of payrolls and note maturities into one giant doomsday which is now scheduled for July 1, 1978. If the assumptions of the financial plan prove false—if an additional $800-million cut in the present annual operating budget cannot be achieved, or if compensating increased revenues cannot be found—doomsday will come ahead of schedule. If the terms of the financial plan and the treasury loan can be extended to five years or, even better, to seven, doomsday will be postponed.

But in any case, doomsday—that day on which all the parties to the deferral of wage increases and cuts in services will be released from their inhibitions, and the city government must stand up on its own—is coming. The gravity of this challenge has not yet been glimpsed by most New Yorkers. Yet their understanding, cooperation, and even their initiative on matters too hot for elected officials to handle are essential if the city is to survive. New York's problems do not spring from trivial mechanical faults that might be rectified with a new accounting system or the prosecution of a few rascals. If the city is to have a proud future, we must be prepared to face the central fact and plan *now* the serious actions needed to deal with it.

Three Responses

The central fact of New York's financial crisis is that the city government does not receive enough wealth to sustain the city at the level to which its citizens have become accustomed. While this is a difficult situation, it is not without remedies. Two are familiar: A successful program of economic development for the city to increase tax revenues and reduce demands for financial aid and services to the needy, and new appeals to Albany and Washington (where a new, perhaps more friendly, spirit will inhabit the White House) to increase the funds supplementing those generated by the city's commerce.

A third is less familiar: We could simply accept the fact that the city's population is going to shrink, and we could cut back on city services accordingly, realizing considerable savings in the process.

These responses are not incompatible, and the city ought to pursue all three of them for whatever benefits they will yield. It is the third, however, that deserves the most attention at this point, for the first two are familiar promises. Planned shrinkage is not a popular idea—for simply suggesting that the department of city planning should study it, I was denounced as a genocidal lunatic and enemy of man. The black and Puerto Rican caucus of the city council adopted a resolution of condemnation. Pickets tried to prevent me from speaking at the Regional Plan Association meetings at the New York Hilton earlier this year. Much of the expressed hostility was based on a genuine fear that somehow the poor would be victimized by this policy. But the oppo-

site is true. The poor, who need the greatest service from the city government, would be worst hurt by a failure of the city to use its resources
economically.

To understand all of this properly, however, it is necessary to take a
closer look at how the city functions when it comes to fiscal matters.

We can think of New York's wealth as being produced by two different
cities that occupy the same boundaries—the Economic City and the
Political City. Most of the excitement over New York's crisis has been
generated by the problems of the Political City, but a precise appraisal
would show that the Economic City is in greater trouble.

The Economic City comprises all of the public and private enterprises
—from the Port Authority of New York and New Jersey, with its airports,
to street peddlers, with their carts—that create goods or services in New
York for which others are willing to pay. Thus, clearly, the Economic
City produces wealth, some of which is turned over as taxes and fees
to the Political City by the vendors of goods and services. The Economic City also employs people. It spreads wealth, though unevenly,
among its residents. To the extent that its exports attract the money
of foreigners (persons or corporate bodies not domiciled within the
city limits), it earns the funds to pay for the city's essential imports.

Part of the Economic City's problem is that its exports have lost their
attraction; in some industries, like beer, the city's once thriving production has shrunk to exactly nothing. In others, like apparel, printing,
baking, the city's production for export and even for its own use has
diminished drastically. Even much of nighttime television production,
once a New York monopoly, has moved to California.

As the tangible exports dwindled, the Economic City paid for its increasing imports by, in effect, selling New York's reputation and its hope
for the future. It did this by persuading investors all over the world
to lend it money.

Most of the Economic City's creditors have no idea of the extent to
which they loaned their savings to New York. Their money, entrusted
to life insurance companies and major banks, was loaned by those institutions to finance the construction of office buildings, hotels, motels
and luxury apartment houses in New York. Only lately have some of
the sophisticated managers of foreign money realized that they mis-
perceived New York City's future. Some major new mortgages have
been foreclosed; other projects were put into the deep freeze even before
they were finished.

When mortgages from commercial sources began to slow down, the
Economic City turned to Government sources. More billions of dollars,

corralled from less sophisticated savers all over the nation, flowed into municipal notes and bonds that paid for revenue-producing projects developed by the Port Authority, the New York State Housing Finance Agency, the Urban Development Corporation and the New York State Dormitory Authority. To the extent that all these developments are self-supporting, New Yorkers will be helped by them. To the extent that they were based on gross underestimates of future revenues, they have increased the burdens of the Political City.

The Political City provides services that people want or require, but for which they are unable or unwilling to pay directly—criminal justice, elementary education, fire protection, for example—or for which it is simply impractical to collect fees, like the use of the public streets. Increasingly, these basic services have been supplemented by the demands of social policy over the years, requiring the Political City to make special provision for those whom the Economic City neglects altogether or mistreats.

It is important to recognize that the Political City also produces wealth. National social policy has empowered Washington to compensate New York, in effect, for its poverty. The federal government provides funds for such casualties of the Economic City as families with dependent children, the indigent ill, the disabled, the poorly housed (some of them, at least), and a host of other burdened human categories. Although selling poverty to the Feds is a business, it is usually a very poor business. In the most favorable cases, the city gets back only three-quarters of the total cost of supporting the intended beneficiaries.

Contrarily, it is sometimes very hard to use federal money for the nonsocial programs of local government. A new administration in Washington may loosen the pursestrings somewhat, but up to now, federal revenue sharing has required a significant matching contribution which the Political City often can't afford. Or it sets standards that can't be met. Or else there may be serious local opposition to major programs that the federal government would be pleased to fund. Such is the case of the Westway, the replacement for the West Side Highway, whose construction would remove many trucks from the city's streets and put thousands of idle New Yorkers to work. As a highway, it qualifies for federal funding, as do highways in all the fifty states. But it is opposed by those who believe mass rail transit is the only moral answer to urban transportation problems.

Traditionally, the Political City has met the rising costs of "normal services" by increasing local taxes imposed on the Economic City. But in New York, that no longer works. To supply the Political City with enough revenue, the Economic City must provide more than 3.5 million jobs, enough to sustain New York's peak population of 8 million. But New York City no longer has 3.5 million jobs to offer. According to the Bureau of Labor Statistics, the city has lost 660,000 jobs in the past seven years alone, so that it now offers somewhat less than 3 million.

As the fortunes of the Economic City decline, the Political City must pick up a far heavier load of social misery. In the late 1960s, the Political City responded to New York's lagging fortunes by hiring 60,000 new workers. Approximately the same number have lost their jobs in the city government's effort to balance its budget. The drop in business income means that higher tax rates are imposed on a dwindling base. As jobs are lost and unemployment benefits expire, the welfare rolls rise. The fears of unemployment spread among the workers in the Political City and stiffen their resistance to cutbacks.

Questionable Assumptions

The assumptions of the three-year financial plan are etched vividly against the facts. The plan assumes that all of the municipal workers will go to the end of the financial plan without receiving cash raises already agreed to (except for the cost-of-living adjustments based on real cash savings), that there can be no increase in the funding of the pension systems, that welfare and Medicaid deficits will not increase and, finally, that the Economic City will be able to continue paying taxes as it does now.

Clearly these assumptions—particularly the last—are questionable. In a recent issue of The City Almanac, published by the Center for New York City Affairs of the New School for Social Research, Citibank economist George Roniger points out that during the 1960s, New York's economy was still so healthy that its employment level remained constant as long as the national employment level remained constant. During the 1970s, that relationship no longer continued. Instead, according to Roniger, New York's employment continues to drop unless the national employment level rises by at least 3 percent per year. While he predicted in his article that the national economy would function that well for 1977, the longer term future will probably not sustain so high a rate of national economic growth. Roniger mildly concluded that for the remainder of the decade "New York may be facing a modest long-term drop in employment." However modest the decline may be, it must be viewed as coming on top of an unemployment rate already at more than 10 percent. Fears for the tax base seem very realistic.

Why can't New York confront this problem directly? Why can't we build up the Economic City to the point that it can once again provide the necessary levels of jobs and revenues? This is certainly the most attractive strategy for New York, but unfortunately, it has already been tried most intensively, and so far, it has not worked.

The reasons for this lack of success are not haphazard or incidental, and they have little to do with the personal qualities of those in charge. Instead, they are basic to the economy of New York City, which grew to its maximum population of 8 million only because it was a very important manufacturing center.

Few New Yorkers think of their city as a factory town; they prefer to imagine that their fellow citizens work in office towers or emporiums of service like hotels and restaurants or magnificent department stores. Nobody notices or remembers that as recently as twenty years ago, the New York region contained a larger number of the 450 Census Bureau classifications of manufacturing industries than any other metropolitan region in the nation. Its factories primarily produced consumer goods; only Detroit concentrated as heavily in one area. The typical New York enterprise employed fewer than 500 people and depended very heavily on a chain of other enterprises to complete the manufacturing process.

Over the years, New York's manufacturing advantages have disappeared. The rail network lies in ruins; truck transportation is more effective for carrying lightweight, high-speed cargoes. Cheap labor for the apparel trades can now be found everywhere in the world, while the costs of manufacturing in the central city—with its traffic congestion, its dependence on the elevator, its tax-inflated energy rates, its social problems—continue to mount. The city's efforts to overcome these disadvantages have never proved sufficient. When the city tries to offer new factories tax exemptions and other favors, existing businesses object that they are being hurt to help the newcomers. Poverty advocates challenge the city for putting "business ahead of people."

(Perhaps the most ominous evidence of the fundamental resistance to development has been the opposition to drilling for offshore oil in the region. Although Mayor Beame has supported it, the state government and many local officials have opposed it, bowing to the assertion of constituents that off-shore drilling endangers the environment.)

Some economists contend that even the city's reputation as the classiest address for a major corporate headquarters is no longer that much of an asset. It may be possible to attract a few more national corporate headquarters to the city, and to name another few office buildings after prime tenants culled from Fortune's list of the 500 largest corporations. But some economists speculate that the headquarters will come with fewer and fewer people. Automated office routines and whizz-bang communications networks allow the vice president for data to stay in Kokomo with his computers and their servants when his boss moves to New York.

There is, finally, the tourist business, not yet fully tapped by New York, and deserving serious attention. It depends on the state of prosperity elsewhere in the world, and on the belief that visitors can come here without risking their necks or their respectability. The city is trying. It has also tried to persuade the national and state governments to locate more of their office functions in New York. The state responded by filling the World Trade Center with state officers that came from other buildings in New York City. The federal government, sensing the same change in the data processing industries that private corporations have noted, has located its back offices in places with names like Holtsville, N.Y.

While one cannot totally discount the possibility that someone, somewhere, has recently invented a product that will revolutionize human life and can be manufactured only in a large city, the prospects for a significant increase in the wealth produced by the Economic City are pretty grim.

Thus one turns to the Political City, with its hope for increased revenues from the state and federal governments. The state government may indeed pick up some cost items in the city's budget, as the mayor has asked, but the prospects are generally wan. The state suffers from many of the same regional economic problems as the city, but even if it did not, the city would be hard to help, for political reasons. The loss of population to the suburbs has shifted constituencies and given the city fewer votes in Albany.

Three Areas of Federal Help

The idea of help from Washington generally inspires hope: Here sits the monster press for printing money with which to wipe out the city's accumulated deficit. But even with a sympathetic president in the White House, Washington may be seduced only by the most carefully contrived courtship strategy, of which the first principle seems to be that New York can be helped only as a side-effect of helping America. The suggestion that the federal government should insure or guarantee New

York's debt appears to be politically hopeless. If it is not to be an outright gift, government insurance requires a precise analysis of the risk—impossible in the case of urban debt—and the building up of common reserves by incremental payments; a guarantee of debt without any contribution by New York City would appear to be a reward for profligacy —a concept that will remain hard for any president to sell to Congress. There are, nevertheless, three areas in which the federal government could help New York together with other cities. These should be quickly explored in company with such urban trade associations as the Conference of Mayors and the National League of Cities.

PENSION SYSTEMS

The first such area involves local government pension systems. Cities across the nation have failed to set aside adequate funds—as measured by actuarial experience and interest earned—to cover their pension liabilities. Mayors of all major cities, including New York, have found themselves on the defensive before the demands of municipal workers. Instead of granting wage increases they cannot afford, each mayor granted pension increases, which would not come due until another mayor took office.

While the federal government has no direct responsibility for local government pensions, it is unlikely that any national government could withstand the pressure to act to alleviate the hardship caused by large-scale defaults on pensions payable by cities to their former employees. Fear of a similar situation in the private sphere sent the federal government deep into the regulation of industrial pension plans. It has not yet involved itself in local and state government pensions, but the difficulties are so widespread and the consequences so serious that pressure to involve the national government should be easy to mount. To induce local governments to accept a measure of regulation, and to place the plans on a sound footing, the federal government might be persuaded to offer a guarantee of the pensions established in a program that meets its approval, and provide for a stretched out preliminary period in which the local deficiency might be made up. Such a program would be of inestimable help to local governments like New York, struggling to set aside pension reserves from an inadequate flow of income. By helping the cities to fund their legitimate pension liabilities, the federal government would free some of their money to meet bond and note obligations. There are cities with pension liabilities in every state.

CARE OF THE ELDERLY

The care of the elderly offers another area for federal intervention that would be of immeasurable help to all of the cities of the United States, especially New York. As the population lives longer and retires earlier, the elderly population that does not require nursing home or hospital care constitutes a growing fraction of the urban population. In New York and other declining older cities, this group faces the most crushing problems of alienation and despair. Occasionally, their suicides, reported in the press, throw a baleful light on the terrors under which they live: fear of strangers in the neighborhood, fear of an increase in rent or a vacant apartment next door, fear of opening the door to a stranger, or attack while fumbling for the key, fear that sudden illness in the night presages a solitary death.

The federal government has made some gestures toward housing for the elderly, but not nearly enough. If its activities in this area were to expand, the result could be a reduction in costs now borne by the city in caring for the aged. New housing programs would also create thousands of new semiskilled jobs in the city.

RESETTLEMENT

Finally, the federal government could resurrect a program from the days of the New Deal: resettlement. Under the New Deal, the Resettlement Administration was established to relocate farm families from areas that had become too infertile to support them, and to relocate families from urban slums into new "greenbelt suburbs." It was greatly influenced by an ideological interest in setting up cooperative settlements, and its record was at best a mixture of success and failure.

In the post-war years, mechanization on the farm displaced southern agricultural workers, sending them north without any federal help. The precedent of resettlement from the used up earth should certainly be applicable to the present urban situation: A national program could encourage people to move voluntarily, and with proper preparation, to places where economic opportunities are opening up. The federal government could, for example, help develop training programs linked to job opportunities in distant states, offer some measure of transportation assistance, and provide some sort of financial back-up so that a family need not fear that it is risking all of its security on an uncertain move. Obviously, such a program would present some unusual problems—not the least being that it treads perilously near the tolerable limit of infringement on the rights of the people to be moved as well as those of the communities that will receive them. But such problems are not insurmountable, and the problems connected with inaction are worse. The social disorganization that follows the concentration of dependent families in the older cities presents the greatest risk of all.

Consistent Density Required

While such initiatives would tend to lighten New York's fiscal burdens, they will hardly close the critical gap between the costs of "normal" city services—police, education, fire protection, sanitation—and the revenue produced by a city that has suffered New York's job loss. And it seems unlikely that the existing trend to "voluntary resettlement"— people leaving homes in New York in order to find jobs elsewhere—will be reversed any time soon. As the number of jobs available declines, population will also decline, and this is a situation beyond the control of either the Economic City or the Political City.

A New York with a population even considerably smaller than the present 7.5 million people could be a very good city indeed; New York would continue to be a world city even with fewer than 5 million. But the Political City cannot survive if the pattern of its costs remains the same for the smaller population as it was for the larger. The same miles of streets cannot be patrolled, cleaned, repaired, and served with public transportation; the same pattern of health care, fire protection, and education cannot be used for a smaller population without bankrupting the city all over again.

Throughout the city, consistent density is a necessary part of building or block survival. It is better to keep one building full than two half full, better to have one full block than five occupied at 20 percent of their capacity. Social cohesion is impossible in sparsely populated areas; buildings that do not have full rent rolls will quickly be abandoned. More important, the city can provide services much more efficiently to fully populated areas. Large parts of the Bronx south of the Cross Bronx Expressway are virtually dead—they have been so reduced in population that block after block of apartment houses stand open to wind and sky, their windows smashed, their roofs burned, their plumbing pilfered. Perhaps only three or four houses in a five-block area are inhabited, with another abandoned five blocks on the other side of them. Yet the city must still supply services to the few survivors, send in the fire engines when there are fires, keep the subway station open, even continue a school. In some of these sections, under the pressure of a local official or a single community group, the city is pressed to make new investments in housing rehabilitation or street improvements whose chances of long life are limited by the surrounding decay.

If the city is to survive with a smaller population, the population must be encouraged to concentrate itself in the sections that remain alive. This sort of internal resettlement—the natural flow out of the areas that have lost general attraction—must be encouraged. The role of the city planner is not to originate the trend of abandonment but to observe and use it so that public investment will be hoarded for those areas where it will sustain life.

Obviously, the few remaining families in a section that is generally abandoned cannot be forced out. Frequently, however, the distress is so general in such an area that whole tax districts can be cleared by taking properties for tax delinquencies. Unsafe buildings can be cleared. The remaining families can be offered relocation benefits to move to areas that remain alive.

Federal housing subsidies can be used to encourage movement away from deteriorating areas; given the wherewithal to move to a better apartment, families begin to question whether the ties that bind them to a grossly deteriorated neighborhood are as important as they seemed.

Gradually, the city's population in the older sections will begin to achieve a new configuration, one consistent with a smaller population that has arranged itself at densities high enough to make the provision of municipal services economical.

Some have argued that New York's densities are too high, and that a spreading of the population should be welcomed. But this recommendation, even if it had merit for an unbuilt city, is irrelevant to a city already built up with apartment houses. These must be occupied fully, or nearly so, if they are to remain in decent condition. The stretches of empty blocks may then be knocked down, services can be stopped, subway stations closed, and the land left to lie fallow until a change in economic and demographic assumptions makes the land useful once again.

Developing Hypotheses

The time to begin planning for a smaller population is now, not after doomsday has come. Certainly the department of city planning can develop alternative schemes based on differing projections of the city's future population at different dates. The department can also develop estimates of the work force needed to provide services to these predicted populations; then it can draw a series of maps indicating which sections, under which hypotheses, are the most likely to attract population and which are the candidates for depopulation. With good predictions for the size and shape of such a future city, it should be possible to design the most economical use of the city's future resources, and to move, step by step, to reach the design based on the most conservative hypothesis, preparing to take more drastic action should it appear necessary. Or to slow down, if the population does not decline due, for example, to unexpectedly heavy immigration.

I surely cannot underestimate the fears engendered by this notion of growing smaller in a social milieu in which growing bigger has been the hope of those who have not had a fair share. And the questions about individual rights posed by national resettlement would also apply to resettlement within the city. But the alternative of living beyond our means is worse for all residents of the city, and in any case, it is the poor who are worst hurt by the loneliness and degradation of the scattered loss of population. (Politicians who oppose planned shrinkage are motivated by the fear that their districts will be depopulated and they will lose their legislative seats as a result. Unhappily, the shrinkage of the population is already causing such a loss of seats through forces beyond anyone's control.)

Essentially, planned shrinkage is a recognition that the golden door to full participation in American life and the American economy is no longer to be found in New York. To advocate control of the shrinking population so that a useful city remains and so that better opportunity is provided elsewhere for those who cannot realistically expect to find it here, scarcely amounts to an assertion that growing smaller is good. Growing smaller happens to have happened. All of the city's historic planning—its rapid transit system, educational facilities, hospitals, and highways—was dedicated to the fulfillment of the dream of constant growth, growth that might last forever. Even if it does not grow, even if the city declines in population, it can continue to provide a richly rewarding environment for millions of its people of every class and race, but they cannot afford the luxury of overestimating the value of their assets and underestimating their liabilities, as we have been doing for the past twenty-five years. Better a thriving city of five million than a Calcutta of seven, destroyed by its internal wrangling. That is today's challenge to New York's leaders—in both the economic and the political cities.

It's Up to Cities to Save Themselves

GURNEY BRECKENFELD

FOR SOME TIME NOW, the mayors of large cities have been begging for massive aid from the federal government. They insist that disaster will befall them and millions of urban Americans unless Washington rescues cities from their economic and financial distress. More recently the mayors have been complaining that they are "extremely disappointed" by President Carter's economic program, which offers indirect help through tax cuts and government-funded jobs. They want a broader and much more costly package of assistance, something like an urban Marshall Plan, including a new federal bank to dispense low-interest loans.

A large new infusion of money is not what our ailing cities need most. States and localities, mostly the latter, will receive some $70 billion this year in federal aid. That already amounts to a Marshall Plan in monetary magnitude, though obviously not in coherence. Over the past quarter century this assistance has totaled some $448 billion, and in some ways the largess has made urban problems worse instead of better. A new dose of federal aid probably would deflect mayors and city councils from their first task—difficult but not impossible—of adjusting to a shrinking population and economy. Those declines have been under way for many years and cannot be reversed quickly, if at all, for they were caused partly by social forces beyond the control of cities, partly by the high costs of living and working in them, and partly by the changing technology of transportation.

Boarded-Up Hotels in Motown

But instead of retrenching and attacking their problems sensibly, most cities have aggravated them. Despite their limited resources, they have, until quite recently, practiced accommodation politics and shown an easy tolerance for swollen, money-guzzling municipal bureaucracies. In every city threatened by insolvency, the mess can be traced to imprudent spending. There has been a pervasive managerial collapse at city hall. Most cities lack the skilled, tough, farsighted public leadership necessary for the long sustained effort that might, in time, revitalize them. Under these circumstances, more federal aid would merely postpone the inevitable day of fiscal reckoning.

The symptoms of ill health are particularly visible right now among the big, old, industrial inner cities of the Northeast and Midwest. In economic terms, Detroit is probably the sickest. The number of people at work there has dropped by 26 percent in five years. Belatedly, a fortress-like, $337-million office-hotel-shopping complex called Renaissance Center is rising along the Detroit River. But an atmosphere of sepulchral menace pervades the nearby streets of the old downtown, which is pocked by vacant stores, boarded up hotels and taverns, and the blank marquees of closed movie theaters. Some office towers are half empty and the next-to-last department store shut its doors this year.

The economies of Cleveland and St. Louis have been floundering for several years, though there are recent signs that the worst may be over. George L. Forbes, president of Cleveland's city council, might be speaking for any of a dozen cities when he says, "We're going to survive, but it is going to be very, very hard."

A Matter of Willpower

New York is still struggling to extricate itself from the thinly camouflaged state-federal receivership imposed twenty-one months ago because of the city's spending binge of the late sixties and early seventies. Though the city has lopped 53,000 jobs from its payroll, it has not yet demonstrated that it has enough willpower to balance its budget.

Financial collapse has become a serious possibility in Philadelphia and Boston, even though both cities have renascent downtowns bordered by elegant old and recently revitalized residential neighborhoods. In Boston, the restoration of historic Faneuil Hall and the adjacent Quincy Market, sensitively carried out by James W. Rouse, the Maryland developer, has created an extraordinary magnet for throngs of shoppers, sightseers, and tourists from all over New England. But Boston has been heading for insolvency, partly because Mayor Kevin White added some 2,000 workers to the city's payroll during his first term, and partly because the school board hired 1,483 new full- and part-time aides, arguably far more than necessary, in the wake of a federal court's controversial cross-city busing order.

Many small and medium-sized cities face even graver difficulties than the big ones. Another ten of Massachusetts's thirty-eight other cities may be as close to bankruptcy as Boston. In January, when an arbitration panel awarded New Bedford's firemen a pay increase that will cost the city $800,000, Mayor John A. Markey demonstrated what that "disaster" will do to the city's budget by stripping off his clothes, down to his yellow shorts and white T-shirt, at a televised press conference.

Yet two cities in the troubled Northeast demonstrate that, with the right kind of local leadership, fiscal disaster can be averted. Both cities are burdened by the familiar afflictions: numerous poor, an eroding job market, and dwindling population. Their resourceful leaders nevertheless have found ways to cut expenses, and even to win battles with militant municipal unions. By a stunning coincidence, the resolute mayors of both cities have personally led squads of volunteers collecting garbage during a successful effort to break a strike by sanitation workers.

For the past seven years, Pittsburgh has been run by a maverick mayor, Peter Flaherty, fifty-one, who holds the remarkable belief that diminishing population should permit a reduction in the municipal work force. The city's population has dropped by one-third from its 1950 peak of 677,000—one of the steepest declines among the nation's leading metropolises—and for several years five dwelling units, mostly abandoned, have been demolished for every new one built. Taking office, Flaherty found the same problems that bedevil cities all over the Northeast: inefficiency, bloated payrolls, and duplication of effort. In his first year, he replaced almost all the city's department heads, froze hiring, restricted overtime, and eliminated 900 jobs, thus turning a threatened $2-million deficit into a $3.7-million surplus.

The following year, a battle with municipal unions erupted when Flaherty wiped out five drivers' jobs in his proposed budget. The drivers, members of Teamsters Local 249 (whose president was also a city councilman), had been operating pickup trucks for plumbers installing residential water meters no bigger than a four-inch flowerpot. But the plumbers refused to do their own driving and their walkout quickly grew to involve more than 2,000 city workers, including street crews, mechanics, and garbage collectors. On television, a medium he uses with considerable skill, Flaherty accused the unions of "trying to take over the city." Then, still followed by TV cameras, he led a garbage collection detail. After ten days the unions capitulated.

Only the Voters Love Him

Since that confrontation, the mayor has relied on attrition to reduce the city's work force. In all, he has cut it by nearly 30 percent. Despite inflation, he has also pared the city's tax take by 3 percent, or $2.4 million below the 1970 level. He is still cutting down. In his 1977 budget, Flaherty did away with 270 vacant jobs to save another $3 million. Despite the manpower reductions, municipal services remain fairly good. People do complain about such items as laggard garbage collection and the condition of the streets, but potholes and parsimony have enabled Pittsburgh to avoid a financial quagmire and enjoy an A-1 Moody's rating on its bonds. Reported crime has dropped a bit, too, thanks partly to a streetlighting program that also contributes to a new afterdark bustle in the central business district.

Pittsburgh's downtown Golden Triangle has the ambiance of San Francisco before World War II. A rich fabric of old and new, it is alive, safe, complete, and above all marvelously compact (you can walk from one end to the other in ten minutes). Electric trolleys still creep through cobblestoned streets, and anachronistic "inclines"—Pittsburgh's funicular counterpart to the cable car—climb and descend a nearby hill. Downtown retail sales, weak in numerous inner cities, have been rising and six new skyscrapers have been built and occupied in the past ten years.

Local citizens like to boast about the fifteen Fortune 500 industrial companies headquartered in their city where they form the nation's third-largest cluster (after New York and Chicago and tied with Cleveland). Their presence has contributed to a recent rise in the number of white-collar jobs. So even though some industrial activity has moved to the suburbs, total employment in Pittsburgh has declined by a comparatively modest 5 percent since 1971.

Flaherty has paid a price for his zealous pursuit of economy and efficiency. At one time or another he has managed to make an enemy of almost every powerful group in town: organized labor, most of the city council, the police, the firemen, the business community, the black community, and both daily papers. Only the voters love him. He was reelected overwhelmingly in 1973 without support from the unions, the Republicans, or even his own Democratic party. He faces considerable opposition this year for a third term, but his chances look good.

A New Magnet in the Old Ruins

By almost every standard measure of trouble, Baltimore should be firmly trapped in the vortex of urban decay. It is an old, conservative, blue-collar industrial place. Though it is the nation's seventh-largest city, only one Fortune 500 company (Crown Central Petroleum, No. 356) makes its headquarters there. Population, falling since 1950, dropped another 9 percent between 1970 and 1975 (to an estimated 830,000), and the number of people at work declined even more (12 percent). More than half the city's inhabitants are black, and the proportion of poor families is high. Yet Baltimore, which H. L. Mencken called "the ruins of a once great medieval city," is making an extraordinary comeback, both physically and—more important—psychologically.

The critical ingredient of that revival is *two decades* of intelligent teamwork between local officials and private business leaders. Their strategy, established at the outset, has been to convert the heart of the city into a culturally rich, architecturally exciting magnet where both affluent and middle-class families will choose to work, shop, and live.

To avoid the bureaucratic torpor that often strangles such efforts, the city wisely turned over its $1 billion urban renewal job to the private, nonprofit Charles Center-Inner Harbor Management Corp., while retaining legal control. Charles Center, now almost completed, has replaced the dingiest part of downtown with a handsome thirty-three-acre complex of office skyscrapers, apartments, a hotel, shops, and tree-lined plazas where, in season, fountains and bands enhance lunch hour for shoppers, office workers, and patrons at open-air cafes. Now the corporation is well along on the much bigger job of joining the city's new skyline to a once wasted shoreline on the Patapsco River, close to Chesapeake Bay. The 240-acre Inner Harbor has been transformed from a jumble of rotting piers and decrepit warehouses into an inviting blend of parks and playgrounds, restaurants, office buildings, an aquarium, a science center, and tourist attractions such as the frigate *Constellation*.

In many cities, downtown empties out at 5 P.M., but Baltimore provides a galaxy of outdoor concerts, ethnic festivals, and boating events that draw crowds—including suburbanites—to the center of town at night and on weekends from spring until fall. Last year, 1.8 million people attended the biggest event, a three-day city fair with seventy-six neighborhood exhibits. All this activity, which symbolizes the changing spirit of the city, is arranged by a downtown coordinating office, which is mainly financed by private contributions. The organization's young director, Mrs. Sandy Hillman, reflects that change herself. "When my husband dragged me here from Washington eight years ago, I figured my life was over," she says. "Now I'd hate to leave."

"Action Memos" in Quintuplicate

Baltimore's yeasty mix of programs has been stirred for the past five years by Mayor William Donald Schaefer, a lifelong bachelor of fifty-five who not only picks young, gung-ho types for key city jobs but prods them to innovate and shows no tolerance for the red tape that frustrates so many good ideas in government. He also checks up on every detail of Baltimore's life and government because, as he says, "little things are important." After driving himself around on weekend inspections, he writes a blizzard of "action memos" to underlings. He gets results, too, because those serially numbered memos come in quintuplicate; an aide follows up every one.

A tightfisted economizer, Schaefer in 1972 imposed a hiring freeze that enabled the city gradually to cut its payroll by 2,200, to 27,000 employees. Schaefer has also continued the city's spartan policy, adopted in 1960, of borrowing no more than $35 million a year, all of it for capital projects. At a time when inflation has prompted most cities to increase their borrowing, Baltimore has for four years been retiring more debt than it has issued. The funding of municipal pensions, swept under the rug in many cities, has been placed on an adequate and systematic basis. Last year, Moody's raised its rating of the city's credit from A to A-1, saving the city some $596,000 in interest costs on its latest bond issue.

Schaefer's turn at heaving garbage helped him tame the municipal unions. When police, city prison guards, and sanitation workers went on strike simultaneously in 1974, the mayor and most of his administrative staff manned garbage trucks while police commissioner Donald D. Pomerleau fired seventy-five patrolmen for ignoring a back-to-work order. Courts eventually fined the unions and some of their officers $157,000 for defying strike injunctions, and the police lost their right to bargain collectively. Last year, the municipal unions signed a two-year contract providing for a modest 4 percent annual pay increase.

Baltimore nonetheless faces many problems. The crime rate, though declining, remains high. Downtown retail sales are weak, and one of four department stores recently announced plans to close. Large sections of the inner city are still black slums. Middle-class flight to the suburbs has slowed, but not halted. So the most crucial part of the city's fight to be reborn has shifted to the rundown historic neighborhoods, many of them close to Inner Harbor or other urban renewal areas whose transformation provides a vital new base to build on.

Some abandoned row houses have been rehabilitated at city expense and resold below cost to private owners. If necessary, the city even provides a twenty-year mortgage with interest as low as 7 percent. Baltimore was one of the pioneers in "urban homesteading" and claims to have had more success at it than all other cities combined. The city sells abandoned old houses for $1 to buyers who agree to fix them up and live in them for at least eighteen months. In one neighborhood, demand from would-be homesteaders proved so strong that the city held a lottery in 1975 to apportion 100 antique threestory brick row houses among 900 applicants.

The most encouraging sign of all is the decline in abandoned housing. Over the past three years, the city has cut its stock of abandoned dwellings from 5,000 units to 4,000, partly because it reclaims some 700 dwellings annually, and partly because the number of abandonments has dropped from 1,500 houses a year to only 400. In-town living has won a small but important new following among the middle class, and property values have increased, sometimes dramatically, in every old inner-city neighborhood. "If we can rev up to rehabilitating 1,000 houses a year, we might do away with vacant houses in five years," says Robert C. Embry, Jr., the city's energetic housing commissioner. "We have a long way to go, but I think the trend is finally in the right direction."

The Pluses and Minuses of Shrinkage

The great lesson of Pittsburgh and Baltimore is that it is possible for cities to shrink successfully. Almost all the central cities of the Northeast and Midwest (and many smaller ones as well) have been losing jobs and population in recent years. For most Americans this shrinkage is by no means a calamity, for it is a consequence of a long-term improvement in their way of life.

There was a time when factories, offices, and dwellings had to be jammed together in cities for access to one another and to river and rail routes. The great shift in moving goods and people by truck and auto and the increasingly complex network of planes, computers, and satellites linking distant places have made it possible for nearly all forms of urban activity to spread out at a lower and more agreeable density across ever wider metropolitan regions and beyond. Rising affluence, moreover, has enabled the rich and middle class to live where they choose, and most of them have demonstrated a preference for more space and greenery.

The thinning-out process inevitably produces minus statistics in old and partly obsolete inner cities, most of which, for political reasons, can no longer grow by annexing their suburbs. This has happened even in some comparatively young and well-run cities with good schools. The population of Minneapolis, for instance, has dropped 30 percent since 1950. Thanks to the recent rapid growth of many big cities in the South and Southwest, this decline is less pronounced for the nation as a whole. Twenty-five years ago, 35 percent of Americans lived in central cities; today about 30 percent do.

The most shocking aspect of city shrinkage—the bombed-out look in half-abandoned slum areas in the older metropolises—has a positive side to it. Generally it means that the worst neighborhoods are emptying out because the metropolitan area as a whole has a housing surplus. Later this process should provide an opportunity to rebuild worn-out parts of cities in ways that fit our new technologies and living patterns.

The declining inner cities will probably continue to experience job and population losses for quite a few more years. Detroit and a few others might even become economic holes in metropolitan doughnuts. But in most cases the outward flow will cease in time and a new equilibrium will be established. As the new vitality in many downtowns and the recycling of historic neighborhoods like Baltimore's suggest, a lot of Americans still choose to live and work in big cities. The elite in particular are tied to such places by their jobs, friendships, possessions, even by clubs and cultural activities.

The No-Win Economics of Perverse Incentives

The real tragedy of our ailing cities is not their shrinkage, some of it unavoidable, but the fact that they have hastened their own decline by a senseless kind of economic warfare against themselves. At every turn perverse incentives created by government give individuals and companies a self-interest in doing what's bad for the community.

Soaring taxes provide a powerful inducement, especially for manufacturers, to leave cities. Even the small "nuisance" taxes so often im-

posed on business can serve as a guillotine for parts of a local economy. New York City belatedly got the message last year after ten
brokerage firms moved key parts of their operations to New Jersey to
escape New York State's stock and bond transfer tax on market makers.
Though the tax was eventually repealed, all ten firms have stayed in
New Jersey.

Rent control has discouraged the building of new apartments and
the maintenance of existing rental units. Thirty-four years of controls
in New York City have brought widespread tax delinquency, decay,
and premature abandonment. Yet despite that disaster, other communities have copied the formula. In the seventies, rent control has been
enacted in about 100 New Jersey localities, Boston and three suburbs,
Miami Beach, Washington, D.C., and Montgomery County, Maryland.

Some of the ugliest consequences of harnessing the profit motive
backwards involve our treatment of the poor. In the name of helping
them, we raise minimum wages, thereby wiping out an important number of low skilled jobs. In many states, moreover, welfare benefits are
set so high that they provide an incentive for not seeking work. Welfare recipients sometimes spurn preferred jobs in the well-founded fear
that they may soon lose them again, in which case they will probably
have to wait a few weeks to get back on the dole. In twenty-eight
states, we also promote the disintegration of families (often feigned)
by providing aid to dependent children only when the father is missing.
Subsidized housing has another perverse effect: it tends to lock the
working poor into fixed locations, removing the incentive to seek a
better job in another town, because a family may face a long wait for
similar tax-supported housing.

An Invitation to the Poor

Misguided altruism has compounded the financial woes of some cities,
most notably New York, which responded with extraordinary zeal to
Washington's great welfare state push in the sixties. Even though the
federal government paid most of the bill for many of the programs,
the costs borne by the city were enormous in the aggregate. Moreover,
the attraction of seemingly "free" money lured New York and other
localities into undertaking projects they could not afford.

Even today, ardent liberals are slow to acknowledge that it is positively ruinous to the economics of successful cities to provide more aid
to the poor than is available in other jurisdictions. When cities or
states use their taxing powers to redistribute wealth, as for instance

with high income taxes, or even when cities allow the poor to occupy valuable land that might be used for purposes that would yield more tax revenue, they impair their fiscal health and over the long run undermine their economies. As recently as last year, Thomas C. Maloney, then mayor of Wilmington, Delaware ran into criticism for using federal revenue sharing receipts to hold down taxes instead of building more subsidized housing. Maloney stuck by his guns, correctly arguing that such expenditures would only invite more poor to congregate in the city.

The cities' afflictions have been mightily aggravated by the great migrations of the post-war era, in which millions of rural poor—mostly black until recent years, but now heavily Hispanic—have arrived with all their hopes and pathologies. Crime-ridden immigrant slums are nothing new for U.S. cities, which in the past absorbed waves of impoverished newcomers from Ireland, Italy, and eastern Europe. In our time, however, misbegotten welfare policies and the disastrous concentration of the poor in subsidized housing have helped to turn great stretches of the inner cities into Kafkaesque reservations for the unemployed and the unwanted, where life can be very dangerous indeed.

Today as in the past, most of the new migrants will make their way up the economic ladder, and millions have already done so. The real problem, which is poisoning life in inner cities, involves a small minority among the minorities: the 15 to 20 percent that belongs to a lower class more or less permanently mired in poverty and malaise. As Harvard's Edward C. Banfield pointed out in his seminal book *The Unheavenly City*, nobody has learned how to change lower class cultural habits any faster than time and circumstance do naturally. The Great Society's effort to short-circuit this slow evolutionary process, combined with an explosion of leniency in the courts toward the thugs who have terrorized large parts of the cities, has made matters far worse.

Some Negative Advice for Washington

A great deal of modesty is in order about any new initiatives to relieve urban problems. We know a lot less about cities, and how they tick, than we were sure we knew fifteen years ago. The most valuable thing the federal government can do for cities is to *refrain* from actions that impair their fiscal health and impede their natural regeneration. Above all, it should curb inflation, which causes cities' costs (64 percent wages and fringe benefits) to gallop ahead of revenues.

Washington should also stop forcing city administrations to pick their way through labyrinthine regulations in pursuit of federal money under the hodgepodge of aid programs that now exist. For a quarter century the federal government has cudgeled, cosseted, and cajoled cities in consistently inconsistent directions through these programs, which recently numbered more than 1,000. In thousands of instances, cities have embarked on wasteful projects simply because Washington was picking up most of the tab and politically potent construction workers stood to get jobs. During the Nixon and Ford administrations, a start was made on amalgamating some of these categorical grant programs and allowing cities more discretion in spending the money. But a comprehensive, Justinian-like recodification is sorely needed.

If the federal government continues to provide temporary loans to New York, or grants them to other cities in acute financial distress, the money should be accompanied by tough restrictions so local officials cannot fritter it away or acquiesce in the exorbitant demands of municipal unions. Any permanent program of loans or loan guarantees would be sheer folly. Even special grants-in-aid to, say, twenty-five cities with the greatest "need" would have the unfair effect of penalizing cities that have done the most on their own to overcome their difficulties. Organized labor has been pressing for a federal law authorizing strikes by public employees. The prospect frightens many city officials, who have good grounds to fear that such legislation would surrender control of their governments to union leaders.

Untangling the poverty-welfare snarl will require perceptive collaboration by federal, state, and local governments. Only Washington, for example, could impose a nationwide change in the arrangements that trap the working poor in fixed locations if they occupy subsidized housing. It still seems debatable, however, whether the federal government should assume the entire cost of welfare, a move currently espoused, among others, by the U.S. Conference of Mayors and supported with Delphic reservations by President Carter.

Washington already picks up two-thirds of the $42-billion-a-year combined tab for cash assistance, food stamps, and Medicaid. States and counties pay for almost all the rest. Only a handful of cities would be directly helped by the shift: New York, Philadelphia, Denver, San Francisco, Baltimore, and Washington, D.C.—all of which double as counties. To be sure, a federal takeover would save states about $14 billion a year, enabling them to cut taxes or provide more aid to their cities. But there is a further catch to the idea. Nobody expects that Washington would set support levels as high as they now stand in New York, Massachusetts, and numerous other states. Unless these states reduced their welfare benefits, their taxpayers would still be stuck with large welfare costs. Their total tax bills might even rise, since federal taxes presumably would go up to pay for more generous welfare in the South.

Taking the Profit out of Crime

Curbing crime is a job for state governments, which generally run the courts with jurisdiction over street crimes, as well as the correctional facilities to which the miscreants are sent. Crime has proliferated because it is the most rewarding way of life available to those involved, especially jobless teenagers with low skills. Entry-level jobs have moved to such places as the South and rural areas where labor costs are lower. And because the courts are overworked and judges have been loth to commit felons to crowded and dangerous prisons and juvenile detention centers, the chance of incarceration for violent crimes has become minuscule; for juveniles in New York State it has been only one in seventeen among those who are both arrested and brought into court.

The opportunities for work and the punishment rate for crime should be increased at the same time. The Carter administration is already tackling the first half of that equation, though the public service jobs it envisages have up to now generally proved an ineffective way to instill work habits in high school dropouts. If we want to have civilized cities again, it is time that repeaters and violent criminals including teenagers be imprisoned for lengthy terms. The courts could be expanded, and humane prisons could be built, for a fraction of what urban businesses and residents are spending to fend off crime or move away from it. The main objective would not be to rehabilitate offenders but to increase public safety, which after all is the foremost job of government.

By now the evidence is overwhelming that society is cowering before a relatively small number of habitual adult and juvenile criminals. Plagued by an epidemic of juvenile crime, Wilmington, Delaware last year compiled police statistics showing that just sixteen local youths had committed 384 felonies in three years, including 93 separate burglaries, 64 robberies, 48 auto thefts, and 1 rape. The same records showed that more than half of the robberies by juveniles involved youths who had escaped from state correctional institutions. This evidence moved the state legislature to require a one-year sentence for offenders aged fourteen to eighteen for any two robberies, muggings, or residential burglaries within a year. For three such crimes in three years, the term is three years. Although the law is still being challenged in court, it is expected to reduce juvenile crime considerably.

The Upside-Down Property Tax

A rollback of the crime rate, however, will not suffice to return cities to economic health. Instead of raising taxes and driving business and industry to parts of the country where costs are lower, cities must give businessmen a reason to stay. Both the state and city of New York are struggling to cut the tax burden, but the proposals up to now have been quite timid. The worst problem is that the combined state and city tax rate on incomes above $25,000 is more than double the average level in other industrial states. Governor Hugh Carey recently proposed reducing state income taxes, but he would grant virtually all the relief to low- and middle-income taxpayers. Mayor Abraham Beame's plans to reduce business taxes would be negated by a probable rise in property taxes, so his promise of no increase for five years thereafter has a hollow ring.

Among disincentive taxes, the property tax by a wide margin has the largest and most pernicious effect on cities. It accounts for 82 percent of the $61 billion localities raise from their own taxpayers, but the trouble is not what it is commonly perceived to be: soaring tax bills that burden hard-pressed homeowners. The real problem is the basic structure of the tax—a confusing and little understood fusion of two separate levies, one on the building and one on the value of the location.

Most cities collect two or three times as much tax from buildings as from the site value of land. The low taxation of land rewards speculators; they can easily afford to keep idle or underutilized sites off the market until urban growth drives the price up enough for a fat profit (which then qualifies for concessionary treatment as a capital gain on their federal income taxes). The high tax on buildings (or improvements to them) discourages both construction of new buildings and maintenance of aging ones. Recognizing this, city after city has offered tax exemption in order to get new buildings put up, but the arrangement reduces the growth of the revenue base and forces other taxpayers to make up the difference.

The remedy is to turn the property tax upside down so it hitches the profit motive to the right objective. States should adopt legislation allowing localities to lighten or abolish the levy on buildings and impose a corresponding increase in the tax on land. The total tax take need not be affected. Most homeowners, several studies have found, would pay less; owners of valuable but well-developed downtown property would pay about the same; owners of valuable but vacant or under-utilized property would pay more. More important, the incentive for private investment in really good buildings would increase while the lure of land speculation would diminish. By raising carrying costs for land, site value taxation might well drive down inflated land prices, which are a major reason why costs are so high in many big cities.

Such a change should be phased in gradually to avoid disruptions, for it would be potent economic medicine. In a study a few years ago, economist Mason Gaffney found that if property taxes had been based entirely on land, downtown Milwaukee would have been rebuilt after World War II without a penny of subsidy for urban renewal. More recently, Philip Finkelstein, director of the Manhattan-based Center for Local Tax Research, concluded that if New York City continues its present arrangement, taxing buildings twice as much as land, "we will accomplish the apparent goal of New York's critics—breaking it off and letting it sink."

Needed: Risk Takers, Not Time Servers

A restructuring of incentives could also help overcome the managerial deficiencies of governments. Civil-service laws and regulations must be rewritten to end job protection for the slothful or incompetent, and eliminate the cumbersome procedures that create delays and drive up costs. As John Dyson, New York State commissioner of commerce, recently suggested, the top 1 or 2 percent of middle-level managers should be stripped of civil service status entirely and made subject to dismissal or demotion if they flub their work. Says Dyson, "We need . . . risk takers not time servers. In too many cases, civil service insulates the middle manager from direct control by the department head, creates a fiefdom mentality, and frustrates any new initiatives that are at variance with the self-interest of the bureaucracy itself."

Ultimately, cities will also have to induce their rank-and-file municipal workers to choose between unions and civil service protection. Given the fiscal bind cities are in, they cannot afford to provide both the high wages exacted by unions—$17,000 a year for a Boston bus driver, for example—and the job security that goes with civil service status. Moreover, as Boston City Councilman Lawrence DiCara contends, "When union power is combined with the equally strong protection provided by civil service, a point of total insulation for the public employee is reached."

The same approach should be applied to public schools, which consume 40 percent of all state and local government spending. There is no way central cities can reattract large numbers of middle-class families with children until the quality of their schools is perceived to equal those in the suburbs. Today, we foolishly couple a no-incentive system for educators with coercion for students who are forced to attend even after they have demonstrated an inability to profit from school. The mandatory school attendance age should be lowered to fourteen (ninth grade), and incorrigible disrupters should be expelled even earlier. A free public education is a costly privilege, not to be denied the majority by supine tolerance for barbarians.

Even Politicians Can Learn Economics

Before New York tumbled into insolvency, the chances were probably nil that cities might rediscover the unused potential of the individual profit motive for regaining their economic and financial health. But the shock waves from that event have prompted leaders in many cities to re-examine old assumptions. Some are beginning to recognize that cities must think about their economies in foreign trade terms: either they "export" enough goods and services to pay for their "imports" or the economies will wither. Costs, in short, are crucial. They are so far out of line in New York, says Alan K. Campbell, dean of the Lyndon B. Johnson School of Public Affairs at the University of Texas, that "if the city were a sovereign country, there would be no way for it to survive unless it devalued its currency."

The message is beginning to register that New York can no longer afford to spend $4.8 billion a year on welfare, health, and hospitals, and billions more on excessive pay and fringe benefits for city employees. Felix G. Rohatyn, the Manhattan investment banker who has helped steer the city through the financial shoals as chairman of the state-created Municipal Assistance Corporation, is encouraged by the change in thinking. "It's a very slow process," he says. "It's only been about a year since some politicians began to realize that there's a limit to taxing and borrowing, that there are such things as economic laws and market forces. The unions caught on before the politicians, maybe even before the bankers. Now the unions talk of going with us to Albany to see about getting tax cuts for higher-bracket executives. We've taken a halting few steps, but it's a beginning."

Appendix

Regional Development: Strategy from Theory

THOMAS A. CLARK

Intent

THE PURPOSE OF THIS DISCUSSION is to survey current theoretical perspectives on regional development in the United States and to assess their usefulness in defining national and regional strategies for regional development. Within this focus some stress will be given to the particular problems of the Northeast. Throughout, the various strategic alternatives will be considered in the context of the economic, institutional, and power relations which span the nation, influencing the ultimate impact which any developmental policy might have.

Many subjects of public policy relate to the welfare of regions. Transportation policies govern the ease with which people, capital and resources can be brought to places of production, and the products of these places distributed to local and distant markets. Agricultural policies influence the use and product of the land, the shape of farming, and the ultimate quantity, variety, and price of farm produce. Defense, housing, energy, environmental, welfare, recreation, public facilities, communication, and land use policies likewise have importance for the status of individual regions and their role within the interregional framework. But while these categorical policy *subjects* concern

407

features of regions, their *objects* are seldom explicitly regional. It is consequently useful to distinguish "policy in regions" from "policy of regions" (regional policy).

Defining Regions

Regions served by regional policy are sometimes formal and other times functional in character. Formal regions are legally demarcated. They are spaces to which certain activities, powers, and responsibilities of government are related. Whatever the spatial delimitation of these regions, their legal powers are seldom fully commensurate with their legal responsibilities. The imposition of developmental responsibilities on such regions may exceed their powers, administrative capacities, and resources. In the United States, the administrative hierarchy of localities, counties, and states is rigidly bureaucratic. Governmental offices are generally categorical and ill-suited to devise and implement coordinated regional strategies. The spatial imprint of such a region is often inappropriate given the current configurations of population and the economy. Still, it may be easier in the short run to work within this structure than to change it. Some progress, of course, has occurred through sharing and consolidation within single tiers of the administrative system and through the establishment of new administrative tiers.

The alternative to the formal, political region is the functional region delineated according to mappings of geographic interaction revealed in patterns of trade and travel. To the extent that such a region encompasses the places whose mutual interaction determines the path of regional evolution, the task of devising and implementing regional policy may be easier. Of course, not all the places among which critical interactions occur may exist within a single region. In addition, current and desired patterns of interaction may change over time. Consequently no particular pattern of spatial administration can be expected to remain forever satisfactory. In any case, different areal logics apply to economic, service, and environmental regionalizations. The criteria of delineation must be appropriate to the policy perspective.

Exactly how regions should be delimited is seldom so obvious as it might seem. It is clear, however, that their functional content, size and even shape may influence the ease with which various regional policies might be devised, implemented, and measured. Most possible regional policies are developmental in character. They address regional income level and distribution, economic output, employment, and other measures of welfare.[1] Their intent is to achieve levels of regional performance which are derived in relation either to local conditions or to the status of other regions. Developmental policies imply the existence of regions at various successive stages along the developmental continuum. One approach to classification would be according to current levels of development plus earlier developmental trends and future potential. Such a scheme might include these successive categories:

1. Depressed, rural regions—very limited development potential
2. Lagging, rural regions—moderate development potential
3. Dispersed multinucleated urban regions—moderate development potential
4. Slowing-growth and declining metropolitan or megalopolitan regions
5. Flourishing (stable or growing) urban-rural regions having a dominant agricultural or natural resource base
6. Progressive (stable or growing) urban-centered metropolitan or megalopolitan regions endowed with propulsive, high-growth industries.

In the short run, regions may move marginally up or down portions of this continuum.[2] Each position along it implies distinct bundles of strategies intended to accomplish at least these general categories of objectives: [3]

1. Sustain essential functions and minimal living conditions within the status quo
2. Accommodate to a probable or inevitable back-sliding to a less satisfactory future state
3. Prepare for the possible or probable future advance to a more satisfactory state by hastening its arrival and insuring a smooth transition.

The first would be an essential ingredient of any policy, in combination with either the second or the third. In certain regional situations, the region itself may be unable to act because it lacks either the will or the resources. Back-sliding is seldom willingly accepted; as a consequence limited resources are misinvested, and the ultimate decline is even more painful. When the will is lacking, external incentives may be required. When resources are in short supply, more may be accomplished when there is inter-regional cooperation, perhaps with national assistance. In the short run, of course, neither advance nor decline is inevitable. In such situations the predominant regional objective might be to sustain essential functions while perfecting the status quo and insuring that the delicate balances of the regional mechanism are maintained even as they evolve.

Regional theory does not serve all regional situations or objectives with equal facility. Certain regional theories are intended to guide the attainment of simple or complex equilibriums within or among regions, with or without "increase" or development. Others are intended to stimulate development, sometimes through deliberate disequilibration. Most treat regions as "points" lacking interior space and capable of instantaneous internal adjustment to mobilize their resources as opportunities occur. A few, however, explicitly recognize the lag of internal adjustments caused by the friction of distance and the immobility of people and resources.

Regions of the Northeast

The North Central and Northeast states contain a diversity of regional types. As a whole their infrastructure is well developed, if occasionally in disrepair. The larger urban areas are dense but politically fragmented. Between neighboring central cities bordering the Great Lakes and the Atlantic Coast are vast stretches of urban settlement. Inland, beyond these megalopolitan regions lie subsidiary striations along major transportation corridors which join together the cities of the interior. Agricultural, recreation, and resource lands remain only where urban encroachment has been forestalled due to inaccessibility, difficult terrain, governmental conservation, or a vigorous rural resource economy. Once the entire region was dotted by smaller towns and cities. Today much of this structure has been absorbed functionally, if not politically, into the denser urban sphere. The remaining rural places of an earlier era have selectively risen in size and rank to provide suburban or exurban residential functions, or to become distinct urban economies within the regional hierarchy of such places. The older, denser urban industrial cores of this region are also economically diverse. Some have responded to "post-industrial" opportunities of the tertiary and quaternary sectors far more energetically than others. All, however, retain an aging base of manufacturing industries, few of which remain nationally dominant. Within these urban cores reside significant black and other minority populations living disproportionately in poverty, geographically isolated from the politically distinct, more prosperous suburban rings. In summary, the region's urban geography has three dimensions:

1. Megalopolitan—continuous settlement along the transportation—communication corridors at varying urban densities.
2. Central city-suburban—dense inner cities surrounded by a succession of age-graded suburban rings.

3. Interior urban hierarchy—urban places of varying sizes partially dominating surrounding territories whose extent roughly corresponds to the size of the urban place while engaging selectively in longer distance trade. The smallest such places are towns whose function is as a central place for dispensing goods and services. Larger places tend to have disproportionately larger secondar sectors.

These dimensions of the urban geography are embedded within the larger geography. The placement, function, and inter-relation of urban places in each regional type has much to do with its strategy, goals, and prospects.

In summary, the northern and eastern portions of the United States are not one but many regions. Only the most general regional objectives pertain to the whole. Any developmental strategy intended to reverse decline, stimulate stagnating regions, or foster change without "growth" will have to address the unique situations of each single type of region. Of course, since these various types share a common geographical position within the nation as a whole, maximum effectiveness will be achieved if there occurs broad geographical coordination. This is so for the following reasons:

1. The various subregions of the northern and eastern states are not closed systems. They are highly interactive. Policies in any one must therefore account for policies in the others.
2. Without coordination, needless competition for scarce resources may occur to the advantage of none.
3. Growth of the whole region depends significantly upon events in, and policies of, other national regions. Regional coordination will insure a more united front in securing a fair share of national resources in the form of federal grants, subsidies, investments, and procurements. Coordination maximizes the opportunity for effective political representation.

Certain theories of regional development are so general as to suit the requirements of such large, internally diverse regions. These, as will be demonstrated, pay no heed to the interior spatial configuration of development within regions. Consequently their assumptions appear quite unrealistic. They offer little insight into the partially distinct mechanisms by which development and change occur in each regional type. Such intra-regional ambiguity, of course, might have political appeal to regionwide policymakers confronted by competing client regions.

National Regional Policy: The United States

While many, perhaps most, national policies have differential regional impacts, few have been explicitly "regional." Possible reasons for this include the traditional deference to laissez faire capitalism, pervasive attitudes of local-regional autonomy, the relative cultural uniformity of all subnational regions, and the limited role in regional mediation which the national government has been perceived to play. Despite significant regional economic differences the less-advantaged have been slow to utilize political power to shift national policies and priorities. This is not surprising since lagging regions within New England, the South, Midwest and West are themselves diverse and unable to coordinate political initiatives. Of course, political representation and tenure in Congress have favored rural interests, and today, despite reapportionment, the more rural states retain an advantage which is disproportionate to their populations. The current shift of population and resources from the Northeast to the South and West undoubtedly is influenced by national policies originating in these regional biases; however, in a nation so vast, decentralization is inevitable and would occur though at a slower rate even without redistribution at the national level. Today service and even some manufacturing industries are increasingly foot-loose and therefore less bound to traditional urban locations. People, likewise, seem increasingly to favor less dense, "newer" residential environs. This preference, whatever its roots, is long-standing. With the opening of the suburbs, cities lost hold of their households, setting in motion residential filtering to poorer households, physical decay, and an outflow of employers. Suburbs grew, aged, and cycled from one resident generation to the next. Meanwhile the opening of new regions more recently has afforded more distant settings in which to fulfill these preferences. The national impact on the process has largely occurred through the funding of the public infrastructure and economic activities. These, in turn, make it possible for larger numbers of households to be satisfactorily housed and employed outside the Northeast. Their shift reflects changing residential opportunities more than changing preferences.

Modern day national policies having distinct regional emphases date from at least the New Deal of the 1930s (TVA, Civilian Conservation Corps, Reconstruction Finance Corporation, and Rural Electrification). The primary objective of these was to provide employment and upgrade the economies of lagging regions. Perhaps most comprehensive of all was the Tennessee Valley Authority whose initial purpose was to develop an entire region through direct federal intervention. In later years its purposes became more diverse. The region itself became a center for nuclear research and development during World War II, and the TVA's energy role became dominant. Today hydroelectric dams, coal-fired furnaces, and nuclear plants generate energy for use in Tennessee and neighboring states. Its current responsibilities are many, including development planning in tributary areas, environmental management, agricultural improvement, transportation, and water supply, in addition to energy. This model for national regional intervention is unique for several reasons. It is governed by a board of directors advised by federal managers, and is therefore administratively distinct from local authority. It is supported by federal grants and local grants, payments, and purchases. It has both central and ancillary responsibilities and can therefore influence longer chains of events by which initial investments in infrastructure and directly productive activities are translated into regional development gains.

During World War II, New Deal initiatives were compounded by the war economy. Defense spending tended to favor established centers of settlement if only because minimal time lags in production could be afforded; less-favored regions lacked infrastructure. Following the war, cyclical more than regional issues dominated economic planning. During the 1960s, however, renewed concern for the lagging, rural regions of the nation led to passage of important legislation. These acts augmented previous federal programs intended to meet narrowly conceived needs (roads, dams, waterways, harbors, and so on) and specific problems of regions having low incomes, high unemployment, and declining population. Such programs applied to any regions meeting specified criteria. By contrast, programs established during the 1960s created regional commissions in specific areas. They were empowered to coordinate federal investment to satisfy pressing human needs and develop the economy. The first program enacted was the Appalachian Regional Development Act (ARDA) of 1965.[4] It established the Appalachian Regional Commission, the most active of all such commissions. Under the leadership of two co-chairpersons, one representing the federal government and the other to be chosen from among the board of governors representing the thirteen participating states (only West Virginia was wholly contained within the region), this federal-state partnership pursued two general goals after 1970: first, achieve self-sustaining development and higher incomes; second, provide people with skills to live anywhere in the nation.

The region has been divided into four distinct planning regions within which is designated a four-tier hierarchy for investment in health, housing, vocational education, resource development, environmental management, water and sewer facilities, and highways. During the early years of the program the bulk of all expenditures was devoted to previously programmed highway development. This TVA-like program has from the start pursued a growth center investment policy whereby a critical development mass is achieved through concentrated investment.[5] Each state, however, was charged with devising its own regional development plan, and the number of centers has become quite large. The resulting pattern places centers of varying sizes within fairly convenient reach of the dispersed, rural populations, but the economic advantage of concentration perceived to exist by growth center proponents has been somewhat compromised. Among centers, more recent policy has favored those having the greatest growth potential except in Georgia, Tennessee, and North Carolina where growth away from the larger metropolitan areas was apparently preferred.

Also in 1965, companion legislation, the Public Works and Economic Development Act (PWEDA) established regional commissions for other major lagging or depressed regions.[6] These today include the Ozarks, the "Four Corners" of the Southwest, New England, the Coastal Plains, the upper Great Lakes, the Old West, and the Pacific Northwest. A mid-Atlantic Regional Commission (New York, New Jersey, Pennsylvania, Maryland and Delaware) has also recently been proposed. Relative to their Appalachian counterpart, these commissions have been less well funded, their plans less systematic; and they have not achieved a tight coordination of the plans and policies of individual states—the possible exception being the more aggressive New England Commission. The PWEDA commissions can fund planning and demonstration projects, and offer supplemental grants, but unlike the Appalachian Regional Commission they have no fully independent programs.

The same legislation which established these commissions also renamed and redefined the Area Redevelopment Administration which was created by the Area Redevelopment Act of 1961 to serve rural regions having suffered the depletion of a significant natural resource on which their economy was heavily dependent, or a declining market for certain key natural resources. The newly created Economic Development Administration was to provide grants for building or improving facilities, long-term low-interest loans for these facilities and commercial and industrial firms, and technical assistance for planning and trial demonstration projects. The program was addressed to redevelopment areas (counties, labor areas, and some cities), redevelopment districts (multicounty groups), and development centers (areas having less than 250,000 population). Many of these resided within the regional commission areas; and, though both the PWEDA commissions and the EDA were administered within the Department of Commerce, there was little coordination between them. Generally the EDA has pursued a "worst first" policy. That is, areas qualifying according to the criteria of persistent unemployment, low income, and falling employment rates are taken from bottom to top, in effect frustrating the growth center approach of the third development category.

Aside from the innovative regional commissions established during the 1960s, recent federal legislation has in other ways fostered rural development and more generally, coherent regional planning. Several acts stress the rural deployment of federal activities, offices, and facilities in rural regions: the Agricultural Act of 1970, and the Rural Development Act of 1972. In addition, the Office of Management and Budget's A-95 circular establishes mechanisms to coordinate federal assistance to regions, though most regions still lack overall plans by which this coordination would occur. Perhaps most important are the provisions for federal revenue sharing whereby federal revenues are allocated according to various distributive criteria to states and localities. A significant fraction of these revenues are made available for use outside the formats of categorical programs. The full, long-term impact of such a strategy has yet to be determined. Indeed this concept of "fiscal federalism" is still not completely formulated. At the least the approach insures greater state and local autonomy though the ultimate impact will be governed primarily by these three factors: the relative burden incurred by individual regions as federal revenues are raised, the criteria by which these revenues are disbursed among regions, and the manner in which states and localities will elect to spend them.

In addition to the categorical and block grants, loans, subsidies, and direct investments of the federal government affecting regions, there are the policies and politics of government procurements of defense and other items produced within the private sector. These represent often massive investments which are highly concentrated in space and therefore inevitably redistributive in character, inasmuch as the revenues devoted to such purchases are generated throughout the nation. Of course, since major private contractors in defense and other industries receive a large portion of these funds, the effect of procurement is to concentrate societal capital in firms dedicated to self-preservation and able to divert capital among the various corporate arms without regard to the regional systems they transcend. Whether effective regional development planning can occur without directly influencing these nonregional federal expenditure patterns will largely depend on the extent to which they operate at cross purposes.

This brief review of federal regional programs, policies, and impacts stressed the role of selective inter-regional redistribution in securing regional development, primarily in lagging, rural regions located beyond the immediate reach of the nation's major urban centers. Recently the government has begun to formulate objectives and strategies for a national settlement policy which presumably would stress the limitation of further growth in more densely populated regions, while fostering the growth of smaller centers and more rural regions.[7] These objectives are in many ways implicit in the national programs and policies intended to bring development to lagging rural regions, since rural gains are largely if not entirely the equivalent of urban regional losses. To promote rural development is to deny developmental resources to more urban regions while drawing from them both population and employment opportunities. To this time, in any case, legislative proposals for national land use, settlement, and growth policies have had little success in Congress.

In summary, national regional policy in the United States is still in its infancy. Generally, programs embodying regional policy have won legislative approval only when they have been perceived to serve a meliorative role in redressing severe deficiencies in single regions, or when many regions are perceived to share in program benefits. The PWEDA and Appalachian programs secured approval largely as a result of these perceptions.

The TVA was born in national economic crisis made more severe by regional isolation. It has been sustained by federal largess, the maintenance of local prerogatives, and opportunistic flexibility. The Appalachian and other regional commissions have followed a similar approach; but they are internally more diverse, and in many, the financial incentives have been too few and insufficiently conditioned upon mutual cooperation to achieve a truly regional policy. Even in Appalachia the states retain considerable autonomy and plan separately.

Regional Policy Suppositions

It is difficult to find examples of the deliberate application of development theory in any of these regional efforts. There are, however, certain general suppositions which inform them. In summary these include the beliefs that:

1. Maximum advantage will accrue to policies concentrating development in growth centers or sectors which are sufficiently large to be pushed above the threshold of self-sustaining growth.

2. Investment in growth centers already above the threshold of self-sustaining growth will accelerate growth to an extent determined by the content of investment and the conditions of the center including its size and economic structure.

3. Investment in growth centers will tend to have positive consequences for the center's regional hinterland, though these will to some degree be offset by negative consequences of central expansion.

4. The strength of positive and negative hinterland impacts due to central growth will tend to decline, though not necessarily at the same rate, with increasing distance from the center.

5. The shorter the period of time over which external investment in growth centers occurs, the greater the net growth return.

6. Infrastructural investment will tend to yield a higher economic return than investment in facilities and services which bypass the private economy to meet human needs (housing, health, protection, and skills).

7. Investment in the development of firms engaging in the export of natural resources (mining, energy, forestry, fishing, farming), manufactured products, and services will tend to yield a greater growth return than investment in output for local consumption.

8. Imbalances among categories of investment (human oriented facilities and services, production oriented facilities and services, and directly productive activities) may stimulate subsequent investment in the less well financed categories.

9. It is easier and/or preferable to bring jobs to people rather than to bring people to jobs located beyond commuting distance of their initial place of residence.

10. Despite inevitable differences in the economic structures and sizes of regions there may occur movement toward equalization of real incomes and living standards if:

    a) There is economic convergence between centers and their respective hinterlands.

    b) The various regions of the nation become more similar in economic composition.

11. Certain smaller and/or more remote places will yield a smaller return per unit of investment than would certain larger and/or less-remote places.

These beliefs are not shared by all theorists nor are they acknowledged uniformly by all development programs. Some are implicitly derived from more thorough statements of regional development theory. Most troubling, they are ambiguous and often too general to guide many of the critical planning and investment decisions which must be made.

Where they have been systematically tested, the evidence has seldom been fully supportive. The proposition of growth center proponents that central gains will be regionally localized is one good example of fact denying theory, at least in some important situations. It is probably unreasonable, of course, to expect any general theory to fit all occasions. At the same time theoretical propositions regarding development should be explicitly conditioned to fit some definite domain of relevance. The major theoretical orientations from which the previously summarized developmental propositions would seem to be derived will be discussed later in this paper.

National Versus Regional Policy

There are many different roles which the federal government might play in regional development. These can be grouped into these involvement "postures":

1. Directive—federal control over key development decisions according to a national-regional development plan to which political localities may contribute but over which they have limited influence once its main structure has been determined.
2. Cooperative—joint planning by federal and regional governments and agencies. General federal fiscal and substantive guidelines would be established within which regional governments would operate with little federal intervention except to insure that the plans and programs of neighboring regions do not conflict. This approach would probably require a two- or three-tier structure of decisionmaking, with the lower tiers being assembled from existing state or local governments.
3. Indicative—federal government provides categorical and block grants to regions, shares revenues, and makes certain direct investments and procurements according to overall national development guidelines while monitoring regional performance and providing information to individual regions regarding possible consequences of policies they might pursue.
4. Programmatic—federal government provides categorical and non-restricted funds to regions and localities. National objectives would remain categorical and not explicitly coordinated while regions and localities would create development plans using federal and local resources.
5. Remedial—similar to programmatic involvement but with the federal role even more restricted, except when regions are beset by exceptional, debilitating events (socioeconomic collapse, natural catastrophes, inter-regional and international discord, and the like).

These alternative postures differ according to the inter-governmental distribution of decisionmaking authority, the overall extent of functional governmental responsibility, and the means for coordinating the categorical functions of government. The list is not exhaustive nor is it unambiguous. Most alternatives are structural and each could be fitted to a variety of different fiscal formats. Each would entail a different political-administrative approach, but none is stated in sufficient detail to constitute a theory of decision. It is interesting to speculate regarding the consequences of a system with complete regional autonomy, in which national directives would be few and no public sector redistribution would occur among regions. Even the remedial alternative, however, does not go so far.

In most recent examples of federal involvement in regional development planning, participating political jurisdictions have been willing collaborators. The sacrifice of some measure of local autonomy apparently has been offset by actual or perceived development gains. Often, however, it has been difficult to trace precisely the impacts which individual policies have had. Consequently on many occasions regional gains attributed to the pursuit of certain policies may, in fact, have resulted quite naturally from independent trends or events within individual regions themselves. It is unlikely, however, that all legitimate regional policy objectives can be attained without national coordination and resources.

In the United States today there exists a partnership among national, regional, and local governments. Within this partnership authority does not in all instances flow from top to bottom. Autonomous actions of subnational governments are often decisive in establishing the developmental course. Any future mechanism for regional planning will also have the characteristics of a partnership, with essential coordinative and redistributive roles retained by the upper levels of the governmental system, and the remainder largely performed by the lower levels.

Strategy from Theory

This section explores the problem of development apart from the political-administrative context in which it occurs. Various developmental theories will be suggestively, not exhaustively explored, to determine their real value for regional planning. Of course, though all such theories pertain to the same "standard" region, more or less, the factors they incorporate and the perspectives they embody are often quite different. However the meaning of *development* is defined, different theories may suggest widely different approaches to stimulate it. The strategies embodied in different theories, furthermore, are not equally relevant to all decisionmaking systems. That is, sometimes key variables in the development process are beyond the control of existing systems for decision. In the short run, the political-administrative system is usually quite stable, at least structurally. But as national and regional conditions change even this system must be adjusted to fit new requirements. In the long run, regional development is perhaps best conceived as both a political and a socioeconomic phenomenon. The following discussion briefly characterizes each theoretical perspective, then discusses its strategic implications.

EXPORT-BASE THEORY

Most regional development theories drawn from regional economics premise stable short-run numerical relations among key economic dimensions of regional economies. These relations take the form of multipliers which are specified for one period of time and applied to the next. Export-base, input-output, and most regional simulation models are successively more sophisticated applications of the concept. All measure dimensions of the economy according to measures of money, physical quantity, or employment. The export-base model presumes a stable ratio between the level of exports (basic production) per unit of time from a region and the level of local (nonbasic) production for local consumption. Given estimates of basic production during the next unit of time, the model will determine the amount of additional nonbasic production which this expansion would entail.[8] Exports and local production are logically related. Each additional amount of production for export will increase the regional income leading to greater demand for local production.[9] To operate the model it is generally assumed that levels of employment correspond to levels of production in basic and local industries. Unfortunately the multiplier has been shown to be unstable over time in single economic regions and among regions having equal export levels at any moment in time. Also, it does not necessarily apply in the same way to declining areas as it does to growing regions.[10]

Though empirical tests of the model indicate serious shortcomings, the importance of exports for regional development seems undeniable. Generally, regions endowed with any natural resource which exceeds local demand are well advised to exploit external markets, but only if two key conditions are satisfied. First, the quantity of the resource, whether renewable or not, should be sufficiently large to warrant its extraction (farming, forestry, mining, and the like). Second, since there may exist alternative outlets for the expenditure of local energies and capital, the optimal allocation of resources would require that investment alternatives be pursued according to potential yields. If certain of these alternative opportunities reside outside the region, it must be decided whether the potential gain from such pursuits more than offsets direct plus secondary (spin-offs favoring the region itself) consequences of alternate local opportunities. Local investment, of course, tends to allow the community to capture these secondary consequences while external investments do not.

Exports, in any case, are not limited to partially or unprocessed raw materials. Both goods and services may also be marketed directly or through a chain of inter-industry connections outside the region. Similar reasoning pertains to these alternative opportunities. Over time, many argue, the long-run viability of a regional economy depends upon its ability to invent or innovate new export bases either through the discovery of new natural resources or the application of technical knowledge to improve the process by which current or new products are made.[11] Technical knowledge, however, tends to disperse quite quickly either through imitation or the decentralization of a parent firm's production into new regions to gain access to new markets or cheaper inputs.[12] Technological monopolies are therefore short-lived, and continuous product and process development must occur.

The importance of exports for a regional economy seems largely governed by its size, its economic diversity, and the character of external demand and competition. Very large regions tend to have relatively diverse economies whose structures approach that for the nation as a whole. A significant portion of total regional production therefore serves internal demands. Today many economic activities, particularly commerce and services, seek locations maximizing access to consumers. These will generally be present wherever accessible demand exceeds industry-specific size thresholds. However, those types of activities having significant scale economies may tend to concentrate in certain regions, exporting some portion of their output to other exterior regions. This will tend to occur only when cost savings due to increased firm size are not offset by the added costs of transporting outputs to external markets.

The export-base multiplier is also a key feature of many recent regional econometric simulation models.[13] The most ambitious would link a national model to one or several interactive regional models in which the role of exports is usually critical. Since the relations within these models cannot normally be expected to be stable over longer

periods of time they are currently most appropriate for short-run fore-
casts. Few are truly analytic, most being consumers, not producers,
of theory.

Input-output analysis is a far more disaggregated application of the
multiplier concept.[14] The input-output model, developed by Leontief
and applied in many national, regional, and urban contexts, is probably
the most reliable method for forecasting economic change. The model
conceives the regional economy as a set of industrial sectors each of
which produces and consumes its own and others' products. In addition there exists a final demand sector formed of all purchases by
households, government, and external (export) consumers. Given
estimates of future final demands in each sector, the model will then
convert these into levels of production in each industrial category.[15]
Larger models apply to several regions simultaneously.[16] All such
models assume constant rates of inter-industry exchange according to
the level of output in the consuming industry. Simple versions of the
model are now in frequent use in evaluating possible impacts of proposed developments in single industries or sets of industries. As with
other models using multipliers, input-output models are less reliable
in long-run forecasting. The method and detail with which they conceive the forward and backward linkages of industries, however, remains very helpful in envisioning the full impact of expansion or
contraction in any one.

GROWTH CENTER THEORY

Growth center theory has provided a loose rationale for regional
development strategy in many nations.[17] Simply stated, the theory
assumes that a growth center, or pole, will influence surrounding territory, and that the degree of influence will diminish with increasing
distance.[18] Maximum advantage will accrue to investments in infrastructure and directly productive activities within these centers. At
any point in time, furthermore, certain industries within them will
tend to dominate because of their scale, potential market, and extensive connections with other regional industries. Investment in these
propulsive industries and in infrastructure on which they depend will
yield the maximum regional benefit if it is concentrated in centers rather
than dispersed throughout the region. This is so because of the greater
economy with which central infrastructures can be built, and the other
advantages gained by larger firms in larger centers. Regions may
have several such centers whose effects overlap in some localities.
Centers, it is generally assumed, must be sufficiently large to afford

firms these advantages, though no single critical size pertains to all regions.

Central place theory entails a somewhat similar conception of space.[19] As growth center theory, it envisions regions as divided into overlapping urban spheres of influence. Larger centers perform the widest variety of activities, and their commercial hinterlands are most extensive. Smaller centers within the regional hierarchy of such places perform fewer commercial functions, and these are a subset of those performed at larger centers. Though one version of the theory emphasizes agglomerative advantages in industrial production, the theory is burdened by several restrictive assumptions and currently lacks the dynamic qualities needed in policy formulation.

Despite their current limitations, however, the theories of growth centers and central places are the two general approaches most able to assist in planning regional investments, at least in relatively more rural lagging regions.[20] Most alternatives are aspatial, and though they may provide some help in deciding what should be the content of investment, they fail to indicate where within the region it should occur. Generally *what* and *where* are mutually dependent and must be simultaneously determined. Growth center theory begins to suggest what types of propulsive (often manufacturing) industries might be most helpful in generating future growth and attaining improved regional conditions. It also begins to suggest in what places such industries would be not only feasible but also bring the greatest advantage. The feasibility of alternate locations within a region of moderate size is determined primarily by conditions within centers while the degree of favorable regional impact of a new investment will depend somewhat more upon the relative location of the center.[21]

In the past the pursuit of growth center development in the United States has been primarily the responsibility of the Economic Development Administration which was created in 1965. The principal recipient of its financial and technical assistance was the multicounty development district formed of counties having low income or high unemployment. Though alternate investment criteria within the same agency stressed a policy of "worst first," this assistance often went to districts (centers) with development potential. Some of the assistance was devoted to existing firms and improvements in existing infrastructure. Additional resources were applied, however, to induce the establishment of new businesses in the district. This took the form of indirect inducements (to improve physical facilities, upgrade labor productivity, and the like) and direct incentives in the form of guarantees, grants, loans, and tax advantages for which new firms might apply.

It is one thing to attempt to expand existing businesses, and quite another to persuade new ones to locate within the area. Many plants are established each year, but there are many areas in which to locate. It is exceedingly difficult to anticipate which businesses will be drawn to an area by any particular set of investments and incentives. An area must reckon not only with the actual change in its relative attractiveness resulting from these (in light of conditions in competing areas), but also with the way they are perceived at a distance by prospective firms. Given this uncertainty, areas generally can do no more than adopt a general development strategy, then respond more specifically as real opportunities arise.

In larger urbanized regions experiencing economic stagnation or decline, the growth center investment strategy has a different meaning. Within these regions are often many politically distinct but functionally related jurisdictions. Private or public investment in any one will stimulate both gains and losses in others. The problem is that these tend to result in cumulative imbalances in liveability, public sector viability, and overall development potential.[22] Gains in progressive exurban and suburban communities, or even in some central cities tend to create the conditions for further growth. This growth, of course, will slow even in prosperous communities as limits on land, environment, and other capacities are approached. As gains establish the preconditions for further growth, neighboring communities may become less able to resist the negative consequences which it would engender.

In such urban regions the developmental problem is not necessarily one of securing additional increments of growth in the form of increased output or income. Instead it may be to achieve a more favorable or equitable distribution of resources among people through governmental redistribution (among jurisdictions or among income groups), deliberate depopulation or disinvestment of failing jurisdictions, or shifts in access to economic opportunities in the private sector. Redistribution generally does not occur easily. More importantly, to redistribute may mean to lessen, at least in the short run, the region's economic potential since productive resources would quite possibly be less efficiently used. It is even possible to imagine a situation in which redistribution among political jurisdictions would produce a less equitable distribution among individuals.

In any case, when regional resources are insufficient to achieve equity at an acceptable level throughout the region, or when redistribution is impossible to achieve, each separate community may have to pursue its own development strategy according to local conditions. Here, as in the case of rural regions, the measures for securing additional growth reduce to two: improve conditions within the community, and offer direct inducements to existing and potential new firms.[23]

Finally, consider the relation between the export-base and growth center theories. Both concern the relation between a local and external region. Indeed, if we treat the growth center as the local economy, then all exports from it would drive its economy within the multiplier relationship. Growth center theory, however, assumes the territorial impact of the center will diminish with distance. If this occurs too abruptly, the impacted territory would be too small to constitute the market required if exports are to dominate. It would seem that the larger the center, the more potentially important would be production for export; and that proportionately less important would be the role of the center as a central place having a distance-diminishing relation to its surrounding territory.

MACROECONOMIC THEORIES

Included within the macroeconomic category are theories initially conceived in relation to whole nations. They are highly aggregated and not all are developmental. They are mentioned almost in passing since they cannot easily be translated to the subnational scale without considerable distortion. All pertain to "point economies," that is regions having no internal spatial dimension. All ignore transportation costs and the frictional effects of distance, opting instead for the assumption of perfect mobility.

The first group of these are Keynesian models of regional economies.[24] The most prominent of these conceives the economy to be governed by the interaction among four components: investment, savings, income, and output. At equilibrium, income equals output in money terms, and savings equal investment. Equilibrium, however, does not automatically occur. Government therefore must intervene to insure critical balances are maintained. Despite its intuitive plausibility, the model has failed to solve the problem of "stagflation." Regional variants retain the same ingredients while incorporating migration and inter-regional trade.[25] There is great appeal in so simple a model. If a region's welfare could so easily be maintained by manipulating such macro variables the task of regional development would be much less demanding than it, in fact, seems to be. Generally, however, regions have no direct control over these particular variables, and since the model assumes perfect mobility and is mute regarding developmental content or resource distribution, other models have greater current usefulness.[26]

A second macroeconomic approach is international trade theory, as applied to subnational regions. In its several forms the theory attempts to determine the conditions of regional economic specialization. The classical thesis is that with free, unimpeded trade among regions, each region will produce for export those commodities which it can produce at a comparatively lower cost while importing those in which other regions have the comparative advantage of lower production cost.[27] The theory is largely contradicted by the evidence, but even if it were not, the neglect of the specific mechanisms by which growth impulses are transmitted over space within and among regions limits its usefulness in defining policy.[28]

Neoclassical theory, a third macroeconomic alternative, is an extension of inter-regional trade theory. It assumes full employment, instantaneous mobility of production factors, and perfect competition. As such it has dominated regional growth theory in recent years. These models stress the conditions of ecomnomic production (supply) and are therefore different in emphasis from export-base and Keynesian models which stress demand. They assume that sufficient demand will automatically arise when a region's output is increased. Output, in turn, must be stimulated for growth to occur. According to one prominent formulation, growth has three main sources: increased use of available capital and labor, increased productivity through technological advances, and the reassignment of capital and labor from less to more productive industries.[29] These, of course, suggest actual strategies which regions might pursue. Because of this, such models seem much closer to developmental solutions than do the Keynesian or trade models. In fact, from the perspective of a small region having large, potential external markets, the assumption of unlimited demand is not unrealistic.[30] To the extent that growth depends on demand, in any case, regional planners can directly influence only local demand, but this will be quite small in rural regions. The bulk of regional development policy consequently has stressed supply, not demand, factors.

Two historical models having macroeconomic characteristics are also potentially relevant to regional development. One of these, Rostow's stage theory of national development, defines a sequence of stages through which nations proceed at varying rates.[31] The critical stage is that of takeoff during which productive investment increases and social and political changes occur enabling the emergence of leading industries. If persistent growth ensues, progress will eventually become self-sustaining. Analogous regional stages might also exist though the generality and relevance for policy decisions is at this point uncertain, and the prospect of irreversible development is doubtful. There is quite possibly, however, an investment-resource threshold beyond which development becomes far more likely. The correspondence between these and the critical size thresholds of growth center theory is not known.

Unequal exchange theory is a second historical model claiming regional relevance.[32] The disparity between rich and poor regions is attributed to differences in regional wage rates. Wealth in the form of wages and surplus value (profits) will flow to the richer from the poorer regions due to the purchase of imports in poor regions and the investment in rich regions of profits produced in the poor. Accordingly, inter-regional disparity will continue until the poor region is depopulated or wages are equalized. Regional development policy would therefore attempt to elevate wage rates. Such a policy, in reality, might accelerate the decline of the poorer region unless the higher wage rates result from rising productivity.

THE THEORY OF LOCATION

Nearly all regional development theories contain important, often critical, assumptions about the locational behavior of individual firms engaged in primary resource extraction (mining, forestry, fishing, agriculture, and the like), secondary industrial processing, and tertiary commerce (wholesaling and retailing). Most assume that production factors are perfectly mobile.[33] The direction of a regional economy, in fact, can be viewed according to decisions of firms and households to locate and relocate, and operational decisions (to expand, contract, or change) once locations have been chosen. Of course, in reality production factors (land, labor, and capital) cannot move instantaneously in response to new opportunities, and there is frequently a cost penalty in the move itself.

Most regional development strategies, ultimately, are centered on attempts to include unwanted activities to leave, and to convince desired activities to come or to stay within the region. There are several different approaches to location theory. Some assume locational decisions will be made rationally (usually minimizing one, several, or all facets of production costs including for site and transportation) with full knowledge of the consequences. Others assume only that the final locational decision will fall within the subset of all possible places at which profits would be positive (higher profit places perhaps having a higher probability of being chosen). It is relatively easy to determine which kinds of firms might find a particular region profitable. With more effort it is even possible to determine how one region stands against all others. It is not easy, however, to determine in advance which firms will actually be drawn to the region in question. Consequently regional planners may follow a strategy of local investments in physical facilities and human resource development while holding out to potential new firms the prospect of additional incentives. In theory it is possible to determine how much the region's relative attractiveness would change for given activities due to any set of investments and inducements. The fact remains, in any case, that firms seldom optimize location. Either they are behaving irrationally using known locational criteria or they are considering additional factors, acting rationally in this expanded context. It is possible also that, for some, the locational alternatives are hardly different. For these footloose industries non-economic factors may be more critical, and regional promotion a possible success.

MIGRATION: THEORY AND INDUCEMENT

The theory of migration is no more than a general explanation of the factors which motivate people to move, the way these are considered, and the ultimate choices which individuals or households make. Some moves are sequential as households cycle through stages of identity and residential need. At any point in time a household will have certain residential preferences related to house type, neighborhood, location relative to places frequently visited, and region. As preferences change, the utility of any residence may change. Of course, the residence itself may also alter as the house, its neighborhood, or its effective location change. At some point unsatisfied preferences may stimulate the search for an alternate place of residence in light of household resources. Over time certain predominant migration patterns may become established. These may define the movements of similar households from house to house or region to region. They may also reflect chain migrations over several generations. Related theory indicates the likely impacts on both origins and destinations of migrations.

Patterns of population are basic to patterns of labor supply and final economic demand. Though these are only a single facet of regional economic potential, they are one of the most critical dimensions of the space-economy. Though Americans are highly mobile, regional policy has traditionally stressed moving jobs to people, not the reverse. It is clear, however, that this is often neither feasible nor desirable. All the nations of western Europe now subsidize certain migrations, primarily from rural to urban areas. These take several forms: (1) inter-regional job banks, (2) travel and moving assistance, (3) allowances to visit distant families from whom individuals have been separated, (4) living allowances during job training or prior to starting a new job, and (5) allowances to become established in the vicinity of the new job.[34] The expense of such programs usually is offset at least partially by savings in unemployment compensation. These savings can be considerable when great distances separate the unemployed from potential jobs, and inter-regional migration is considered only as a last alternative.

In the United States, relocation projects have been tried in the past. Pilot projects, for example, were funded under amendments to the Manpower Development and Training Act of 1963. Recipients of this assistance were drawn from various known groupings of the unemployed for ease of identification. Though the results indicated the feasibility of such a program there is no permanent, comprehensive program of relocation assistance now available in the United States. Since the development of employment opportunities is extremely difficult and costly in some lagging regions, the only realistic alternative is migration. Even in some more prosperous regions there are too few employment opportunities. A more comprehensive strategy might attempt to encourage some of the urban unemployed to migrate elsewhere. This would seem desirable in the short run only when the area lacks the capacity to generate new jobs in appropriate categories. Sometimes, of course, there are adequate jobs within the urban area for the un- and under-employed, yet geographic, sociocultural, and institutional barriers isolate them from able applicants.

There are, in any case, many governmental policies and programs exercising a significant, if unintended, influence upon national settlement patterns. Welfare provisions in particular have long been recognized as having a major impact upon the distribution of recipient households, often causing overloads in regions with minimal residency requirements and comparatively well-funded programs. Similarly, many other actions of government lead to population dislocations, but the total effect is seldom planned.

OVERVIEW OF REGIONAL THEORIES

As this review of regional theory shows, several distinct developmental perspectives exist.   These at varying times emphasize:

1. Dynamic economic equilibrium models.

   Objective: maintain a dynamic balance among certain macroeconomic dimensions such as saving, investment, output, and input to insure full employment and stable prices during periods of increasing population.

   Strategy: regulate the rate of productive investment.   This rate depends on the availability of capital generated in or out of the region by income gained in selling the regional output.   Investment may be most directly influenced through incentives to invest.   The spending by government of its revenues gained from the economic surplus of the private sector is also a form of investment.

   Comment: regional versions of this model sometimes allow the inter-regional movement of certain production factors (including labor) and products but do not provide a convincing rationale for the forces determining these movements in the short run.   Disparities among people and places within regions are not considered, nor is the explicit content of the economy.   Major structural economic transformations by which lagging regions might evolve are not addressed.   Many of the key policy variables of the model are not controlled within the region itself.

2. Export oriented models.

   Objective: increase total regional economic output in the form of goods and services, and thereby increase regional income.

   Strategy: increase the level of production for export to other regions.   To do so, external demand for the region's products must be stimulated.   This may be accomplished by the following:

   a) Generate new products for which there is no immediate "foreign" competition.

   b) Concentrate investment in industries having a comparative advantage over those of other regions due to market access, lower production costs, abundant natural resources, marketing efficiency, and regional product identification.

   c) Foster the transfer of productive resources from certain non-export to export industries, from nonproductive to productive activities, and from weak to strong export industries.

   d) Strengthen export marketing systems.

   Comment: not all industries have equal export potential because local production capacity or the external market is limited.   Care must be taken that the potential scale of production be sufficiently large.   Lagging regions often emphasize exports of natural resources while gradually substituting local production for imports to gain capital for further expansion. One key means of expansion is through the processing of resource exports. Whole vertical industries may later evolve from this base. Developed regions in decline may already have a great diversity of industries. There the objective would be to sort out industries, favoring those with the largest potential external markets and the greatest ability to stimulate the regional economy through the export-base multiplier relationship.

3. Spatial development models.

Objective: achieve a more equitable balance in development levels and/or rates among regions while spreading the wealth of individual regions more evenly among urban and rural places within them.

Strategy: growth within single regions may be stimulated through inter-regional governmental redistribution and/or more effective spatial organization of productive activities within regions. Government redistribution through tax and spending policies is, of course, most necessary when a whole region lags. When poverty pockets exist within otherwise wealthy regions, however, only internal redistribution of resources by government may be necessary. Lagging regions or subregions may, it is argued, make the best use of limited resources by concentrating them in centers of growth (towns, smaller cities, or sets of such urban places) to achieve scale and urbanization economies. The prime benefit accrues to the growth centers, themselves, but if these are located within or proximate to lagging rural places, then center over time will act as a lever, uplifting the rural hinterland. In the short run the center's impact on its hinterland may be more negative than positive, though the region as a whole would likely have a net gain. In summary, the spatial development strategy entails:

a) Inter-regional governmental redistribution through various formulas for taxation and spending.

b) Stimulate the emergence and/or expansion of propulsive industries in growth centers either directly or through infrastructural and human resource development.

c) Prepare the hinterlands of these centers to contribute to development of the center itself. This would entail efforts to influence the quantity and quality of rural resources and the settlement pattern of the entire region.

d) Prepare the hinterlands to receive the benefits of expansion at nearby growth centers. To do so will prevent spread effects from leaping over the immediate hinterland to more distant places less well connected to the local economy.

Comment: growth centers historically have been urban places. Many of these depend primarily on exports to generate further growth. Usually the maximum advantage is gained through exports to other regions since their own hinterlands are often too small. Growth centers are members of the regional-national hierarchy of urban places. They are economically connected simultaneously with smaller, equal, and larger such places. Some consider development to be a two-part spatial process in which growth "impulses" move up and down (pri-

marily) the urban hierarchy and spread outward from city to countryside.

Each of these three summary development perspectives relates to a
bundle of distinct theories. The dynamic equilibrium perspective is
most closely associated with the Keynesian viewpoint, particularly the
Harrod-Domar model. The export oriented perspective joins the predominant themes of the export-base, trade, neoclassical, and unequal
exchange models. The spatial development perspective is most closely
associated with the growth center and settlement policy approaches. It
is also similar to aspects of the sequential model of national-regional
development insofar as two themes are stressed. First, most sequential
models of regional development premise certain stages through which
a region might evolve. Similar reasoning has been applied to growth
centers, which some presume will advance through several stages of
evolution (defined according to their internal economic composition
and relation to surrounding territory). Second, certain national-regional
models include a stage at which takeoff into self-sustaining growth will
occur. The regional variant corresponds to the attainment of the critical
size above which growth center development will be sustained through
cyclical and cumulative processes of economic transformation.

Lagging, Developing and Declining Regions

In this concluding section are considered the major difference among
three major regional types, and the strategies which might be useful in
each. Among the objectives which these strategies might pursue are
the following:

1. Satisfy critical current human needs
    a) Increase incomes (purchasing power)
    b) Provide subsidies and welfare services
    c) Stimulate development of needed private commercial and service
        establishments which are accessible and affordable

2. Moderate cyclical tendencies within the economy
    a) Maximize employment opportunities
    b) Minimize inflation

3. Establish the preconditions for growth
    a) Encourage saving and investment
    b) Accumulate resources generated outside the region in the private
        and public sectors

    c) Develop the necessary infrastructures (roads, buildings, facilities, and the like)

    d) Develop the region's human resources

    e) Redirect and recycle the region's resources from less to more productive pursuits

    f) Stimulate social, political, and institutional changes to accommodate and direct needed economic transformations

4. Maximize the opportunity for attaining an equitable distribution of new wealth among people and places within the region

    a) Insure that individuals at all skill levels have access to employment

    b) Insure that no matter how low on the wage-job ladder an individual enters the market there are both incentives and opportunities to rise within an upward career track

    c) Insure that those unable to work have adequate care

    d) Among subregions insure that the benefits of growth in progressive core regions can be channeled to those which lag behind.

All of these objectives may not have equal priority at any point along the development path of any particular regional context.[35]

LAGGING REGIONS

The syndrome of a lagging rural region is a familiar one. Certain of its resources are depleted thorough exploitation or mismanagement. Its population has ceased to grow, and may in fact be declining. Younger, more educated, and highly motivated people are leaving behind an older, less productive, more dependent population. Its industries are small, often ill-equipped, and seldom in the fast-moving sectors of the economy. Beyond the reach of its towns and cities, population is too dispersed to allow for efficient distribution of goods and services; and in these areas there is generally insufficient demand for some of the higher value, less often needed consumer goods and services. Even its urban places may be relatively small, often specializing in local commercial functions. A few industries may serve regional and external markets though these may be relatively small in scale, and if the market potential is great, it may be experiencing severe external competition. Still, there may be certain activities in which there is development potential. Some firms may be drawn to the area to allow its workers access to the area's amenities. Others may seek out low-wage labor or access to local markets.

In this setting development policies would in the short run tend to favor two key objectives: satisfy the most pressing needs of people living in the region, and establish the preconditions for accelerated growth. The strategy for achieving these objectives might include some of the following measures:

1. Accelerate the accumulation of capital in the form of individual savings and corporate surplus while enlisting external investors
2. Establish quasi-public development institutions to manage the accumulation of capital and its investment
3. Identify general sectors of activity in which the region may have economic potential and develop some portion of the necessary infrastructure
4. Concentrate investments in infrastructure and industries within designated growth centers
5. Where feasible and necessary to gain sufficient economic thrust, designate certain areas for deliberate decline through assisted out-migration
6. Stimulate the movement of resources from certain less productive industries serving local demands to progressive industries which have great external demand potential and pay higher wages

In initial stages it may be necessary to encourage selective out-migration and the diversion of resources from less to more productive activities. One consequence may be that the region reverts temporarily to a less-developed state in which certain amenities are sacrificed and a greater portion of locally consumed goods and services is actually imported. In this early development phase the multiplier effect of export industries might be temporarily suppressed in order that the local income they produce can be turned back into the export sector. Eventually, of course, imports will again give way to local production, and the other regional goals of economic stability and equity can be pursued.

DEVELOPING REGIONS

Actually several distinct regional types might fit this category. The prime criterion for inclusion would be an economy having experienced sustained development over a substantial period of time. Such an economy would presumably have satisfied many of the most pressing human needs and at least begun to attain equity conditions. If the duration of sustained growth is quite long, such an economy may have developed certain burdens of old age including seriously underproductive economic sectors, some physical deterioration of public and private facilities, and a measure of under- and unemployment in the low-wage labor market. These economies, however, have both the opportunity and the resources to begin the process of economic invigoration of lagging subregions and sectors while at the same time taking steps to prevent the problems which may attend too much growth over too short a period of time and the surpassing of regional environmental capacities. Among the specific strategies which may be pursued in this regional situation are:

1. Decentralization of past growth or the channeling of future growth which might be destined for the most congested regions to others which have both the need and capacity.
2. Regional integration of economic and political subregions through quasi-public and/or public institutions capable of effective planning and redistribution according to regionwide objectives.
3. Ameliorate the effects of too rapid growth in earlier years. These effects may include excessive population concentration, the failure to achieve balanced development minimizing cyclical propensities, and insufficient development in certain consumer and service industries.
4. Preservation of regional amenities such as clear air and water, open space, stable neighborhoods, historical attractions, and the like.
5. Redevelopment of deteriorating public and private facilities.
6. Industrial sorting to redirect resources to the more productive and regionally suitable industries serving both export and local markets. Even in the more remote regions this may entail shifts from certain extractive and resource dependent activities to those of the tertiary and quaternary sectors.
7. Deliberate attempts to discourage further concentration of impoverished households in ghetto areas while insuring adequate alternatives.

The major theme of regional objectives pertaining to such regions is that further growth may not be in the regional interest. Instead current and prospective resources should be devoted to the development of both spatial and economic equilibriums. The ultimate objective would be a self-sustaining, equitable distribution of regional resources beneath the levels of excessive concentration. Whether or not regions will have the wisdom to know when excessive concentration is approaching is unclear.

DECLINING REGIONS

Declining regions are those which have already experienced some duration of sustained growth during which the economy became fully if not excessively developed. There are many potential causes for decline, not all of which originate within the region itself. Among these are decreases in residential amenities, failure to develop and sustain new export bases, deterioration of public and private facilities and services, political fragmentation without mechanisms for intra-regional redistribution, excessive concentration of impoverished households, changing tacit or explicit national priorities, and the rise to economic prominence of alternative regions to which new increments of national growth are being drawn. All of these in different degrees have contributed to the current losses of people and jobs in the Northeast.

Understanding of the reasons for regional decline is a necessary but not sufficient condition for devising future regional policy. It is seldom possible simply to reverse a prior causal condition to restore regional vigor. *Ameliorative policies are not usually symmetric to causal policies and conditions.* Regions which may have experienced prior excessive growth (by any objective standard) might use decline as an opportunity to foster some measure of out-migration and resource redistribution within the public and private sectors. If decline occurs, it may be useful to channel losses to emphasize sectors and subregions which have the least opportunity for making a significant contribution to economic recovery. When decline appears inevitable in the short run the preferable strategic stance may be to ease the human burden of downward transition while planning for the attainment of some future stable state at a scale somewhere beneath that achieved before decline began.

Strategies to be pursued by declining regions may differ in kind from those of lagging regions attempting to establish the pre-conditions for sustained growth, and in degree from those pursued by developing regions. Among them are:

1. Selective withdrawal of resources from certain sectors and subregions
2. Concentrating limited resources in propulsive industries serving regional and national markets
3. Re-balancing the political economy to insure effective regionwide developmental coordination, perhaps directed by a quasi-public regional council having its own resources and powers to implement its policies
4. Direct investments to maximize economic opportunities and living conditions at the ultimate level at which the post-decline economy may reside

In any case, the quality of a region as a place to live bears no direct relation to its overall population or its prior development path. Perhaps the most difficult task in easing the pain of decline is to reshape current outlooks and institutions to meet future needs. This is as much a question of political will as of resources and strategies.

NOTES

1. These objectives are infrequently wholly compatible yet the conflict is seldom acknowledged in theory or strategy. See also M. E. Conroy, *The Challenge of Urban Economic Development* (Lexington, Mass. Lexington Books, 1975), chapters 3-5 regarding income level, stability, and distribution in urban economies. See also B. Massam, *Location and Space in Social Administration* (New York: John Wiley-Halsted, 1975).

2. Categories along this continuum are more or less exhaustive. Their significance depends on their scale, delimitation, and functional composition. The more urban regions along this continuum have often been omitted from similar typologies, probably because their economic problems have seemed different in kind or degree and less amenable to regional solutions.

3. Each of these can be further characterized according to three alternate planning postures suggested by Ozbekhan. These are: (1) operational or tactical planning in relation to short-term goals which are ameliorative or trend-modifying, (2) strategic planning serving longer term, multifaceted goals, and (3) normative planning to shape the long-term future through the reconsideration of means and ends. H. Ozbekhan, "Toward a General Theory of Planning," in *Perspectives of Planning*, E. Jantsch, ed. (Paris: O.E.C.D., 1969).

4. For a review of this program and its impact see D. N. Rothblatt, *Regional Planning: The Appalachian Experience* (Lexington, Mass.: Health, Lexington Books, 1971). Also D. A. Rondinelli, *Urban and Regional Development Planning: Policy and Administration* (Ithaca, N.Y.: Cornell University Press, 1970), part 2, and N. M. Hansen, *Rural Poverty and the Urban Crisis: A Strategy for Regional Development* (Bloomington: Indiana University Press, 1970), chapter 4. Evaluation of the program's impact has been hampered by the long lead time required for investment impacts to occur, the lack of explicit and sustained objectives, and the simultaneous impacts of autonomous economic events including regional shift in the national system and recovery in the coal economy.

5. The growth center approach and its sectoral counterpart are reviewed later in this paper.

6. See D. A. Rondinelli, *Urban and Regional Development Planning*, chapter 4, and for a review of an early urban application of PWEDA in Oakland see J. L. Pressman and A. Wildavsky, *Implementation* (Berkeley: University of California Press, 1973), which demonstrates one major model for generating urban jobs for the urban disadvantaged and the bureaucratic entanglements which may attend the effort.

7. The emergence of a national debate regarding growth and settlement policy was stimulated by two major events during the 1960s: the development of legislation for lagging rural regions, and the increasing awareness of urban poverty and minority expectations. The environmental debate likewise stimulated interest in land use policy though national initiatives remained distinct from those involving urban development. Passage of the Urban Growth and New Community Development Act in 1970 even went so far as to require periodic reports on national urban growth, but the prospects for an explicit national growth policy remain very doubtful. For an overview of the Ameri-

can policy issue and the experiences of other nations from whom a U.S. approach to national growth policy might be derived see J. L. Sundquist, *Dispersing Population: What America Can Learn from Europe* (Washington, D.C.: The Brookings Institution, 1975) and L. S. Bourne, *Urban Systems: Strategies for Regulation—A Comparison of Policies in Britain, Sweden, Australia, and Canada* (New York: Oxford University Press, 1975). Prospects for national involvement in regional planning institutions appear somewhat more promising in the United States to the extent that the sacrifice of local autonomy is in proportion to the perceived benefit of regional cooperation.

8. Among the earliest formal statements of the model were R. B. Andrews, "Mechanics of the Urban Economic Base," *Land Economics* 29, (1953), and W. A. Mackintosh, "Innis on Canadian Economic Development," *Journal of Political Economy* 56, no. 2 (June 1953): 185-94. See also C. M. Tiebout, *The Community Economic Base Study,* Supplementary Paper no. 16 (New York: Committee for Economic Development, 1962).

9. The relationship is the basis for the theoretical justification of the model as presented in H. O. Nourse, *Regional Economics: A Study in the Economic Structure, Stability, and Growth of Regions* (New York: McGraw-Hill, 1968), 155-63.

10. Application of the model was most extensively documented in R. W. Pfouts, ed., *The Techniques of Urban Economic Analysis* (West Trenton: Chandler-Davis, 1960).

11. See for example W. R. Thompson, *A Preface to Urban Economics* (Baltimore: The Johns Hopkins Press for Resources for the Future, Inc., 1965), 15-18. Analysis of the economic and export orientations of the major subnational regions of the United States may be found in H. S. Perloff, E. S. Dunn, E. E. Lampard, and R. F. Muth, *Regions, Resources, and Economic Growth* (Lincoln: The University of Nebraska Press, 1960), and more recently in B. J. L. Berry, "The Geography of the United States in the Year 2000," *Transactions* no. 51 (November 1970): 21-53. See also J. R. Borchert, "American Metropolitan Evolution," *Geographical Review* 57 (1967): 301-32, and Borchert, "America's Changing Metropolitan Regions," *Annals, Association of American Geographers* 62 (1972): 352-73.

12. Development conceived as a process of diffusion of people, firms, ideas, and products (wealth) from urban centers to other centers and outlying regions is a theme pursued in A. R. Pred, *The Spatial Dynamics of U.S. Urban-Industrial Growth, 1800-1914* (Cambridge: The M.I.T. Press, 1966); Pred, "Diffusion, Organizational Spatial Structure, and City-System Development," *Economic Geography* 51, no. 3 (July 1975): 252-68; M. P. Conzen, "The Maturing Urban System in the United States, 1840-1910," *Annals, Association of American Geographers* 67, no. 1 (March 1977) 88-108; and B. J. L. Berry, "Hierarchical Diffusion: The Basis of Development Filtering and Spread in a System of Growth Centers," in *Growth Centers in Regional Economic Development,* N. M. Hansen, ed. (New York: The Free Press, 1972).

13. See L. R. Klein, "The Specification of Regional Econometric Models," *Papers of the Regional Science Association* 23 (1969): 105-15, and subsequently, N.J. Glickman, "Son of 'The Specification of Regional Econometric Models,'" *Papers of the Regional Science Association* 32 (1974): 155-77, but especially page 172. The coefficients of these linear models can be inter-

preted as multipliers which weight the additive contribution of several simultaneous explanatory variables in projecting the dependent variable. Glickman suggests the use of the economic base hypothesis in projecting nonbasic production within individual regions. Since longitudinal (time series) data are usually inadequate and major statistical problems (autocorrelation, multicollinearity, and minimum degrees of freedom) exist, most models compromise theoretical elegance for operational necessity and are therefore forecasting rather than analytic. They are, therefore, most often consumers, not producers, of theory; and few even now are fully suited for policy analysis.

14. One of the first statements of the approach was W. W. Leontief, "Quantitative Input-Output Relations in the Economic System of the United States," *Review of Economics and Statistics* 18, no. 3 (1936): 103-25. More recently see W. Isard, et al., *Methods of Regional Analysis* (Cambridge: The Technology Press, 1960). The export-base model is a two sector model with similar characteristics.

15. A brief symbolic statement of the input-output model follows. Define (X) to be a matrix dimensioned (nxl) representing the total number of units of output from each sector per unit of time (say one year). Next define (Y) to be a matrix of total units of final demand for each sector's output per unit time. This matrix is also dimensioned (nxl). Finally, define (A) to be an (nxn) matrix of technical coefficients representing the rates at which each sector consumes another's output per unit of time. For example, one member of the matrix, (A), can be defined to be (a_{ij}). This coefficient indicates the level (units) of immediate, direct demand by sector (j) for the output of sector (i) per unit of output of (j). Consequently, in the algebra of matrices, $X = (AX + Y)$. And if the matrix (I) is defined to be an (nxn) identity matrix with ones on the diagonal and zeros elsewhere, then $X = (I - A)^{-1}$. This is the key equation for the one-region inter-sectoral model. The term, $(I - A)^{-1}$ is an (nxn) matrix whose elements are multipliers which when applied to independent estimates of final demand (Y) yield the levels of total output per unit time in each sector.

16. An inter-sectoral, inter-regional model does not exist for the United States, however Leontief and Isard have proposed a procedure for linking all regions which does not require inter-regional coefficients. This involves applying the model to the nation as a whole, then allocating the projected national output to regions, and, finally, applying the inter-sectoral model to each region to convert final demands including exports to local production levels by industrial sector.

17. The earliest statement of this concept dealt with abstract economic spaces (not geographical regions) containing interactions among related industries regardless of their actual, geographical locations. The seminal work was F. Perroux, "Note sur la notion de 'pôle de croissance,'" *Economie Applique* (1955), 3-7-20. It is conceptually similar to the industrial complex addressed in W. Isard, E.W. Schooler, and T. Vietorisz, *Industrial Complex Analysis and Regional Development* (Cambridge: The M.I.T. Press, 1959). Growth centers are the geographical counterparts of these abstract poles.

18. A useful demarcation of U.S. growth centers and their respective hinterlands is B.J.L. Berry, *Growth Centers in the American Urban System,* Volumes 1 and 2 (Cambridge: Ballinger, 1973). A major proponent of growth center

strategies in the United States is Niles Hansen. See N. Hansen, *Rural Poverty and the Urban Crisis: A Strategy for Regional Development* (Bloomington: Indiana University Press, 1970), and N. Hansen, "An Evaluation of Growth-Center Theory and Practice," *Environment and Planning* 7 (November 1975).

19. The two semifinal statements of central place theory are these: W. Christaller, *Central Places in Southern Germany*, trans. C.W. Baskin (Englewood Cliffs, N.J.: Prentice-Hall, 1966), and A. Losch, *Die räumliche Ordnung der Wirtschaft*, translated as *The Economics of Location* by W.H. Woglom and W.F. Stolper (New Haven: Yale University Press, 1954).

20. The correspondence between central places and growth centers was first explored in J.-R. Boudeville, *Problems of Regional Economic Planning* (Edinburg: Edinburg University Press, 1966). Central place theory, however, remains essentially static whereas growth centers are by definition in evolution through interactions with their hinterlands. The correspondence is further evaluated in J.B. Parr, "Growth Poles, Regional Development, and Central Place Theory," *Papers of the Regional Science Association* 31 (1973): 173-212, especially 173-4.

21. Recent elaborations of growth center theory go beyond the purely economic to consider the social, political and institutional factors through which growth is generated and its impact distributed. Perhaps the most extensive, though subjective, of these is J. Friedmann, "A General Theory of Polarized Development," in *Growth Centers in Regional Economic Development*, N.M. Hansen, ed. (New York: The Free Press, 1972), pp. 82-107.

22. Hirschman has argued that in developing regions such imbalances are both inevitable and desirable since they stimulate remedial action in both the public and private sectors. The development process then becomes a process of rebalancing as scarce resources are devoted first to one development facet then another. To the extent that imbalances arise between subregions (center and periphery, or among distinct segments of the center) some such as Hirschman argue that equalization will later occur, whereas Myrdal finds the process to be both circular and cumulative, resulting in sustained inequality. See A.O. Hirschman, *The Strategy of Economic Development* (New Haven: Yale University Press, 1958), and G. Myrdal, *Economic Theory and Underdeveloped Regions* (London: Duckworth and Co., 1957). See also J.G. Williamson, "Regional Inequality and the Process of National Development: A Description of Patterns," *Economic Development and Cultural Change* 13, no. 4: part 2.

23. See A. Pred, "The Interurban Transmission of Growth in Advanced Economies: Empirical Findings Versus Regional-Planning Assumptions," *Regional Studies* 10 (1976): 151-71. See also P.O. Pederson, "Innovation Diffusion within and between National Urban Systems," *Geographical Analysis* 2 (1970): 203-54, and E. Casetti, L.J. King, and J. Odland, "The Formalization and Testing of Concepts of Growth Poles in a Spatial Context," *Environment and Planning* 3 (1971): 377-82. At issue is the degree to which growth centers of various sizes and types exercise an influence upon their respective hinterlands which is spatially localized. Casetti et al. find some evidence supporting the thesis of an inverse distance relationship whereas Pred points to contrary evidence. Regional planners would be well advised not to accept

without investigation the inevitability that new development will benefit their locality through forward (supply) and backward (demand) inter-industrial linkages. The spatial imprint of impact may indeed be extensive rather than intensive.

24. This perspective stems from J. M. Keynes, *The General Theory of Employment, Interest and Money* (New York: Harcourt, Brace, 1936). Today this viewpoint is no more than a general orientation permitting a great variety of interpretations. Theorists freely borrow from it, often discarding elements lacking empirical support. The most widely utilized Keynesian model has been that developed independently by two theorists whose names are now synonymous with the model (Harrod-Domar model). E. D. Domar, *Essays in the Theory of Economic Growth* (Fair Lawn, N.J.: Oxford University Press, 1957), and R. F. Harrod, *Towards a Dynamic Economics* (London: Macmillan, 1948).

25. A regional (subnational) version of the Harrod-Domar model has been articulated by H. W. Richardson, *Regional Economics: Location Theory, Urban Structure, and Regional Change* (New York: Praeger, 1969), pp. 321-3. The assumptions of this regional model are severely restrictive and necessarily inappropriate in many developing contexts. Whether or not these assumptions might be relaxed while retaining the major characteristics of the model is uncertain, though doubtful.

26. The Harrod-Domar model was one of the first widely used development models. In many of the lagging regions and nations in which it was applied, however, the workforce was unskilled, under-productive and underemployed. Additional increments of capital could not always lead directly to increased production in the manner specified by the model. In opposition to its capital orientation arose a number of labor oriented models stressing mechanisms by which labor could be drawn into nonagricultural pursuits to increase productivity and enable further savings and investment. See, for example, W. A. Lewis, "Economic Development with Unlimited Supplies of Labor," *The Manchester School of Economic and Social Studies*, May, 1954, and R. Nurkse, *Problems of Capital Formation in Underdeveloped Countries* (New York: Oxford University Press, 1953). These studies primarily addressed Third World nations. The problem of capital formation, however, is often the most critical in stimulating lagging regional economies of the more developed world, many of which have or might attract relatively substantial numbers of workers. In many instances, though, the necessary capital may be imported through outside investors rather than being generated through local savings.

27. Merchantilist concepts of the seventeenth century marked the early beginnings of trade theory, but it was Ricardo who gave the perspective an intellectual base. His was the theory of "comparative advantage." Subsequent neoclassical theories expanded his model while providing alternate geometric solutions to trade problems.

28. Renewed interest in trade theory in this century led to two distinct attempts to apply trade theory to subnational regions. These abandoned Ricardo's labor theory of value while introducing nonlabor production factors such as land, capital, and entrepreneurial ability. These factors were assumed immobile among regions. Heckscher (1919, 1949) explained regional dif-

ferences according to inter-regional variations in production functions whereas Ohlin proceeded from the assumption that production functions and factor quality were identical among regions. For Ohlin, differences among regions were due to variations in factor supply. Heckscher claimed factor prices would equalize with free trade while Ohlin claimed full price equality would be approached but never achieved. See E. Heckscher, "The Effect of Foreign Trade on the Distribution of Income," in *Readings in the Theory of International Trade,* H. S. Ellis and L. A. Meltzer, eds. (Philadelphia: Blakiston Co., 1949), pp. 272-300, and B. Ohlin, *Interregional and International Trade* (Cambridge: Harvard University Press, 1933). The comparative advantage concept was recently tested yielding no definitive conclusion by J. R. Moroney and J. M. Walker, "A Regional Test of the Heckscher-Ohlin Hypothesis," *Journal of Political Economy* 74 (1966): 573-86. The theory is ill-suited to specify strategies for regional development, in any case, since it is aspatial, nondevelopmental, and an incomplete specification of a regional economy.

29. G. H. Borts and J. L. Stein, *Economic Growth in a Free Market* (New York: Columbia University Press, 1964). More recently Muth has elaborated this model. His algebraic model determines employment and migration simultaneously in a two-sector (export and local) urban economy. Prices of exports and capital goods are determined in national markets. Increased demand for exports at these national prices may draw local workers from nonbasic to export production if the wage rate in these export industries is higher than that for nonbasic production. Total employment, he argues, would be expected to increase following increases in export activity only if there were natural increases in population, or increased labor participation rates, or immigration. Recall that in the export-base model increased employment automatically follows increased export activity. R. F. Muth, "Differential Growth Among Large U.S. Cities," in *Papers in Quantitative Economics,* J. Quirk and A. Zarley, eds. (Lawrence: University of Kansas Press, 1969), 311.

30. Siebert has developed a deductive development model blending the neoclassical and export-base perspectives. This two-region model admits both economic and institutional factors. Regions having the highest rates of immobile invention will attain the highest growth rates. H. Siebert, *Regional Economic Growth: Theory and Policy* (Scranton, Pa.: International Textbook Company, 1969).

31. W. W. Rostow, *The Stages of Economic Growth: A Non-Communist Manifesto* (New York: Cambridge University Press, 1960).

32. A. Emmanuel, *Unequal Exchange* (New York: Monthly Review Press, 1972). See also, E. Malizia and D. Reid, "Perspectives and Strategies for U.S. Regional Development," *Growth and Change* 7, no. 4 (October 1976): 41-47.

33. See D. C. North, "Location Theory and Regional Economic Growth," *Journal of Political Economy* 63, no. 3 (June 1955): 243-58. A brief overview of location theory is W. Alonso, "Location Theory," in *Regional Policy,* J. Friedmann and W. Alonso, eds. (Cambridge: M.I.T. Press, 1975), pp. 35-63. Two texts covering the rudiments are: B.J.L. Berry, et al., *The Geography of Economic Systems* (Englewood Cliffs, N.J.: Prentice-Hall, 1976), and W. Isard, *Introduction to Regional Science* (Englewood Cliffs, N.J.: Prentice-Hall, 1975).

34. See N. M. Hansen, *Location Preferences, Migration, and Regional Growth* (New York: Praeger, 1973), chap. 2.

35. For an overview of the U.S. regional setting and a summary of recent dynamics see G. Sternlieb and J. W. Hughes, eds., *Post-Industrial America: Metropolitan Decline and Inter-Regional Job Shifts* (New Brunswick: The Center for Urban Policy Research, Rutgers University, 1975). See also G. Sternlieb and J. W. Hughes, "New Regional and Metropolitan Realities of America," *Journal of the American Institute of Planners* 43, no. 3 (July 1977): 227-41.

About the editors:

George Sternlieb is director of the Center for Urban Policy Research and a professor of urban and regional planning at Rutgers University.

James W. Hughes is a research associate at the Center and an associate professor of urban planning and policy development at Rutgers.

About the Center:

The Center for Urban Policy Research, a part of Rutgers, The State University of New Jersey, promotes multidisciplinary investigations into urban and suburban development. The Center is concerned with both research and its application to policy problems. Under the directorship of George Sternlieb, a staff of economists, geographers, sociologists, and urban planners studies the environment, housing development, public administration, municipal financing, urban and suburban growth, and other problems of key significance to practitioners, administrators, and concerned citizens.

In recent years, the Center has undertaken studies sponsored by federal, state, and municipal agencies and private organizations on the subjects of fiscal impact analysis, municipal tax delinquency, housing costs and financing, rent control, land use, and economic development. Studies are now underway on redlining, historic preservation, remote sensing, and loft conversion.